IN VISIBLE ARCHIVES

IN VISIBLE ARCHIVES

Queer and Feminist Visual Culture
in the 1980s

Margaret Galvan

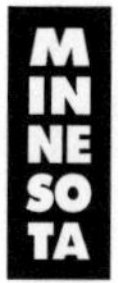

UNIVERSITY OF MINNESOTA PRESS

MINNEAPOLIS | LONDON

The University of Minnesota Press gratefully acknowledges the financial assistance provided for the publication of this book by the University of Florida College of Liberal Arts and Sciences and Center for the Humanities and the Public Sphere (Rothman Endowment).

Published by the University of Minnesota Press
111 Third Avenue South, Suite 290
Minneapolis, MN 55401–2520
http://www.upress.umn.edu

 Available as a Manifold edition at manifold.umn.edu.

ISBN 978-1-5179-0323-7 (hc)
ISBN 978-1-5179-0324-4 (pb)

A Cataloging-in-Publication record for this book is available from the Library of Congress.

Printed in the United States of America on acid-free paper

The University of Minnesota is an equal-opportunity educator and employer.

Legacies have everything to do with the future of feminism.
—Nancy K. Miller, *Getting Personal*

CONTENTS

MAKING VISIBLE ARCHIVES

Visualizing Collective Action

Across the 1980s, women in feminist and gay and lesbian movements in the United States celebrated their sexuality as one of the interlocking parts of their identity in response to constraining cultural phenomena like the feminist sex wars, conservative political norms, and the HIV/AIDS crisis. Forty years later, we widely remember their words in essays, manifestos, and march chants, as they shifted the feminist movement toward the sex-positive third wave and participated in gay and lesbian organizing that fed into groups like ACT UP, Queer Nation, and Lesbian Avengers. By contrast, we have overlooked how women wielded images to theorize their embodied sexuality directly, and their art, created within grassroots networks, has been mostly forgotten. The eight artists I study in this book collectively depicted sexuality by embedding their own individual experiences within a larger framework. Through collages, cartoons, drawings, and photographs, Hannah Alderfer, Beth Jaker, Marybeth Nelson, Roberta Gregory, Lee Marrs, Alison Bechdel, Gloria Anzaldúa, and Nan Goldin represented their own perspectives and those of a wider range of people around them in order to document the intersectional diversity of bodies and sexual identities that made up their communities. Within the past twenty years, newly processed collections within archives have begun to make these women's powerful visual contributions available once more.

And yet, visibility is tenuous and not guaranteed. These women exist in visible archives, both present and precarious. The paradox of this book's title reflects the hard-won and narrowly kept conditions of visibility for diverse sexual identities. As the artists featured in this book were trying to make their lives and sexualities visible, they were facing censorship and critique, even from within their own movements. The call was all too often coming from inside the house. Further, we are at a historic moment now where a number of the social advances discussed in this book are on the verge of collapse, underlining just how much women's sexuality and LGBTQ identity remain both dangerous and revolutionary. These women and countless others are preserved in visible archives, but their memory and legacy are not guaranteed. It is my hope that recovering the grassroots tactics for how these artists made their communities visible and advocated for their rights amid unprecedented adversity may inspire future activists.

By building worlds around their individual experiences, the artists analyzed in this book insisted that their experiences be seen and valued as universal. Their art functions as collective autobiography in how they drew themselves within a larger community and then welcomed others to imagine themselves within that world. By foregrounding the importance of community in their visual representations, their approaches encouraged women and LGBTQ viewers who encountered their work to reflect on their own experiences of sexuality and feel like they were part of something larger than themselves. The artists deployed these visual tactics not only to bring people together in community, but also to recognize how their own individual work grew out of, reflected, and was supported by a collective of individuals.

The career trajectory of each of the artists in this book shows how they anticipated later developments in feminist as well as gay and lesbian thinking and artwork. This forward-looking artwork sometimes set them at odds with their contemporaries, but the community they invoked supported their values in future years. Though repudiated in their time during the feminist sex wars, the precepts of the sex-positive feminists were woven into the fabric of the third wave in the 1990s and the visual style of the artists behind the censored *Diary* (1982) from the Barnard Sex Conference—Hannah Alderfer, Beth Jaker, and Marybeth Nelson—prefigured the DIY style behind zines that would become so popular during the riot grrrl movement in the 1990s. Moreover, the lesbian and bisexual content within the underground comix movement as captured in solo works by Roberta Gregory and Lee Marrs would find a home and flourish in the *Gay Comix* series of the 1980s and 1990s and facilitate a lesbian comics boom among a new generation of artists in the 1990s. From its local beginnings in the pages of grassroots newspapers in the 1980s, Alison Bechdel's *Dykes to Watch Out For* comic strip would become such a subcultural phenomenon that many young women in the 1990s and beyond would tell Bechdel they learned what it meant to be a lesbian from the strip. Gloria Anzaldúa's editorial work with *This Bridge Called My Back* (1981) and individual writing in *Borderlands / La Frontera* (1987) were immediately successful and would continue to be so in subsequent years as she was invited to talk at multiple public lectures annually, where she illustrated her popular concepts in drawings that have not yet been examined as vital sites of visual theorization and community formation. At the time that Nan Goldin began to show her photography in the 1980s, color photography was not standard in the high art world, but her work and its snapshot aesthetic became widely influential in subsequent years, such that the groundbreaking, defiant nature of her formal choices is no longer as immediately apparent to modern eyes.

They created their work against the backdrop of the 1980s, which began with some measure of hope to continue to build on the social progress that feminists and those invested in gay liberation had achieved in the 1970s. As the Village People put it in "Ready for the 80's" (1979), a party anthem send-up in anticipation of the new decade, "In the eighties we will travel far / We will realize just who we are / We can move as one." Despite external challenges like the election of conservative Ronald Reagan in November 1980 and internal fractures within social movements, artists rallied the spirit of collective possibility in their work.

In this vein, Mary Wilshire's one-page comic from early in the decade that appeared in *After/Shock: Bulletins from Ground Zero!* (1981) speaks to its moment in time, encapsulating the potential for social change that the major artists in this book would embrace with their art (Figure I.1).[1] Here, a topless, masked superheroine breaks the fourth wall, interrupting a series of short strips on earlier pages where white women objectify men in office settings and claiming the final page for a public service announcement. Across the top row of panels the superheroine calls for political reengagement, and the following nine panels depict more than a dozen different individuals—diverse in terms of their race, sexuality, profession, and age—gathering to collectively rally for social justice. These figures present a stark contrast to the upwardly mobile white women seen on earlier pages, who have effectively leaned in for their own advancement but have forgotten about the cause. Together, these diverse individuals identify a wide range of pressing social issues—racial equality, abortion, nondiscrimination of homosexuality, freedom of erotic art— that need attention. In a contemporary review of the comic that appeared in *The Comics Journal* (1982), Bill Sherman reads Wilshire's piece as "reemphasiz[ing] the initial feminist impetus behind" women's comics, reminding the "white-collar class of women" of "the movement that opened many offices for them."[2] Within the comic itself, Wilshire identifies the need for renewed political activism due to the election of Ronald Reagan, who took office as U.S. president at the beginning of 1981, by having a female newscaster intone, "These are radical privileges—and they're in jeopardy. Just look at the eyes of Nancy Reagan!" The superheroine demarcates the new decade as another opportunity for change if people pay attention and join together. Like a lot of the art discussed in this book, this comic was produced within grassroots networks and is all but forgotten today, but it underlines the power of visual art to advocate for social change.

All these women's artwork shaped feminist futures, but how they mobilized image and text together to plant the seeds for future community to bloom has been overlooked, such that the full impact of their feminist community-building tactics has yet to be assessed. This book is that reckoning, connecting the dots from the past to the present by unpacking the powerful collective potential of visual rhetoric, contextualizing it within its time, and tracing its influence forward through the archives that preserved these artworks and made them available for research. Throughout their careers, these artists actively conceived of their own work as documenting and preserving sexual experience at a time when many feminists were uncovering the forgotten work of earlier influential women artists and others were endeavoring to build archives of their own. The following two sections outline how this book engages both visual analysis and archives in order to recover the political impact of these women's artwork.

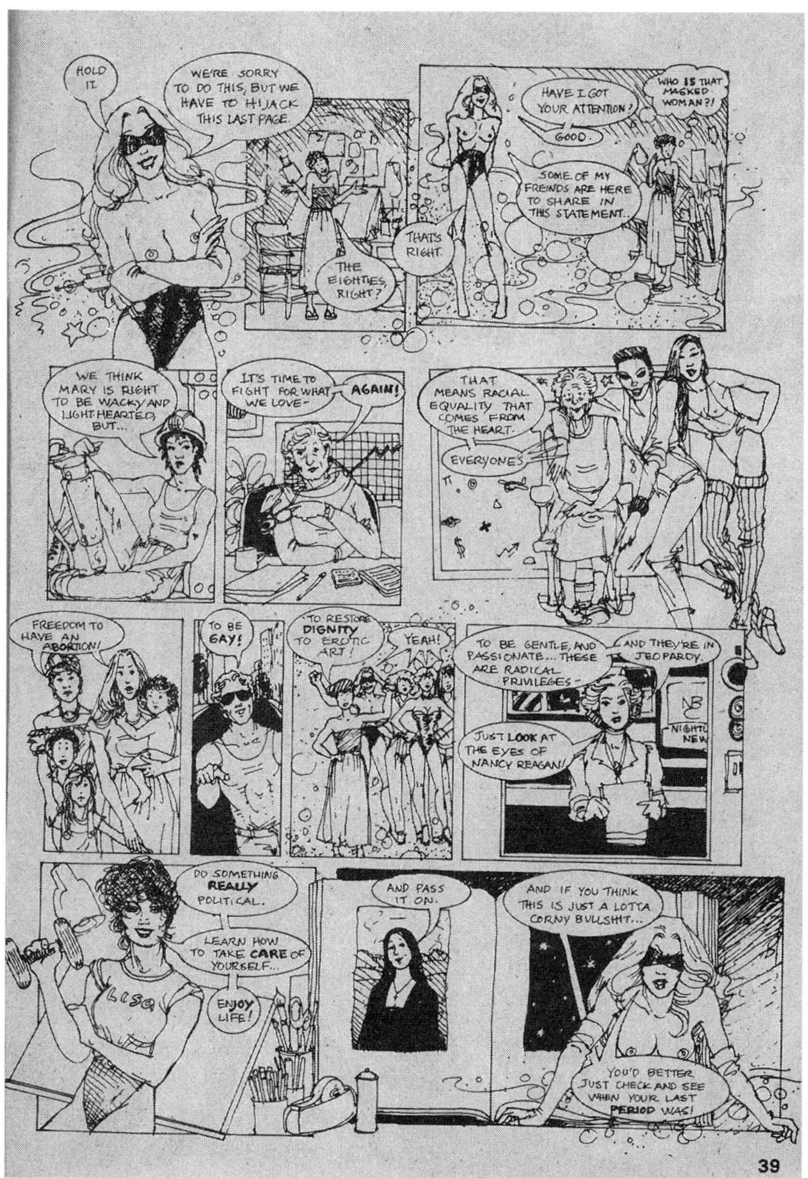

Figure I.1. Final page of Mary Wilshire's "More Nasty Women's Humor" comic in *After/Shock* (1981), which shows a topless, masked heroine joined by an intersectional array of individuals making a public service announcement in support of social justice in the face of Ronald Reagan's election as U.S. president. Copyright 1981 by Mary Wilshire.

From Sequence to Collectivity: Theorizing Comics and Other Image–Text Artworks

The visual forms I analyze across five chapters—multimedia collage, comic books, newspaper comic strips and spot graphics, notebook doodles and transparency drawings, and photographs—allowed women to represent and examine the sexuality of their bodies within feminist as well as gay and lesbian movements, but these formats have often been ignored as crucial sites of theoretical engagement. The fusion of image and text together within these artworks is especially powerful as it allowed women to control the conversation through both of these registers. Not only were they able to visualize diverse bodies on their own terms, but they also supplied textual commentary that foregrounded their own interpretations rather than letting anyone else speak over or for them.

To analyze the critical heft of these images and their multilayered relationships to text, I deploy close reading that is informed by my training in comics studies. As fellow comics scholar Ramzi Fawaz observes, "Comics is an object of inquiry that invites or elicits a method of reading for multiplicity. Put simply, comics teaches us to read lots of different things—words, images, aesthetic styles, characters, panels, colors, textures, formats, and page layouts—in lots of different sequences, patterns, and juxtapositions: in a single panel, on a full page, between and across pages in a narrative arc, and often across numerous serial installments."[3] This interactive "multiplicity" embedded in how we look at comics guides my analysis throughout the book. By coining the term *comicity*, which denotes comics-like properties inherent in other works of art, Colin Beineke offers terminology for a comics-focused way to engage analytically with other artistic formats that would benefit from similar image–text analysis or that have properties that align them with comics in some way.[4] Indeed, all the artworks in this book benefit from a comicitous analysis where I investigate the multilayered relationships between image and text, considering their spatial orientations on the page and how they are sequenced together to formulate a larger collective. Gathering these works into one artistic lineage allows us to draw connections between how women leveraged the affordances of their different art forms in order to assemble a visual vocabulary of sexuality and embodiment within the feminist and gay and lesbian movements.[5]

These women's artworks often appeared in collective publication contexts like newspapers and anthologies, where other words and images interacted with and shaped the interpretation of their pieces. In her scholarship about the important role that periodicals played in feminist movement culture, Agatha Beins foregrounds how items on a single page spread or in an individual issue or publication were in dialogue with one another: "A piece about a local film festival could appear next to an announcement about an upcoming election and in the same issue as a page full of poetry, a graphic of a woman with her fist raised in a Black Power salute, and an editorial requesting help putting out the newsletter. . . . Discourses outside a particular article or image shape its meaning: a single issue is in conversation with previous issues and anticipates future ones."[6] In this book, I expand Beins's premise about how to look capaciously at the content of a periodical to contextualize a range of visual culture as it was produced and disseminated in a wide variety of formats. For example, when a cartoonist like Alison Bechdel publishes her comics within specific grassroots newspapers or a photographer like Nan Goldin arranges her photos into a book with a textual preface that she pens, these publication venues frame our reading of the images and affect their reception and circulation both directly in the moment and indirectly thereafter.

By bringing together women who made art in different media, we can understand how visual formats were vital spaces of theorization within activist circles. This book builds on comics scholarship like that of Hillary Chute and Ramzi Fawaz, who have reshaped the critical landscape in the last ten years by centering women creators and queer perspectives.[7] Also important is the social justice–minded work of scholars like Rebecca Beirne, andré carrington, Yetta Howard, and Darieck Scott who have engaged comics as a site of critical discourse within a larger ecosystem of many artistic forms.[8] Together with these thinkers and others, my scholarship is part of an emerging subfield of queer comics studies that examines both LGBTQ creators as well as how the comics form itself can be queerly mobilized.[9] While various scholars have engaged comics as local sites of activism, this book conceptualizes how diverse visual cultures (that include comics) were important to feminist as well as gay and lesbian movements.

In their depictions of women's sexuality, each artist draws on the power of sequence, which is seen as one of the bedrock traits of comics.

Cartoonist Will Eisner penned an early book analyzing the medium that he titled *Comics and Sequential Art* (1985), and Scott McCloud built from Eisner's work when he defined comics as "juxtaposed pictorial and other images in deliberate sequence" in *Understanding Comics* (1993).[10] Both of these texts are foundational to the discipline, and McCloud's work is one of the most cited and taught pieces of comics scholarship. When Chute engages how McCloud and others have foregrounded sequence in their definitions of comics, she observes that "the prioritizing of sequence allows for a rich history of forms, some of them ancient, such as cave paintings, to be understood as applicable to the history of comics," a lineage that McCloud advocates for within his book.[11] I mobilize sequence to underline the comicity of Alderfer's, Jaker's, and Nelson's multimedia collages, Bechdel's spot graphics, Anzaldúa's drawings, and Goldin's photographs and how they belong together in conversation with Marrs's and Gregory's comic books and Bechdel's comic strips. All these artists embraced how sequence allowed them to create relationships between images and individuals and show how they were on the same page, whether literally, metaphorically, or both.

Even more important, sequence allowed these artists to visualize collectivity, as Wilshire's comic at the opening of this introduction demonstrates when she uses a single comics page to depict many women and LGBTQ individuals rallying together for social justice. By putting multiple images and people into sequence artists were able not only to create visibility for many identities and link these perspectives by forming them into a community, but also to welcome their audience into affinity with them. In McCloud's book, he draws himself as a narrator on the page to create a connection with his reader, a tactic that some of these artists adapt, illustrating themselves or analogs of themselves among an even larger community populated by diverse individuals with whom readers can identify. All the artists created relationships among many images, but they at times defied "deliberate sequence" by rearranging, recontextualizing, and revising their images, speaking to how relationships between individuals and particularly individuals within social movements are always shifting and changing. In Fawaz's scholarship, he sees comics sequence as "a site of open-ended multiplicity" that queer cartoonists can wield to "[express] and translat[e] shifting understandings of queer sexuality across time and in different cultural and political contexts."[12]

In putting Fawaz's insights together with mine, our embrace of sequence underlines how this formal characteristic can be deployed to celebrate how "people are different from each other," one concept with which Eve Kosofsky Sedgwick helped launch the field of queer theory in *Epistemology of the Closet* (1990) by demonstrating the infinite differences (or sequences) within people as opposed to binary ways of thinking that would prefer to fix individuals into limited, knowable categories.[13]

Roberta Gregory invokes the power of sequence in her comic *Dynamite Damsels* (1976) to comment on the shifting norms in feminist culture in the late 1970s. On the back cover, she depicts the major characters in her comic together in one group in order to reimagine their relationships (Figure I.2).[14] At a glance, this image of ten women standing under the banner "We're women and we're beautiful" is a utopian vision of a feminism that harmoniously gathers a diverse grouping of individuals. By depicting her protagonist, Frieda, hugging an anonymous woman whose shirt back proclaims, "And this includes YOU, too!" Gregory invites the reader to put her face on this woman and join the cause.

Despite the welcoming tone of the text, the image reveals how the whole group isn't as accepting as they declare. At the edges of the image, we see the butch lesbian Doris shocking Marylou by grabbing her breast. Gregory's narrative complicates our reading of Doris's assault by showing how Marylou is consistently a source of oppression, threatened by Doris's lesbianism and other women who are not like her. Throughout the comic, Marylou enacts microaggressions against other members of the group, including from the outset where the first words out of her mouth subtly attack Edie, a Black woman who is asking about the whiteness of the feminist movement, and derail the potential for a nuanced discussion about race in their consciousness-raising group.[15] With this boob grab, Gregory irreverently signals that white women like Marylou who dominate the movement need to be woken out of complacency to recognize and value the individuality of the women around them. The shared, friendly facial expressions of all the other women on the page, including Marylou's daughter, visualize the potential for feminist solidarity while simultaneously acknowledging that its reality is not a given, as Gregory's narrative examines and as this back cover echoes. Marylou represents the straight white feminism that many women, including the artists in my book, organized in reaction to in the 1980s, in order to

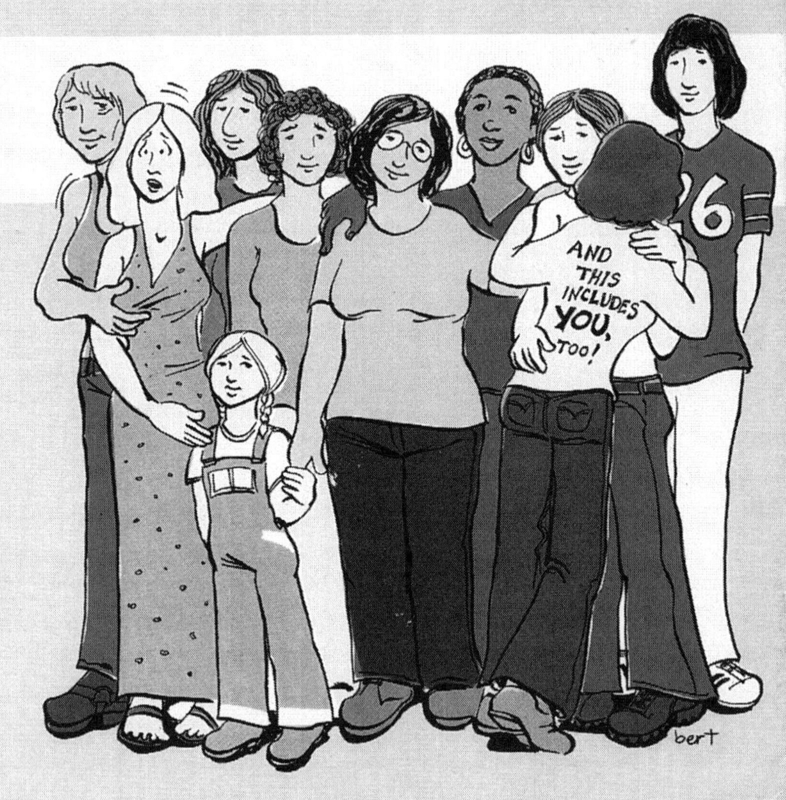

Figure I.2. Back cover of Roberta Gregory's *Dynamite Damsels* (1976) where the cast of characters stand together under a banner that affirms "We're women and we're beautiful" and welcome the reader to join them. Courtesy of Roberta Gregory.

hold the movement accountable for the experiences of a broader range of women.

Beyond how the visual form of the works allowed artists to visualize and critique collectivity, their handmade materiality also contributed to welcoming the audience into movements for social justice. In *Graphic Women* (2010), Chute analyzes how the "rigorously handmade" quality of the women's comics she studies establishes intimacy as "the subjective mark of the body is rendered directly onto the page and constitutes how we view the page."[16] Alongside comics studies, zine studies has been particularly adept at describing how the materiality of artwork was vital in forming community. The artists in this book produced their visual artwork in formats that emphasize their personal, handmade nature—the collage, the comic, the diary, the doodle, the grassroots newsletter, the snapshot. All these visual forms would later live side by side in zines. In her landmark study *Girl Zines* (2009), Alison Piepmeier articulates the concept of "embodied community": how "zines' materiality helps form a particular kind of connection between zine readers and creators."[17] As much as zine makers created connections on the page through the intimate, handmade nature of their content and its format, and solidified those connections by building postal networks of other individuals producing zines, so also did the artists in this book create and broadcast their content within communities in order to further develop these groups. In focusing on how each artist facilitated an "embodied community" through her work, I show how these artists were deliberate in designing and sharing their creations in specific ways that would highlight the larger community they were a part of and welcome new individuals into the fold.

Situating Collectivity in Women's Lives and Archives

Over the past ten years, I have researched the artwork of these eight women in over a dozen grassroots archives and university special collections across the United States and drawn on some newly digitized resources as well. Attesting to how they touched on multiple discourses with their art, their work can be found in wide-ranging archival collections devoted to women's history, sexuality, popular culture, ethnic studies, and art movements. By thinking across these many archives, I reconstitute the multivalent legacies of these women and examine the crucial role of the archives in how they preserve and shape our memory. My engagement with archives builds on the archival turn in critical theory, particularly the feminist and queer thinking on archives that has consolidated around the work of Ann Cvetkovich and Kate Eichhorn.[18] When I discuss archives in this book, I mean archives in the very material and concrete sense that Michelle Caswell delineates as "collections of records, material and immaterial, analog and digital . . . , the institutions that steward them, the places where they are physically located, and the processes that designated them 'archival.'"[19] How archivists have welcomed these women's artwork into collections has been vital in shaping their legacy.

The richness and nuance with which I can visually analyze and contextualize each artist's work is thanks to how these materials have been preserved in archives. Because their art circulated in small numbers through grassroots and independent contexts in the late 1970s and 1980s, it has been mostly forgotten in the decades since. In this book, I engage the archives not only to examine the impact that the art made in its time, but to explore its continuing relevance as these materials migrated into archives to be preserved. Interference Archive, a grassroots archives formed in 2011 that collects the print culture of social movements, operates according to the principle of "preservation through use." The organization makes activist art broadly available to organizers today so that they can learn about and draw strength from earlier generations of activists, which is so crucial particularly since activist histories are not always well documented.[20] By making the art, histories, processes, and tactics of the artists I study more widely available through this book, I transform the ethos of the Interference Archive into a principle guiding my scholarship.

Through analyzing how the women's artwork and artistic processes were shaped by other women involved in the social movements around them, this book fashions a vision of how collective investments undergirded their careers. A collective understanding of artistic production often remains as opaque to us today as it did to feminists in their time—as a group of women involved in the production of the feminist magazine *Heresies* lamented in the late 1970s, "We haven't yet learned to analyze 'women working together.' . . . Women need to develop ways of thinking, looking, talking about our processes."[21] We are now in a moment when popular visual art forms like comics and photography are more widely dispersed throughout culture than ever before and often used for the purposes of social activism, such that it's crucial we reconnect to and make these earlier visual activisms visible for new generations of artists. That is, I am reactivating these artists' work for what they might tell us about collective activism in their time but also for how making visible this visual activism might inspire and shape future artwork.

In the past two decades, archivists have been critical in recruiting and processing collections containing the artwork of these women and other social movement materials from the 1970s and 1980s, making possible the recovery work of this book. In her groundbreaking monograph *The Archival Turn in Feminism: Outrage in Order* (2013), which has quickly become a touchstone for myself and many other scholars, Kate Eichhorn examines how "feminists born since the late 1960s" who entered the archival profession have become invested in preserving the traces of second- and third-wave feminism.[22] She focuses the bulk of her analysis on a select group of archivists and librarians who have collected third-wave zines from the 1990s and related feminist ephemera in university collections, positing that "the archival turn in contemporary feminism is as much about shoring up a younger generation's legacy and honoring elders as it is about imagining and working to build possible worlds in the present and for the future."[23] These same zine librarians and archivists—Kelly Wooten, Lisa Darms, and Jenna Freedman—and others—like Milo Miller and Christopher Wilde, who founded and run the grassroots Queer Zine Archive Project, and Karen Green, who serves as the comics curator of Columbia University—have been critical in my thinking about how radical visual materials are preserved within archives and remembered as a part of social movements and how the intersection between these two ideas shape their legacy.[24] Their work in archives elevating marginalized voices and formats fits within the emerging field of critical archival studies, which "broadens the field's scope beyond an inward, practice-centered orientation and builds a critical stance regarding the role of archives in the production of knowledge and different types of narratives, as well as identity construction."[25] How they thought through the challenges of developing collections replete with comics, zines, and other grassroots image–text material encouraged me to think critically about how archives necessarily frame and make visible otherwise inaccessible visual artwork—even as the materials of the major figures I study were mostly found in other collections. In the grassroots and university collections engaged across this book, which centralize documents concerning women's sexuality and LGBTQ community, archivists have had to "take one of two approaches to dealing with the uneven power dynamics inherent in the structure of archives: either they subvert the power structures in order to re-build and reclaim them, or they build their own, more democratic or non-hierarchical alternatives."[26] Archivists' critical perspective has been key to allowing the artwork of the women to survive in visible archives and remain relevant in the present, thanks to how archivists collect, process, and preserve the work for researchers.

Engaging the archives reveals how each woman took on multiple roles to produce and share visual artwork, including ones we often overlook or don't spend enough time critically examining. We remember these women as artists, but they were also teachers, organizers, editors, and curators. They uplifted and influenced the artistic imagination of a larger community not only through their individual art, but also the labor they performed in these other vocations. For example, in their studies of Anzaldúa's archives, AnaLouise Keating and Suzanne Bost discuss how her expansive collection reveals entirely new dimensions of Anzaldúa as a writer—not only through the proliferation of unpublished writings she left behind but also through the additional roles Anzaldúa took on.[27] In my scholarship on Anzaldúa in this book, I examine her as a visual artist and pedagogue and analyze how she mobilized these callings to build a larger community of support from those who were already invested in her writing. Too often in our analyses, we don't fully value the community-minded labor that many artists undertake; these women demonstrate how fundamental such labor was to how they conceived of and occupied the role of an artist.

The archives further reveal how the women themselves were invested in documenting and preserving—not only within their own individual artwork but also more broadly as they gathered the work of others as editors and curators and saved the work of others in their own collections. This multivalent archival impulse is perhaps no surprise, given that the feminist and gay and lesbian social movements of the 1970s and 1980s were broadly engaging with print media to make their experiences legible and, further, that there were groups of individuals starting grassroots archives to collect these documents and others from earlier moments of activism.[28] By the end of the 1980s, institutional and university archives had started to collect LGBTQ materials into their collections to preserve them in the face of the HIV/AIDS crisis.[29] That is, this book spans a historical moment during which documenting, preserving, and eventually archiving diverse voices was a part of the cultural consciousness and inflected the art that these women produced.

In 1980, as lesbian feminist poet and activist Adrienne Rich averred that "lesbian existence has been written out of history," these women were doing their part to *draw* lesbian existence back into history in greater variety and scope, nesting it within a larger world of experience that valued women's sexuality as a core part of their identity.[30] As Bechdel put it in a retrospective interview, she began making comics to visually affirm her lesbian identity: "When I started drawing the strip in the early eighties, my primary motivation was that I wanted to see a cultural reflection of my life, of my humanity. An actual, visual reflection. A lot of books about lesbians were starting to appear, but there still weren't many visual images."[31] In a monumental review of photographer Nan Goldin's career, Hilton Als details her "passion to document," and it is this passion, not only to document but also to represent and preserve, that defines the artwork of all these women.[32]

Throughout the book, each chapter analyzes how specific archives have preserved and made visible the women and their artwork. I develop a theoretically informed section for each chapter that foregrounds the archival dimensions of each woman's artistic praxis, contextualizing her work in its time by connecting her to contemporaneous thinkers and further theorizing its continuing resonance by putting her in conversation with contemporary archival theorists. These sections build from my own experiences researching each woman's work in one or more archival collections and considering what larger lessons could be drawn from where and how the woman's visual work was present within the archives. I began to see, as I've detailed in the above paragraphs, how the women themselves were deeply invested in preservation. Through the archives, we can reconstitute a fuller story about these women's contributions and how they laid the groundwork for future communities of sexually diverse individuals as feminist as well as gay and lesbian social movements further developed beyond the 1980s. As much as we can

glimpse the women's collective commitments through their visual artwork, the archives allow us to map out further the role and histories of
those communities in the women's lives, art, and activism.

Chapter Overview

In the following five chapters, I analyze the artwork of eight women,
examining how they theorized across a range of visual print forms and
showing how these forms belong together in one genealogy. Through
their multifaceted image–text artwork that visualized the bodies and lives
of women and queer individuals, they were making space for the representation of more diverse sexual identities within the women's liberation
and gay and lesbian movements in the late 1970s and 1980s. Every chapter investigates how the published location of the artist's work shaped its
reception and legibility within the larger feminist and gay and lesbian
movements and, later, within archives. By juxtaposing how their artwork
has been preserved in archives and how they themselves were invested
in documenting and preserving the movement around them, each chapter contends with the paradox of how they actively created conditions
for visibility while they also constantly risked invisibility in the moment
and thereafter. These theoretically attuned archival sections frame close
readings of the women's work where I trace the evolution of how they
wielded both image and text to theorize and represent their communities at multiple points throughout their careers. All the chapters underline how artists dealt with critique they faced for their representations
of women and how they searched for more hospitable audiences and a
larger community of like-minded individuals for later work.

In chapter 1, I examine how the *Diary of a Conference on Sexuality*
(1982) catalyzed the feminist sex wars in the early 1980s when Barnard
College administrators confiscated and censored the document, which
served as the program for Barnard's annual Scholar and Feminist conference. Many scholars who discuss this event focus on the women at the
conference like Dorothy Allison and Gayle Rubin who were targeted by
anti-porn feminists for their views on sexuality, but they pay relatively
little attention to the confiscated *Diary* that artists Hannah Alderfer, Beth
Jaker, and Marybeth Nelson designed. I analyze how this trio of artists
wielded collage and recontextualized images to discuss the multifaceted

nature of women's sexuality, which threatened the anti-porn protesters. The contemporaneous development of grassroots LGBTQ archives is significant for how they safeguarded controversial visual materials, providing the images that the artists themselves deployed in their collages and later preserving the *Diary* and other similar works from the period. In examining the *Diary*'s collage aesthetics and how Alderfer, Jaker, and Nelson sourced images from archives and collectors, I explore how they further developed their visual activism with *Caught Looking* (1986), where they continued to counter the anti-porn feminists with sexually explicit imagery.

Looking back to the underground women's comics of the mid to late 1970s, chapter 2 considers the career trajectories of Roberta Gregory and Lee Marrs, whose feminist comics bildungsromane, *Dynamite Damsels* (1976) and *The Further Fattening Adventures of Pudge, Girl Blimp* (1973–77), respectively, represent their protagonists' involvement with the feminist movement alongside their developing queer sexuality. I examine how the way these comics are preserved on the margins in various archives echoes both artists' struggle to fit their work into the feminist and underground comix movements, and how it is important to look across multiple kinds of archival collections of comics to piece together an understanding of artwork like theirs that existed at the intersection of various movements. Their comics crucially illustrate how 1970s feminism sparked sexual discovery, but critique how women of color and lesbians were excluded from full participation. Through close-reading their solo comics and then discussing their pioneering work in the *Gay Comix* (1980–98) series, I show how Gregory and Marrs ultimately made a new generation of women cartoonists feel welcome to explore women's sexuality in comics form. By casting back to the 1970s, this chapter demonstrates how women worked to create venues that would support their representations and facilitate newly emerging communities of artists in the 1980s.

Chapter 3 takes up one of the best-known lesbian cartoonists, Alison Bechdel, who was inspired by early issues of *Gay Comix* to start cartooning in this period. Partly because she was of a younger generation than the other artists in this book, Bechdel faced less initial pushback in creating her work and was able to build off the foundations that earlier cartoonists like Marrs and Gregory had created. I close-read her little-known beginnings in the early 1980s as a comics artist, documenting how her participation in the collective of the *WomaNews* (1983–85) grassroots feminist periodical shaped her career. Because this research was completed fully outside of comics collections and within queer grassroots archives and university collections dedicated to sexuality and women's history, I show how these spaces, which I collectively term queer comics archives, are necessary to trace the career and influence of queer cartoonists like Bechdel and give us ways of framing and analyzing such work. I examine how Bechdel developed an intersectional visual politics through advertisements and other art she produced in *WomaNews* and track how her work was in conversation with contemporaneous lesbian feminists. Through analyzing comics-adjacent visual print material, this chapter serves as a link to the following chapters that contend with a wider array of image–text media.

Chapter 4 reconceives the legacy of Gloria Anzaldúa, who is well-known for her challenge of white feminism in *This Bridge Called My Back* (1981) and creation of new subject positions for Chicana women in *Borderlands / La Frontera* (1987) including her theorization of mestiza consciousness. I reclaim Anzaldúa as a visual queer theorist and show how drawing was an important part of her theorizing across her career, examining how she used drawings in her early classroom notes from the 1970s to trace ideas she would more fully explore in her celebrated texts in the 1980s. She illustrated these concepts when she gave public talks about her scholarship, and I examine how her drawings of mestiza consciousness radiated intersectionality avant la lettre and welcomed a diverse grouping of other individuals into community with her. By engaging with the visual materials she produced and kept in her own personal archives and how her practice echoes that of other Chicana women in social movements, I theorize how individual archival collections can act as bridges that preserve and connect the individual artist to a larger community.

Finally, chapter 5 analyzes the work of photographer Nan Goldin, who documented alternate queer kinships in *The Ballad of Sexual Dependency* throughout the 1980s, taking photos and showing them in different slideshow configurations before she published a smaller set as a book in 1986. While her photos initially circulated in conversations around sexual liberation, by the time she published her book HIV/AIDS had devastated her community, and she reconceptualized her artwork as attempting to preserve the memory of those she had lost. While the artwork of Alderfer, Jaker, and Nelson was informed by the contemporary development of LGBTQ grassroots archives, Goldin's photographic and curatorial activism is marked both by the HIV/AIDS crisis and echoes how archives started to collect and preserve this moment. I examine Goldin's AIDS activism through her curation of *Witnesses: Against Our Vanishing*, a 1989 exhibit featuring the work of artists meditating on the AIDS crisis, and link her curatorial practice with her earlier photography. Through closing the book with the trajectory of Goldin's work across the decade, I foreground how she and the other women in the book were able to circumvent censors who sought to curtail the visual expression of sexuality and effectively document the diverse community of individuals around them.

1

THE COLLAGE ACTIVISTS

Hannah Alderfer, Beth Jaker, and Marybeth Nelson
Frame the Feminist Sex Wars

Making Visible the Visual

In late April 1982, just two days before an academic conference in New York City, the confiscation of a slim black handbook provided the kindling necessary to set the feminist world ablaze, igniting what became known as the feminist sex wars.[1] Just over seventy pages long with a simple cover that included a visual simulation of a diary lock, *Diary of a Conference on Sexuality* contained both drawings and text and, crucially, was the program for Scholar and the Feminist IX: Towards a Politics of Sexuality. The Scholar and Feminist conferences, which had been held annually at Barnard College since 1974, brought together feminist activists and scholars. The 1982 conference, coordinated by Carole S. Vance and planned by a committee of twenty-four women, aimed to "address women's sexual pleasure, choice, and autonomy, acknowledging that sexuality is simultaneously a domain of restriction, repression, and danger as well as a domain of exploration, pleasure, and agency" and ultimately featured eighteen workshops encompassing a wide range of perspectives on sexuality.[2] Feminist activists who opposed pornography called Barnard College administrators and trustees in the week before the conference to protest. They were aiming to prevent the participation of a handful of individuals, including both those involved in planning the conference as well as those who were scheduled to speak and who represented organizations—No More Nice Girls, Samois, Lesbian Sex Mafia—that supposedly promoted pornography, sadomasochism, and pedophilia and were positioned as out of step with "a major portion of the feminist movement."[3]

21

Rather than censor the conference presenters, Barnard College administration reacted against the *Diary* and its radical, punk aesthetics and sexually evocative imagery; Barnard president Ellen V. Futter worried "that the appearance of Barnard's name in the publication implied endorsement of particular points of view—inappropriate for a college."[4] The confiscation of the *Diary*, which not only served as the program for the conference but also included documentation of the conference planning, did not prevent the event from proceeding. However, in the absence of the *Diary*, anti-porn feminists warped perceptions of the conference as they stood outside of Barnard's gates on the day of the proceedings, handing out leaflets composed by Women Against Pornography and endorsed by Women Against Violence Against Women and New York Radical Feminists listing the women and organizations they were denouncing under a large handwritten banner that proclaimed "We Protest."[5] In a retrospective account, Vance called this handout "a masterpiece of misinformation, as the politics of feminist groups were misrepresented and women were accused of promoting pornography."[6] While the conference continued as planned, with the controversial speakers still presenting their papers, these personal attacks on Brett Harvey, Ellen Willis, Gayle Rubin, Dorothy Allison, and Patrick Califia "caus[ed] lasting pain and damage."[7]

The *Diary* finally became available after the conference, but it was unable to make the same impact that the papers from the conference did and its important visual activism has gone largely unremarked on in the years since.[8] It was only months after the conference that the 750-plus conference participants received an edited version of the *Diary*, which redacted the Barnard logo and other related content that would affiliate Barnard with the Scholar and the Feminist IX conference and the *Diary*.[9] Two years after the event, conference coordinator Carole S. Vance edited *Pleasure and Danger* (1984), a collection that gathered together talks from the conference. Many of the texts from this anthology continue to circulate; some, like Gayle Rubin's "Thinking Sex: Notes for a Radical Theory of the Politics of Sexuality," have become cultural touchstones. Rubin's essay opened the field-defining anthology *The Lesbian and Gay Studies Reader* (1993) and is considered foundational to queer theory, which had started to coalesce as a field around this same time following Teresa de Lauretis's coining of the term in her 1991 essay "Queer Theory: Lesbian and Gay Sexualities."[10] By contrast, the original *Diary* remains rare. Though it went through a second printing in February 1983, it was never released in a larger print run or by a more major publisher, so it is largely accessible only in archives.[11]

Many scholars have retrospectively referenced the feminist conflicts around the Scholar and the Feminist IX: Towards a Politics of Sexuality, colloquially remembered as the Barnard Sex Conference, as a pivotal flash point of the feminist sex wars where feminists broadly clashed over issues related to sexuality, including pornography and sadomasochism.[12] Comparatively little attention is given to the graphic artists—Hannah Alderfer, Beth Jaker, and Marybeth Nelson—who came together to design the *Diary* and how they continued their visual activism throughout the decade. Their graphic works within the *Diary* were central to the debate around sexual expression that occurred in the 1980s. Consequently, this event also demonstrates the key role that visual imagery played in the development of feminist discourse during this time, as the confiscation of the *Diary* heightened the conflict between the opposing groups of feminists. But the genealogy of this visual document and its role in theorizing women's sexuality has not been thoroughly explored.

The story of the *Diary* highlights the difficulties that many feminist visual works that engaged sexuality faced in their production and circulation during the 1980s, threatening both their immediate reception and enduring legacy. Across the book, I trace similar stories of how other artists mobilized images to build a community of discourse, while they simultaneously found it difficult to make their visual feminism legible. In the following two chapters, echoes of the *Diary*'s difficulties can be found in how women cartoonists like Roberta Gregory, Lee Marrs, and Alison Bechdel struggled to find receptive venues for their feminist comics and had to create opportunities through self-publication. In the final two chapters, I demonstrate how even more immediately recognized artists, like Gloria Anzaldúa and Nan Goldin, faced critique that influenced how they shared their visual work and shaped their careers. The nuance of visual politics lies at the core of these difficulties, as visual representations of sexuality were attacked both from within and outside the feminist movement across the decade. This chapter shows how these forces united as anti-porn feminists joined with conservative lawmakers to attempt to criminalize the circulation of obscene materials in both local and national ways.

Alderfer, Jaker, and Nelson further developed their visual feminist activism across the 1980s. Even before the *Diary*, they were invested in examining women's sexuality together. As undergrads, they studied at the School of Visual Arts in New York City and, after graduating in the late 1970s, formed the collaborative artist collective Group Material with other classmates and a small coed network of other young artists.[13] They fully participated in Group Material's shows and other artistic efforts, including the feminist leaning "It's a Gender Show!" in early 1981, but they ultimately left the group that May to commit more fully to feminist artwork and principles.[14] As Alderfer opined in her departure letter, "Briefly stated; sexual politics, issues of sexual difference and preference, and feminism are met within this group with disinterest and hostility which seems irresolvable with continued participation and struggle."[15]

They quickly found opportunities around them to examine sexuality within a feminist frame, including in the feminist journal *Heresies*, whose twelfth issue focused on issues of women's sexuality and was cheekily titled the "Sex Issue" (Figure 1.1).[16] All issues of *Heresies* juxtaposed feminist visual art and writing together throughout the roughly hundred-page volumes. Though Alderfer, Jaker, and Nelson's visual work is uncredited in *Heresies* #12 (1981), we can glimpse their work in a handful of unattributed collages throughout the issue, including in one roundup of archival images from the theater collection at the New York Public Library for the Performing Arts, a source that they would continue to draw on in future work.[17] Together with the *Diary*, these publications gave the three women a platform to explore and theorize women's sexuality as represented in, determined by, and transgressive of visual media. This trio continued to collaborate on this topic in the wake of the Barnard Sex Conference, producing the book jacket design for Vance's *Pleasure and Danger* (Figure 1.1). This multimedia collage combines two personal photographs of Alderfer's leg and Jaker's stairwell with the other details drawn in or sourced from advertisements. Originally collaged in black and white, the work was then xeroxed in color.[18] Together these visual elements and duplication process recreate the feel of a midcentury pulp novel to echo the tenor of the collection's title.

In 1984, the same year that *Pleasure and Danger* was published, a number of women joined together to form the Feminist Anti-Censorship

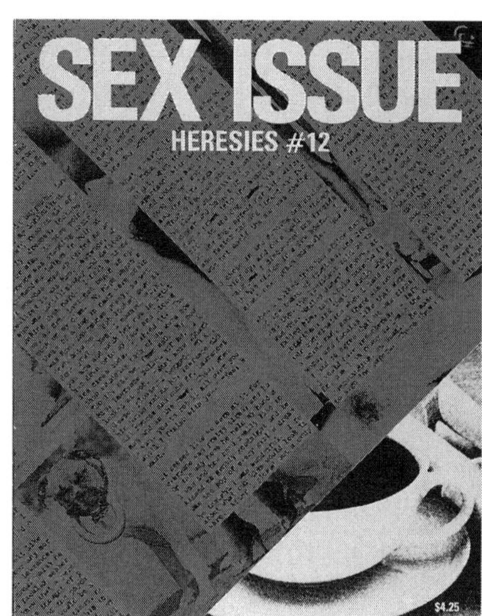

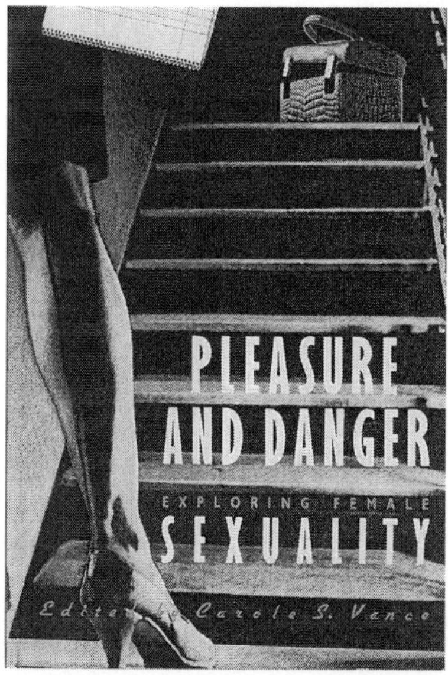

Figure 1.1. Front covers of *Heresies* #12 (1981) and *Pleasure and Danger* (1984), both of which Hannah Alderfer, Beth Jaker, and Marybeth Nelson composed via multimedia collage. Images reprinted with permission of Hannah Alderfer and Marybeth Nelson. Cover design Hannah Alderfer, Beth Jaker, and Marybeth Nelson with the Heresies Collective. *Heresies* scan courtesy of Visual Resources Center, Stanford University. *Pleasure and Danger* scan courtesy of the Lesbian Herstory Archives.

Taskforce (FACT), which was created to challenge the feminist anti-pornography efforts to have their ideas enforced by the state. In the years since the Barnard Sex Conference, feminists like Andrea Dworkin and Catharine MacKinnon, together with the support of conservative politicians, had been working to institute anti-pornography ordinances across the country.[19] In response, FACT took legal action, drafting and filing a legal brief that "was co-signed by the Women's Legal Defense Fund (WLDF) and eighty individual feminists."[20] FACT also took artistic action by creating *Caught Looking: Feminism, Pornography and Censorship* (1986), a multimedia text that Alderfer, Jaker, and Nelson visually designed over the course of eighteen months.[21] FACT compiled *Caught Looking* to bring together feminist writings "on the issues of pornography and pleasure, censorship and the impulse to control, sexual politics and sexuality in women's daily lives" framed through Alderfer, Jaker, and Nelson's visual design.[22] The trio of artists responded to the ongoing efforts to restrict sexual expression among anti-porn feminists and conservatives by creating a densely visual book that was both more erotic and more political. While *Heresies* #12 and the *Diary* were visually suggestive, *Caught Looking* directly incorporated and recontextualized pornography from across history.

The use of archival materials was critical to the visual and political interventions of these vital feminist works. Both the *Diary* and *Caught Looking* are indebted to personal archives and the proclivities of collectors for their images. For example, both publications made use of the Lesbian Herstory Archives, a lesbian feminist grassroots archives inspired by conversations among members of the Gay Academic Union that launched in 1974 when Joan Nestle and Deb Edel decided to house the collection in their own apartment, where it grew exponentially until they found an independent location in the early 1990s.[23] To the present day, the Lesbian Herstory Archives remains an important source on which many artists draw. For the *Diary*, Alderfer, Jaker, and Nelson also made use of the New York Public Library Picture Collection and the Schomburg Center for Research in Black Culture Photographs and Print Division. For *Caught Looking*, they also searched out images from "the porn shops of 42nd Street, [their] corner newsstands, back-date magazine sellers, out-of-print bookshops and . . . private dealers in New York where explicit sex-photos are for sale."[24] Looking at the intersection of archives and artistic production, specifically through the groups of women who produced the *Diary* and *Caught Looking*, shines a light on the way these artists were able to argue for a wide-ranging understanding of sexuality by recontextualizing materials from archives and collectors.[25]

Responding to anti-pornography feminists, Alderfer, Jaker, and Nelson wielded collage as a tactic to combat censorship, creating a new visual platform to express their political disagreement. Building from the *Diary*, where they visually augmented the conference planning notes and program, they further amplified the textual theorizations of women's sexuality in *Caught Looking* by their dense use of recontextualized images from archival sources. Archives and collectors played a critical role in supporting this activism by safeguarding controversial images. In the next section, I map out how archives intersected with this artistic production. I then further interrogate how Alderfer, Jaker, and Nelson's collaged approach innovates a new visual form of feminist discourse while embedding familiar feminist forms—in many ways, the artists I study in the later chapters will follow this approach by responding to feminist rhetoric through visual artwork. These two sections feed into how I close-read both the *Diary* and *Caught Looking* and theorize the visually articulated feminist theory that Alderfer, Jaker, and Nelson deploy through collage.

Alderfer, Jaker, and Nelson's continued feminist activism across the 1980s not only brought these works into the world, but also, in their work with FACT, successfully advocated against anti-pornography ordinances. They created space within the feminist movement for explicit visualities, thereby supporting other artists' visual innovations within feminism in the years to come, including Goldin's sexually explicit photography that I discuss in the final chapter. Ultimately, their activism fed into the sex-positive strand of the third wave in the 1990s, but their visual creations—especially the *Diary*—had already begun to retreat from public focus, out of print and discoverable only within the archives through which they emerged. Despite renewed attention to this period in recent years, the *Diary* and *Caught Looking* remain largely inaccessible.[26]

The Role of Archives and Collectors in Safeguarding Controversial Images

Grassroots or community archives preserve material from marginalized groups that might not otherwise be saved. The creation of spaces dedicated to the preservation of LGBTQ material in particular paralleled the feminist and gay liberation movements of the 1960s through 1980s.[27]

The ONE National Gay and Lesbian Archives was founded as the Western Gay Archives in 1971, the Stonewall National Museum and Archives began in 1973, the Lesbian Herstory Archives was created in 1974, the Sexual Minorities Archives began with the creation of the New Alexandria Library for Women in 1974, the Ohio Lesbian Archives was started in 1978, the June L. Mazer Lesbian Archives was started as the West Coast Lesbian Collections in 1981, and the GLBT Historical Society was founded in 1985. This handful of examples from across the United States illustrates the proliferation of new archives during this period.[28] While many have become more official and some have joined with university collections—like the Mazer did with the University of California, Los Angeles, in 2009 and the ONE did with the University of Southern California in 2010—all of them began as personal collections, often started in their founders' own homes. The personal nature of these spaces persisted as they grew into grassroots archives staffed by volunteer archivists. Further, as Angela L. DiVeglia has noted, "community archives play an important role in the larger LGBT community; not only do they provide an alternative to often exclusionary archives, but they also allow a greater focus on community- and identity-building through the reclamation and self-production of history."[29] These archives were created in the absence of more official archives collecting such material, but they and the social movements affiliated with them subsequently inspired traditional spaces to take notice, such that some of the artists that I study in this book (e.g., Alison Bechdel and Gloria Anzaldúa) have their personal papers collected within long-established collections dedicated to women's and Latin American history.

Grassroots archives like these are especially protective of controversial images because the archivists involved—including the volunteers who join later and donate their time to maintaining and growing the collection—feel a personal connection to the material. Often, materials documenting LGBTQ lives and art are under threat, so grassroots archives operate like a safe haven. Safeguarding involves archivists preserving the materials for posterity within the archives in order to actively support the discovery of these materials and their continued use in contemporary social justice movements. The space of the archives extends beyond the walls of its physical space and feeds back into various social movements. In Ann Cvetkovich's discussion of the Lesbian Herstory

Archives (LHA), she shows how LHA has served as a source for films and documentaries, slideshows, and external exhibits.[30] Grassroots archives like LHA work to make their materials more accessible not only by removing barriers to public access but also by participating in and curating exhibits and other public-facing events. The materials collected within LHA and other grassroots archives remain active as living materials rather than forgotten documents.

More than just archives, Alderfer, Jaker, and Nelson relied on individual collectors when locating sexually explicit images for *Caught Looking*. One of their major sources was Vasta Images/Books in Lower Manhattan whose images appear on most pages of *Caught Looking*. In thanking Joseph Vasta for the many photographs he supplied, Alderfer, Jaker, and Nelson noted, "We encountered imaginative erotic images and a rare compassionate sexual vision."[31] Vasta Images/Books was particularly helpful in providing a wide historical range of sources, including many of the earliest pornographic images in the chronological "100 Years of Porn" feature. Though the trove of erotic photographs from Vasta Images/Books was overwhelmingly heterosexual in nature, the role of such collectors is similar to grassroots archives like the Lesbian Herstory Archives in how they safeguard images portraying sexual diversity. Moreover, as the next chapter will discuss in further detail, individual collectors have been an important source in preserving marginalized media that later finds a place within established archives.

Because archives keep materials available for use, when you engage materials there, you cannot think of them as having been deposited there just once. Rather, you must consider how these materials circulate back and forth between archives and individuals who repurpose them for new art and thought. Attending to how multiple mediations continually shape archival materials—which Eric Ketelaar terms "recontextualisation"—supersedes the notion of provenance that prioritizes a document's origins.[32] For example, in both the *Diary* and *Caught Looking* Alderfer, Jaker, and Nelson source and rework images from archives and collectors by putting them in new collaged configurations. Their artistic interventions and archival sources matter just as much as the provenance of the images. The art they use in the *Diary* and *Caught Looking* depend on the archives for visibility and vice versa, as the images' repurposing enacts the mission of those organizations and people who deliberately preserved them. While this chapter focuses on visual documents created by sourcing images from archives, later chapters look to how archives preserve not only artworks and legacies but also the activism surrounding these works.

In maintaining materials for continual repurposing, archives disrupt the notion of a finished product just as manuscripts within archives more generally can challenge the idea of a definitive version. This disruption is a key component of these materials, as social justice movements operate on a need for futurity rather than finality. That is, movements work to continue advocating for their cause, so it is paramount that the materials also remain active. In her study of archivists who preserve third-wave feminist materials, Kate Eichhorn demonstrates how contemporary archivists themselves conceive of the archives as an active space: "For a younger generation of feminists, the archive is not necessarily either a destination or an impenetrable barrier to be breached, but rather a site and practice integral to knowledge making, cultural production, and activism."[33] By conceptualizing the archives as a space "integral to knowledge making, cultural production, and activism," archivists facilitate how visitors to the archives can research, encounter, and reactivate the materials they come across. In short, activist archivists are essential not only in collecting and organizing the material but in facilitating its reentry into the critical discourse. How the materials from the feminist sex wars themselves are maintained underlines both their living nature and the precarity that all movement documents face. While the visual interventions of the *Diary* and *Caught Looking* were formed through the archives, their low-circulation, independently produced, and ultimately out-of-print status means that they are now largely a form of the archives themselves.[34]

Fittingly, then, one of the copies of the *Diary* within Barnard's own archives, maintained as part of the documentation of the event, has been marked up by the college for the purposes of its eventual censorship. Barnard administration wanted to distance the institution from being affiliated with the *Diary*, but much of the *Diary* remains relatively untouched. Administrators' biggest edit involved the page dedicated to the history of the Barnard Women's Center (Figure 1.2). On this page of the archived version of *Diary*, a penciled hand annotates the page, seeking to remove the necessary affiliations from the textual description of

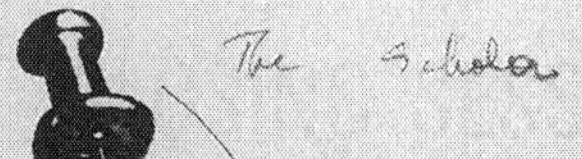

The Barnard Women's Center, 1971–1982

In the fall of 1981 the Barnard Women's Center celebrated its tenth anniversary. Founded in 1971 by a task force of administrators, faculty, trustees, alumnae, and students, its purpose was to create a physical and psychological space for women within and outside the university. Through its resource collection, its up-to-date information on women's programs and events, its discussions, lectures and conferences, the Center encourages a continuing dialogue on feminist theory and practice. Staffed by a director, associate director, and administrative assistant, it is governed by a 12-member Executive Committee composed of equal representation from students, faculty, administrators, and alumnae. Barnard College provides 2/3 of its annual budget and the remaining third comes from gifts and grants. A link between the college and women of the larger community, the Women's Center is an important meeting ground for feminist activities.

As part of its commitment to the new scholarship on women, the Women's Center holds an annual Scholar and the Feminist Conference each spring. Initiated in 1974 and funded by the Helena Rubinstein Foundation, the conferences provide a useful framework for the investigation of the impact of feminism on traditional scholarship. The Women's Center works closely with an academic coordinator and planning committee--composed of scholars and activists from Barnard and the larger community--in developing the theme, selecting speakers and organizing the conference. During the past eight years the Scholar and the Feminist Conference has become a New York City feminist event, bringing together over 600 people, mostly women--scholars, artists, and activists.

The first Scholar and the Feminist Conference, 1974 (academic coordinator, Susan R. Sacks), raised the fundamental question, can feminism and scholarship be integrated? Themes of subsequent conferences reflect the continuing dialectic between feminist consciousness and women's studies: 1975, (II) "Towards a New Criteria of Relevance" (Nancy K. Miller); 1976, (III) "The Search for Origins" (Hester Eisenstein); 1977, (IV) "Connecting Theory, Practice and Values" (Mary Parlee); 1978, (V) "Creating Feminist Works" (Elizabeth Minnich); 1979, (VI) "The Future of Difference" (Alice Jardine); 1980, (VII) "Class, Race and Sex: Exploring Contradictions, Affirming Connections" (Amy Swerdlow); and 1981, (VIII) "The Dynamics of Control" (Hanna Lessinger). "Towards a Politics of Sexuality," coordinated by Carole S. Vance, is our ninth conference.

Papers from three of the earlier conferences, (1976, 1977 and 1978) have been published in pamphlet form by the Barnard Women's Center. The Future of Difference edited by Hester Eisenstein and Alice Jardine, an anthology of essays from the 1978 conference, was published by G.K. Hall and Company in December, 1980. Class, Race and Sex: The Dynamics of Control (G.K. Hall), papers from the 1980 and 1981 conferences, edited by Amy Swerdlow and Hanna Lessinger, will appear in late 1982.

Jane S. Gould, Director

Janie Kritzman, Associate Director

Maria La Sala, Assistant to the Director

70

Figure 1.2. Original, pre-censorship copy of the *Diary*, edited by Barnard in order to remove Barnard's affiliation from the document by deleting the page describing the history of the Barnard Women's Center. Image reprinted with permission of Hannah Alderfer and Marybeth Nelson. Copyright 1982, 1983 by Hannah Alderfer, Beth Jaker, and Marybeth Nelson. Box 5, Folder 10, Barnard Center for Research on Women records, 1962–2019, Barnard Archives and Special Collections, Barnard Library, Barnard College.

the Center through hefty line edits. However, these focused actions are insufficient in erasing Barnard's complicity, so the hand ultimately strikes the page entirely—a penciled *X* recommends the wholesale removal of the page, reinforced by striking this item from the table of contents as well.

The edited version that Barnard eventually sent out removes the description of the Barnard Women's Center not simply by producing a blank page in its place, but by including a large gray rectangle occupying the body of the page, filling the space in a way that makes its emptiness conspicuous (Figure 1.3).[35] There are other pages throughout the *Diary* that were intentionally left blank for conference attendees' notes, but Alderfer, Jaker, and Nelson designed them with see-through background images—hair, safety pins, matchbook, keys, condom, rose, et cetera—that float in free space and elliptically relate to the conference theme.[36] Because the page is styled differently, the gray blankness noticeably hides something. Barnard's decision to distance themselves from the *Diary* further demonstrates the need for independent archives and activists, as the women involved had to find other avenues for their activism around sexuality. Across the 1980s, visual artists laid claim to broadly representing sexuality, broadcasting their creations through grassroots networks affiliated with feminist as well as gay and lesbian movements rather than more official or mainstream channels.

Figure 1.3. Blank page that replaces the history of the Barnard's Women Center in the edited version of the *Diary* that was mailed to participants. Image reprinted with permission of Hannah Alderfer and Marybeth Nelson. Copyright 1982, 1983 by Hannah Alderfer, Beth Jaker, and Marybeth Nelson. Scan courtesy of Visual Resources Center, Stanford University.

In the coming years, major feminist works focused on sexuality were also produced by and within communities of artists and activists, particularly radical hybrid image–text documents, as I examine in subsequent chapters. The *Diary* and *Caught Looking* foreshadowed the visual aesthetics of riot grrrl zines in the 1990s, demonstrating the connection between the feminist sex wars and the pro-sexuality politics of third-wave feminism that the zines exemplify. The *Diary* was produced in conjunction with an academic event that heightened a growing division between opposing forces, so there was a utopian, circumspect quality to the production, while *Caught Looking* was an unabashedly activist document, produced through a feminist group, that contains sexually explicit imagery directly confronting the anti-pornography ordinances of the day.[37] These contexts shaped Alderfer, Jaker, and Nelson's selection and deployment of images from archives, and just as these publications professed a wide-ranging acceptance of sexual expression, the images themselves also conveyed the importance of archives and collectors who preserved them.

Theorizing the Aesthetics of Politically Controversial Visual Forms and Visual Scholarly Discourse

By deploying collage in designing both the *Diary* and *Caught Looking*, Alderfer, Jaker, and Nelson created richly textured and hybrid artworks that shaped feminist discourse on sexuality through the juxtaposition of varied visual and textual forms. The stakes of sexually controversial visuality that resulted in the confiscation and censorship of the *Diary* by the Barnard administration in April 1982 was heightened by the time *Caught Looking* was published in 1986. In the intervening years, Andrea Dworkin and Catharine MacKinnon had been proposing local anti-pornography ordinances in a number of U.S. cities, prompting the formation of FACT and the creation of *Caught Looking*.[38]

For both publications, their hybridity helped them effectively counter the anti-pornography feminists. As Carole S. Vance described in an epilogue to *Pleasure and Danger* that looked back at the Barnard Sex Conference, "Illustrated by witty and evocative sexual images, the *Diary* contained minutes and bibliographies from planning committee discussions; personal statements from committee members; the conference concept paper; and abstracts and suggested readings from workshops.

Juxtaposing text and image, the *Diary* invited readers to consider their inter-relationship."[39] Similarly, Ann Snitow, a member of FACT, described the hybrid composition of *Caught Looking* in a retrospective review: "The texts of *Caught Looking: Feminism, Pornography and Censorship* [1986] are polemics, histories, and analyses. . . . The artists turned the collection into much more: a powerful collage of words and images that is still circulating in the world, a distinguished instance of collective, political art."[40] Both of these accounts emphasize the diversity of the textual makeup of the books and how the visuals amplify the overarching argument. As writers themselves, Vance and Snitow foreground the textual variety, yet the visual elements also ranged widely—Alderfer, Jaker, and Nelson meticulously detailed the visual credits across multiple pages at the back of *Caught Looking*.[41] How they sourced their images from a variety of archival sources, as described in the above section, also contributes to the range of visual imagery in both volumes.

Through the various juxtapositions that collaging offers, Alderfer, Jaker, and Nelson evoked and drew strength from the diary form that was important within second-wave feminist discourse and foreshadowed the popular third-wave feminist form of zines. Moreover, their hybrid, image–text works fit in a lineage alongside notable female cartoonists like Erika Lopez and Lynda Barry who have employed collage-like aesthetics and unexpected fusions of image and text to great acclaim.[42] All of these formal juxtapositions—among varieties of texts and images—determined how readers understood their feminist messages. Alderfer, Jaker, and Nelson's collaged approach meant that viewers could not simply determine what individual images meant; they would also need to contemplate the full constellation of images and how they existed in coordination with text. Beyond individual page compositions, readers were invited to consider the interactions of different styles of image and text present and also how the sources of the images and texts, including those gathered from archives, shaped the overall message. The collective form of collage allowed Alderfer, Jaker, and Nelson to bring many sources together into conversation around women's sexuality and illustrate the complexity of the topic, showing how variously it had been visually represented across time and contexts. Though the artists in subsequent chapters created works in other media, they also brought a collective of voices and juxtaposition of formal elements into the space of their artistic works to weigh in on women's sexuality.

Within second-wave feminism, many writers turned to using the form of the diary in their public writing due to how it allowed women to express how the personal was political through sharing their experiences. The diary was wielded by many within the movement including well-known contemporaneous thinkers like Gloria Anzaldúa, Audre Lorde, Cherríe Moraga, and Adrienne Rich. These women used the diary to facilitate a closeness between author and reader through direct address as well as to highlight the political nature of everyday, personal occurrences. Through their collaged approach, Alderfer, Jaker, and Nelson transformed the genre. With the *Diary*, they reimagined it as a public, collective form. In a short note included alongside personal messages from the other conference organizers, Alderfer commented on the use of a diary: "My secret desire was to write in a personal diary yet where could I write what I wanted but in a diary that must be made public?" (Figure 1.4).[43] With this statement, Alderfer demonstrates how a public diary was necessary to reveal certain truths that had been waiting to be told. She writes in plain block letters to proclaim her position more boldly than the typewritten or cursive script entries of the other conference organizers featured on the same page. Her choice to convey her message in such a straightforward, handwritten manner underlines its personal nature, while also allowing her message to be easily readable by a larger public. That is, she translates her message to fit the form of a public diary.[44] As she gestures to with her remarks, the metamorphosis of the conference program into a diary that was shared and public shapes the academic material reproduced within. Framing public, scholarly discourse through the diary genre underscored the usually private nature of sexuality and how feminists were transforming these topics by making them public and scholarly. By adopting the diary format, though, Alderfer, Jaker, and Nelson also underlined how personal this topic remained for all involved. While *Caught Looking* did not explicitly draw on the diary form, it invoked the personal in its written accounts and inclusion of pornographic images from private collectors.

The diary format is most evident in how the preliminary meeting minutes of the conference planning committee are styled as diary entries, opening these discussions to conference-goers and allowing them to learn from and think alongside these women. These nine entries at the outset span the first half of the handbook and document the initial weekly sessions from mid-September to late November 1981 during which the

The committee asked many more questions than it could possibly begin to answer, or find "experts" to address. Nevertheless the questioning was itself valuable.

One issue not overtly raised was that of the difficulties of a common lesbian and heterosexual feminist discussion of sexuality. Avoiding debate by assuming that an issue is recognised, and being recognised, settled, is not necessarily a good tactic. The debate goes on.

Julie L. Abraham

MY SECRET DESIRE WAS TO WRITE IN A PERSONAL DIARY

YET WHERE COULD I WRITE WHAT I WANTED

BUT IN A DIARY THAT MUST BE MADE PUBLIC?

WITH MUCH LOVE TO MY COLLABORATORS AND THIS DIARY Hannah

Why talk about "sexuality" and not "sex"? At the beginning, we had trouble even defining "sexuality" so that we could work with it. For me, sexuality is inseparable from its representation (visual, linguistic, psychic). We can only talk about sex across culturally-given metaphors that encode the dominant ideology, that mediate our own "experience" and are embedded in the very words we have to use because there are no others (yet). To say "sexuality," not "sex", is to acknowledge that our perspectives are partial.

/M. Altman

Being a part of the planning committee has provided new ways for me to see some important connections among the personal, political, feminist, social, sexual and academic parts of my own life - Jan Boney

HETEROPHILIA: ITS CAUSES AND CURES
A pioneering conference that removes the stigma from heterophilia by considering it as a clinical entity in the light of the most recent research. Originated and planned by the 192 St. John's Place Research Institute; Tee Corinne, concept; Alma Routsong, Frances Doughty, Tee Corinne, panels. THE SOCIAL WORLD OF THE HETEROPHILIAC: WHAT HETEROPHILIACS DO IN THE DAYTIME   A CURED HETEROPHILIAC: A CASE STUDY   HORMONE IMBALANCES IN HETEROPHILIA   PRO-BLEMS OF SELF-CONTEMPT AMONG HETEROPHILIACS   DIFFERENCES BETWEEN MALE AND FEMALE HETEROPHILIA Closing Ceremony: Gala Banquet--The conference will feature reports from four heterophiliacs themselves: men and women who have the conscience and courage to appear, disguised by paper bags, as witnesses to the agony of heterophilia in today's society.   Frances Doughty

9

Figure 1.4. Handwritten message from Hannah Alderfer about the *Diary* format amid personal messages from other members of the conference planning committee. Image reprinted with permission of Hannah Alderfer and Marybeth Nelson. Copyright 1982, 1983 by Hannah Alderfer, Beth Jaker, and Marybeth Nelson. Scan courtesy of Visual Resources Center, Stanford University.

conference planning committee met to formulate the event.[45] While these entries originated as minutes, they're designed to look like diary entries where "Dear Diary" and that week's date were styled in a visual font beginning each narrative entry that described that week's meeting and thematic focus. The diary entries recorded the group's discoveries in the present tense as their thoughts were still in the process of being formed and shared through group discussion. The present-tense tenor of this form would encourage readers to engage, particularly as they examined how the words connected to images on the page through the stylized look of "Dear Diary" and that week's date. By intersecting with and often quite literally framing the words, the images were touched by the personal revelations and obliquely echoed them. Given that none of the images directly illustrated textual material, readers would have to dig into their associational ties to understand the interrelationship.

In these pages and throughout both volumes, the personal surfaces through the visual and forms community, as when Alderfer's choice of handwriting highlights her personal message and invites readers to ponder her question about the possibility of diaries. The signaling of the personal through visual elements that foreground the work's handmade nature positions both the *Diary* and *Caught Looking* as proto-zines that also are in conversation with the sex-positive politics central to zines when they became popular amidst the riot grrrl movement of the 1990s associated with third-wave feminism. This formal similarity means that the insights of zine scholars are also relevant to these creations. As mentioned in the introduction, Alison Piepmeier's theorization of "embodied community," which describes how zinesters form community with their readers through the zine itself, resonates with these texts. Piepmeier further expounds on this concept in her monograph *Girl Zines* (2009) when she writes, "The materiality of zines creates community that is embodied because it activates bodily experiences such as pleasure, affection, allegiance, and vulnerability. . . . These qualities emerge in various ways in the medium itself."[46] In this formation, it is the materiality of the zine itself as well as its handmade aesthetics that initiate "bodily experiences" among readers who become part of the community through engaging with the zine. The intimate, personal subject matter of the *Diary* and *Caught Looking,* in particular, amplifies this exchange as women reflect on their own bodies and sexualities and also are encouraged—through image and text—to think through how broader culture represents these entities. That the books are produced by many individuals also shapes the resulting community as it is not a matter of one woman connecting to another, but of a woman being recruited to join a constellation of feminists and their multifaceted and varied understandings of sexuality rather than with the limited view of the anti-pornography crew.

Both volumes operate as fusions of communities—namely, those of the varied groups that come together to create them, including Alderfer, Jaker, and Nelson, who visually designed each book and engaged broader communities of archives and collectors to do so. By designing an all-encompassing visual register, Alderfer, Jaker, and Nelson create literal frames on each page that are positioned as looking glasses for the readers to see through. Their various layouts shape the reading experience and encourage readers to reflect on the multifaceted and complex nature of sexuality as they group individual images together to illustrate the experiences of multiple women. The kinship of the *Diary* and *Caught Looking* with these other popular feminist forms—diaries and zines—allows Alderfer, Jaker, and Nelson to foreground formally the intimate nature of women's sexuality while also facilitating a public, collective conversation. The following two sections will look more closely at how Alderfer, Jaker, and Nelson deployed collage to examine the politics of women's sexuality, and how their tactics evolved across the 1980s in response to the concurrently shifting tactics of the anti-pornography feminists.

Collaging Feminism in the Barnard Sex Conference's Diary of a Conference on Sexuality

Despite the confiscation and editing of the *Diary* by the Barnard administration, its visual representations were fairly tame. Within them, though, there was the kernel for later, more explicit representations in *Caught Looking* with their open approach to interrogating and representing women's sexuality and other interlocking matters. As Judith Butler described in a review of the *Diary* published in *Gay Community News* in December 1982, they had high expectations for the lascivious content of the *Diary*, given its censorship, "so when I opened it to find photos of women in bed with the sheets pulled up to their chins, the let down was considerable."[47] Indeed, while there are small peeks at nudity throughout the *Diary* with a titillating breast or butt cheek here or there, overall the images were more suggestive than erotic. Rachel Corbman summarizes the relatively innocuous visual content of the *Diary* in an article about the planning and aftermath of the conference: "While some of the graphics are intentionally provocative, the overall effect of the handbook seems within the limits of appropriateness for an academic publication on feminism and sexuality."[48] Yet, within these limits, Alderfer, Jaker, and Nelson were able to visually introduce a complex conversation on sexuality and include the diverse perspectives of the conference planning committee and workshop leaders on the page.

The *Diary* represents a key moment in the history of women theorizing their sexuality through images and reclaiming the power of the visual that had been so often used to objectify them. While this chapter focuses on how the visual approach of the *Diary* laid the groundwork for the sexually explicit visual innovations of *Caught Looking*, it is crucial to emphasize that these works influenced and were shaped by the visual tactics of the other artists featured in this book and are a vital touchstone in that broader political and artistic history. Indeed, Alderfer, Jaker, and Nelson's collage aesthetics integrates comics, drawings, and photographs—the media that the other artists in this book create—throughout both the *Diary* and *Caught Looking*.

Reimagining the conference program genre through the diary genre's ethos of meticulous recording provided a more in-depth, behind-the-scenes look at the work the academic coordinator and conference planning committee did in conceptualizing the event. Typically, Barnard's annual Scholar and Feminist conferences produced only minimal, four-page conference pamphlets that listed the schedule of the conference, so this production was exceptional.[49] The *Diary* recreated the conference program genre by more extensively documenting the organization of the conference itself in addition to more thoroughly representing the conference schedule, devoting a page to each of the eighteen workshops planned for the afternoon of the conference. The handbook opens with the September 2, 1981, letter that Vance sent inviting scholars and activists to participate in planning the eventual conference, which outlines the potential questions the planning committee and the conference itself might tackle (Figure 1.5).[50] Rather than simply reprinting the letter's text in the booklet, the letter itself is reproduced on Barnard letterhead

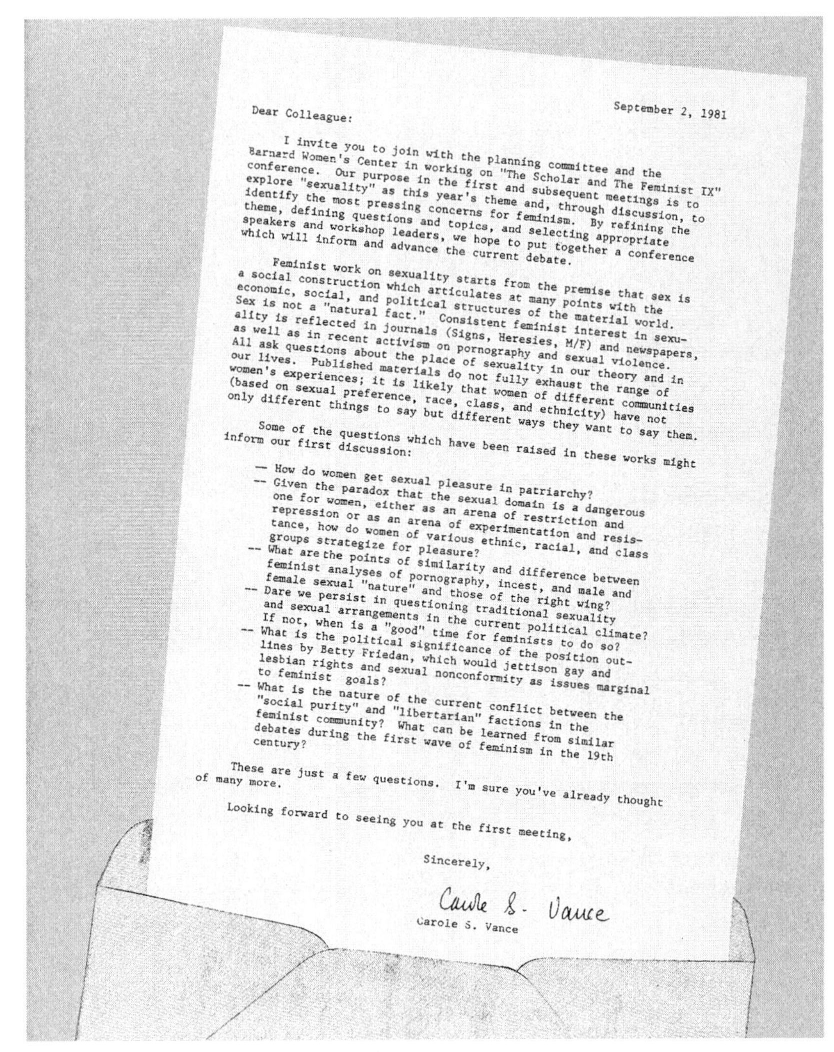

Figure 1.5. Carole S. Vance's letter inviting scholars and activists to participate in planning the conference and the following copyright page of the *Diary* featuring the lip prints of the three designers accompanied by their signatures and a handwritten inscription. Images reprinted with permission of Hannah Alderfer and Marybeth Nelson. Copyright 1982, 1983 by Hannah Alderfer, Beth Jaker, and Marybeth Nelson. Scan courtesy of Visual Resources Center, Stanford University. Letter courtesy of Carole S. Vance.

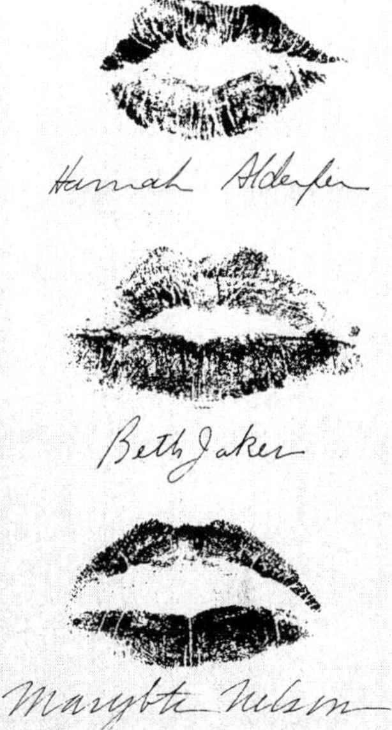

For your pleasure
your thoughts...
consider sexual choices—
erotic possibilities, now
and for the future,
With Love,

ACKNOWLEDGEMENTS

EDITORIAL WORK
Hannah Alderfer, Meryl Altman, Kate Ellis, Beth Jaker, Marybeth Nelson, Esther Newton, Ann Snitow, Carole S. Vance

CONSULTATION AND REVIEW
Diane Harriford, Amber Hollibaugh, Andrew Tyndall, Paula Webster

VISUAL RESOURCES
Lesbian Herstory Archives, Deb Edel and Joan Nestle
New York Public Library Picture Collection
Schomburg Reference Library Photography Archives

SPECIAL THANKS
Tony DiCiaccio *for preliminary typing assistance*
Dorothy Jaker *for visual research*

VERY SPECIAL THANKS
Meryl Altman *for editorial assistance*
Anne Drillick, *without the contribution of her invaluable production work and long hours this diary would not have met its deadline*
Carole S. Vance

Set in Memphis and Helios by Brooklyn Bridge and igloo graphics
Printed by Faculty Press.
©copyright Hannah Alderfer, Beth Jaker, Marybeth Nelson

Second Printing, February 1983

**THE SCHOLAR AND THE FEMINIST
TOWARD A POLITICS OF SEXUALITY**

Saturday, April 24, 1982

Carole S. Vance, *Academic Coordinator*

Conference Planning Committee
Julie Abraham, Hannah Alderfer, Meryl Altman, Jan Boney, Frances Doughty, Ellen DuBois, Kate Ellis, Judith Friedlander, Julie German, Faye Ginsburg, Diane Harriford, Beth Jaker, Mary Clare Lennon, Sherry Manasse, Nancy K. Miller, Marybeth Nelson, Esther Newton, Claire Riley, Susan R. Sacks, Ann Snitow, Quandra P. Stadler, Judy R. Walkowitz, Ellen Willis, Patsy Yaeger

Barnard Women's Center
Jane Gould, Janie Kritzman, Maria La Sala

emerging out of an envelope, mimicking the moment when every woman first read the letter and considered participating in planning the event. In the censored version of the page reprinted here, Barnard removed their letterhead. Turning the page, the publication information and table of contents follow, and it is here that Alderfer, Jaker, and Nelson announce their collaborative artistic authorship by each leaving a signed lipstick print on the publication information page, alongside a joint message to the readers, "For your pleasure / your thoughts . . . / consider sexual choices— / erotic possibilities, now / and for the future / With Love."[51] They prompt readers to embrace pleasure and amplify that message by sealing their message with a printed kiss, much as one might sign a letter to a lover. Together, these lips and Vance's letter frame the rest of the *Diary*, encouraging participants to seriously weigh the matter of women's sexuality without forgoing their embodied responses to erotic stimuli.

Alderfer, Jaker, and Nelson's handiwork is visible in the following pages as they reconceive the nine sets of minutes from planning meetings as collaged diary pages.[52] As discussed in the previous section, these entries make evident their group discussion with many of the interspersed remarks of the conference planning committee members reflecting on how they learned to speak together about difficult and complex topics through these sessions. By making the planning process transparent through the letter and diary entries, all participants are made to feel like they can join the conversation. Following the entries in the first half of the *Diary*, the latter half is mostly devoted to the descriptions of the conference workshops. Also included throughout the *Diary* were the personal statements from every member of the planning committee, a detailed history of the Barnard Women's Center that was ultimately censored, blank pages for notes, an address book page where attendees could collect the information of fellow conference participants, and a concept paper where the planning committee articulated a "politics of sexuality" formed through their planning meetings.

The diary entries set the aesthetic tone for the handbook. Their collage format facilitated an openness in readers' interpretation and encouraged them to think capaciously about sexuality. Here is where we find the fairly innocuous images of women in bed that Butler gestured to in their review, which first appear with the September 22 and October 6 entries (Figure 1.6).[53] In these early meetings, the women are still discussing sexuality broadly, responding to Vance's engagement with the topic and tracing out their own. In both of these entries, we see photographs of women alone and in small groups peeking their faces out from under the bed covers in the bottom outer corners of each page. To add another layer of visual complexity, these images are presented as if they are the hidden content under each page as, above each image, we see an illustration of a rolled-up corner. This design suggests that each meeting allows the participants to fold back the corners and see these women and their sexual experiences just as the women themselves are peeling back the covers to reveal themselves to the photographer. As the first entry of the *Diary* on September 16 only showed a hand beginning to write on a blank page, these images set the tone for the representation of women throughout the handbook.

The entries that follow don't always show women in bed, but the next one that does, November 10, illustrates how the conference committee had broadened their conversation to consider the multivalent ways in which women engage sexuality in their lives.[54] This entry includes a photo-collage comic that unfolds in two panels apiece across the top of three pages (Figure 1.7). During that meeting, the women discussed how Black and white feminists engaged sexuality differently, and the comic also follows that theme and represents their shared conversation. It depicts a Black and white woman, both hidden under a bed, who encounter each other and work through their internal biases in order to emerge out from under the bed and talk together about sexuality.

The women and bed are inked in a cartoon style, while photographs in the space above the bed illustrate the mental images that each woman works through in order to engage the other.[55] The photographs depict how race has separated the women, while the internal dialogue of each woman emphasizes how sexuality has kept them from being in solidarity with each other. The photographs transition from the historical to the contemporary, emphasizing how the legacy of the enslavement of Black people in America shapes their encounter. The first photograph shows the white children of a slaveholding family who are accompanied by their enslaved caretakers; this image is contrasted with the white and Black woman tentatively peeking their heads out from under the bed and sighting the other woman. The second panel contrasts images of Black and white suffragettes, including an iconic image of Sojourner Truth, while the third panel features a photo from the 1968 sanitation workers strike in

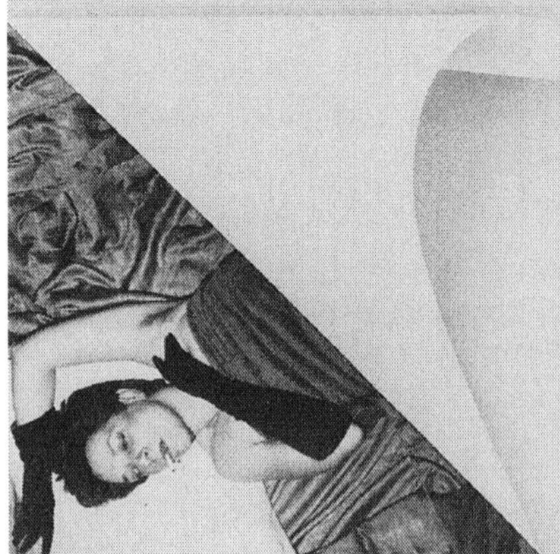

        Carole described briefly the nature and development of her interest in the
topic of sexuality. Following the round-robin method, each member described her
responses to the first meeting and thoughts during the intervening week: comments flew thick and fast.

        -A recent workshop on sexuality at the Communist University in London was
dominated by the "politics of rage," not just an expression of anger, but the
embodiment of the anti-intellectual premise that thought is not necessary to political action; feeling will suffice. This is a heritage of feminism.
        -Important and interesting topics for further discussion: the question of
"political correctness" in sexuality; the links between sexual "political correctness" and other forms of "political correctness" both on the Left and the
Right; the silence of heterosexual women and reasons for it; implications of
celibacy.
        -What do we mean by "sexuality"? What is sexual? How can we have a confer-
ence without defining what it means? Who determines sexuality and for whom?
Is all pleasure sexual? Is all sexuality pleasurable? What is the relationship
between the two?
        -Are the issues mentioned at our first meeting specific to a particular cohort
or generation of women? Examples: the issue of orgasm (difficulty in obtaining
an orgasm; vaginal versus clitoral) was a larger one for women over forty than
for nineteen year olds today.
        -What is sexuality? Is it defined by specific organs (the genitals) or spe-
cific physiological reactions? This definition would have no room for the pros-
titute, who may be experiencing little or no "sexual" sensation, yet the act is
surely a sexual one in some respects.
        -Without being totally utopian, what are feminists' expectations for sexual
change?

                                        -In our dislike of biological
                                        reductionism, have we been unwill-
                                        ing to consider biological or phys-
                                        iological features of sexual re-
                                        sponse? What about Masters and
                                        Johnson's work? Is it an error to
                                        think there is an irreducible phys-
                                        ical bedrock to all or some sexual
                                        experience?
                                        -Are we going to focus exclu-
                                        sively on genital sexuality? Scyl-
                                        la and Charybdis: sex is only the
                                        most orgasm-directed and genital
                                        behavior, which leads to talking
                                        about little but technique versus
                                        such a broad definition of sexual-
                                        ity/sensuality that it includes
                                        seeing a good movie. A discussion
                                        followed, with the following exam-
                                        ple offered as a rough guideline
                                        for our group: maternal sexuality

Figure 1.6. First page spread of September 22 minutes in the *Diary* in which the conference planning committee discusses their preliminary thoughts on the topic of sexuality; visually the designers style the meeting as a diary and there are photographs showing women in bed under the lower outside corners of the pages. Image reprinted with permission of Hannah Alderfer and Marybeth Nelson. Copyright 1982, 1983 by Hannah Alderfer, Beth Jaker, and Marybeth Nelson. Scan courtesy of Visual Resources Center, Stanford University.

would include women's specifically sexual response to nursing and issues of sexuality between mothers and daughters but would not include viewing nurturance as a generalized form of sexuality.

-In the current debates within the feminist community and with the New Right, the issue _is_ genital sexuality. The conference must address this issue.

-Why and how is human culture the agent of sexual repression?

-We need to include infant sexuality, which surely is continuous to some degree with adult experience.

-Observe the following contrast: feminists explain why women can't get any pleasure in patriarchy, at the same time a popular literature proliferates instructing women on how to get sexual pleasure. Who is buying these books? Are women succeeding in obtaining pleasure? If so, why don't we know much about their experience? On the other hand, who writes these books and, more generally, what does "popular culture" represent?

-What is the relationship between lesbian separatists and the anti-pornography movement? Do both groups share a vision of a world made safe for women? Why was "violence against women" (campaigns against rape, battering and incest) superseded by "women against pornography" (campaigns against pornographic visual representation)?

-The anti-pornography movement poses a problem regarding male sexuality, in that it is presented as "naturally" different from that of women. If so, what is to be done?

-Feminists' criticism of psychoanalysis and psychodynamic explanations has led to throwing the baby out with the bathwater. Feminists need to give more attention to psychological dynamics.

-What is the relationship between gender and sexuality? Why are women attracted to men? What creates attraction? Why women are attracted to women seems evident (Chodorow, Dinnerstein). What causes the exclusivity of attraction to men or women? Where does that leave bisexuals who are really violating a rigid dichotomy? Do sanctions against bisexuality (not only by moralists, but by those who find them politically disloyal) illustrate the point that taboo is always present in some form, even though it may move around from one area to another? Why do we in our categories always construct binary oppositions (female/not male)? (See Levi-Strauss, Mary Douglas.)

-The Women Against Pornography (WAP) Times Square tour featured a porno supermarket, the ultimate in capitalist production, display and consumption. What is the relationship between capitalism and sexuality? Pornography in past centuries had been the prerogative of the elite; now it is available to all for democratic consumption.

-Can one say anything good about capitalism? It permitted women, especially daughters, to get out of the family. It permitted the formation of sexual minorities.

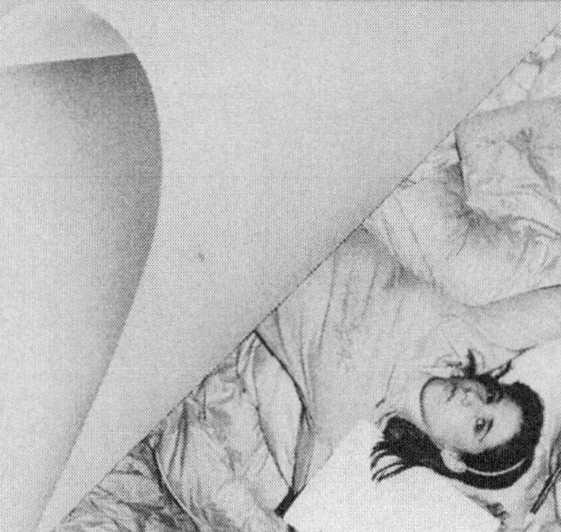

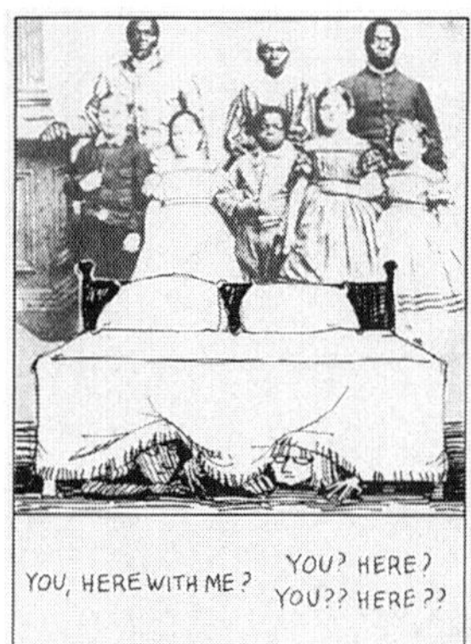
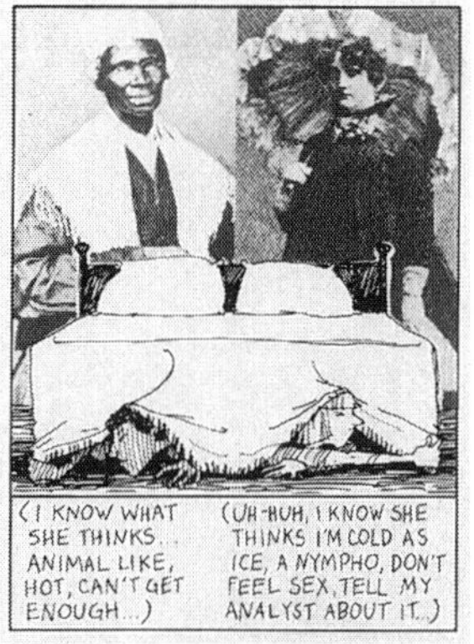

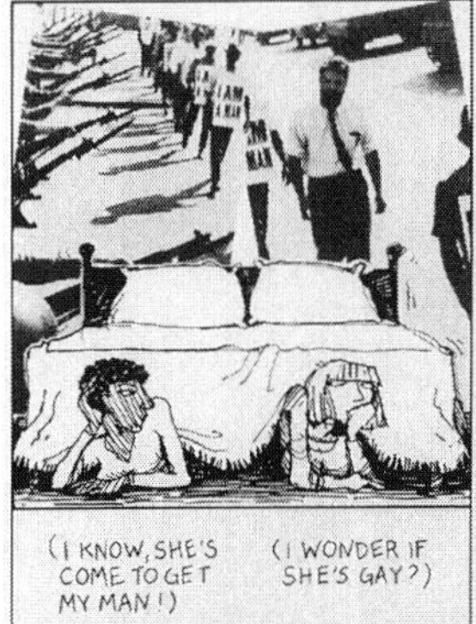
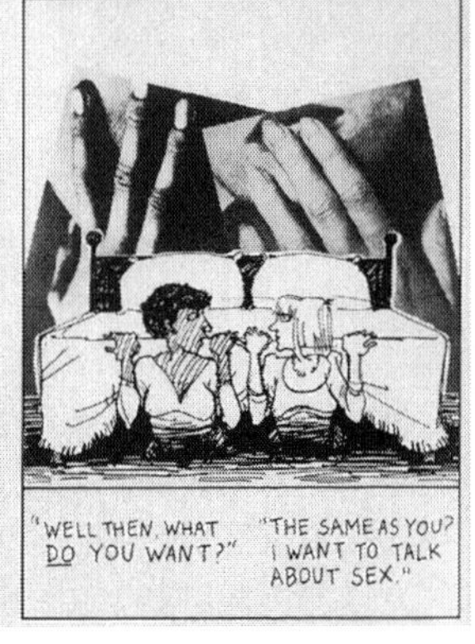

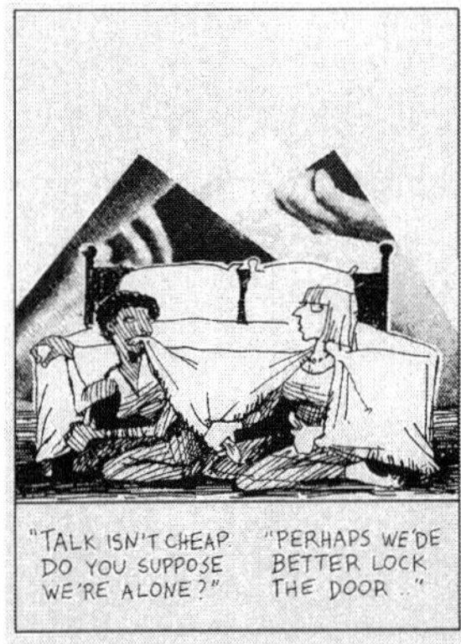
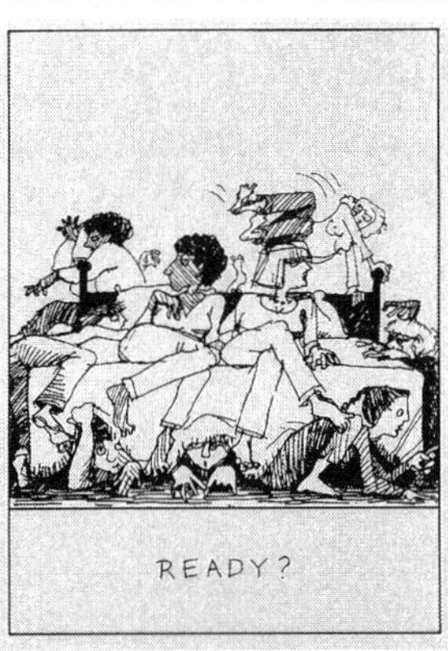

Figure 1.7. Six-panel comic in the *Diary* depicting Black and white women figuring out how to talk together about race and sexuality unfolds, two panels at a time, over the pages of the November 10 meeting minutes. Images reprinted with permission of Hannah Alderfer and Marybeth Nelson. Copyright 1982, 1983 by Hannah Alderfer, Beth Jaker, and Marybeth Nelson. Scan courtesy of Visual Resources Center, Stanford University.

Memphis, where Martin Luther King Jr. was assassinated. In these panels, each woman wonders to herself how the other woman is perceiving her on the basis of racial sexual stereotypes. Starting with the civil rights photograph, which is split in half, the women grow bolder and begin to emerge out from under the bed, as the photographs continue to tilt and recede, such that they're almost imperceptible in the fifth panel and nonexistent in the sixth. Across these panels, the women start to directly speak with each other, acknowledging that they want to talk about sex. In the sixth and final panel, as the two women sit on the edge of the bed and ask, "Ready?" in unison, a surprising number of other Black and white women spring out from under the same bed. Just as the meeting described in the entry was a starting point to having a discussion about sexuality and race, so, too, does this "Ready?" signify the start of a conversation that would continue at the conference itself.

Alderfer, Jaker, and Nelson shaped the visual language of the *Diary* not only by sourcing their images from a wide variety of archives, including the Lesbian Herstory Archives, the New York Public Library's Picture Collection, and the Schomburg Center for Research in Black Culture Photographs and Print Division, but by also calling on the workshop facilitators to contribute images to introduce their workshops. As the table of contents entry for the workshops states, "Each workshop leader was asked to provide a description of her workshop, a postcard illustration with a brief description, and bibliographic suggestions for future reading on her topic."[56] Due to the fact that the topics of the workshops varied widely, so did the visuals. The shared postcard format for the workshops links them together and addresses potential attendees as friends receiving personal messages that encapsulate the workshop topic in more accessible language. Just like the letter at the outset, the postcards position each session as a friendly exchange awaiting a response. Both the postcards and the personal messages from the members of the planning committee situate each woman's connection to the conference and encourage the attendees to do the same. The address book that Alderfer, Jaker, and Nelson included on the back inside cover would have—if the *Diary* had been distributed at the conference—further facilitated these personal links by giving attendees a space where they could record the names, addresses, and telephone numbers of new connections so that they could continue to be in dialogue following the event.[57] These gestures highlight and seek to broaden the community represented with this handbook.

Even the visuals that Dorothy Allison and Gayle Rubin—two of the women that the anti-pornography feminists protested—provided for their workshops were suggestive but not explicit. For her "Politically Correct, Politically Incorrect Sexuality" workshop that she organized with Muriel Dimen, Mirtha N. Quintanales, and Joan Nestle, Allison contributed a collaged postcard that showed an aghast Dorothy Gale standing in the middle of a gay bar as leather-clad men embrace and play pool around her (Figure 1.8). A couple of the men look back at her with wondering glances. Her presence in this space slyly nods to the fact that gay men are euphemistically known as friends of Dorothy. The pre-printed message on the flipside of this cheeky postcard reads, "Toto, I don't think we're in Kansas anymore," reinterpreting one of her famous lines from *The Wizard of Oz* (1939) for this new context. With a flourish of cursive script, Allison signs her name, Dorothy, signaling her solidarity with this subculture of gay men as well.

Rubin's postcard for her "Concepts for a Radical Politics of Sex" workshop also depicts an image of leather-clad gay men. Here, in a cartoon image from the famed Tom of Finland, whose drawings had been popular among gay men since the 1950s, a naked man lying suggestively on a tiled floor looks out at the viewer as he's lovingly trampled by and delights in a series of leather boots belonging to at least four other individuals that surround him. On the flipside of the postcard, Rubin typed up a quotation from Michel Foucault's *The History of Sexuality* (1978) and printed a stamp that features the phrase "thought crimes," which was coined by George Orwell in his dystopic novel *Nineteen Eighty-Four* (1949) that depicts a society so oppressed by the ruling class that individuals are surveilled and punished for even an "incorrect" thought. Both of their postcards subtly nod to the leather subculture that often went hand in hand with sadomasochistic sexual practices that the anti-pornography feminists protested as deviant when they targeted both Rubin and Allison and their respective associations with the Samois and Lesbian Sex Mafia organizations. Their perspectives, conveyed through curated image and text, joined alongside a wide range of others at the conference that aimed, in Vance's words, "to allow more information about the diversity of women's experiences to emerge."[58]

As a whole, the *Diary* presents a vision for women's sexuality where the images themselves play an important role, setting the stage not only for Alderfer, Jaker, and Nelson's later work with *Caught Looking*, but also for the work of the other artists discussed in this book. Especially through their repurposing of photographs, Alderfer, Jaker, and Nelson underline how women and their sexuality have been represented and emphasize the need for a different approach, which subsequent artists provide. In their more explicit work in *Caught Looking*, Alderfer, Jaker, and Nelson show how to reclaim and understand these images as empowering, outlining a visual theorization of women's sexuality that embraced rather than censored erotic representations of women's bodies.

Evolving Explicit Collage Aesthetics in Caught Looking

First published in 1986, *Caught Looking* was a groundbreaking work that brought together essays and innovative, sexually explicit visual material in a direct attempt to fight against the anti-porn feminist movement that had worked to create restrictive ordinances in the years since their protests of the Barnard Sex Conference. Alderfer, Jaker, and Nelson visually designed this volume as part of the activist FACT organization, which was formed in 1984 to advocate against the anti-pornography legislation championed by Andrea Dworkin and Catharine MacKinnon. Though a number of the women involved with FACT and those who contributed essays to *Caught Looking* were academics, *Caught Looking* was an activist rather than academic project, which meant that Alderfer, Jaker, and Nelson could deliver on the erotic content hinted at in the *Diary*, evolving explicit collage aesthetics to do so. Their reclamation of sexual imagery echoed the actions of feminist creators of erotica and pornography whose artwork they also included in the collection alongside more patriarchal sources.

The overall aesthetic project of *Caught Looking* counters the slideshows that anti-pornography groups across the nation put on in the late 1970s and 1980s to "raise public consciousness and to let audiences see for themselves the kind of offensive and abusive media images that the organizations denounced."[59] Groups like the San Francisco–based Women Against Violence in Pornography and Media started in 1976 and the New York City–based Women Against Pornography, which was

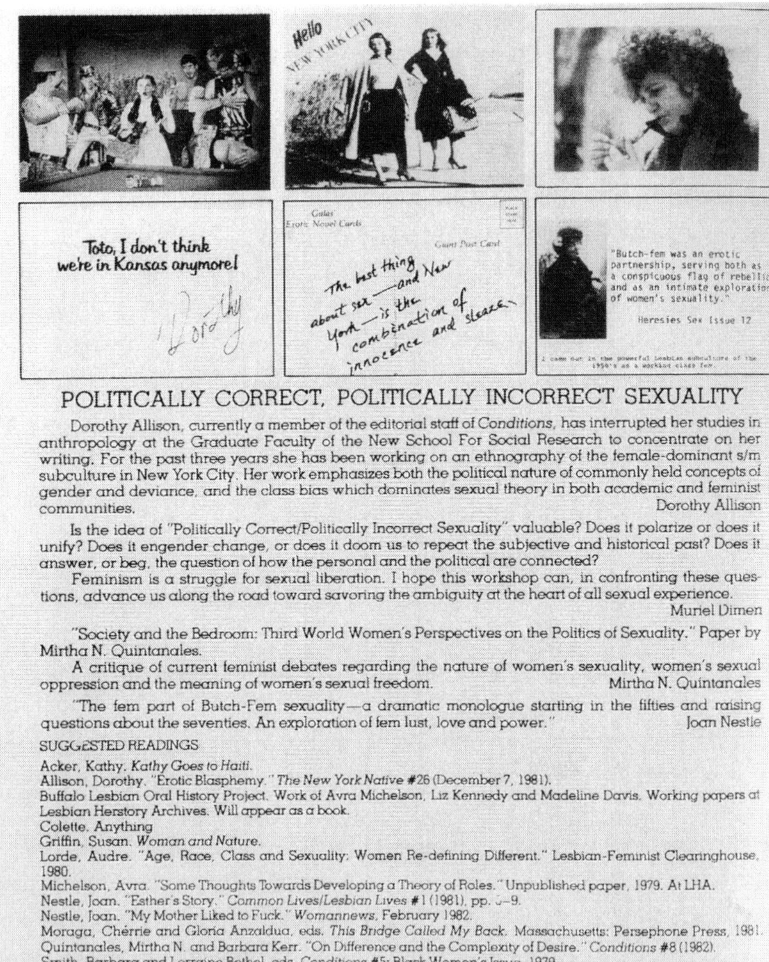

POLITICALLY CORRECT, POLITICALLY INCORRECT SEXUALITY

Dorothy Allison, currently a member of the editorial staff of *Conditions*, has interrupted her studies in anthropology at the Graduate Faculty of the New School For Social Research to concentrate on her writing. For the past three years she has been working on an ethnography of the female-dominant s/m subculture in New York City. Her work emphasizes both the political nature of commonly held concepts of gender and deviance, and the class bias which dominates sexual theory in both academic and feminist communities.

Dorothy Allison

Is the idea of "Politically Correct/Politically Incorrect Sexuality" valuable? Does it polarize or does it unify? Does it engender change, or does it doom us to repeat the subjective and historical past? Does it answer, or beg, the question of how the personal and the political are connected?

Feminism is a struggle for sexual liberation. I hope this workshop can, in confronting these questions, advance us along the road toward savoring the ambiguity at the heart of all sexual experience.

Muriel Dimen

"Society and the Bedroom: Third World Women's Perspectives on the Politics of Sexuality." Paper by Mirtha N. Quintanales.

A critique of current feminist debates regarding the nature of women's sexuality, women's sexual oppression and the meaning of women's sexual freedom.

Mirtha N. Quintanales

"The fem part of Butch-Fem sexuality—a dramatic monologue starting in the fifties and raising questions about the seventies. An exploration of fem lust, love and power."

Joan Nestle

SUGGESTED READINGS

Acker, Kathy. *Kathy Goes to Haiti.*
Allison, Dorothy. "Erotic Blasphemy." *The New York Native* #26 (December 7, 1981).
Buffalo Lesbian Oral History Project. Work of Avra Michelson, Liz Kennedy and Madeline Davis. Working papers at Lesbian Herstory Archives. Will appear as a book.
Colette. Anything
Griffin, Susan. *Woman and Nature.*
Lorde, Audre. "Age, Race, Class and Sexuality: Women Re-defining Different." Lesbian-Feminist Clearinghouse, 1980.
Michelson, Avra. "Some Thoughts Towards Developing a Theory of Roles." Unpublished paper, 1979. At LHA.
Nestle, Joan. "Esther's Story." *Common Lives/Lesbian Lives* #1 (1981), pp. 5–9.
Nestle, Joan. "My Mother Liked to Fuck." *Womannews*, February 1982.
Moraga, Chérrie and Gloria Anzaldua, eds. *This Bridge Called My Back.* Massachusetts: Persephone Press, 1981.
Quintanales, Mirtha N. and Barbara Kerr. "On Difference and the Complexity of Desire." *Conditions* #8 (1982).
Smith, Barbara and Lorraine Bethel, eds. *Conditions* #5: Black Women's Issue, 1979.
Rubin, Gayle. "The Leather Menace: Comments on Politics and S/M." *Coming to Power.* San Francisco: SAMOIS, 1981.

62

Figure 1.8. Pages from the *Diary* that introduce two conference workshops, featuring annotated postcards from the workshop leaders. Images reprinted with permission of Hannah Alderfer and Marybeth Nelson. Copyright 1982, 1983 by Hannah Alderfer, Beth Jaker, and Marybeth Nelson. Scan courtesy of Visual Resources Center, Stanford University.

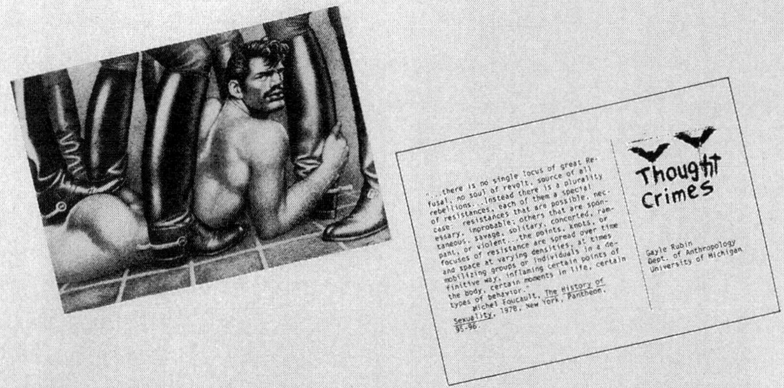

CONCEPTS FOR A RADICAL POLITICS OF SEX

The social relations of sexuality have always been as political as the social relations of class, race, gender, and ethnicity. However, at certain periods of time, in certain societies, the organization of sexual behavior is more actively contested, and in arenas more visible and centrally located. Since 1977, in the United States and in much of the western capitalist world, sexuality has become the locus of intense, focused, and bitter political struggle. A generation of political activists, veterans of the 1960's and 1970's, have been taken by surprise by attempts to reimpose tighter standards of sexual morality.

There has been a lack of conceptual tools with which to record, analyze, and position the events of the many discrete battles in the new sex wars. Many radicals have assumed that the body of feminist theory contained the necessary concepts. But feminist analysis was developed to describe and criticize oppression based on gender. While sexual experience is affected by the social relations of gender, sexuality is nevertheless not the same thing as gender. Just as gender oppression cannot be understood by an analysis of class relations, no matter how exhaustive, sexual oppression cannot be conceptualized by way of an understanding of gender relations, no matter how complete.

We need to develop an analytical apparatus specifically engineered to see, describe, and criticize sexual oppression. This workshop will propose some elements of a radical political theory of sex. The agenda for building such a body of thought about sexuality would include the following items: (1) It is essential to learn, albeit critically, the existing body of knowledge about sexuality. Sexological work contains useful empirical information, as well as material from which some of the structures of erotic oppression can be inferred. (2) It is important to get rid of the idea of sex as an asocial or transhistorical biological entity. (3) The persistence of the western (and especially Anglo-American) idea of sex as a destructive force needs to be explored. (4) The idea that there is a single kind of "good" sex that is "best" for everyone needs to be criticized. (5) Above all, we need to understand that there is systematic and serious mistreatment of people based on sexual behavior. Oppression generated out of sexuality is just as real, unjust, and barbarous as are the oppressions of class, race, gender, and ethnicity.   Gayle Rubin

SUGGESTED READINGS

Califia, Pat. *Sapphistry*. Tallahassee, Florida: Naiad Press, 1980.

English, Deirdre, Amber Hollibaugh and Gayle Rubin. "Talking Sex." *Socialist Review*, July–August 1981, pp. 43–62.

Foucault, Michel. *The History of Sexuality*. New York: Pantheon, 1978.

Gagnon, John. *Human Sexualities*. Glenview, Illinois: Scott, Foresman and Co., 1977.

Samois. *Coming To Power*. San Francisco, California: Samois, 1981.

Walkowitz, Judith. *Prostitution and Victorian Society*. New York: Cambridge University Press, 1980.

Weeks, Jeffrey. *Coming Out*. New York: Quartet Books, 1977.

established in 1979 and was the main group behind the Barnard Sex Conference protest, frequently hosted slideshows that presented hard- and softcore pornography paired with text to interested groups of women.[60] These organizations also used a script they read in conjunction with the slideshow, which was very deliberate in interpreting all of the images as harmful.[61] Some of the groups also hosted walking tours, presenting women with a guided experience of their local red-light districts and exposing them to sex shops and peep shows.[62]

While *Caught Looking* drew on some of the same images as these groups did, Alderfer, Jaker, and Nelson did extensive research and broadened the scope of material included. Rather than dictating singular analyses of given images as the slideshows demanded, the artists allowed readers to interpret the images for themselves. Alderfer, Jaker, and Nelson also paired images with text in order to make meaning of pornographic images, but their deployment of images allowed readers more freedom in decoding them. The fact that the images were included in a series of feminist essays did prompt readers to understand them as part of a feminist project, but just how to negotiate them was left open. Indeed, as theater scholar Elinor Fuchs, who admitted her "ambivalence" toward the feminist sex wars in a review of *Caught Looking*, asserted, "At a programmatic level, some feminists have been working to break down barriers between the two populations of women [the 'good girl' and the 'bad girl'] and their representations. *Caught Looking* performs the merger by making readers look at 'dirty' pictures in order to read feminist texts (or encounter feminist texts in order to gaze at dirty pictures)."[63] While Fuchs posited that "*Caught Looking* performs [a] merger" of disparate contexts, Alderfer, Jaker, and Nelson utilized collage to challenge the notion that the "'dirty' pictures" were separate from the "feminist texts." By organizing images together in sets—so that there were multiple on the page—Alderfer, Jaker, and Nelson encouraged the reader to move away from ascribing individual meaning to images, the very tactic the anti-pornography groups used in their scripted, didactic slideshows. Moreover, in addition to the images they included with articles, Alderfer, Jaker, and Nelson also reproduced nine sets of images as visual collages devoid of textual meaning aside from short descriptive titles given to them in the table of contents: "power," "powder puff," "comfort," "sex cafe & tender," "gaze," "spread," "fuck," "liquid," and "fantasy outfits." Letting the images collectively speak for themselves communicates Alderfer, Jaker, and Nelson's feminist stance against censorship, but it also echoes the work of the other artists discussed across this book as they theorized visually through sequences and accumulations of images.

Alderfer, Jaker, and Nelson further complicated Fuchs's binary between the "'dirty' pictures" and the "feminist texts" by including feminist erotica and pornography alongside traditional pornographic images. Combining all the disparate sources together further troubled the binary by not making a judgment call on some images as correct and others as fraught. Alderfer, Jaker, and Nelson incorporated images by women creators including Lynda Barry, Lizzie Borden, Louise Bourgeois, Betty Dodson, Nan Goldin, Morgan Gwenwald, Cindy Sherman, Kiki Smith, Nancy Spero, and Anita Steckel. In addition, they featured the photography of Honey Lee Cottrell and Annie Sprinkle multiple times throughout the collection, acknowledging these artists' depth of commitment to understanding explicit portrayals of a wide range of sexual practices as part of the feminist project. Both artists' works were published regularly in the lesbian erotica magazine *On Our Backs*, founded in 1984. By offering up images from a wide range of sources and cultural locations—from museum walls to mail-delivered erotica—*Caught Looking* welcomed readers by creating an associational web that affirmed these images and held them all on an equal plane.

The book includes two introductions: one from three of the editors—Kate Ellis, Barbara O'Dair, and Abby Tallmer—and one from the designers—Alderfer, Jaker, and Nelson.[64] Rather than having one introduction follow the other, they instead interleave these texts together, mirroring the rest of the collection. The designers' statement occupies one page whereas the introduction by the editors unfolds over three pages. Sets of images face each of the subsequent pages of the editors' introduction, foregrounding how the designers will speak throughout the rest of the volume through complex visual–textual layouts. These introductory texts center the primacy of images, with Ellis, O'Dair, and Tallmer averring, "In creating this book, we found it necessary to address the lack of exposure most of us have had to sexually explicit materials, and to turn to the materials themselves for a beginning definition."[65] This "turn to the materials" is a turn to the visual that is key here and throughout the volume; letting the images not only define themselves but also set the definitions allows readers to understand sexuality in a more nuanced and fluid way. Moreover, through this turning, the editors encourage the readers to do their own by turning each page and formulating their own definitions from this constellation of images.

Both the editors and designers not only see *Caught Looking* as an argument in support of explicit material but as an introduction to it, as well, which shapes Alderfer, Jaker, and Nelson's selection of images. In their designers' statement, they transform this process of "turn[ing] to the materials," positing, "In making our final selection, we considered that for some this book would be an initiation into the world of sexually explicit images. We chose images that are both strong and appealing. We also included images that would impart a history of the envisioning of sex. And, ultimately, like all consumers of pornography, we chose those images we found erotically powerful, the pictures that turned us on."[66] When selecting images, Alderfer, Jaker, and Nelson prioritize ones that encourage the readers to turn yet again—not only to turn the pages of the book, but to turn back to their own bodies and be "turned . . . on" by them. This nesting set of turns outlines a series of readerly actions to be set in motion by *Caught Looking*—with an attention to the body at the center of both the images and the readers' actions. These turns seek to position the readers and the representations in parallel pleasure. Just as Ellis, O'Dair, and Tallmer suggest that readers should turn to the materials to understand better both sexual pleasure and its representations, so do Alderfer, Jaker, and Nelson recommend that readers turn to their own bodies to solidify that understanding by indulging themselves in sexual satisfaction. Where the anti-pornography slideshows wanted the audience to turn away with disgust, this collection stimulated a turning toward to understand matters from the inside. *Caught Looking* thus argues for a horizontal, collective self-knowledge rather than the hierarchical, authoritative lessons of the slideshows, and it is this same ethos that undergirds the visual production of the artists in subsequent chapters.

Alderfer, Jaker, and Nelson's arrangement of images within the volume amplifies that collective pleasure. They often include multiple renderings of any one action on a single page, and the multiplication of the action there and across the collection suggests a diversity of approaches to pleasure. For example, one of the imagistic arrays of photos titled "Pictures (Spread)" illustrates six different methods of vaginally focused foreplay—from self-love to digital and oral penetration to face-sitting.[67] To wit, readers encounter a buffet rather than a set menu of sexual pleasure. Across *Caught Looking*, Alderfer, Jaker, and Nelson amplify that buffet by including a temporal range of historic and contemporary pornography, foregrounded in their "100 Years of Porn" feature where they include an image in the "low right corner of each right page" that tracks the development of porn from the 1890s "in an approximate chronology to the present."[68] These images intertwine with the layouts that Alderfer, Jaker, and Nelson design for each essay.

Alderfer, Jaker, and Nelson also arrange sets of images into sequences within page spreads. The images accompanying Lisa Duggan's essay "Censorship in the Name of Feminism" are arranged in a sort of faux sequencing that encourages the reader to consider a whole cornucopia of sexual scenarios (Figure 1.9). While the photos on the first spread are largely gathered from contemporary feminist sources including Sprinkle's photography and Borden's filmic oeuvre, the images on the following pages come from geographically and temporally disparate sources. Across eight pages, these images operate as snapshots into twenty-one worlds of individual experience. The images grow marginally in size with each sequence, bringing us closer to these worlds but never close enough to understand the entirety of the moments captured. Juxtaposed with these images are those in the bottom right-hand corner of each page spread that form part of the "100 Years of Porn" feature. The contribution to this feature on the fourth page of Duggan's essay takes us to four images from a circa 1950s photo shoot of a scantily clad man showing off his muscles in a desolate outdoor setting.[69] These photographs, like those sequenced throughout Duggan's piece, do not show a progression of action. Together, these orderless series embody a refusal to prescribe that pleasure progress in one way or another—readers are encouraged to imagine their own entry and exit points to sexual gratification.

In their essays, many of the writers directly discuss the arguments of the anti-pornography activists; the accompanying collages refract the limited views into a more multifaceted prism of experience. In Paula Webster's essay "Pornography and Pleasure" she recounts attending one of the Women Against Pornography's slideshows and then joining the group in a walking tour of the seedy Times Square pornographic district thereafter. When originally published in *Heresies* #12 (1981) as part of

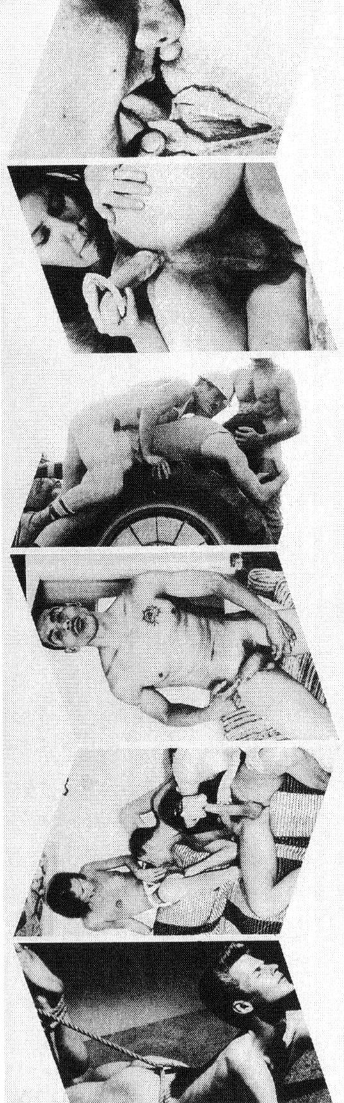

their neighborhoods to a vision of sex leading to Armaggedon.

Pressure this past year from the motley collection of anti-porn groups in Indianapolis led Mayor Hudnut, a Presbyterian minister, to look for new ways to battle pornography. Obscenity laws hadn't proved effective. Although the city's zealous antivice prosecutor and police department had been willing to make the arrests, their cases repeatedly failed to persuade juries or were thrown out on technicalities. The zoning law used to restrict "adult businesses" had been tied up in court challenges as well (there is now a new zoning law, however). Mayor Hudnut finally received inspiration from an unlikely source—the progressive city of Minneapolis and radical feminists Dworkin and MacKinnon.

Dworkin and MacKinnon didn't plan to write a new municipal law against pornography. In the fall of 1983, they were teaching a class at the University of Minnesota, presenting and developing their analysis of the role of pornography in the oppression of women. Each woman is known for her advocacy of one of the more extreme forms of anti-pornography feminism—the belief that sexually explicit images that subordinate or degrade women are singularly dangerous, more dangerous than nonsexual images of gross violence against women, more dangerous than advertising images of housewives as dingbats obsessed with getting men's shirt collars clean. In fact, Dworkin and MacKinnon argue that pornography is at the root of virtually every form of exploitation and discrimination known to woman. Given these views, it's not surprising that they would turn eventually to censorship—not censorship of violent and misogynistic images generally, but only of the sexually explicit images that cultural reactionaries have tried to outlaw for more than a century.

Dworkin and MacKinnon were invited to testify at a public hearing on a new zoning law (Minneapolis's "adult business" zoning law had been stricken in the courts also). When they appeared, they testified *against* the zoning strategy and offered a surprising new idea instead. Dworkin railed at the City Council, calling its members "cats and dogs" for tolerating pornography; MacKinnon suggested a civil rights approach to eliminate, rather than merely regulate, pornography. City officials must have enjoyed the verbal abuse—they hired the women to write a new law and to conduct public hearings on its merits.

In Minneapolis, Dworkin/MacKinnon were an effective duo. Dworkin, a remarkably effective public speaker, whipped up emotion with sensational rhetoric. At one rally, she encouraged her followers to "swallow the vomit you feel at the thought of dealing with the city council and get this law in place. See that the silence of women is over, that we're not down on our backs with our legs spread anymore." In contrast, MacKinnon, a professor of law, offered legalistic, seemingly rational, solutions to the sense of panic and doom evoked by Dworkin. In such a charged atmosphere, amid public demonstrations by anti-porn feminists—one young woman later set herself on fire to protest pornography—the law passed. It was vetoed by the mayor on constitutional grounds.

Indianapolis, though, is not Minneapolis. When Mayor Hudnut heard of the Dworkin/MacKinnon bill at a Republican conference, he didn't think of it as a measure to promote feminism, but as a weapon in the war on smut. He recruited City-County Councilmember Beulah Coughenour—an activist in the Stop ERA movement—to introduce the law locally. A Republican conservative, she is a member of the lobbying group Pro-America; she sent her children to Reverend Dixon's Baptist Tem-

Figure 1.9. Two pages from Lisa Duggan's "Censorship in the Name of Feminism" in *Caught Looking* that show scenes of sexual intimacy in sequence in increasing proximity as the essay progresses. Images reprinted with permission of Hannah Alderfer and Marybeth Nelson. Copyright 1986, 1988, 1992 by Caught Looking Inc. Scan courtesy of Visual Resources Center, Stanford University.

MacKinnon/Dworkin approach by asserting that pornography causes "sodomy" and "destruction of the family unit," as well as crimes and immorality "inimical to the public good." In Washington, Pennsylvania senator Arlen Spector is broadening his congressional hearings on child pornography to investigate the effects of adult porn on women. President Reagan has also announced his intention to establish a federal commission to study pornography and offer legislative action. Imagine the administration that brought you the Family Protection Act introducing measures to control pornography. Imagine anti-pornography feminists helping to legitimate such a nightmare.

In Canada, the conservative Fraser Committee on Pornography and Prostitution has been holding hearings across the country, while some city governments have already been prosecuting prostitutes, rounding up gay men in bathhouses, and bringing charges against gay publications for obscenity. Canadian anti-porn feminists, joined by some American sympathizers, have testified in favor of more restrictions on sexual representation.

If the discussion of sexuality surrounding the anti-porn law in Indianapolis had resulted in increased awareness of feminist issues, in the increased visibility and social/political power of feminists, in the enhanced ability of feminists on both sides of the issue to define and control the terms of debate, perhaps it could have been useful. But it didn't. Instead, Catharine MacKinnon joined with the right wing in invoking the power of the state against sexual representation. In so doing she and her supporters have helped spur a moral crusade that is already beyond the control of feminists—anti-porn or otherwise. And that moral crusade can only be dangerous to the interests of feminists everywhere, and to the future of women's rights to free expression.

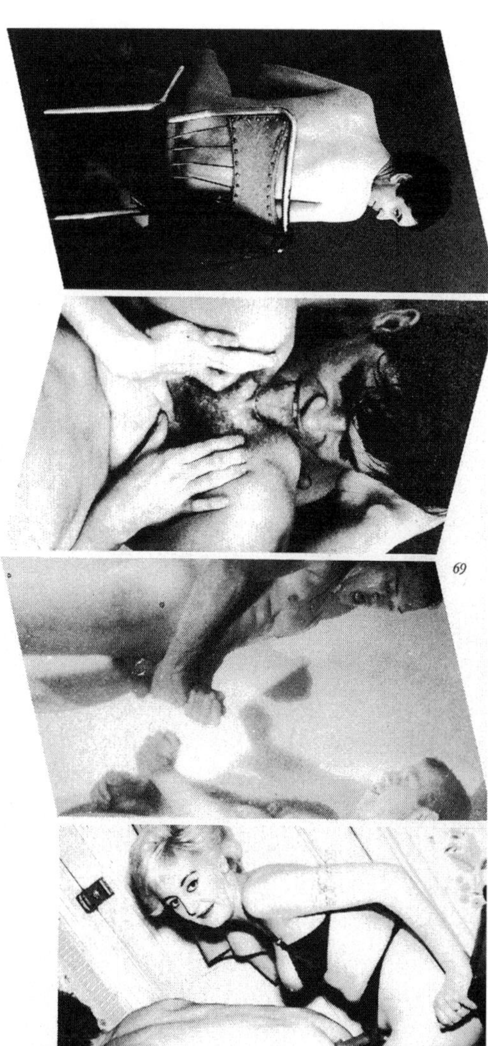

its "Sex Issue," erotic feminist comics were included alongside the piece.[70] When Webster's essay was reprinted in *Caught Looking*, Alderfer, Jaker, and Nelson transported the reader to Forty-Second Street. More so than elsewhere in the volume, the essay is surrounded by images, echoing Webster's own experience that she recounts. Yet, even amid neon signs offering up "live sex acts," "fantasy," "sex play," and "live" "nude" "adult" "girls" displayed on each of the essay's pages, Webster finds "important messages for women" in pornography and admits that "it is true that this depiction is created by men, but perhaps it can encourage us to think of what our own images and imaginings might be."[71] A handful of the images are Sprinkle's "own [feminist] images and imaginings" of this seedy sexual milieu, but Webster's words juxtaposed with Alderfer, Jaker, and Nelson's collage also cast the rest of the images in a new light as not simply replicating the author's experiences of exploring Times Square with Women Against Pornography but, rather, envisioning how women can reclaim such myriad images for their own pleasure.

On the two middle pages of the essay, the most heavily imagistic spread demonstrates this reimagining through photographs that link women with wild animals (Figure 1.10).[72] They aim to find new life in this well-worn cultural pairing by reproducing photographs that date from the 1940s and 1950s when this pairing was used in many B horror films like *Cat People* (1942), *The Curse of the Cat People* (1944), *Jungle Woman* (1944), and *The Cat Creeps* (1946), in which a femme fatale threatened horrific violence whenever she transformed into a wild animal.[73] This small collection of images underline how pervasive this trope is and how subtle it can be, by showing women with wild animals alongside those who are clothed in or photographed against animal print. Important within such a constellation of images, this relationship is deployed only in ways that facilitate ecstasy—two of the women pictured have their heads tilted back in a likely moan. These photos that imply an unbridled female sexuality through this association with wild animals are but one pornographic trope that Alderfer, Jaker, and Nelson reclaim.

In reimagining images through collective collage and synthesizing materials from different times, the designers highlight persistent themes within pornography as they shift or reclaim these tropes and feature contemporary feminist pornography that also does this work. The essays participate in creating that shifting ground by documenting and advocating

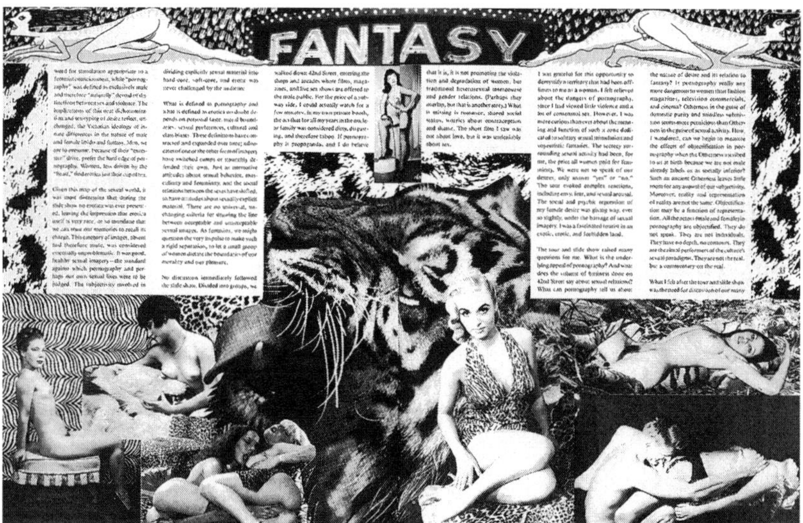

Figure 1.10. A page spread from Paula Webster's "Pornography and Pleasure" essay in *Caught Looking* that combines animal print with images of women receiving pleasure. Image reprinted with permission of Hannah Alderfer and Marybeth Nelson. Copyright 1986, 1988, 1992 by Caught Looking Inc. Scan courtesy of Visual Resources Center, Stanford University.

against the anti-pornography activists. As *Caught Looking* went into production, anti-pornography efforts began to be stymied on a national level when the Supreme Court affirmed the U.S. District Court for the Southern District of Indiana's decision that the Indianapolis ordinance was unconstitutional in *American Booksellers Association, Inc. v. Hudnut*.[74] Yet, unlike the *Diary, Caught Looking* transcended its immediate moment in part because of how its creators understood it "as a sourcebook from which to derive new questions regarding these topics."[75] Though it documented the current debate about the role of sexually explicit images, it also acted "as a guide for further activism."[76] The women of FACT wanted readers to return to the text again and again rather than understanding it as a snapshot of a particular time, and its hybrid nature facilitates that action. The many juxtapositions on any single page position the volume as speaking across time.

Three further reprintings of the book—in 1988, 1992, and 1995—attest to the collection's enduring relevance as the feminist sex wars itself waned in the face of third-wave feminism.[77] In each of these editions, new prefatory remarks on the inside of the front cover engage with high-profile court cases involving women's sexuality to demonstrate its continued need. The second edition marked the collapsing of the anti-pornography movement through the repeal of the ordinances and looked ahead:

> With the 1986 Supreme Court decision invalidating the Indianapolis antipornography ordinance, the momentum behind such ordinances dissipated. The effort to defeat one antipornography ordinance was over; the larger struggle to change the overwhelmingly sexist environ-ment in which we all live continues. For us, sexual issues remain fun-damental to feminist debate and sexual liberation implicit in women's liberation. We offer this second edition of *Caught Looking* as both a document of a heady time and a fluid dialogue about women and sex.[78]

With these words, FACT claimed victory while articulating how these issues and images remained active rather than resolved. With the third edition in the early nineties, the editors identified three recent legal cases in which women spoke out publicly about sexual harassment and assault:

> Increasingly, issues of women's freedom and credibility in the realm of sexuality are reshaping our institutions and our relationships. . . . The testimony of Anita Hill in the Thomas confirmation process, Patricia Bowman in the William Kennedy Smith trial, and Desiree Washington in the Mike Tyson trial aroused virulent attack as well as impassioned defense. They also brought into sharp focus the complex web of race and class that underlies any discussion of sexuality in our culture.[79]

This April 1992 preface points to how these cases outlined a "complex web of race and class." A full ten years after the events of the Barnard Sex Conference, these cases highlight the enduring nature of the issues that the *Diary* raised and that *Caught Looking* further explored. Following this passage, the editors espouse "hope" that "this collection will contribute to a dialogue about sexuality and its representation." However, that hope is largely unrealized, as demonstrated by the treatment of Hill, Bowman, and Washington and the results of their testimony in each of the cited cases—not to mention the treatment that even more contemporary women have received in similar cases. Despite Alderfer, Jaker, and Nelson's artistic activism across the 1980s, sexuality and its representations remained a contentious debate. Despite its continuing relevance, *Caught Looking* went out of print following its fourth edition in 1995.

Archives and Afterlives: Creating Space in the Feminist Movement for Explicit Visualities

In the late 1990s and subsequent decades, both the *Diary* and *Caught Looking* faded from recognition, while the issues that animated them remain unresolved. In the last decade and a half, the Barnard Sex Conference's importance within the feminist sex wars has come under renewed attention, including in special issues of journals like the *Communication Review*'s 2008 "Commemorating the Barnard Conference," *GLQ*'s 2011 "Rethinking Sex," and the 2016 "Pleasure and Danger: Sexual Freedom and Feminism in the Twenty-First Century" installment of *Signs*.[80] In reviewing the Barnard Sex Conference in these accounts, scholars mainly focus on the textual rhetoric, only briefly mentioning the image–text productions. Not only is the centrality of the *Diary* to this historical fracture overlooked, but the significance of the *Diary*'s visual legacy is also cast aside.

The *GLQ* issue did pay some attention to the *Diary* by reprinting various sections through "The *GLQ* Archive" feature where the journal makes available "previously unpublished or unavailable primary materials that may serve as sources for future work in lesbian and gay studies."[81] This issue focused on the feminist sex wars and the Barnard Sex Conference through Rubin's famed "Thinking Sex" essay, illustrating how, thirty years after the fact, Rubin's supposedly antifeminist ideas were integral for queer discourse. This contemporary interest in Rubin's views was further underlined by the release of *Deviations: A Gayle Rubin Reader* (2011) by Duke University Press that same year. It took only a little over ten years for Rubin's thought to be valued as important and recast as foundational for the emerging discourse of queer theory. As mentioned at the outset of this chapter, Rubin's import is further acknowledged through the inclusion of "Thinking Sex" in the groundbreaking *Lesbian and Gay Studies Reader*.[82]

GLQ focused on the conference through Rubin's participation as a workshop facilitator, so the editors reproduced mainly the latter pages of the *Diary* concerning the events of the conference itself. Across the twenty-eight pages of the seventy-plus-page *Diary* reproduced within *GLQ*, they printed ten of the eighteen pages devoted to conference sessions as well as the two pages detailing the opening and closing sessions, but only two of the nine entries documenting conference planning. The two diary entries reproduced in *GLQ* are the October 20 entry discussing issues of S–M and taboo sexualities and the November 10 entry focusing on the role of race within feminism and sexuality.[83] These choices echo those foci of the conference that would receive attention within the feminist movement across the 1980s and that the artists I study across this book engage in their visual theorizing. While these entries are representative of the other entries, we miss how Alderfer, Jaker, and Nelson captured the wide range of theoretical conversations that animated the conference planners through the sheer visual variety that all nine diary entries provided in their succession of different layouts, fonts, and visual media. Despite the limitations of this reproduction, the issue indicated that the *Diary* would soon be fully digitized and housed at a dedicated website, but that promise never materialized.[84]

Where archives once served as the source material for the *Diary* and *Caught Looking*, they now serve as its primary residence. This is true even more so for the *Diary*, as it was produced for the roughly 750 conference attendees and was never released by a larger publisher in a format that would earn it shelf space in a library collection.[85] Though also rare and currently out of print, the multiple editions of *Caught Looking* with print runs of up to five thousand foreground its aim to reach communities beyond those initially imagined. While their liminal existence stifles the ability of either book to stir contemporary readers to consider the complexity of women's sexuality and its representations through engaging with and thus viscerally responding to the images that first instigated debate, women have continued to examine their own sexuality through graphic depictions. But it is critical that we pay attention to these earlier, obscured creations, in order to see how foundational these materials were to feminist debate and how they still resonate and reverberate, despite their peripheral status in mainstream culture.

Looking anew at image–text creations from this era is essential for allowing us to begin to trace a genealogy of representations of women's sexuality that started with these works, and that continued throughout the 1980s in the work of other important feminist artists. The following chapters track this history in more detail. The next chapter steps back in time to the late 1970s to examine the feminist underground comics of Roberta Gregory and Lee Marrs. They were using the visual format to critique the feminist movement's limitations while also wielding it to create a more capacious feminist community that would embrace women of color and lesbians. At first, they struggled to have their work accepted within the feminist movement until they started publishing in *Gay Comix*, a series started in 1980 that allowed them to inspire and build a larger community of women cartoonists. Like this chapter, this second chapter and the ones that follow trace the trajectory of an artist's career and how they ultimately figured out how to grow supportive communities.

2

THE COMICS VISIONARIES

Lee Marrs's and Roberta Gregory's
Underground Feminism

*Historicizing Women's Comics within the
Feminist Movement*

Though the Barnard Sex Conference is understood as the catalyst of the feminist sex wars in the 1980s, the tensions that caused the schism had been building over the course of the 1970s. Scholars have traced how the different groups debated this topic at separate conferences and events across the late 1970s,[1] and both factions of feminists participated in key events that marked the widening gap between these groups: in San Francisco, for example, the newly formed lesbian BDSM group Samois marched in 1978 in the Gay Freedom Day Parade, while that same year anti-pornography feminists involved in Women Against Violence in Pornography and Media organized a national conference around "Feminist Perspectives on Pornography."[2] As the divide between these groups grew, the *Diary*'s dramatic censorship at Barnard in 1982 made it clear among sex-positive feminists that new networks that would support their ideas and their innovative visual forms were needed. The story of how the *Diary*'s artists—Hannah Alderfer, Beth Jaker, and Marybeth Nelson—continued their activism, honed their visual presentation, and eventually collaborated on *Caught Looking* in 1986 is an important example of how women built artistic networks in this period to support their visual politics. But there are numerous other important stories of network building and artistic production, many of which have remained submerged deep in the archives, including important collaborations in comics and feminist anthologies, as well as innovations in representing feminist politics in photography and other visual media.

65

Just as certain feminists rejected the *Diary*'s collage aesthetics in the 1980s, leading to the curtailment of its circulation and reception, so, too, did some feminists reject the aesthetics of women's comics throughout the 1970s. Some of these comics anticipated and critiqued the feminist movement's shortsightedness, especially with regard to including lesbians and women of color in the movement, which the *Diary* and *Caught Looking* and the artists in the following chapters would continue to focus on in the following decade amid a larger conversation about sexuality. Due to popular understandings of the form as a misogynist enterprise, comics existed at the margins of feminism and struggled for broader recognition in movement bookstores and publications.[3] While women cartoonists broadly adopted feminist ideals in their work, the independent scene in which they created these comics—known as the underground— was populated predominantly by straight white men who often produced comics that centered retrograde and offensive depictions of women and gender relations.[4] At this time of rich, multifarious social revolutions, there were a number of women cartoonists who frequently worked to counter the patriarchal underground ethos. Among them, cartoonists Lee Marrs and Roberta Gregory were particularly important for pushing boundaries in the way they directly represented the exclusions of both the underground and feminism in their comics, illuminating why new spaces for artistic production were necessary.

Marrs's and Gregory's comics were part of a lively domain of independent comics produced by women in the 1970s in coordination with the larger countercultural underground comics movement.[5] Two long-running feminist series emerged out of this space: *Wimmen's Comix* (1972–92) and *Tits & Clits* (1972–87). *Wimmen's Comix* ran for seventeen issues and nearly two decades, while *Tits & Clits* ran for seven issues and a decade and a half. In that time, the series collectively featured the work of over one hundred women cartoonists and often served as the entry point for new generations of women entering the field. While Marrs and Gregory were contributors to both series, their involvement with the *Wimmen's Comix* collective across the run of the series more clearly demonstrates the depth of their participation in the comics scene. Marrs was not only a founding member of the *Wimmen's Comix* collective but also an editor of the second issue and one of the most prolific contributors to the series, producing images for the front and back covers of three issues.[6] Gregory was notably the first openly nonheterosexual contributor, depicting same-sex attraction in her first comic in the series, "A Modern Romance," which appeared in *Wimmen's Comix* #4.[7] Both women contributed to over a third of the seventeen issues, participating across its full run.

Outside these two series that operated as safe spaces for women's content, the larger underground comics scene was known for its frequent misogyny. Prominent underground cartoonist Trina Robbins, self-appointed herstorian of the movement, claims that "it was almost de rigueur for male underground cartoonists to include violence against women in their comics, and to portray this violence as humor."[8] Working in the same medium, women's underground comics challenged misogyny as form by producing a range of liberated women's bodies on the page. In so doing, these works also pushed back against the limitations of feminist discourse in the 1970s, particularly with their open focus on and embrace of many forms of sexuality. Both the *Wimmen's Comix* and *Tits & Clits* series were important interventions that set the stage for Marrs, Gregory, and countless other artists to create works elsewhere. For Marrs and Gregory, their resulting individual comic books, *The Further Fattening Adventures of Pudge, Girl Blimp* (1973–77) and *Dynamite Damsels* (1976), respectively, allowed them to specifically examine the space for women's sexuality within the feminist movement.[9]

Marrs's and Gregory's individual comics and their collective participation foreshadow their later trailblazing work creating representations of women's LGBTQ experiences in the *Gay Comix* (1980–98) series in the coming decade, as discussed later in this chapter. In tracing the arc of their careers, we can see how their investments in multiple movements echo the shifting social landscape around them. Scholars like Hillary Chute, Susan Kirtley, Sam Meier, Leah Misemer, and Nicholas Sammond have analyzed the underground feminist comics series' influence.[10] This chapter extends those conversations by tracing how two artists who developed through *Wimmen's Comix* and *Tits & Clits* responded to their affiliated social movements and provided a platform for emerging artists interested in LGBTQ expression, both in their individual comic books as well as in their foundational comics in early issues of *Gay Comix*. This chapter also contends with how the social position of these comics and their resulting location in archives have often circumscribed how we understand their contributions to histories of both comics and feminism.

Despite directly engaging feminist issues, these comics and artists struggled to find support from the broader women's movement. The artists contemporaneously cited how couching their political critiques in this visual, often humorously irreverent form presented an insurmountable barrier. In a 1980 interview in *The Comics Journal*, Robbins opined, "It's really weird the way leftists and militant feminists don't seem to like comix. I think they're so hung up on their own intellect that somehow it isn't any good to them unless it's a sixteen-page tract of gray words."[11] Here, Robbins identified genre tunnel vision in which only text in a certain form passed ideological muster. In an interview from 1979 printed in the grassroots publication *Cultural Correspondence*, Marrs expanded on the practical consequences of that prejudice: "But we got totally rejected by the women's movement, for the most part. . . . Not just that *Ms.* magazine wouldn't run us, but bookstores across the country wouldn't carry us, because we did not have a heavy, traditional, feminist political line."[12] Marrs equated these concrete examples with rejection, for they foreclosed the ability of the collective to reach a broader feminist audience despite their varied attempts to participate.[13] Her quotation also foregrounded their comics as something done differently from the feminist norm in their content, even though later in the same interview Marrs went on to compare their comics with the "work[ing] through" that happened in "consciousness-raising groups."[14] Notably, these feelings of frustration came at the close of the decade when women broadly felt disillusioned by the promise of feminism, as Marrs and Gregory recorded in their solo comics.[15]

Within this social landscape, Marrs's and Gregory's comics document the frustrations with second-wave feminism by depicting the movement within their pages. The intersection of the coming-of-age narrative with representations of grassroots feminist organizing allowed both artists to review and critique the first half decade of women's liberation in the early 1970s. Their comics bildungsromane, Marrs's *The Further Fattening Adventures of Pudge, Girl Blimp* and Gregory's *Dynamite Damsels*, both feature a young female protagonist coming into her own sexuality as she grows in her involvement in the feminist movement.[16] While coming-of-age tales, particularly around sexual knowledge, were common in women's underground comics, Marrs's and Gregory's linkage of this growth to the feminist movement is relatively unique. Across their comics, they represented the early movement through its grassroots organizing spaces—consciousness-raising groups, demonstrations, self-help clinics, and more—often alluding to historical referents in these moments. The close readings later in this chapter put these comics back into conversation with their contemporary feminist interlocutors, demonstrating the limits of these movement forms in supporting a range of women's experiences. The juxtaposition of text and image in these comics allowed them to realize and challenge more viscerally the tenets of feminism through women's own bodies. In visualizing and interrogating feminist forms, Marrs and Gregory theorized new possibilities for women engaging their politics with their bodies.

While Marrs's and Gregory's comics illustrated how much feminism in the 1970s sparked sexual discovery, they also documented how the movement did not serve women who were not heterosexual, white, and middle-class. Both comics featured white-coded protagonists who struggled with their sexuality, so Marrs and Gregory centered critiques of how feminism did not support such women. Each artist's own personal identification as a bisexual woman also plays a role in this critical focus, especially given that their comics sometimes read as semi-autobiographical accounts.[17] In each comic, we see how feminist spaces facilitate each protagonist's first sexual experiences and embrace of nonheterosexual identities and practices. Though the characters gained sexual knowledge through intimate experiences with women affiliated with women's liberation, there were limits to how much overt lesbian or bisexual representation was welcomed in the movement proper. These plot points echo the early movement's struggle with lesbian feminism, as documented by Victoria Hesford in *Feeling Women's Liberation* (2013), in which she charts "the emergence of a new figure—the feminist-as-lesbian—which, in turn, has had a defining effect on the way in which women's liberation in particular and feminism in general has been remembered and represented."[18] It is through the stories of these protagonists and their struggles with squaring their same-sex desire within the movement in the works of artists like Marrs and Gregory that we begin to see how women were frequently disregarded due to their difference from a straight, white, middle-class norm.

Marrs's and Gregory's representation of race relations in both comics provided a strong counterpoint to the general lack of regard for women of color in the broader feminist movement at the time. Both artists represented women of color, and Black women in particular, in their work more than other contemporaneous feminist media did, and in the process they demonstrated how these women felt their concerns were not prioritized within the feminist movement. As they documented elsewhere in interviews and comics, their focus on race relations within feminism and representing diverse bodies arose, in part, out of their own upbringing in 1950s America: Gregory grew up biracial in a Southern California, Latinx–Caucasian household, while Marrs was raised white in the South amid the backdrop of the civil rights movement.[19] In her book *Liberation in Print* (2017), which surveys the early feminist movement through grassroots periodicals and their affiliated collectives, Agatha Beins establishes how women of color often had to navigate "implicit racism in dominant narratives characterizing the women's liberation movement."[20] As Beins surveys, in the 1970s feminists were debating the limits of sisterhood in grassroots feminist periodicals across the United States; but comics such as Marrs's and Gregory's, in their position somewhat outside the movement, could comment holistically, coalescing years of movement debate in their visual forms.[21] The coming-of-age narrative structure facilitated their critiques of how the feminist movement was heterocentric and white-dominated by showing how women had their consciousness raised through the movement yet grew to realize its limitations. Alongside these critiques, both Marrs's *Pudge, Girl Blimp* and Gregory's *Dynamite Damsels* simultaneously charted a pathway forward, gesturing to the conditions of possibility that would allow for the full participation of Black women and lesbians in the feminist movement. Not only did these artists lay the groundwork for future cartoonists in these comics and in their later work in the 1980s, but their concerns about feminism's exclusions anticipate the networks that future artists created to address these issues across the 1980s, including Alison Bechdel, Gloria Anzaldúa, and Nan Goldin, all of whom are discussed later in this book.

Because most of Marrs's and Gregory's comics—like women's underground comics in general—were released in small print runs and have not been republished, archives are essential in accessing these works and writing these histories. However, these comics surface unevenly from archives. Since their contexts and histories have often been overlooked, this chapter in some ways is a work of feminist recovery, reaching back from the contemporary scholars also working on this period to the second-wave feminists themselves who reached even further back in history to rescue feminist foremothers. However, in surveying the varying archival contexts in which these comics are preserved, this chapter puts pressure on the limits of recovery for marginalized media. We read, in the spirit of Ann Laura Stoler, along the archival grain to suss out the frameworks behind how these comics were collected in archives and how that has affected how they're positioned on the margins or not at all in histories of feminism and comics.[22] In then analyzing these comics anew and putting them back into conversation with their contemporaries in the feminist movement, this chapter identifies a new pathway through feminist thought in these overlooked comics. The archiving of these and other feminist comics from this period reflects how they were stuck between movements and modes of feminism, threatening their legacy.

Reading across Archives, Working between Movements

The marginalization that feminist underground comics faced in the 1970s from both the larger underground comics scene and the feminist movement continues today. As Susan Kirtley reflects in the middle of a recent essay in which she untangles the different ways that underground women cartoonists responded to the feminist movement and its ideologies in their work, "Perhaps as a result of this 'outsider' status in both feminist and underground circles, these important, influential comics have rarely been studied, which is another example of an unfortunate double standard, for these comics most certainly bear additional examination, both for historical research and to further our understanding of the craft and form of comics."[23] Kirtley's observation echoes that of Chute's eight years earlier in her landmark monograph *Graphic Women* (2010), where she roots her lineage of contemporary women cartoonists in the underground, asserting that these works had not received ample attention.[24] In the time between Chute and Kirtley, many scholars have begun to focus more intently on the underacknowledged role of women as creators of comics—both in the underground and more broadly.[25] And yet the "'outsider' status" persists. In this section and throughout the book, I insist that these works and our reception of them are affected by their marginalization in archives, and it is no different here. How their position is inscribed in the very archives through which scholars access and write about these works shapes this scholarship.

Feminist underground comics are found within many collections, but it is how they are organized in these spaces that keeps them on the margins of discourse. Indeed, if we not only look to their status within one archives but instead analyze their position in multiple archival locations, we start to understand their persistent marginalization. This tactic of reading across archives is one that I develop here as a practical and theoretical notion that works to understand the cultural positioning of objects. Many archival research projects analyze objects through their collection in one location; this chapter and book insist that for those materials collected across many locations—as grassroots materials and comics often are—we must consider how these various collections tell us different stories of how these materials were understood in their time and pay particular attention to the way these varied tellings of the past continue to influence how they are understood in the present. To read across archives also requires that we look outside the collections that often contain just the comics and locate connections to other materials in archives that speak to how comics participated in larger cultural discussions.

For example, tracking the seventeen issues of *Wimmen's Comix* (1972–92) in its various archival locations demonstrates how it and its fellow feminist underground comics were stuck between and subsequently marginalized by both the feminist and underground movements. Although there are some archives that maintain archival records and papers from individual cartoonists—such as the Billy Ireland Cartoon Library and Museum at The Ohio State University and, increasingly, in the Rare Book and Manuscript Library at Columbia University—most comics materials within archives are simply copies of the original comics themselves assembled together by avid collectors. Thanks to these kinds of collectors, issues of *Wimmen's Comix*—though often not the complete run—exist in a number of university and grassroots archives across the United States, including at Harvard University, Iowa State University, the Lesbian Herstory Archives, Michigan State University, ONE National Gay and Lesbian Archives, Pennsylvania State University, Stanford University, University of Connecticut, University of Virginia, Washington

State University, et cetera. The politics and proclivities of the individual collectors who donated their comics to these institutions matter a great deal, as Nicholas Sammond identifies in a recent essay: "Who collects or does not collect a given title, how they identify themselves, can shape the presence, absence, and location of that title in an archive. Likewise, the conditions under which that archive was created and is structured will, obviously, determine both the nature of its holdings and how they are organized and encountered. This often replicates in the archive the very history of marginalization that gave rise to women's and queer comix in the first place."[26] In this passage, Sammond describes the interplay between collectors and archives and how an archival collection is shaped by a collector's biases in addition to the leaning of the archives as a whole. The upshot of these forces, Sammond posits, is that marginalized works are again often sidelined. Depicting the situation that Sammond alludes to with these insights, many of the archival collections that contain *Wimmen's Comix* and other progressive titles do not center these works, leaving them dispersed and obscured, both organizationally and historically, to contemporary researchers.

In many prominent collections of underground comics, which have been put together by avid collectors who are men, *Wimmen's Comix* and other feminist titles are few and far between, eclipsed by a hefty dose of misogynist portrayals prevalent in many underground comics. While this context usefully explains some of the formal barriers that women were working against in their comics, progressive titles can get lost amid this retrogressive cacophony, seeming peripheral or secondary to the movement. These underground comics collections often contain a brief description seeking to describe all of the collection's content—for example, both of Washington State University's comics collections provide this summation: "They frequently depict graphic violence, and many are sexually explicit."[27] While this portrayal rings true for many underground comics—feminist ones included—how progressive titles address sex and violence sets them apart in ways not recognized by this reduction. They seem like outliers not only in terms of their content and how they handle it, but also in terms of their production history, as they continued to be created well after the heyday of the underground in the 1960s and early 1970s. This difference in periodization likely contributes to the fact of their being incompletely collected—for *Wimmen's Comix*, roughly two thirds of the seventeen issues were published after 1975, the year that Patrick Rosenkranz marks as the cutoff in his history of the underground comics movement.[28] Because these comics had a different orientation to content and time than the bulk of the underground, they are often not well served or as completely collected in such archival collections.

For this reason, feminist collections of comics, including those at Harvard University and the University of Virginia or lesbian collections at the Lesbian Herstory Archives, provide a useful counterpoint. In these collections, feminist underground comics are positioned in the archives as being in dialogue with other comics by women and broader feminist works, locating them in a genealogy of works that extend out of the underground. In such groupings, one can see how *Wimmen's Comix* has shaped decades of feminist women's comics and continues to shape contemporary women's work in the medium—something that is otherwise obscured in the incomplete or marginalized organizational schemes in other archives. However, while these feminist collections allow for a careful tracing of the artistic evolution in women's comics and show how *Wimmen's Comix* and other underground feminist works like those of Marrs and Gregory were formative for future artists, these collections also isolate these works as innovators who were ahead of their time. To wit, these titles are peripheral in different ways in both underground and feminist collections because they seem, in part, stuck between movements—too late for the underground and too early for feminist comics.

Feminist underground comics represent important critiques of the feminist movement in comics form. But women produced other comics at the time that have also been overlooked by archives and scholars. As this chapter and the next shows, there were a number of feminist comics that women published that explicitly responded to and critiqued feminist as well as gay and lesbian activism. Marrs, Gregory, and other important women underground cartoonists inspired subsequent generations of women who published their comics within feminist and gay and lesbian periodicals in the 1980s, as the next chapter examines through cartoonist Alison Bechdel, who self-syndicated her *Dykes to Watch Out For* comic strip (1983–2008) in an impressive array of grassroots and independent newspapers. Even in the 1970s, though, there were women, many of them anonymous or pseudonymous, producing comics in feminist newspapers in local and unacknowledged ways.[29] At that time, there were numerous local, independent feminist newspapers around the United States. However, although these women's comics were important for illustrating feminist principles in a different form within those local collectives, these cartoonists did not, by and large, connect to or participate in the larger comics communities in major urban areas or based around publications with national distribution. In recent years, many scholars have taken up Kate Eichhorn's call for the archival turn in feminism and gone to the archives to nuance our understanding of the contemporary feminist movement and tell stories of local collectives that have been excluded from the major narratives.[30] While these scholars have deftly worked through grassroots sources, they have yet to fully account for the rich visual culture of feminism and how such works unfurl different theories and histories of feminism.[31] It is one of the primary goals of this book to provide this account.

Moreover, when comics are collected solely alongside other comics, they are separated from the cultural conversations and communities that supported this work. Similarly, when comics are discretely collected as primary document collections without further historical context in the collection itself, it severs important connections to that context. Their history has to be reassembled by again working across archives to grasp how different people within these social movements both understood and collected these comics. Reading the comics solely within comics collections reduces our understanding of their impact. On the other hand, reading them across these spaces reveals how their precarious historical position emerges precisely out of how they were stuck between the feminist and underground movements in their time, which later shapes how they were collected.

This chapter, drawing on the holdings of multiple archives, reconnects these contexts and locates these connections in order to describe this larger social framework. These archives include underground comics collections at Washington State University, a broader comics collection at Michigan State University, digital collections of comics including the Alexander Street Press Underground and Independent Comics database, grassroots archives including the Lesbian Herstory Archives and the ONE National Gay and Lesbian Archives, and digital collections of grassroots newspapers and ephemera including Reveal Digital's Independent

Voices, Gale's *Archives of Sexuality and Gender*, and others. Reading feminist comics in these multiple locations reveals how they were important to many different communities. It also underscores how and why they were and remain peripheral to these conversations.

The different understandings of these comics in their varied archival locations demonstrates why we should always examine how materials are structured within archives. Reading across archives with these comics in particular, we learn something about the multiple, intersecting nature of social movements, which is deepened when we turn to Marrs's and Gregory's comics that mediate these intersections. Where the previous chapter discussed how grassroots archives and independent collectors safeguarded marginalized images, this section broadens that conversation by thinking through how all sorts of archives organize material in ways that promote different histories. The following chapters will further this conversation by examining the varied visual production of three artists active in the 1980s in order to demonstrate how we can theorize the collectivity of feminist and queer visual cultures within many kinds of archives and show how they were in dialogue with archives. The visual cultures discussed in this chapter and the ones that follow nuance our conceptions of feminist and other affiliated histories. For Marrs and Gregory, they leverage the comics form to document and challenge the feminist movement, deploying visual tactics to theorize the role of sexuality with feminist circles.

Pudge, Girl Blimp: *Feminist Collectives Shift the Sexual(ity) Conquest*

Published in three issues in the 1970s—the first in 1973, the second in 1975, and the third in 1977—Marrs's *The Further Fattening Adventures of Pudge, Girl Blimp* is, on its surface, an amusing romp in counterculture San Francisco through the eyes of a seventeen-year-old virgin newly arrived from the Midwest. At the center of most of the narrative, the protagonist, an unconfident and heavyset young woman, constantly faces barriers and setbacks on her ultimate quest to be deflowered. This general plot structure and its irreverent tone is in keeping with the underground comics form that Marrs both adopts and critiques. Through infusing her comic's form and content with feminist politics, Marrs dramatically reconstitutes both Pudge and her quest over the course of the narrative. Marrs renders the comic in a densely illustrated fashion that depicts Pudge within crowds as she negotiates different countercultures. All these characters exist within heavily annotated surroundings, which articulate a shared visual politics that embed Pudge's experiences among the many people and groups she encounters.

As Pudge attempts to lose her virginity, she simultaneously acquires a more positive sense of her body and a more dynamic sense of what losing her virginity might mean through these interpersonal encounters. The trajectory of how she strives to lose her virginity reflects this growth of meaning, as her first two failed attempts within the opening pages of the first issue involve her trying to get herself taken advantage of and trying to take advantage of someone else, showing very little respect or thought for herself or others.[32] After this second try, a textual panel asks if Pudge will have her "consciousness raised" and if she "will . . . ever see herself as whole person, female?"[33] This moment, which happens on the sixth page of over a hundred pages of content across three issues, marks an explicit departure from the narrative structure with which Marrs begins her comic. Up until that point, her character would have easily fit in a raunchy underground comic that sexualized and objectified its women characters. Though the series remains comical and irreverent, Marrs employs feminism to shift the underground narrative incrementally over the course of the three issues through the protagonist's exposure to and participation within feminist collectives.

A variety of feminist collectives play a role in raising Pudge's consciousness, transforming her relationship to sex, consent, sexuality, and her body. Her change issues from her interactions with other characters who challenge her to think more critically about her actions and more generously about herself. She accidentally encounters feminism through a self-help clinic when she finds a notice posted on a community bulletin board in the Mission neighborhood.[34] When she enters the room, she finds women clustered around a slide presentation about their cervixes before the group breaks up to help each other perform self-examinations with speculums and mirrors (Figure 2.1). Quickly pulled into the action, a woman helps Pudge examine her cervix in the bottom right of a panel crowded by other legs splayed in the air and accompanied by the faces of other women who assist the reclining women.

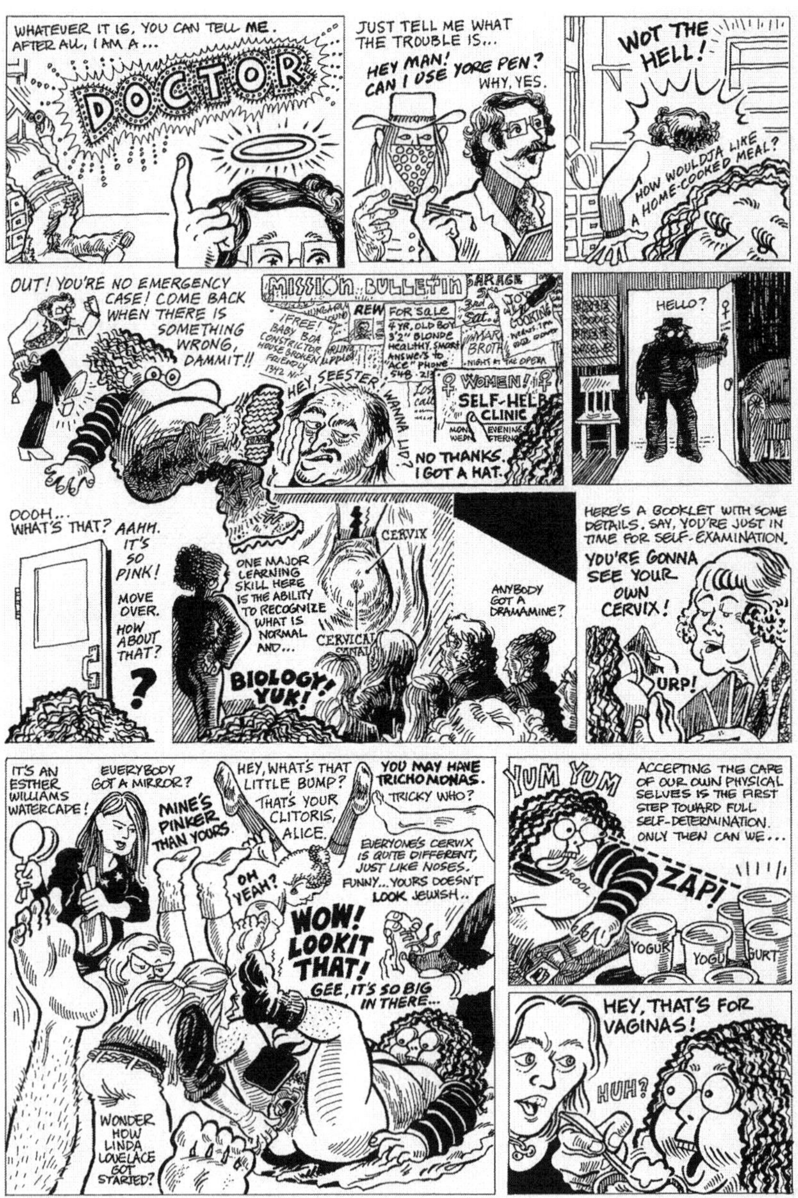

Figure 2.1. Pudge encounters a women's self-help clinic where she learns about her physical anatomy in Lee Marrs's *The Further Fattening Adventures of Pudge, Girl Blimp* #1 (1973). Copyright 1973–78 by Lee Marrs.

Among this crowd of women, we see a diverse group all working together. Compared with her mainstream feminist contemporaries, Marrs represents such collectives as more racially integrated, positioning an intersectional avant la lettre feminism as necessary for Pudge's growth. As Shilyh Warren points out in her analysis of the second-wave feminist documentary *Self-Health* (1974), which depicts a group of women learning about reproductive health and performing cervical examinations together, the required solidarity of sisterhood produces the "sameness in the bodies of women who are all white."[35] Warren invokes Carla Kaplan's work *The Erotics of Talk* (1996), which untangles how consciousness-raising groups compelled homogeneity through "subtle pressures to conform to particular viewpoints or to avoid taboo subjects, especially about race and class."[36] In Marrs's rendering, however, text and image strongly promote difference, especially along racial lines. In the panel where various women examine their cervixes, not only do the sheer number of legs and faces accompanied by exclamations like "Mine's pinker than yours!" promote difference on the most basic level, but other comments more explicitly affirm such values. Explaining speculum use to Pudge, a Black woman facilitating the meeting declares, "You see, every woman looks different inside."[37] Through these differences, Marrs embraces heterogeneity rather than enforcing a sisterhood of sameness.

In illustrating this collective, Marrs not only creates a self-help group with more progressive politics than mainstream depictions but also comically renders a contemporary moment of feminist history—in September 1972, Los Angeles police arrested Carol Downer and a number of other women who had been leading self-help workshops on the rationale that these services constituted unlicensed medical practice.[38] Because Downer had been charged with helping treat women's yeast infections with yogurt, the case became known as the Great Yogurt Conspiracy, as a report of the case in the feminist newspaper *off our backs* called it.[39] In the aftermath of Downer's acquittal and the attendant press coverage, a 2004 article in *Feminist Studies* understands this case as "the now comical police bust over yogurt."[40] By alluding to this moment in feminist history, Marrs connects to her feminist readers and suggests that her comic and character are part of that history.

While the seizure of strawberry yogurt that was a staff member's lunch and not intended for the treatment of yeast infections is already funny,[41] Marrs heightens the humor in her account of the event. In these panels, a character resembling Downer suggests yogurt as a treatment method, prompting an undercover cop to cry out, "You're all under arrest!!" while trying to yank up her pants and ineffectually search her purse for her badge.[42] Although the actual arrests happened in a police raid, this rendering captures the humorous manner in which the event was received by the general public. Marrs conveys her support of feminism by heightening the ridiculousness of the cops in this telling. This self-help clinic exposes Pudge to more perspectives and open dialogues about women's bodies and pleasures before she joins a consciousness-raising group, which she faithfully attends over the rest of the series.

Pudge's participation in a consciousness-raising group across all three issues shapes her perspective about her eventual sexual encounters. Through the depiction of these group settings, Marrs creates the space for conversation while simultaneously foreclosing the possibility of fully engaging any one woman's issues. In her introduction to the group in *Pudge, Girl Blimp* #1, Marrs fashions this spacious lack of listening by fracturing sequential paneling: the recursive flow of the women's conversation sets the panels spiraling (Figure 2.2).[43] At the center of this spiral, Marrs insets a "start" arrow, as if to suggest a deliberate order to read, from inside out. However, this order clashes with the traditional left-to-right movement of a page, which is still in play: the first and final rows are not canted into the spiral structure. These two conflicting orders underline the directionless movement of the group's conversation. In each section of panel we see a different woman speaking of her gendered frustrations, and in the spiraled section these moments overlap each other so that the women's sentiments cannot be deciphered in full. In other panels, characters trail off in ellipses, such that no thought is closed or resolved, regardless of whether fully spoken on the page. Just like Marrs's depiction of the women's self-help group where panels were filled with many voices and bodies, here we see various groupings and conversations afloat as Pudge makes her first introductions. As the panels start to spiral, these voices are fragmented into their own panels, verbalizing their frustrations without any space for real response. In a space outside the tilted panels, Marrs annotates the encounter: "the weeks go on . . . ." What we're seeing, particularly in the central spiral, is not one consciousness-raising session but many. The women circumnavigate

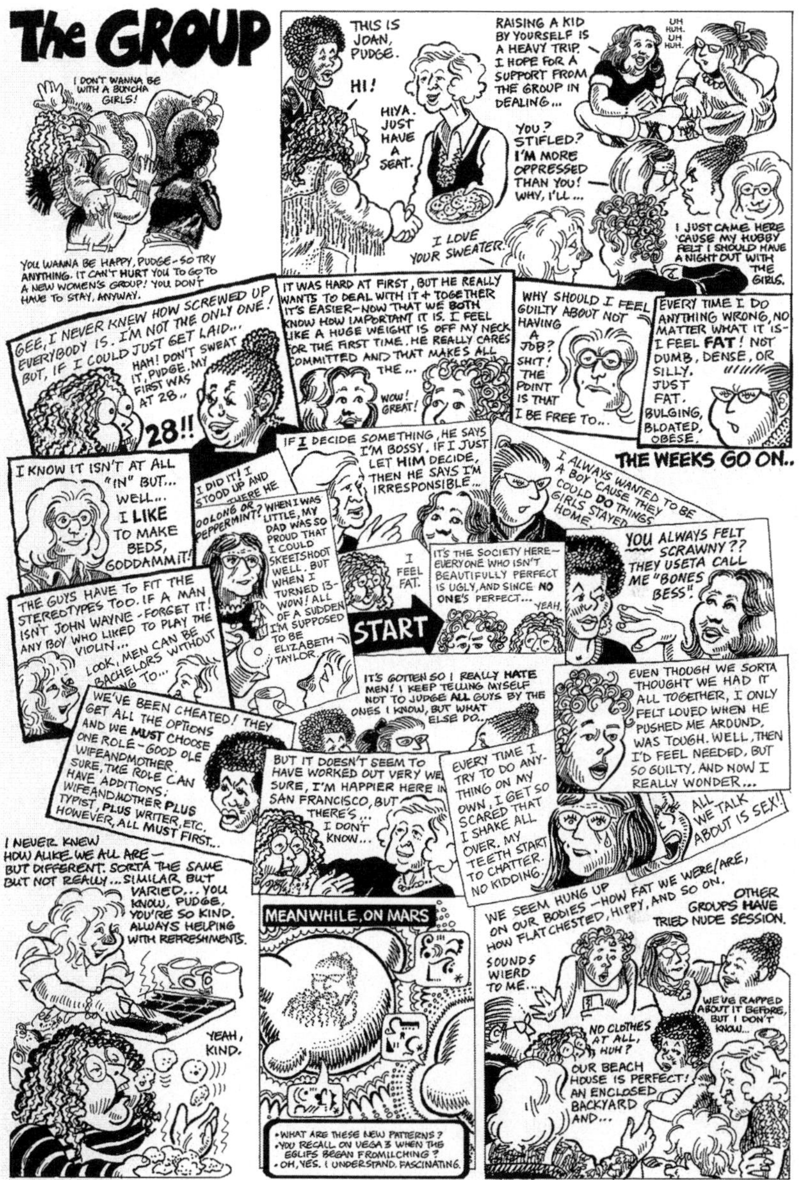

Figure 2.2. Pudge joins a consciousness-raising group and the page layout starts spiraling, showing a montage of many group sessions in Lee Marrs's *The Further Fattening Adventures of Pudge, Girl Blimp* #1 (1973). Copyright 1973–78 by Lee Marrs.

their ideas amid a crowded audience. This sequence acts as a temporal montage fast-forwarding us through Pudge's first consciousness-raising sessions, underlining her participation and suggesting, with the temporal marker, her potential growth at the sequence's end.

Since her interactions with the consciousness-raising group occur within the last few pages of the comic, it is not until the second issue that the personal impact on Pudge can be tracked. That is, *Pudge, Girl Blimp* #2 is the issue in which we can start to see how the seeds of feminism planted in the first comic are starting to shift Pudge's actions and goals. She continues to interact with the group in scattered moments that punctuate the text, indexing how the group becomes as much of a continual presence in her life as her goal to lose her virginity. When we see Pudge spend extended time with the consciousness-raising group, the formal panel layout begins to spiral once again. Unlike the inside–out spiral of *Pudge, Girl Blimp* #1 that conflicted with the left-to-right reading of the top panels, this spiral reads outside in, moving more seamlessly from the top row of panels across the page (Figure 2.3).[44] Here, rather than indicating multiple sessions, arrows lead the reader through a single spiraling conversation in which the women discuss their anger. Because of the many women in attendance, no one woman can do much more than simply register her anger, suggesting this group as a place to start consciousness-raising but not one that will allow for full processing.

This spiral is simpler—in its specified direction and illustration of one session—yet both spirals mark the women's space as formally discrete from the rest of the comic. Not only are these spiraling panels distinct, but also, in their troubling of traditional panel layout and subsequent overlapping and simultaneous collapsing of voices and moments, they are destructive to the comics page. While these spirals evoke the psychedelic culture that was often part of the underground scene,[45] this sense of disruption also resonates with the notion of *écriture feminine*, developed contemporaneously in Hélène Cixous's "The Laugh of the Medusa": "[Women] take pleasure in jumbling the order of space, in disorienting it, in changing around the furniture, dislocating things and values, breaking them all up, emptying structures, and turning propriety upside down. . . . A feminine text cannot fail to be more than subversive. It is volcanic; as it is written it brings about an upheaval of the old property crust, carrier of masculine investments; there's no other way."[46] Disorder

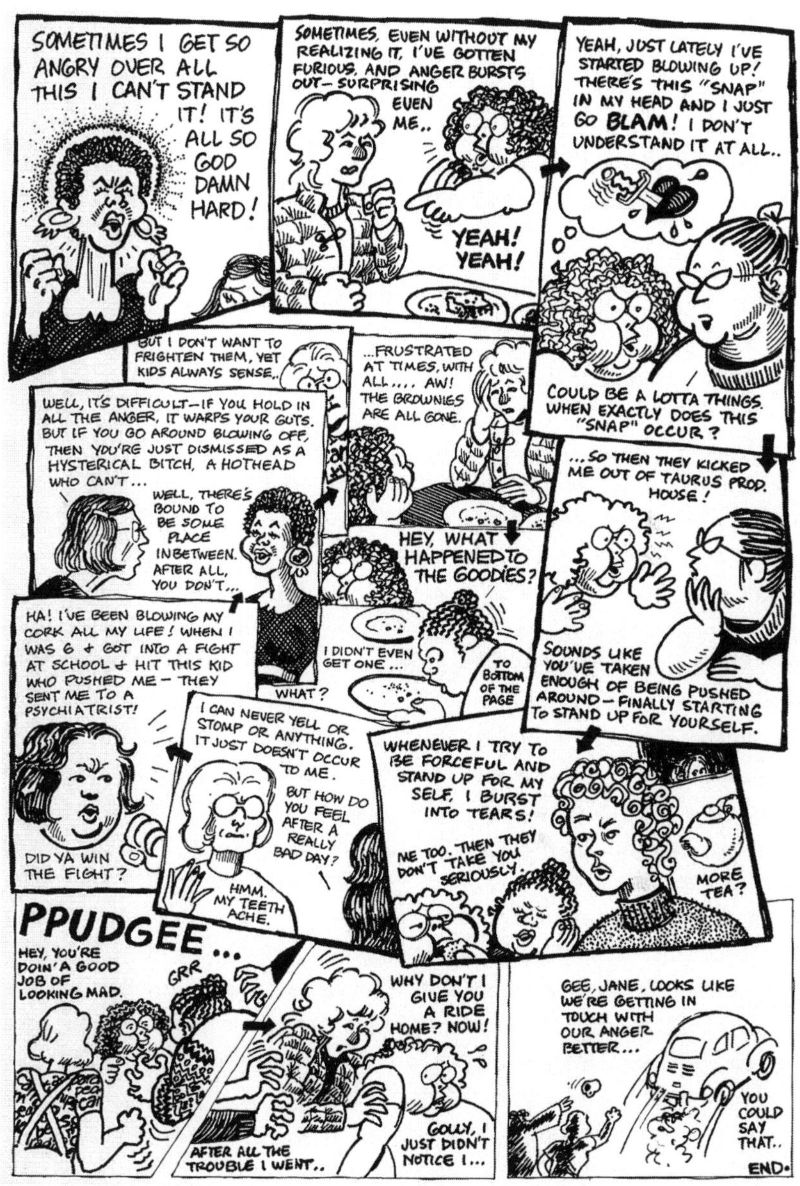

Figure 2.3. Pudge attends another consciousness-raising session where women discuss their anger in Lee Marrs's *The Further Fattening Adventures of Pudge, Girl Blimp* #2 (1975). Copyright 1973–78 by Lee Marrs.

emanates not just out of the writing, but also out of the women themselves, whose deep conversations jump-start the spirals as they perform the gestures that Cixous enumerates. They rhetorically "jumbl[e] the order of space" by reconsidering their values and reflect on how they have already "empt[ied] structures" through changes instigated in their group discussions. While this "volcanic" force only "brings about an upheaval" of the format of two pages, its energy suffuses the rest of the plot, redirecting Pudge's focus.[47] Not only do these moments of feminist collectivity change Pudge's trajectory and the ways she eventually achieves her goal, but also the series itself—with a lusty yet conventionally unattractive and unconfident protagonist—challenges a whole subset of misogynist underground comics featuring graphically attractive women drawn for the purposes of objectification in sexual situations. Through these representations, Marrs subtly disrupts the prevailing structures that constrain and contain comics and suggests innovative possibilities for the form and the characters therein.

Moreover, this feminist sensibility shapes how Pudge's eventual encounters with sexuality are illustrated and how Pudge participates in them outside of the received beliefs with which she begins her narrative. At first, her feminist engagement seems to act as a potential hindrance to her goal, as she rejects the further advances of her first suitor, Jethro, an undercover cop who devalues her as a "suspect" when their vehicular tryst is interrupted by other policemen.[48] However, her personal growth in the consciousness-raising group opens Pudge up to a more wide-ranging and satisfying engagement with her sexuality. Her next two partners demonstrate more progressive mindsets: Jane, a lesbian in her consciousness-raising group, and Skeets, a straight male activist. Her sexual connection with these two partners moves beyond the simplistic quest of losing her virginity, and this change underlines her evolving ideas. From her continuing explorations in feminism, she has gained a sense of self-worth and bodily respect for herself and her partners.

Both of these sexual experiences transpire in the third issue. Her encounter with a woman, however, which happens within the first few pages, shapes the arc of the installment, setting the tone for the heterosexual encounters to follow. With Jane, Pudge first experiences an orgasm and, during this shared intimacy, the two women discuss Pudge's initial, fraught forays with men. For Marrs, lesbian desire nestles comfortably alongside both the feminist movement and heterosexuality and amplifies Pudge's conceptions of sexuality. In Marrs's multipage depiction of Pudge's intimacy with Jane, she shows both women actively exploring the contours of each other's bodies for the purposes of pleasure.[49] Pudge's experience is especially heightened, likely because this represents her first successful sexual encounter with another person and, therefore, fulfills her goal—albeit not in a manner she could have originally conceived of. When Pudge turns to satisfy Jane, Pudge's figure occupies most of the panels as we watch her eager and curious face learning how to give pleasure.[50] Pudge also dominates the panel space during her own orgasm (Figure 2.4). As Jane disappears, we zoom into a row of three panels that show Pudge's orgasm as a fire in her loins that races up her body and shoots out the tips of her hair into a star-filled eruption. In the orgasmic moments, bodies dissolve into psychedelic, wavy lines surrounded by stars and curved shapes. When Pudge later sleeps with Skeets on multiple occasions, her pleasures there stylistically echo and thereby refer back to those with Jane.[51]

While this narrative in three parts begins as a comical, over-the-top sexual conquest, Marrs employs feminism in the form of collectives to nuance Pudge's trajectory and sexuality. On the very last page of the comic, following her birthday, Pudge thinks forward to her future. Here, she realizes, "I can be anything at all!!" picturing career trajectories in six circular panels that overlap each other and the rectangular panels (Figure 2.5).[52] This revelation results from her new progressive politics rather than the loss of her virginity: these realizations forecast career possibilities now open to women because of feminism. The six imagined scenarios not only speak to feminism's impact on real women, but also open up new narratives for female characters.[53] As Pudge raises her consciousness and the series therefore moves away from a misogynistic plot, Pudge's story can be read both as her personal bildungsroman as well as a treatise to underground comics, entreating change.

The impact of Marrs's comics can be seen in how they reached a wide audience, who then saved the comics for posterity within collections that became part of archives. Finding *Pudge, Girl Blimp* in many archival locations, as noted in the previous section, confirmed the breadth of Marrs's message and how her character's journey spoke to both the underground and feminism as it critiqued both movements.

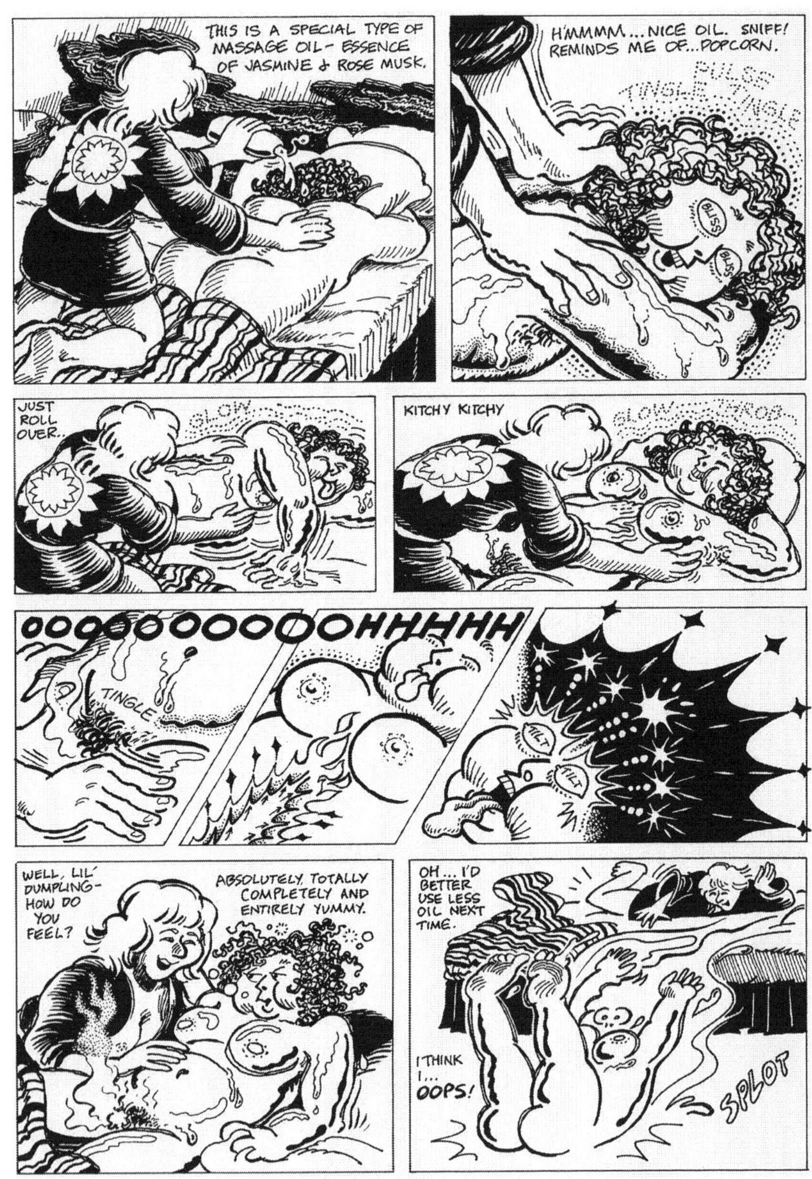

Figure 2.4. Pudge receives a sensual massage from Jane that results in Pudge's first successful orgasm and sexual encounter in Lee Marrs's *The Further Fattening Adventures of Pudge, Girl Blimp* #3 (1977). Copyright 1973–78 by Lee Marrs.

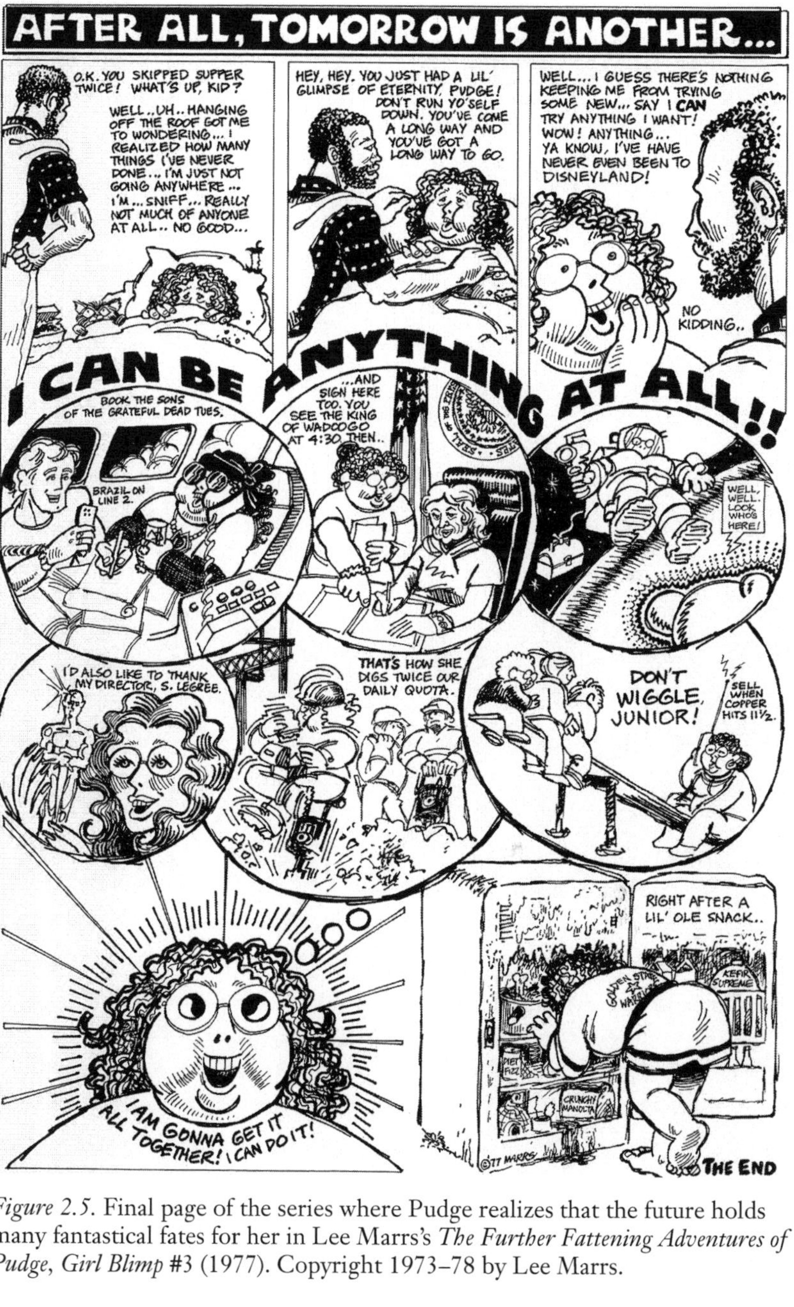

Figure 2.5. Final page of the series where Pudge realizes that the future holds many fantastical fates for her in Lee Marrs's *The Further Fattening Adventures of Pudge, Girl Blimp* #3 (1977). Copyright 1973–78 by Lee Marrs.

Reading across archives helped excavate the different stories that Marrs was nesting within her narrative and how her story was received, even if it remained rather marginal to either movement.

Dynamite Damsels: *Reckoning with Feminist Rhetoric*

On the front cover of *Dynamite Damsels,* Roberta Gregory positions her comic in relation to watershed moments within the feminist movement. While the front covers of *The Further Fattening Adventures of Pudge, Girl Blimp* always centrally situate Pudge in the middle of a crowded, countercultural San Francisco milieu that wraps around onto the back cover, Gregory's protagonist, Frieda, is decentered. Both the front and back covers of *Dynamite Damsels* illustrate collectives of women representing the feminist movement. The contrasting placements of the protagonists is suggestive of how they encounter and convey feminism to their readers. In Marrs's story, Pudge is solidly the main character; these are her adventures, and she serves as a node through which we learn not only about feminism but also about other countercultures that crowd around her on the covers. For Gregory's text, although Frieda is the protagonist, the covers spatially locate feminism as the main character. Frieda changes and grows throughout the narrative, but her transformation simultaneously tells feminism's story, for which Frieda acts as a filter.

While *Pudge, Girl Blimp* functions as an introductory primer to feminism, showing how it can positively reshape someone's experience, *Dynamite Damsels* speaks to those already in the feminist movement and depicts its shortcomings. Gregory formulates this critique both through the experiences of the characters and how she illustrates those happenings. Like Marrs, Gregory's pages are dense, but text, rather than bodies, commands space. That is, the women process their feminism through sizable speech and thought bubbles that entangle them and crowd their bodies. Even moments of pleasure are mediated through and curtailed by feminist rhetoric on the page. While feminism provides these women with the initial platform to raise their consciousness, we can see on the page itself how it becomes a stifling force. Together, both comics outline the potential of the feminist movement while also locating in their representations the seeds for change.

By referencing key texts and moments within the feminist movement, Gregory both celebrates and challenges feminism through her irreverent representation. The cover depicts the protagonist dreaming of a group of armored women riding horses and carrying the banner of feminism on shields that show a ♀ with a fist inside the circle (Figure 2.6). This symbol had become an icon of feminist empowerment when it was chosen for the cover of one of the first widely available mass-market anthologies of the women's liberation movement, *Sisterhood Is Powerful* (1970), which was edited by Robin Morgan. On both Gregory's and Morgan's covers, the centrally located symbol pulsates in red.

In addition to referencing Morgan's anthology, the cover of *Dynamite Damsels* inscribes another contemporaneous event. In May 1970 at the Second Congress to Unite Women, a group of lesbians took over the stage prior to the opening session, demanding that lesbianism be accepted by the Congress following Betty Friedan's recent admonition of lesbians as a "lavender menace."[54] The protesters wore T-shirts bearing the phrase "LAVENDER MENACE" across the bust and held up signs that proclaimed, "THE WOMEN'S MOVEMENT IS A LESBIAN PLOT!"[55] This action led to greater lesbian visibility and to the National Organization of Women passing legislation in favor of lesbians in the following year.[56] Gregory's cover humorously revises this key moment in early feminism. As Frieda dreams, her cat Pumpkin stays awake, wondering, "Is the women's movement really a lesbian plot?" Although the lavender menace succeeded in its immediate goal, Gregory suggests that, over half a decade later, lesbianism's relationship with feminism remains open to debate by transforming the exclamation into a question silently considered by a cat. By unraveling this query in the narrative, Gregory presciently previews one of the conflicts that would further erode the cohesion of the women's movement in the 1980s.

The major narrative within the self-published *Dynamite Damsels* is divided into nineteen vignettes that primarily revolve around Frieda's sexual awakening and her commitments as a feminist activist, though they sometimes also focus on other key characters.[57] Following a couple of prefatory comics, the story begins in the middle of a feminist consciousness-raising session, as Frieda brings a Black woman, Edie, who is interested in joining the group.[58] Edie asks about the whiteness of the

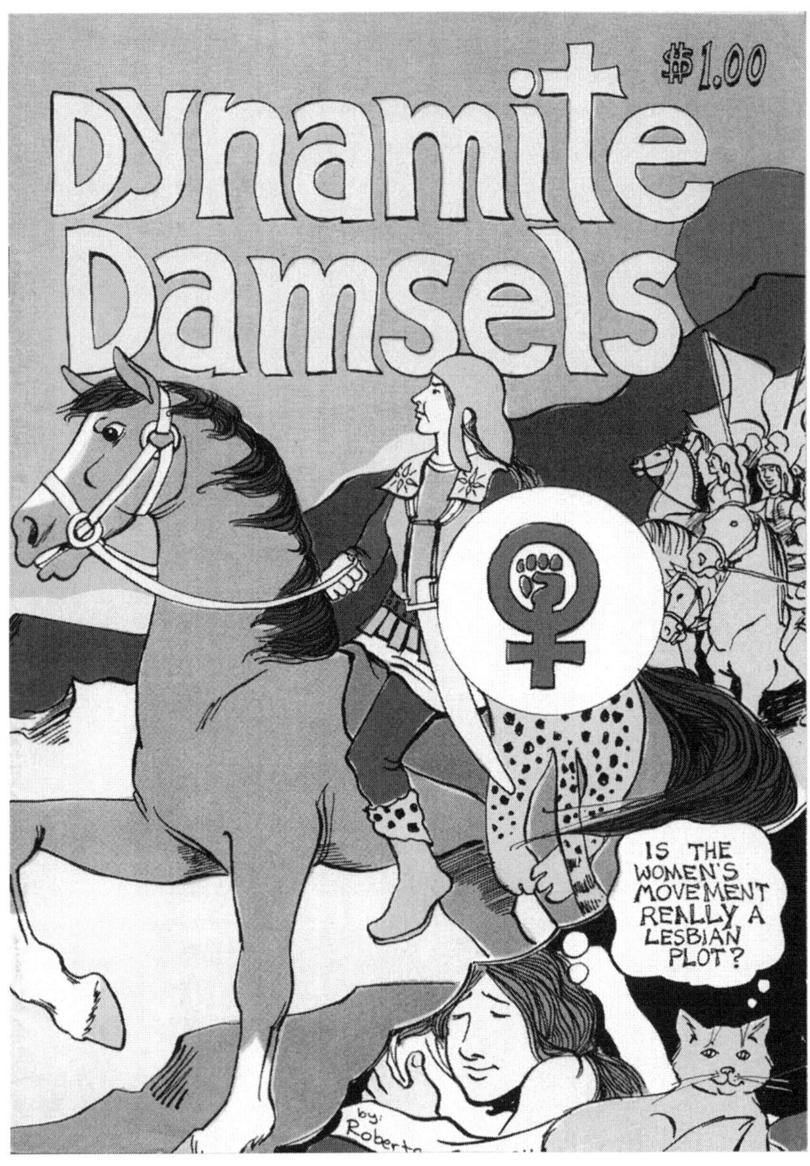

Figure 2.6. Front cover of Roberta Gregory's *Dynamite Damsels* (1976) that shows Frieda, the protagonist, dreaming of a feminist warrior on a horse leading a battalion while her cat wonders, "Is the women's movement really a lesbian plot?" Courtesy of Roberta Gregory.

feminist movement and participates in the session after she's quickly answered, but there is an uneasiness to this exchange among the members and the group forecloses a fuller consideration of race.[59] The women then turn to discuss sex in this and subsequent sessions, so that this vignette, titled "Group Dynamics," positions sex—not race—as the main vector of interest for this feminist plot.[60] The marginalized role of race within this feminist group foreshadows the frictions that Frieda faces as her sexuality shifts, as well as the work that feminists of color would continue to do in the following decade to challenge the perceived centrality of whiteness within the movement, as I discuss in further detail in the chapter on Gloria Anzaldúa.

As the group discusses sex, Frieda, the twenty-three-year-old virgin protagonist, has little to contribute and blushes at her admission of inexperience.[61] Three vignettes later, however, Frieda meets Doris, a stereotypical masculine dyke, who jump-starts Frieda's sexual desires.[62] Frieda negotiates her burgeoning sexual feelings through textual rhetoric. As this more prominent text often limits figural representation, much of the comic is told through reactive faces rather than fuller forms. Even moments of intimacy are crowded by sizable speech and thought bubbles, unlike *Pudge, Girl Blimp*, where text recedes to make space for bodies on the page.

The sheer volume of words on the page becomes stifling when Frieda contemplates her sexual and activist identity while she's alone in her bed, suffering from sleeplessness in two vignettes aptly titled "Insomnia I" and "Insomnia II."[63] In the first vignette, Frieda names feminism as the reason she cannot sleep, reflecting that she has "so much on [her] mind" now that her consciousness has been raised (Figure 2.7). When she finally falls asleep, a dream of embracing Doris wakes her abruptly and her whole body reveals her feelings as she viscerally reacts: she gasps and trembles, her heart pounds, and her cheeks flush. Her immediate thoughts, "Not again! . . . I gotta stop havin' those dreams!" disclose that this is not the first time that she's had this dream; the fact that this comic vignette starts and ends with the same panel reinforces this ceaseless repetition. In the penultimate panel, a dejected Frieda rests her head on her hand, mulling over the implications of this fantasy, first wondering, "Am I O.D.'ing on feminism?" Following thoughts—"Am I carrying it [i.e.,

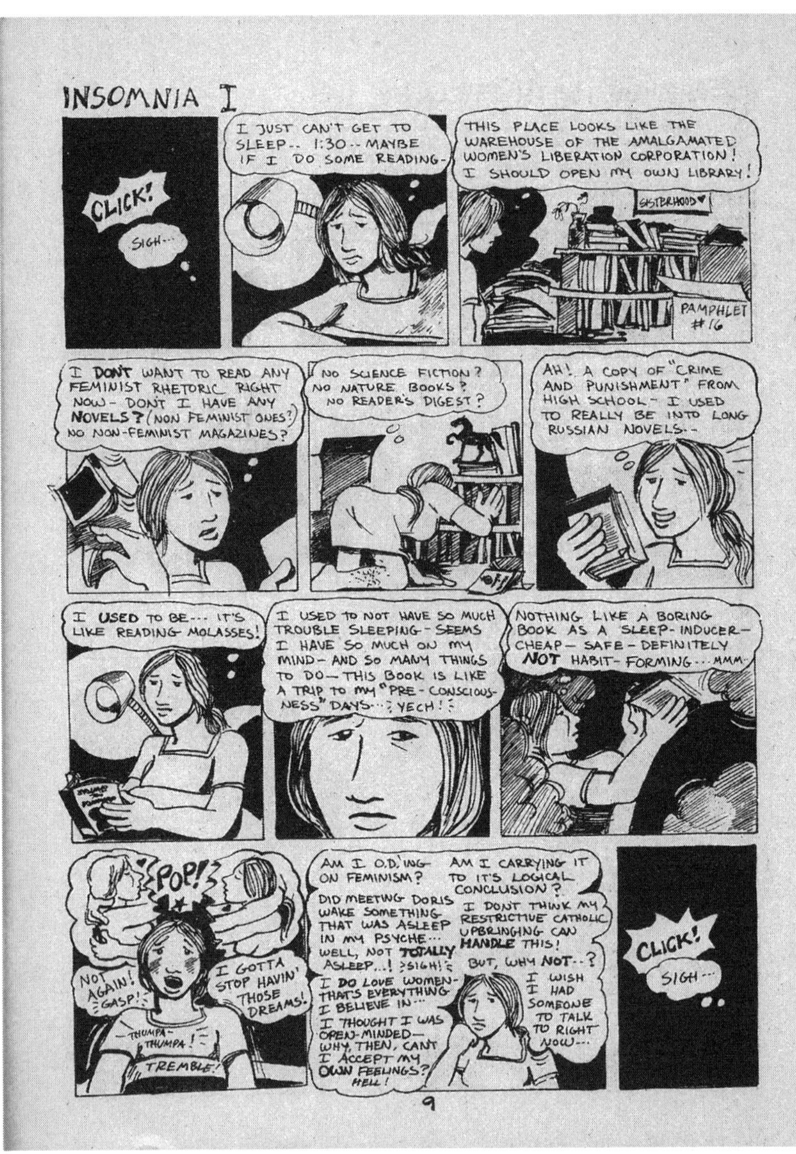

Figure 2.7. "Insomnia I" vignette in Roberta Gregory's *Dynamite Damsels* (1976) where Frieda struggles to fall asleep and considers how her feminist activism and unrequited attraction to a woman play a role. Courtesy of Roberta Gregory.

feminism] to its logical conclusion?"—corroborate that her politics may have germinated this desire. Yet she manifests discomfort with how these feelings challenge her politics, causing her to ask, "I thought I was open-minded—why, then, can't I accept my own feelings? Hell!"[64] She cannot escape the contradictory considerations that collapse around her; she cannot push them to the side (of the panel). These solitary moments of feminist self-reflection illustrate the feminist battle cry that "the personal is political" by unfurling the political in hefty speech bubbles in the most intimate of spaces, Frieda's bedroom. In this and her following bout of insomnia, Frieda endeavors to synthesize her feelings and her politics, yet she cannot find any reprieve from the words on the page.

In "Insomnia II," Frieda experiences broader feminist discontent (Figure 2.8).[65] Here, she tallies the difficult economics of being a full-time feminist activist after a tough and demoralizing demonstration. Her textual worries dominate even more of the page space in this second episode. In a close-up panel, Frieda gazes with furrowed brow directly out at the reader, wondering if she could make a difference by "writ[ing] another bookful of rhetoric."[66] In "Insomnia I," as she attempts to resolve her earlier sleeplessness, she initially turns to her bookshelf but quickly tosses a work of feminism over her right shoulder, deciding, "I don't want to read any feminist rhetoric right now."[67] Her visceral response to feminism in both "Insomnia I" and "Insomnia II" bespeaks her fatigue with the movement, and the qualifying adjectives "another" and "any" collapse the vibrancy of feminist voices into a dull chain of sameness. Yet this feminism is her life force; through Frieda, rhetoric lives and breathes on these pages.

Is Frieda's direct gaze in "Insomnia II" as she considers writing a book an autobiographical rupturing of the fourth wall? Is *Dynamite Damsels* Gregory's "bookful of rhetoric," and is that even possible if it's in comics form? If anything, although Gregory's comics form is overrun with textual rhetoric, her pages confront these words, illustrating their potential stranglehold on bodies and discourse but also working through this impasse in a different medium that allows body and language to reckon directly with each other. Parsing her life run by feminist rhetoric, Frieda tosses and turns in bed. The comics page heightens this motion by alternately zooming in and out from a variety of angles

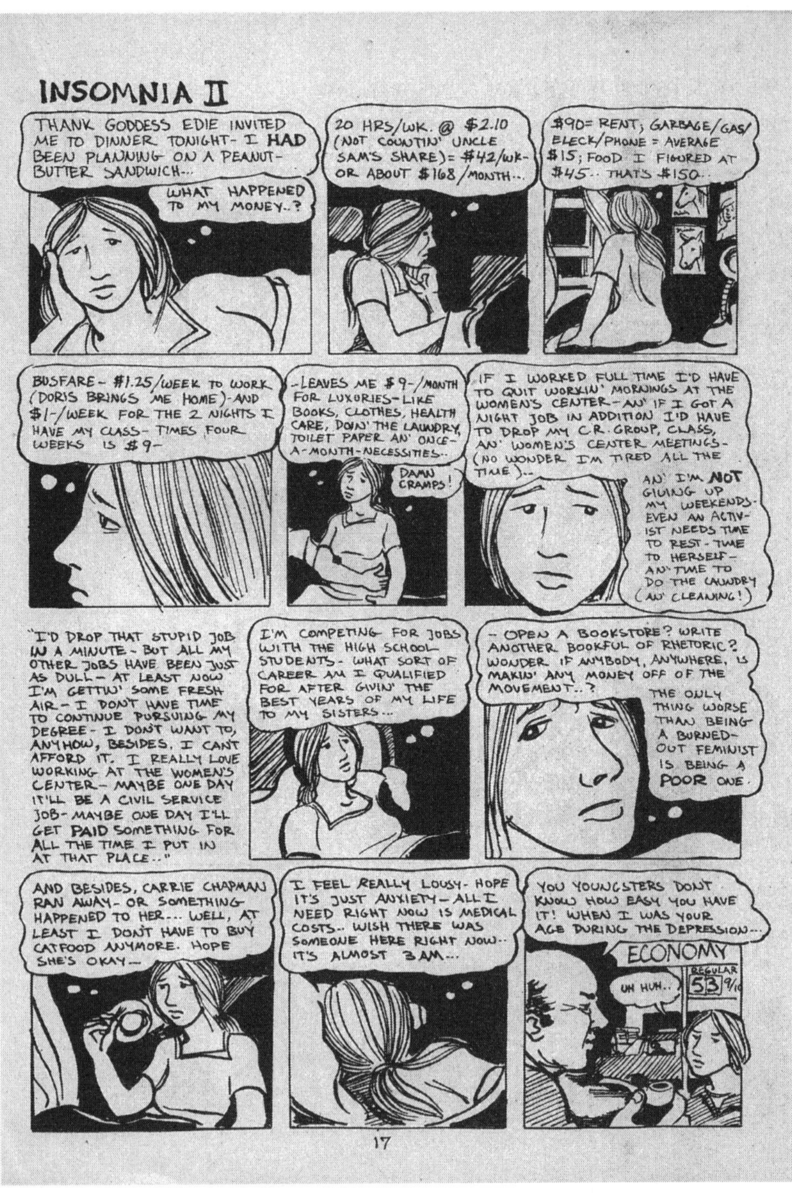

Figure 2.8. "Insomnia II" vignette in Roberta Gregory's *Dynamite Damsels* (1976) where Frieda worries over how she hardly makes enough money to cover her expenses through her feminist activism and wonders if it is worth it. Courtesy of Roberta Gregory.

on her frustrated face. In "Insomnia II," Frieda tackles her feminism face-to-face (or, rather, face–to–thought bubble), and her circular ruminations achieve forward motion in the following vignette when she admits her lesbian feelings. The vignette, a nocturnal interlude between leading a feminist demonstration and coming out, allows Frieda to relate the tangible issues that undergird her daily existence apart from these climatic instances. In this second bout of insomnia, she faces her feminist hardships before her sexuality propels her into renegotiating the terms of her political engagement.

In her waking life, her commitment to feminism brings her fulfillment, but she also feels compelled to deny her sexual orientation. This strain reaches a breaking point at the center of the narrative during a feminist demonstration that Frieda leads, which is portrayed across three pages in "The Unity Show," the longest vignette in the comic. This demonstration immediately precedes her second bout of insomnia.[68] Before the march begins, Frieda is unabashedly positive, blushing at the thought of the feminist action while clasping her hands and verbalizing, "Sisterhood is beautiful—oh, god, I'm so jazzed—it's just like the early days of the movement—."[69] Her burgeoning sexual desire prompts her blushing earlier in the narrative, likening it to a joyous postcoital glow. In these panels, she is positively bubbly—gushing, "We gotta get 'em all together an' then turn 'em into fanatical feminists!"—rather than bothered by any of her insomniac concerns.[70] When the march starts, Frieda's exuberance builds and she proclaims, "It's beautiful! It's all beautiful and perfect!" (Figure 2.9).[71] Mid-demonstration, her mounting energy climaxes as she floats above the crowd with her arms open and eyes closed, surrounded by stars and ♀s. In the following panel, her fellow feminists gaze on her bliss, confirming the sexual undertones by declaring her "positively orgasmic."[72] This moment represents the first time that Frieda finds release when flushed. At this point, Frieda is still entering into sexual self-knowledge, but she finds equivalent fulfillment through her organizing. Yet, in the following panels, the demonstration takes a turn for the worse as female counterprotesters start to assault Frieda physically. In their accompanying verbal attacks, they notably deride Frieda and her compatriots with stereotypes, saying, "They're probably all lesbians . . . and know karate!"[73] This event crushes Frieda's spirit, since she tried to play it straight for the purposes of the march and is aware that homophobia is also replicated within her feminist group.

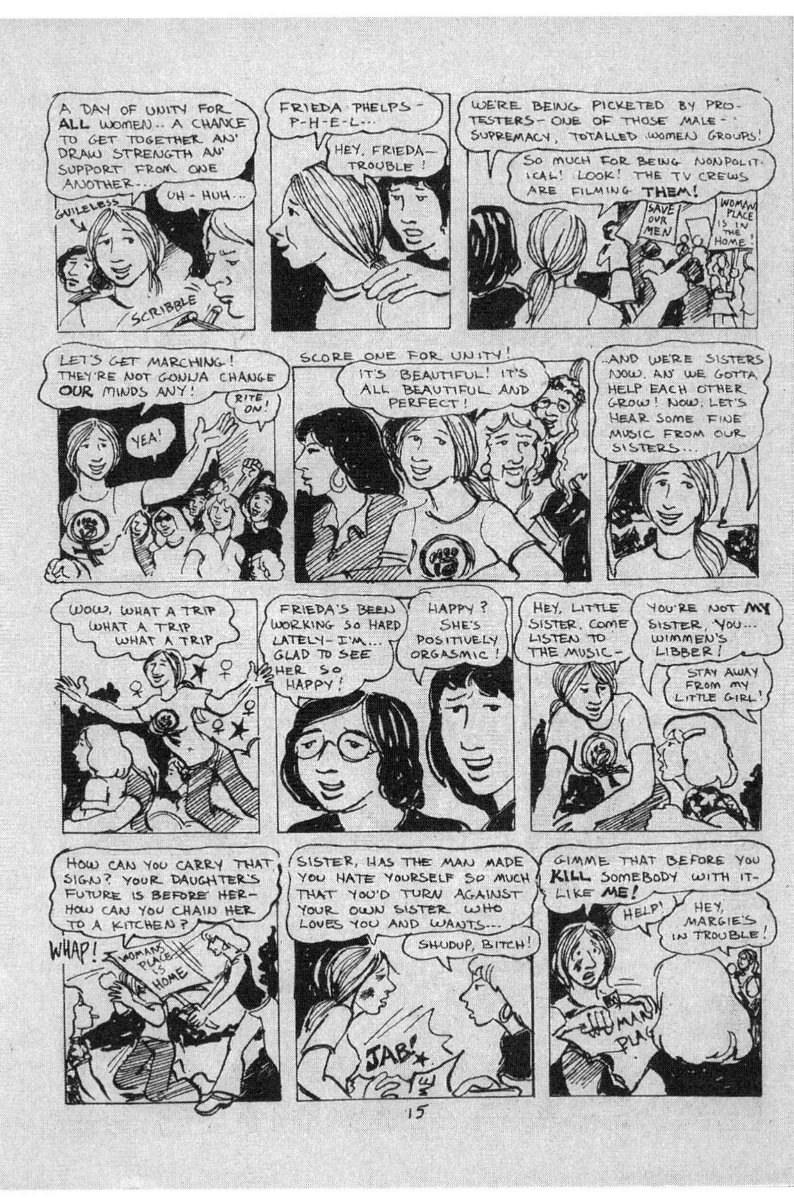

Figure 2.9. The middle page of "The Unity Show" vignette in Roberta Gregory's *Dynamite Damsels* (1976) where Frieda is optimistic about their feminist march before being physically attacked by counterprotesters. Courtesy of Roberta Gregory.

Following this difficult march and the anxiety and agitation of her sleepless night, Frieda comes out as a lesbian, an admission that radically reconfigures her relationship to feminism. Throughout, feminism leaves little space for Frieda's newfound sexuality, and this is no more evident than when she receives a phone call during an intimate moment. The telephone rings as she is in bed discussing lesbian relationships with Doris and her partner, thinking to herself, "What a beautiful moment— if only it could last forever!"[74] The "RING-GG!" splays vertically between panels, viscerally cutting off the intimate exchange from Frieda's harried conversation about the women's center in the next panel. Two very different Friedas exist on either side of the ring. By this point in the story, she is fed up with feminism, such that these phone calls are strenuous affairs. The feminism on the phone calls her into unhealthy sacrifice and no longer recognizes her fully. In response to the phone call, she sends Doris, the most visibly lesbian character, in her stead.[75] She has already come out to her fellow feminists, but by answering the call with Doris, Frieda learns that they do not embrace her new identity and community as fully as they claim.

The final two pages culminate in a face-off between Frieda's feminism and her lesbianism through the figure of Doris. When Doris arrives at the women's center to fill in for Frieda, the women literally shove her into a closet to hide her, not wanting her to appear in a television show they are filming about the center (Figure 2.10).[76] Although they do not physically accost Doris, their actions echo those that Frieda suffers at the march, when hateful women try to silence her. When Frieda arrives and learns what has happened to Doris, her response is to quit her work with the women's center and leave the consciousness-raising group—opting to take time to reassess her own identity, independent of activist work.[77]

Frieda's actions are not a full-scale rejection of feminism but a recalibration. Her soul-searching transformation throughout the comic illustrates the malleable mentality that feminism must strive for if it does not want to alienate its lesbian sisters, not to mention women of color. If *Pudge, Girl Blimp* acts as a treatise to underground comics and feminist newcomers, then *Dynamite Damsels* is a didactic manual for feminism, depicting methods of alienation to avoid. In the comic's visuality, Gregory wields feminist rhetoric and associates it with bodies, indexing who commands which rhetorics to both include and exclude.

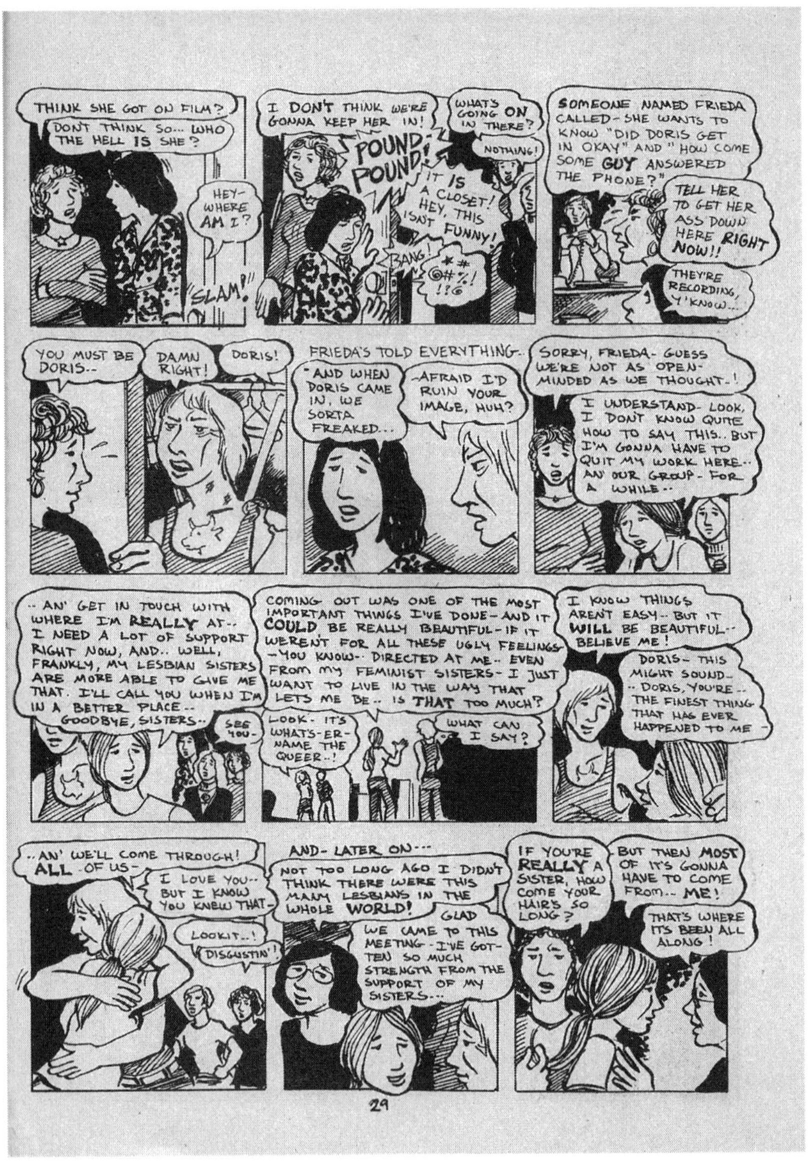

Figure 2.10. The second page of the "Changes" vignette and final page of the main narrative of Roberta Gregory's *Dynamite Damsels* (1976) where Frieda quits her job at the women's center after learning that the women there homophobically locked Doris in the closet so that she wouldn't appear in a film they were shooting. Courtesy of Roberta Gregory.

As with Marrs, how Gregory's comic exists across archives situates its feminist contributions. Both comics were collected variously and paired with newer comics by women outside of underground collections, which suggests how they inspired and shaped this future work. One surprising archival location of *Dynamite Damsels* is as one of the earliest artifacts on the online Queer Zine Archive Project, which collects zines that queer people made, starting in the late 1980s through the present. Though the visual style of *Dynamite Damsels* differs from the DIY aesthetics of many of the zines, which are closer to the look and feel of the *Diary* and *Caught Looking*, it echoes the personal nature of many zines and gives insight into lesbian and feminist lives in the 1970s. Because the comic documents not only the feminist movement but also the life experiences of the many women involved, Gregory's comic adds to the collection's understanding of the evolving language and everyday histories of queer social movements.

As I will discuss further in the conclusion, both Gregory's and Marrs's comics were also collected at the Lesbian Herstory Archives. In addition, a research binder on early lesbian comics put together by photographer Tee Corinne included Gregory's letters and early comics, revealing the development of her comics feminism.[78] All of these details scattered across archives grounded the comics contributions of these women and showed how they were embedded within multiple communities interested in issues of social justice.

Creating Networks for New Generations with Gay Comix

Following these solo works, Gregory and Marrs kept making comics within the underground publishing scene, frequently contributing to the *Wimmen's Comix* and *Tits & Clits* comics series. In these comics, both artists continued to explore themes related to women's sexuality, but it is their groundbreaking work in the *Gay Comix* series that would make space for new generations of lesbian and bisexual women cartoonists similarly invested in the project of visually representing women's sexuality. *Gay Comix* was notably the first comics series to feature both gay men and lesbians in its pages. The editors aimed to balance that content in addition to seeking out additional representations from across the gender and sexual spectrum. Running for twenty-five issues across two decades, from 1980 to 1998, *Gay Comix* featured the work of over one hundred artists and served as a launching point for a number of emerging artists. Having a dedicated space where women could explore LGBTQ themes helped facilitate a boom in lesbian comics in the 1990s, as this section illustrates.

Both Marrs and Gregory began participating in the series from its first issue, their contributions solicited by underground cartoonist Howard Cruse, who served as editor of the series for the first four issues. Along with underground veteran Mary Wings, Marrs and Gregory outlined a capacious understanding of female homosexuality in *Gay Comix* #1 (1980), providing generous groundwork for future artists to examine wide-ranging facets of such experiences. In that initial issue, Marrs and Gregory both produced comics that harked back to their earlier comics yet expanded the narrative exploration of sexuality past the coming-of-age beginnings of *Pudge, Girl Blimp* and *Dynamite Damsels*. Their brief comics tackled adult sexuality and showed how sexuality is a fluid, evolving dynamic across many years that can be shaped by the community around you.

With the eight-page "Stick in the Mud," which opens the volume, Marrs traces the love life of a bisexual woman, Susan, from her early childhood all the way through to domestic bliss with Carol, illustrated in a final panel where the two relax together in rocking chairs on their porch, knitting and discussing upcoming social plans while the cat naps between them (Figure 2.11). Whereas Pudge emerges from her narrative as an eighteen-year-old with an evolved sense of sexuality who contemplates her future career, Susan struggles with her sexuality for years from her adolescence through her adult life. She yo-yos from one failed love to another, cycling through a range of relationship types with lovers of different genders. This nonlinear narrative progression shows Marrs drawing on while simultaneously upending the tropes of the romance comic, a popular midcentury form that narrated how a young woman found fulfilling heterosexual love with one perfect partner.[79] Marrs dispenses with the possibility of a traditional heterosexual pairing for her protagonist early on, illustrating the courtship, marriage, and divorce in less than a page, following the depiction of failed female loves and preceding some years of a tumultuous swinging lifestyle. Through subverting the expectations and linearity of the romance comic, Marrs makes

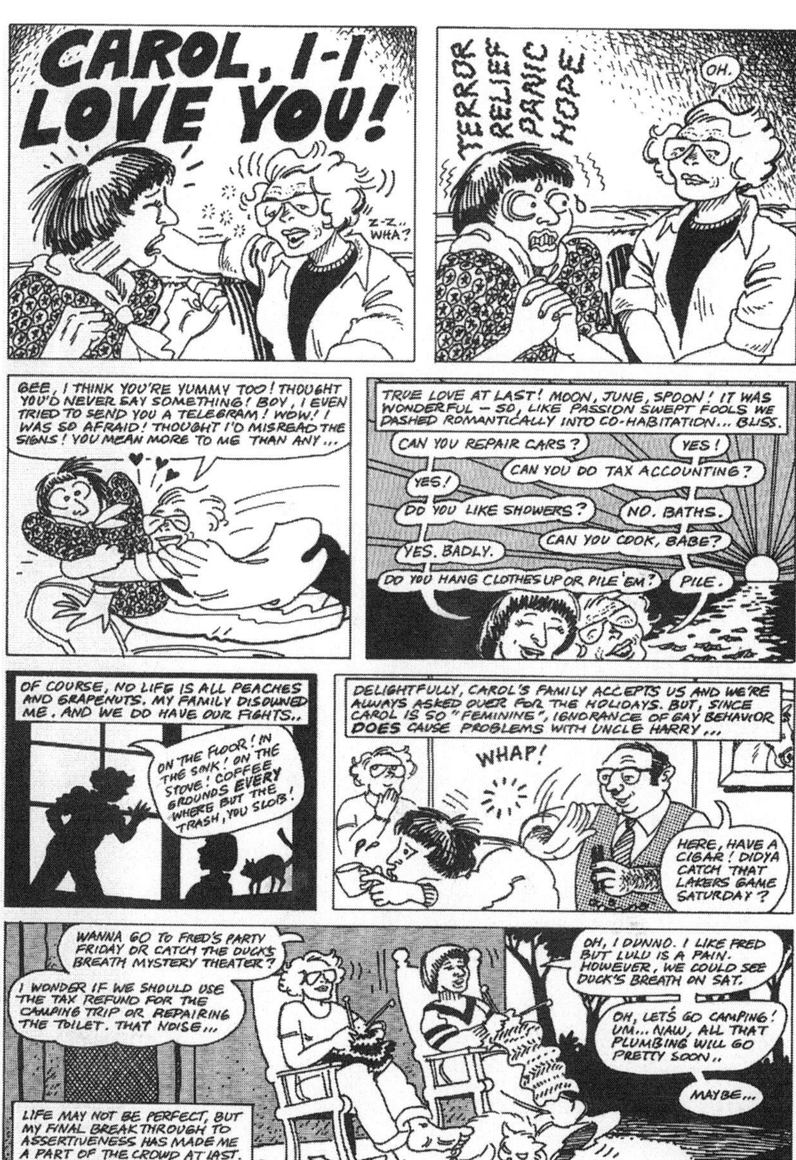

Figure 2.11. Final page of Lee Marrs's "Stick in the Mud" comic that appears in *Gay Comix* #1 (1980) where Susan, the protagonist, professes her love to Carol, and the two women are able to construct a happily ever after together. Copyright 1980 by Lee Marrs.

visible the romantic difficulties for a person who falls outside of accepted sexual norms; yet, in the ultimate subversion of the genre, she offers up a happy ending where the protagonist finds herself in a stable, committed relationship, but with a woman.

A few stories later in the same issue, Gregory's five-page piece "Re-Union" starts from a point that coalesces the beginning and ending of *Dynamite Damsels*, creating a viable lesbian feminist community over the course of the comic. We begin again with a consciousness-raising session, but here, when one woman comes out to the group, not only is she accepted by the group but the comic also traces how this disclosure positively alters the life path for two of her fellow groupmates as they work up the courage to seek female partners also. The comic follows the three women through their love lives until they all bump into one another at a women's concert six years later. This concert is the realization of lesbian–feminist community that Frieda wasn't sure was possible when she left her women's group at the end of *Dynamite Damsels* (Figure 2.12). Three parallel panels at the end of the comic show each woman impressed by the other two while they reflect on how they're still figuring out their own life. The wording of each woman's thought bubble is virtually the same, demonstrating the validity of each path and refusing to judge one woman's experience as more or less evolved. Gregory's image for the back cover of that first issue of *Gay Comix* shares this ethos as she interweaves six scenes of men and women openly expressing and being accepted for their homosexual identities under text that proclaims, "When you're in love, the whole world is lavender." In the space of a few pages each, these comics, together with Marrs's piece, illustrate a multifaceted range of sexual practices and relationship types, opening up the space to tell all sorts of stories of sexuality across the run of the series. Numerous other women soon joined them, inspired by their work here and in subsequent issues.

While Wings and Marrs helped define the developing series in the first several issues, Gregory shaped the voice of the publication over the course of its entire run. Across its twenty-five issues, Gregory was the most frequent female contributor, with pieces in over three quarters of the issues and with half of *Gay Comics* #21 (1993) devoted solely to her work.[80] In addition to influencing the career of Alison Bechdel, as will be discussed in the following chapter, *Gay Comix* inspired many other

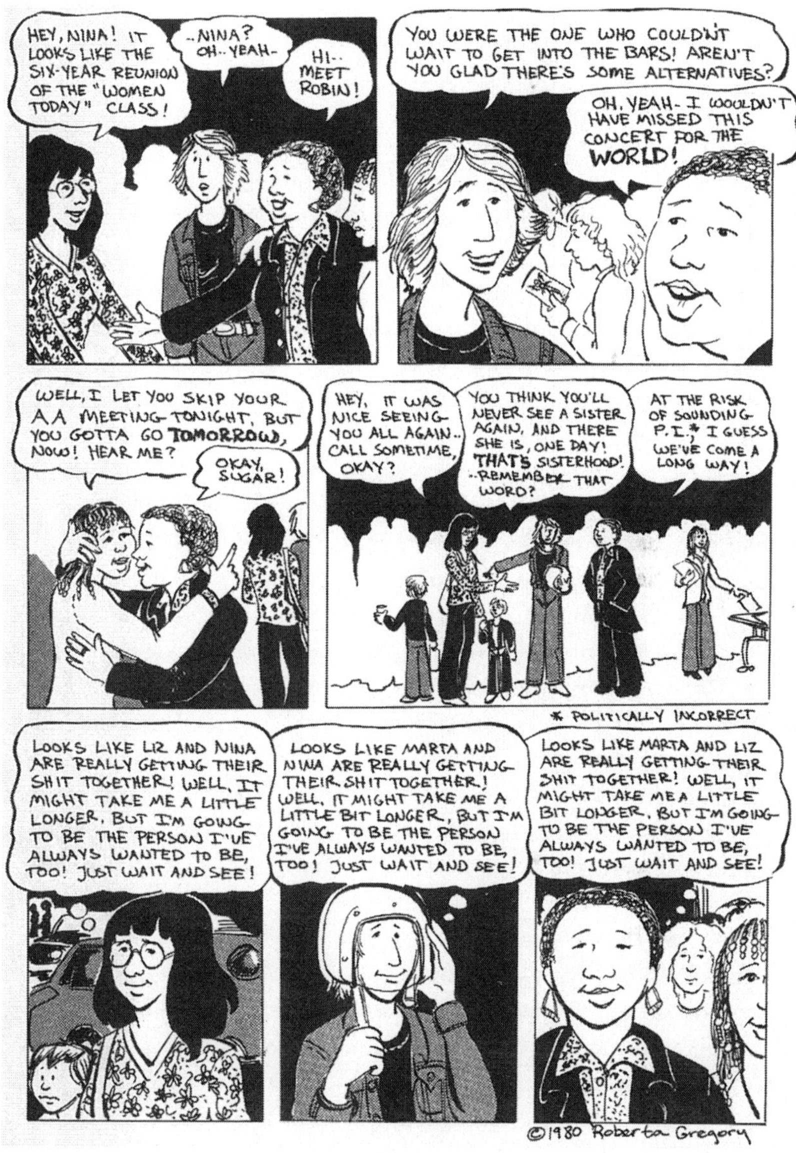

Figure 2.12. Final page of Roberta Gregory's "Re-Union" comic that appears in *Gay Comix* #1 (1980) where three women who met in a consciousness-raising group years ago reconnect at a women's concert, showing that all have learned more about themselves and grown in the intervening years. Courtesy of Roberta Gregory.

women to contribute in subsequent issues, such that the series shifted from portraying the perspectives of veteran underground cartoonists to sharing the work of a younger generation of emerging cartoonists.

This new cohort of lesbian cartoonists included women who would broaden the landscape of lesbian comics in the 1990s with continuing series and collections encompassing strips drawn from their work in *Gay Comix* as well as from grassroots newspapers and zines. The next most frequent female contributors after Gregory—Jennifer Camper, Leslie Ewing, Joan Hilty, and Andrea Natalie—embody this publishing energy and fashioning of a lesbian comics landscape. Starting with *Gay Comix* #2 (1981), Camper published in over half the issues of the series, while Ewing, Hilty, and Natalie began participating in the mid to late 1980s with each artist contributing to roughly a quarter of the issues.[81] All four artists published in a variety of grassroots periodicals across the nation, but it was the *Gay Comix* series that brought them together in print, as in *Gay Comix* #14 (1991), which featured the work of all four artists inside an issue whose fantasy-inspired cover by Gregory depicted a pair of lesbian mermaids, a male faun cavorting with a male centaur, and a lipsticked reptile in dress, heels, wig, and tiara whom a nearby unicorn gazes on quizzically, wondering if she is "a 'drag'-on queen?" (Figure 2.13).[82] All four artists would appear together again in the final issue, *Gay Comics* #25 (1998), which brought together seventy-six of the contributors from across the series for a last hurrah, but their varied work in the series was in dialogue with a wide array of artists as the editors continued to welcome new voices.[83]

Not only did their artistic contributions map out new facets of LGBTQ life from their perspectives as women, but Camper, Ewing, Hilty, and Natalie were also actively community-building through the work they took on alongside the comics they created. That is, their additional community work created infrastructure for future cartoonists and also supported larger queer populations. After a decade of publishing mainly one-off strips that demonstrated her interest in representing LGBTQ community as a multifaceted, intersectional space, Camper curated a selection of these works in *Rude Girls and Dangerous Women* (1994).[84] This collection gestured toward her interest in community building, which would later manifest in her editorship of two comics anthologies, *Juicy Mother* (2005) and *Juicy Mother 2* (2007), where she

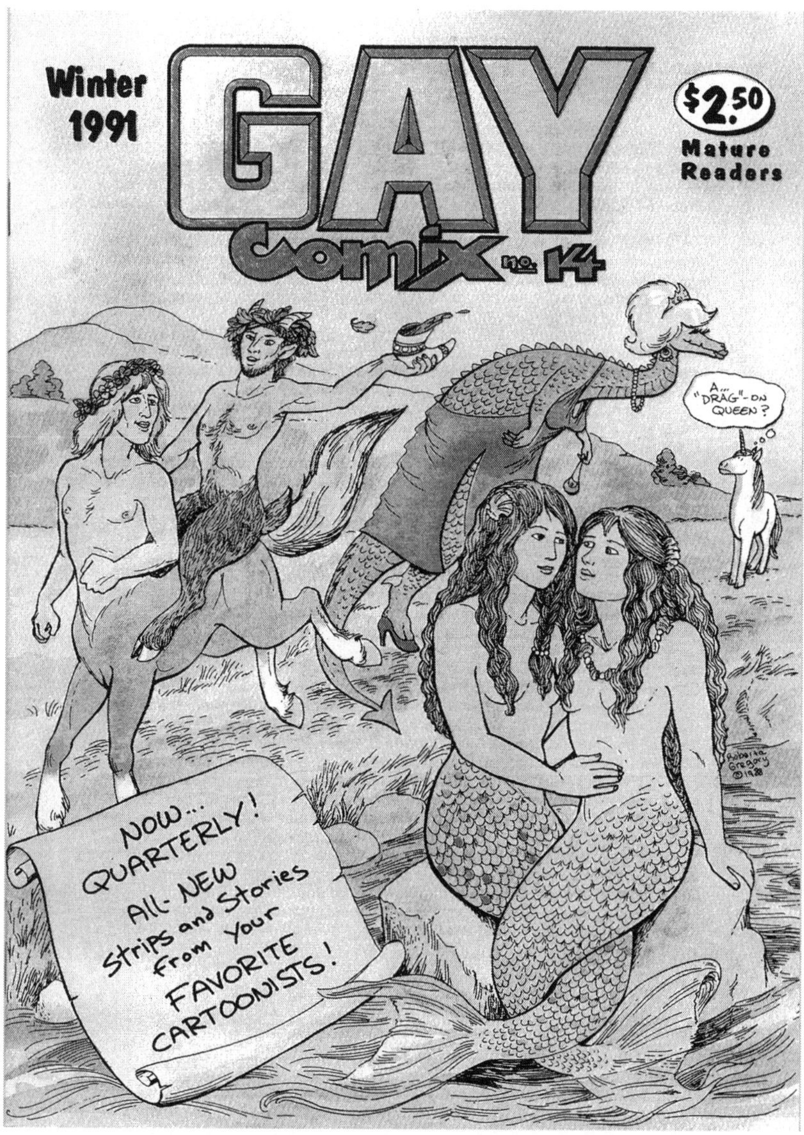

Figure 2.13. Front cover of *Gay Comix* #14 (1991) featuring fantasy art by Roberta Gregory illustrating homosexual couplings of mythological creatures, a dragon in women's drag, and a unicorn wondering over the dragon's punny identity. Courtesy of Roberta Gregory.

brought together a range of established and emerging queer creators.[85] Ewing's recurring strip "Mid-Dyke Crisis," which she published both in issues of *Wimmen's Comix* and *Gay Comix*, represented lesbian relationship dynamics in the contemporary moment and often touched on the HIV/AIDS epidemic, echoing her deep involvement in activism. She organized in the late 1980s with the Names Project AIDS Memorial Quilt and continued thereafter to work in the same sector, including for over a decade as the executive director of the Pacific Center, an LGBTQ community organization located in Berkeley, California.[86] Following publishing comics about lesbian life and even creating a lesbian superhero team, Hilty turned to work in mainstream comics variously as an editor, writer, and artist and was with DC's Vertigo imprint when *Gay Comics* #25 (1998) briefly profiled her career in the history of all contributors to the series they produced especially for the final issue.[87] Natalie founded the Lesbian Cartoonists' Network in 1990, which fostered community for lesbian cartoonists through a newsletter that provided production and publishing resources.[88] In addition to this work, she also published a number of collections of her single-panel "Stonewall Riots" comics in the early 1990s as *Stonewall Riots* (1990), *The Night Audrey's Vibrator Spoke* (1992), and *Rubyfruit Mountain* (1993).[89] All these women were also featured in the collection of lesbian comics that Roz Warren edited, *Dyke Strippers: Lesbian Cartoonists A to Z* (1995).[90] Warren saw this volume as one that would gather together lesbian and bisexual cartoonists and make their work more broadly known beyond the "regional gay and lesbian papers" in which they published.[91] Over half of the thirty-five women included in *Dyke Strippers* also published work in the *Gay Comix* series at one point or another, demonstrating how well the series supported and represented this population.

In creating *Gay Comix*, editor Howard Cruse built a bridge between the underground and LGBTQ lives, drawing out those artists who had been representing these experiences at the edges of the counterculture and welcoming in artists from elsewhere, including those who had been producing comics in grassroots feminist and gay and lesbian newspapers. Though *Pudge, Girl Blimp* and *Dynamite Damsels* may have been outliers in the underground, Marrs and Gregory were central in inspiring future generations of artists in this new context. The capacious vision with which they charted the contours of sexuality in their comics in the underground allowed them to foster an even wider platform of possibility for this comics series. As Cruse wrote at the end of his editor's note for that initial issue, "There's more to gay experience than can be chronicled in 36 pages. So this one's just for starters. Have fun."[92] This sentiment eschews the possibility of being able to definitively represent all facets of same-gender attraction, and similar remarks were found in each subsequent issue, welcoming new participants. The work of the cartoonists further extended that welcome, making good on Cruse's opening remarks by offering representations that moved beyond stereotypes to delve into nuanced contours of sexual experience.

Archives and Afterlives: Resituating Legacies in Archival Space

Just as the *Gay Comix* series facilitated community building that accumulated over the course of its two-decade run, so can comics within archives facilitate future community building. In her scholarship, Eichhorn acknowledges how there's a living presence to activist material within archives being available to resignify and influence future generations of organizers.[93] While she shows how these activists can reactivate the content, Sammond further illuminates how grassroots archives themselves can be dynamic participants in this exchange: "Unlike special collections in larger academic institutions, [community archives] may be (with proper support) better situated to engage critically with their own archiving practices, and to adapt them to changing understandings of the nature of the communities they serve."[94] While the following chapter will look across archives in order to theorize a notion of queer comics archives that identifies how comics operate in tandem with the collections that house them and allow us to understand these places anew through this relationship, one story remains here to tell of the shifting space of feminist underground comics. This adaptation that Sammond identifies happened with the comics collection at the Lesbian Herstory Archives since the time that I started researching there several years ago.

When I began my work there, the comics were tucked away on a bookshelf upstairs, but they have since been moved more centrally downstairs. While the constellation of comics together upstairs did illuminate a genealogy of lesbian comics publishing that informs both this chapter and earlier work, the recontextualization of the comics collection opens up even more possibilities.[95] The comics now sit on a mobile book cart in the front room where floor-to-ceiling shelves are filled with published lesbian literature.[96] This move thereby places the comics in proximity to these literary lineages and suggests that they can perhaps now be understood as part of these feminist genealogies, as they strived for in their time. However, they remain mobile and separate on the cart, acknowledged and visible as their own community rather than subsumed into and lost within a larger whole. This move also acknowledges the import of comics to LGBTQ communities today, as we are currently in the midst of an unprecedented queer comics boom. Because of this popularity, comics that were overlooked in the past, like those of Marrs and Gregory, may have an opportunity to influence new generations of artists in the future.

3

THE NEWSPAPER CARTOONIST

Alison Bechdel's Queer Grassroots Networks

Grassroots Origins and Network Building

Since the runaway success of *Fun Home* (2006), which *Time* named the best book of 2006, comics artist Alison Bechdel's renown has been growing, culminating in Guggenheim (2012) and MacArthur (2014) Fellowships and the creation of a *Fun Home* musical, which won five Tony Awards in 2015.[1] Though these recent accolades foreground the growing appreciation for *Fun Home*—a graphic memoir that details her childhood and coming out in the shadow of a closeted father who ultimately dies by suicide—relatively little attention has been paid to Bechdel's origins decades earlier as a cartoonist, which are sometimes left deliberately vague in her own retrospective accounts. Rather than her singular genius, her beginnings emphasize the collectivity of her work and how her deep understanding of queer life that she documents in her long-running *Dykes to Watch Out For* (1983–2008) comic strip comes from her participation in grassroots periodical networks. Whereas the previous chapter showed how Lee Marrs and Roberta Gregory used comics to represent and critique the feminist movement, this chapter examines how Bechdel embraced the print culture of the feminist movement as a place to publish explicitly feminist comics and other image–text. Together, the chapters demonstrate how these cartoonists developed their artistic visions through connecting to the collectivity of the feminist movement and documenting it in their comics.

Alison Bechdel first began publishing comics after failing to get into graduate school to study art following her graduation from Oberlin College in 1981.[2] After doodling numerous "dykes to watch out for" in

109

correspondence to friends, one of these close friends encouraged Bechdel to submit her work to the New York City feminist newspaper *WomaNews*, where they both volunteered as part of the collective. Her *New Yorker*–esque one-panel *Dykes to Watch Out For* (*DTWOF*) were first published in the periodical in the summer of 1983.[3] For the next two years, Bechdel became more involved with the *WomaNews* collective and continued to publish her cartoons in the pages of the periodical, evolving her *DTWOF* comic into multi-panel thematic takes that humorously weighed in on lesbians' everyday lives, as they dealt with intimate relationships with roommates and partners and also negotiated lesbian subcultures and the experience of being an out lesbian in a straight world. The pages of *WomaNews* evidence Bechdel's growth as an artist not just in her comics but also in advertisements and other graphics she created for the *WomaNews* collective. Following her departure from *WomaNews* upon her move to Northampton, Massachusetts, in the summer of 1985, she began to self-syndicate *DTWOF* in additional grassroots periodicals and published her first collection of comics with independent feminist publisher Firebrand Books in the fall of 1986.[4]

Despite how formative these early years and this grassroots publishing experience were for Bechdel's career, most readers and critics do not know much about them. While some early iterations of her *DTWOF* comic appear in her first two Firebrand Books collections, many, including her single-panel works, do not.[5] Because she transitioned her strip to focus on the lives of a recurring cast of characters in episodic rather than one-off thematic strips in early 1987, none of these early comics is included in *The Essential "Dykes to Watch Out For"* (2008), a seemingly definitive collection of her strips that is now the means through which most fans and scholars access and write about the series.[6] In an introduction to the volume, Bechdel discusses her career and reduces *WomaNews* to an unnamed "local feminist newspaper," further obscuring her early work that is not included in the collection.[7]

These hidden production histories underscore how much Bechdel was in dialogue with and participated directly in the creation of grassroots newspapers. Such activity is not exceptional; indeed, all the artists in this book participated in such networks in ways that have not been fully acknowledged. For Bechdel, that linking of activism to artistic production started at *WomaNews*, but that was just the beginning of her involvement in grassroots networks. In addition to her work on *WomaNews* (1983–85), she served as the production coordinator for the Minneapolis–Saint Paul gay and lesbian newspaper *Equal Time* for four years (1986–90) before she was able to make a living from her comics and associated work.[8] Bechdel also self-syndicated her strip in roughly two hundred periodicals over the course of two decades, which put her finger on the pulse of local social movement politics nationally and internationally over a decade before the Internet digitally networked people together. She chronicled this experience in a short-lived strip, *Servants to the Cause* (1989–90), which appeared in the pages of national gay magazine *The Advocate*.[9] This strip followed a diverse cast of characters who worked together on a fictitious queer periodical, and the plot intersected generational debates and identity politics.

Bechdel, like the artists discussed in this book's other chapters, derived her highly innovative depictions of queer visual politics from her closeness to grassroots networks. The evidence of this history can be found in archives containing Bechdel's comics and other media, including her own papers in the Sophia Smith Collection at Smith College; the records of her longtime publisher, Firebrand Books, held in the Human Sexuality Collection at Cornell University; and the Newsprint Collection at the Lesbian Herstory Archives, which maintains a full run of *WomaNews*. In general, scholars working in comics studies do not make substantial use of non-comics archives when studying cartoonists. This oversight leads to a glossing over or ignoring of specific contexts where comics were prominent—like in grassroots publications, as this chapter shows. As I argued in the previous chapter, it is important to work across archives to uncover new histories and artists. These contexts, especially considering works like queer comics or others with clearly political and discursive objectives, show a rich world of collective engagement where embedded cartoonists were connected to readers and other activists and influenced by the social movements around them.

Bechdel and other cartoonists used grassroots publications to express their politics in varied image–text considerations that were not always explicitly comics, but that benefit from comicitous analysis. As one can tell from a glance at the archives noted above, Bechdel's publications are not kept within archival comics collections, but instead are held within queer-adjacent and queer grassroots archives.[10] Analyzing comics through these kind of archives—which I further theorize as queer comics archives in the following section—make visible the communities and collective practices that shape the production and circulation of queer comics art—unlike more traditional comics archives that focus on preserving the comics of individual cartoonists.

To understand not only Bechdel's queer comics but also those of many of her contemporaries, it is necessary to review the publishing milieux that supported her work. This is particularly important, since many grassroots queer comics have been traditionally overlooked by comics studies because they are often produced outside mainstream comics publishers and not connected to the artists who participate in those communities. Just as there's been more scholarly attention paid to women's comics in the last decade, as described in the previous chapter, so, too, has there been an expansion of focus on queer comics, some of which were produced in grassroots networks, and a constellation of what might now be called queer comics studies as I mention in the introduction.[11] Still, for many years, cartoonists were at the forefront of bringing queer cartoonists together out of their local grassroots contexts and connecting them into larger communities through the use of anthologies, as the last chapter touches on through the *Gay Comix* series.[12] Throughout the years, books like *Gay Comix* (1980–98), *Strip AIDS* (1987), *Strip AIDS USA* (1988), *Gay Comics* (1989), *Dyke Strippers* (1995), *Juicy Mother* (2005), *Juicy Mother 2* (2007), *Gay Genius* (2011), *No Straight Lines* (2013), *Anything That Loves* (2013), *QU33R* (2014), ALPHABET (2016), *Being True* (2018), *We're Still Here* (2018), *Rainbow Reflections* (2019), *Be Gay, Do Comics!* (2020), and *When I Was Me* (2021) have been an important means of gathering queer comics and cartoonists from across their disparate publication contexts.[13] While these venues make the cartoons more visible, we miss a sense of the local politics that intersect with the comics, as when they appear alongside articles in periodicals.

Featured in many of these anthologies, Bechdel is central to this community of queer cartoonists. Roz Warren dedicates *Dyke Strippers* to her, and *Gay Comix* devotes an entire issue to her work.[14] In his introduction to *No Straight Lines*, a collection bringing together four decades of queer comics to chart a shared history among the artists, cartoonist and editor Justin Hall acknowledges both the power of queer periodical comics and the difficulties that have kept them from the recognition they richly deserve: "The weekly strips' publication in the gay news-papers gave them a timeliness and immediacy that was often used for direct political and social commentary. It also placed them even further outside of the traditional comics industry than the queer comic books and tied them in even more strongly to the LGBTQ community and the queer media ghetto."[15] These circumstances separated queer grass-roots comics from the "traditional comics industry" of their time, and these circumstances led to the comics being overlooked and forgotten.

This situation—the separation of queer grassroots comics from the comics industry—neatly characterizes Bechdel's own career as she pub-lished *DTWOF* over the course of more than two decades from 1983 to 2008. People interviewing Bechdel have pointed to the marginal position of queer comics publishing. Anne Rubenstein opened a 1995 interview with Bechdel with this one-liner: "Alison Bechdel may be the most popular American cartoonist who you've never heard of."[16] Six years later, Trina Robbins echoed this sentiment in the introduction to her 2001 interview with Bechdel: "In a better world, she would already be a well-known mainstream creator."[17] In the intervening years, Bechdel self-syndicated her own strip in around fifty periodicals nationally and internationally. Most of these venues were strictly grassroots, but she had more mainstream coverage in a few markets. Her publication list was always in flux, as grassroots periodicals went under with frequency. *WomaNews* stopped publishing in 1991, and *Equal Time* folded in 1994. With such losses, Bechdel would seek out new periodicals with similar geographic coverage so that her local readers would still be able to access her strip.

In March 2006, in advance of the release of *Fun Home*, which rock-eted Bechdel to mainstream acclaim, she assessed her national coverage by labeling a map with the names of her publications and marking key cities she was not reaching (Figure 3.1).[18] Although she had thirty-five big cities and other environs under her belt, she identified fifteen cities where she wanted her work to be published. Because she previously had coverage in these cities, including Phoenix (*Heatstroke*), Anchorage (*Iden-tity Northview*), and Milwaukee (*Wisconsin Light*), finding new publica-tions in these markets would allow her to reconnect to dedicated readers. More than just a snapshot of her coverage in North America, the map presents a sense of her span across the decades. Granted, it does not

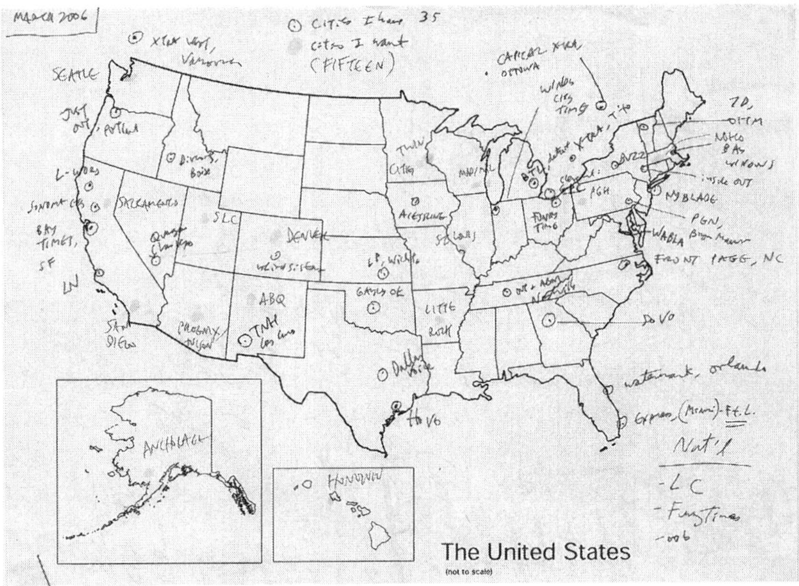

Figure 3.1. A hand-annotated map where Alison Bechdel represents her publication network in the United States in March 2006. Courtesy of Alison Bechdel Papers, Sophia Smith Collection, SSC-MS-00633, Smith College Special Collections, Northampton, Massachusetts. Reprinted with permission of author.

show the whole picture—the roughly two hundred periodicals that published her comic over the course of two decades—but it evokes what both Rubenstein and Robbins are getting at when they cite Bechdel's popularity despite her lack of mainstream renown. When Bechdel ceased publishing *DTWOF* in May 2008, many periodicals had been publishing her work for nearly two decades, including small outfits like *Bryn Mawr College News* (Bryn Mawr, Pa.) and *Sonoma County Women's Voices* (Sebastopol, Calif.) alongside more prominent and national publications like *Lesbian Connection* (East Lansing, Mich.), *Lesbian News* (West Hollywood, Calif.), *off our backs* (Washington, D.C.), and the *Washington Blade* (Washington, D.C.). Through her own extensive efforts reaching out to publications and managing her networks, Bechdel had a presence in grassroots publications across the nation, and her books and associated products were sold in an overlapping geography of independent and feminist bookstores.

And yet, this map and those interviews could have been framed very differently, for in 1993 Bechdel turned down an offer to produce a syndicated strip with the Universal Press Syndicate (UPS), which gets strips like Garry Trudeau's *Doonesbury* and Bill Watterson's *Calvin and Hobbes* into the funnies pages of thousands of major newspapers. In making her decision, Bechdel solicited the advice of fellow queer cartoonist Joan Hilty, who was familiar with different comics markets. Hilty responded by sharing materials critical of the UPS and hedging about her advice, explaining, "So, basically, I'm just flip-flopping about what to tell you. I guess that reflects my own mixed feelings about the profession: the exposure's great but the politics are daunting. . . . On the other hand, your work is so good—putting a lot of other comics to shame on both an artistic and narrative level—it deserves an even wider audience."[19] Bechdel echoed this back-and-forth in notes to herself, in which she drafted questions for the syndicate ("How does the editing process work?"; "How political/sexual/etc. can it be?") alongside questions for herself ("How much time will this take?"; "How bland would it have to be?"; "Could I work in 4 panels??").[20] These personal questions indicate that she was leaning toward no because this opportunity would require her to create a strip format that would have taken time away from *DTWOF* and may have needed to be quite "bland." Based on politics and some well-founded assumptions about what other constraints the strip would face, her refusal demonstrated why LGBTQ comics stayed out of the most visible comics communities until only recently.[21] Bechdel turned down the offer in part because she was able to make a living through self-syndicated cartooning. In the early 1990s, she was also earning money through her stationery business, where she sold a catalog of *DTWOF* items, including mugs, mousepads, and calendars.[22]

The wide popularity of Bechdel's self-syndicated comics in publications around the country and her adept business sense brought her a degree of financial solvency as well as an important connection to the communities represented in her strip. While she was publishing *DTWOF* with smaller periodicals, not only did they send her a copy of every issue, they also frequently corresponded with her. That is, the structures of self-syndication facilitated Bechdel's close communication with each periodical. This correspondence was often warm and friendly, as her activist interlocutors related as much to her as they did to her recurring cast of characters who became a feature of the comic in early 1987.

Yet shoestring finances made funding the comic a continual battle—one that various periodicals put extra effort into solving, thereby proving the import of Bechdel's strip to their readers. For example, in the July/August 1988 issue of *Valley Women's Voice* (Pioneer Valley, Mass.), the paper printed a notice above one of Bechdel's strips: "HELP! Don't let Mo, Toni, Ginger, and friends leave the Valley. Only with your sponsorship ($) can we keep *Dykes to Watch Out For* in the *Valley Women's Voice*."[23] In this notice, the characters are configured as "friends" who might have to move away if financial support doesn't come through. Ultimately, *DTWOF* stayed in the Pioneer Valley periodical through the funding of local cartoonist Rob Ranney and others, whose names were published alongside the comic in future issues.

Across the country, members of the *Lavender Network* (Eugene, Ore.) raised $600 to fund Bechdel's comics through their July 1990 Save the Dykes event. Sally Sheklow, Bechdel's contact at *Lavender Network*, communicated to Bechdel the success of the event through photographs and also included information about her creative project, *The Sound of Lesbians*, a musical comedy parody.[24] Through these items, Sheklow shared the vibrancy of the queer community in the Pacific Northwest and displayed a personal connection with Bechdel. These examples show how personal investment in Bechdel's comic formed the basis for her support among these varied collectives, linking her to diverse lesbian communities.

These grassroots networks infused Bechdel's comic with queer ideas from a range of local and nationally known grassroots periodicals. In letters like Sheklow's, readers shared their responses to the comic, weighing in on its plot and telling her which characters they identified with.[25] The publications themselves also provided Bechdel with information about local queer communities across the nation that she included in her strip. If she had accepted UPS's offer and given up self-syndication, she would have lost her source material.[26] In her strip, Bechdel's characters reflected her readers' lives, reacting to current events and participating in political activism like the 1987 March on Washington for Lesbian and Gay Rights.

Bechdel further demonstrated how much her characters were living in the same world as her readers in an eleven-year graphic time line she included in her retrospective book *The Indelible Alison Bechdel* (1998).[27]

She created five parallel time lines—a general one for national happenings that year; one for Mo; another for Clarice and Toni; yet another for Sparrow, Ginger, and Lois; and a final one for Madwimmin Books. In this chronology, Bechdel included panels and images from her strip and captioned these happenings, arguing for the importance of common lesbian lives by juxtaposing them alongside large-scale events. Through her comic and again through this time line, her readers across the nation could see themselves in her characters, living their lives amid global changes much larger than themselves. To wit, Bechdel used comics to present new ways of thinking about women and queer discourse and to develop politically attuned networks, which she first developed in the pages of *WomaNews* before expanding to other grassroots publications and networks.

Bechdel's use of publication networks, and its influence on her ideological and artistic approaches to her stories and drawings, demonstrate the necessity of considering grassroots contexts when studying comics, particularly with regard to their relationship to feminist and queer discourse. Similar to the way the visual and page-layout contexts affected in-panel representation, as I discussed in the last chapter, Bechdel's comics also interacted with other content on the pages of the periodical, and thus established particular techniques for expressing lesbian experience. Bechdel's comics do visual work akin to what contemporary lesbian theorist Teresa de Lauretis argues that feminist cinema should do in "construct[ing] another (object of) vision and the conditions of visibility for a different social subject."[28] As Bechdel glibly puts it in an interview, "I would love to be the lesbian Norman Rockwell."[29] Further specifying this project in a retrospective comic, Bechdel asserts that her goal is to create "a catalog of lesbians! I would name the unnamed. Depict the undepicted!"[30] That is, to embody Rockwell in a lesbian way, Bechdel seeks to "catalog" a wide array of "undepicted" lesbian experiences, making visible a multiplicity of "different social subject[s]" and creating the possibilities to maintain these "conditions" through her business savvy and persistence. Well-known for the *Saturday Evening Post* covers in which he illustrated everyday U.S. culture for more than five decades, Rockwell further broadened the swath of the United States he covered in later work when he tackled topics like civil rights. In some of her work, Bechdel directly echoes Rockwell, as when she modeled the cover of her 1994 calendar on Rockwell's iconic Thanksgiving painting

Freedom from Want (1943) by positioning the recurring cast of *DTWOF* around a table to celebrate the protagonist's birthday.[31] By naming her comic *Dykes to Watch Out For,* she directed her readers to look at this project and be complicit in making visible these new subjects, an action that included not only reading her comics but also financially supporting her through purchasing calendars and other items.

Not only do Bechdel and de Lauretis theorize each other, but we can build from them a theory of the archives that contain these works. Explicitly queer and queer-adjacent archives are the frame around Bechdel that further sustains these "conditions of visibility," making apparent "different social subject[s]" from those found in comics collections in other archives as the previous chapter discusses. Archives that collect not only personal papers but more extensively a world of queer experience— periodicals, books from grassroots publishers, movement T-shirts and buttons, and so on—allow us to see the process of "construct[ing]" queer subjectivity and make visible not only queer individuals but a truly "social subject" in her investment in collective politics and queer networks. To wit, we can see the quotidian queer community that Bechdel strived to "catalog," taking a page from Rockwell's depictions of everyday U.S. communities. Heather Stephenson, the journalist who solicited the Rockwell sound bite from Bechdel, posits, "Bechdel sees herself as an archivist chronicling her generation through the details of lesbians' daily lives."[32] This embodiment of Bechdel "as an archivist" speaks volumes, for as a lesbian, "her generation" is the queer one that has hitherto not been seen in such fullness or, in de Lauretis's language, as "construct[ed]." It is perhaps little surprise, then, that two decades later the critical reception of Bechdel's *Fun Home* focused on the archival aspects of her work, including her precise reproduction of personal family objects. Though this personal archive reflects individual queer experience, established queer archives make visible political networks that sustain individuals and allow us to understand Bechdel as "the lesbian Norman Rockwell" in a manner that individual autobiography alone cannot grasp.

Queer Comics Archives

Archives are not simply an aesthetics of Bechdel's work: she engages existing archives and, like many lesbian feminists before her, actively creates her own archives.[33] She saved not only her own comics, correspondence, and documentation of her business practices, but also the periodicals that printed her work, effectively preserving the social movement around her that might otherwise not be saved, as other artists in this book did in both their art and files. The next chapter on Anzaldúa will further examine how and why women involved in social movements preserved their community within their own personal archives. Bechdel's archival engagements directly inform her artwork not only in subject matter but also, as scholars like Hillary Chute have discussed, in her rigorous process of drawing from physical examples.[34] Her dual engagement with existing archives and her own practice of saving materials came together in late 2008 when she donated a first accession of archival material to the Sophia Smith Collection at Smith College. She documented this process in a video posted to YouTube titled "The Memoirist's Lament," where she shows her many filing cabinets all over her house before she divulges that Smith College will be archiving these materials.[35] With this reveal, the camera pans back from the material being shown and text appears across the screen: "god help them." She then transitions to looking inside the filing cabinets, culling folders that end up among those materials going to Smith College. She has since donated several more accessions and plans to send along additional materials, so her archival connection is active in the present day.

When she began to identify files to send to Smith, Bechdel was also in the midst of another creative project of organization as she suspended her twenty-year comic strip, *DTWOF*, in May of that year and curated a selection of strips to be published with Houghton Mifflin Harcourt, the same publisher that released *Fun Home*. Both projects were completed in fall 2008, as Smith received twenty boxes of archival materials and *The Essential "Dykes to Watch Out For"* was released. Due to the simultaneity of these endeavors, the archives weigh heavily on *The Essential "Dykes."* And it is not only the space of the Sophia Smith Collection that inflects the book; she also visited two other university archives that spring while giving talks about *Fun Home* at those institutions—the Jean-Nickolaus Tretter Collection in GLBT Studies at the University of Minnesota and the Human Sexuality Collection at Cornell University—that house the papers of her longtime publisher Firebrand Books. She blogged about both visits on her website.[36]

These three archival encounters erupt onto the pages of Bechdel's introduction to *The Essential "Dykes."* As in her graphic memoirs—*Fun Home* (2006), *Are You My Mother?* (2012), and *The Secret to Superhuman Strength* (2021)—in the introduction she re-creates personal documents in the telling of her artistic genealogy, but adds another level to this representation by depicting herself entering a locked room called the archives and accessing the documents there.[37] Once she has entered this space, she starts rummaging through the drawers, seemingly disrupting classification yet retrieving her files in precise chronological order.[38] In the comic, she builds a narrative of how she became an artist through her reading of these archivally housed documents. Key here is her sprawling rendition of the archives itself, pictured in a long vertical panel on the left-hand side of the page. She uses this verticality to great effect, depicting the space as filled with rows of infinitely tall filing cabinets. This image resembles, in part, the back room of the Tretter Collection, where she took a photo of herself in awe during her visit and subsequently shared on her website.[39] However, in her drawing, the shelves of the archival boxes are replaced by impossibly fantastic filing cabinets, more closely resembling giant versions of the filing cabinets that populate her home as shown in the YouTube video about donating her files to the Sophia Smith Collection. As she readies files documenting her own career for the archives, Bechdel imagines the archives as merging domestic and institutional storage in her comic, acknowledging the hybridity of the space where such files are organized and kept. By creating a fantasy archives through which she relates her personal queer history, Bechdel recognizes how institutional repositories collect a larger scope of queer genealogy—as she discussed in her blog posts about her visits to the archives at the University of Minnesota and Cornell University. In nesting three archives into one representation in this comic, she underlines their interconnected nature and how archives not only contain grassroots networks but are themselves also part of a network.

This network of archives that collect intersectional queer and feminist histories comprises grassroots archives started by activists as discussed in the first chapter. Ann Cvetkovich's *An Archive of Feelings* (2003) jump-started critical conversations about radical archives and remains a vital cornerstone, much as Jacques Derrida's *Archive Fever* (1995) did for more general archival concerns. Cvetkovich's delineation of grassroots archival spaces not only illuminates Bechdel's own symbolic embrace of archives, but from Cvetkovich's description we can also fashion a definition of queer comics archives, which preserve this doubly marginalized work—as comics are an art form often not taken seriously that marginalized folks then embrace to represent their experience. Following an extended discussion of the Lesbian Herstory Archives, Cvetkovich defines the shared attributes of queer archives more generally: "Ephemeral evidence, spaces that are maintained by volunteer labors of love rather than state funding, challenges to cataloging, archives that represent lost histories—gay and lesbian archives are often 'magical' collections of documents that represent far more than the literal value of the objects themselves. . . . Queer archives can be viewed as the material instantiation of Derrida's deconstructed archive; they are composed of material practices that challenge traditional conceptions of history and understand the quest for history as a psychic need rather than a science."[40] Throughout this passage, Cvetkovich focuses on different registers of "history" and the "challenges" that grassroots archives present, nuancing and interconnecting both concepts—history and archives—through repetition. Through coalescing ideas of "history" and its "challenges" in the "challenge [to] traditional conceptions of history," Cvetkovich demonstrates how all the items in her opening catalog add up: as "material practices" that can perform these "challenges" through various methods. In Bechdel's representation of archives, we can see how she leverages her "'magical' collection of documents" to narrate the overarching trajectory of her career, selecting items that together culminate into "more than" the sum of their parts. In activating archival objects, Bechdel "challenge[s] traditional conceptions of history" and uncovers her lived lesbian history that shapes her long-running comic. Whereas Bechdel illustrates the multivalent possibility of queer archives, Cvetkovich communicates the ways that archives enact that multivalence.

How queer archives are more personally constructed through the collective labor of individuals committed to making queer histories visible differentiates comics collections in queer and queer-adjacent archives from comics held in other archives. To create a framework for understanding how comics operate in tandem with the queer archives that house them, I theorize the notion of queer comics archives. They "challenge traditional conceptions of history" not only through the comics' content but also in how they open up "material practices" that give us new ways to analyze the documents themselves, conceptualize the affiliated histories, and, ultimately, understand their individual histories as connected to a larger queer community. This analysis enacts de Lauretis's "conditions of visibility," allowing for the recovery of new individual and collective histories.[41] As discussed in the prior chapter through the notion of researching across archives, archives in general allow us to read comics with a new fullness and to see the personal networks surrounding their creation. While some of the archival collections in the last chapter made it seem like women and queer folks were on the periphery— "totally isolated and broken from history rather than being a part of it"—reading across archives and embracing queer comics archives allows Bechdel and other LGBTQ individuals to "see [them]selves as part of a coherent history" and community.[42]

Queer comics archives empower us to see new comics not housed in other comics collections and to understand the importance of social activism to comics through studying them in their original queer publication contexts in addition to examining them as they touch the lives of gay and lesbian folks who donate their ephemera to the archives or who are preserved through their communication with the artists themselves. Collections-building "material practices" embody "queerness as collectivity"—an articulation of the relational queer theory that José Esteban Muñoz theorizes in *Cruising Utopia* (2009).[43] Just as Muñoz maps queer collectivity through close reading, new practices of close-reading comics and other image–text creations that emphasize relationality can map how queer activisms shape such works both in this chapter and others in this book. Departing from the traditional formalism of comics scholarship that "privileges art and artists with more cultural capital, not less," this approach decenters the individual, honoring the rich history of collaboration in comics.[44] This method pairs with the previous chapter wherein cartoonists represented and considered the role of the individual within a social justice–oriented community. Together, these tactics open a conversation about the multiple ways that communities shape even single-authored works.

Reading queer comics as they originally appeared in the pages of grassroots periodicals, and examining how other materials on the page intersect with them, reveals how comics are but one panel on an entire spread of content.[45] In this way, the periodical should be further understood as a space of exploration, which allows us to trace how comics art and styles evolve within grassroots communities. The stylistic freedom of the periodicals themselves also transfers to the visual artwork within, facilitating the making of other image–text creations crucial to the development of the cartoonists who evolved their practices in these communities. That is, these adjacent image–text creations should also be read comicitously. These practices allow us to read beyond the static frame that closets comics. When we fixate on the frame and what's inside, as strict comics formalism would have us do, we fix straight edges to our interpretation rather than considering queerer readings that cross borders—to evoke the theorization of Gloria Anzaldúa, whose hybrid drawings are the subject of the following chapter.[46] Many early exploratory cartoons were never republished outside of queer publication networks, but such works—like comics-infused advertisements—are important to understanding more nuanced takes on feminism and queer theory inflected by the thought of local collectives. These modes of reading comics bring the surrounding community and production history to bear on what is created in the panel.

Such practices are not applicable only to comics that appear in grassroots spaces; rather, we must be generally attentive to original publication histories and to reading across publication contexts—in addition to reading across archives. Whenever a comic is republished in a new venue, its meaning—and sometimes also its content—shifts. With queer comics especially, moments of republication build community as the new setting makes the comic visible to a new audience. As we have already seen, feminist, gay and lesbian, and other alternative grassroots periodicals enfolded Bechdel's comic into their own local communities and inscribed her comic with additional meaning when they raised money to support her work. A growing body of scholarship by Agatha Beins, Julie Enszer, and others acknowledges the importance of periodicals in the development of the women's movement and gay and lesbian organizing, which this chapter extends by examining the role of comics in and as embodying this collective environment.[47]

Because Bechdel's work was published in numerous formats and within highly specific political contexts and publications, close-reading her work within those original contexts is essential to understanding the narrative and aesthetic developments of her work. For example, in the March 1984 issue of *WomaNews,* Bechdel produced an advertisement for two upcoming *WomaNews* workshops where participants would "learn practical skills" like "editing/proofreading" and "layout/pasteup" (Figure 3.2).[48] The women in Bechdel's drawing for the advertisement exhibit serious demeanors as they demonstrate the skills covered in each workshop. Their faces communicate dedication—an attribute that *WomaNews* would want to encourage in potential new collective members. The humor lies in the action of their hands. The writerly type, bent so earnestly over a sheet of paper for the "editing/proofreading workshop," concentrates her energies on marking one big single X on the paper as if to pronounce cheekily, "No, no, and no; all of this has to go!" Below her, the woman engaged in the "layout/pasteup workshop" has been stymied by her overzealous approach to the tools of the trade—glue, paper, and scissors. The glue is all over the table, and cutout paper rectangles of various sizes are stuck all over her. Yet she still determinedly holds the scissors in her right hand as she attempts to wrest control of her left hand from the glue's grasp. That levity and a bit of chaos enter the frame through the working hands implies that the activity of making *WomaNews* is not a mechanical endeavor but rather a creative, open, and human one. There is space for mess and occasionally flip decisions within a fervent framework.

Reading this piece as but one panel in a full-page spread, we can see how its meaning radiates as those looking at the advertisement could imagine the work of their hands carefully editing the news briefs or curating the advertisements to fill space on this and subsequent pages. We can also consider Bechdel's drawing on this page from within the context of her broader artistic development: the social organizations and events referenced here influenced the evolution of her work, and it is pages like these that she edited and organized when she participated in page layout alongside other members of the *WomaNews* collective. Her pithy representations of the women here and in those that she draws for the *WomaNews* letters pages covered in the next section are part of an effort to match her style to fit not only the periodical's politics but also its limited page space.

The matter of space was a constant consideration in her work, as it could vary depending on the nature of the publication venue. For example, when Bechdel worked directly at *WomaNews* and *Equal Time*, she created advertisements that needed to fit into set layout spaces on the page, but when she started self-syndicating her *DTWOF* comic strips, she had to contend with the layouts of a whole range of periodicals. Her *DTWOF* comics blossomed alongside her participation in the collectives of grassroots periodicals. In the Firebrand reprints, we see these comics spanning two slim horizontal pages, while they take up a large full page in *The Essential "Dykes."* When Bechdel sent her comics off to numerous periodicals, she included information about how to print and arrange her work, giving the periodical a few horizontal and vertical possibilities so that the comic could fit various page layouts. When we expand our reading of a comic beyond the edges of the frame, as archives that house vast collections of queer periodicals allow us to do, we activate the notion of queer comics archives that free us to read comics in multiple contexts and fully engage "queerness as collectivity."[49]

Bechdel's development as a comics artist while working as part of the *WomaNews* collective was a formative period in her career. By assessing these archivally held works through the close-reading methods of queer comics archives, it's possible to trace the evolution of Bechdel's work at this time. The following sections focus specifically on her process of deliberate revision and the importance of her comics-adjacent work. These accounts push back on the sense of Bechdel as a singular genius, since they show how Bechdel's participation in queer networks influenced her work. Queer comics archives make visible the networked world that queer comics thrived in and that has heretofore been little discussed in comics scholarship. Moreover, while we recognize the labor of the hands within comics studies, such labor has been theorized through the artist–author who individually creates a work; here we have the opportunity to retheorize this labor as a collective one.

WomaNews *and Revision*

Bechdel started publishing in *WomaNews* in the July/August 1983 issue and spent the next two years evolving her comic in the pages of the periodical while also participating in its production. As she became a member of the collective in late 1983, she produced one comic per issue along with other contributions.[50] As she developed her hand, her earlier

Newsbriefs

compiled by Hennie Spek and Kathy Stener

• Two white North American activists, Shelley Miller and Silvia Baraldini, were subpoenaed last February by a federal grand jury investigating the clandestine Puerto Rican Independence organization, FALN. The two women refused to testify and denounced their subpoenas as an effort at political internment of public activists. Miller, a leader of the New Movement in Solidarity with Puerto Rican Independence and Socialism, stated that the use of the grand jury is "part of a strategy by the U.S. Government to destroy solidarity with Puerto Rican independence at its earliest stages."

The two were to be tried on Feb. 9 for criminal contempt. At a pre-trial hearing, the defendants presented the judge with an open letter from nearly 100 organizations and individuals denouncing the use of the grand jury as a repressive tool of political internment and supporting the stance of non-collaboration. This is the third trial in the past year in which supporters of Puerto Rican independence have been prosecuted for criminal contempt.

• Thousands of women rallied in Ouagadougou, the capitol of Upper Volta, on Oct. 4 to celebrate the changes brought to women by the socialist revolution of Aug. 4, 1983.

The president of Upper Volta, Thomas Sankara, has consistently emphasized the exploitation of women and has urged and aided Voltaic women to organize to accomplish their liberation. In a speech on Oct. 2, he declared that the revolution and women's liberation go together. Since the revolution, women have been increasingly more involved in the Defense Committees, and the Ministry of Social and Women's Affairs has been restructured to take account of the new involvement.

• Two hundred women from the U.S. and Canada were refused entry to Honduras, where they planned to hold prayer vigils for peace in the region near two U.S. military bases and in the capital, Tegucigalpa.

The visit was organized by the Women's Coalition to Stop U.S. Intervention in Central America and the Caribbean. The first group was prevented from boarding a Honduran airline flight in New Orleans, after the company received word of the government's decision. The second group arrived in Honduras on an Air Florida flight, but the aircraft was ordered to return to Miami with the women on board.

Outwrite

• In 1982, Jackie Fourthman, then 20 years old, pleaded guilty to third-degree murder and child abuse in the death of her 7-month-old son. She was sentenced to 9 months in prison to be followed by probation conditional on her not having another baby for 15 years. Fourthman was arrested late last year for leaving Indiana without permission of her probation officer and for giving birth to another son in Nevada.

The probation condition may be renounced as unenforceable because Florida's Second District Court of Appeals called it unconstitutional when James Burcell, Fourthman's estranged husband and father of the dead child appealed the court order that he not father another child for 15 years.

The Guardian

• Rosemary Hernandez, a battered woman and mother of two young daughters, was murdered in Park Slope on July 27, 1983. Her husband, the prime suspect, was arrested in November. A memorial fund has been set up for the children, whose guardians are family members in desperate need of financial help. Contributions from individuals, groups or agencies should be sent to: Children of Rosemary Hernandez, c/o New York Women Against Rape, 231 E. 14th Street, NY 10003.

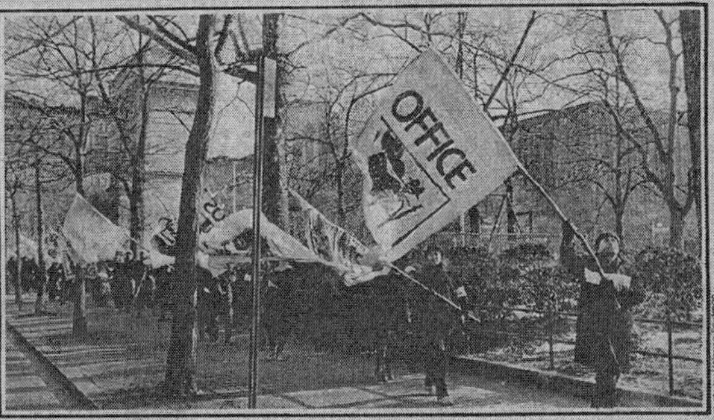

ARTISTS CALL Against U.S. Intervention in Central America staged a silent march on January 28 in New York City, as part of a 3 month calendar of events. Hundreds of artists and their supporters converged at the Battleship Intrepid, and walked in a somber single file procession down the Avenue of the Americas to a rally in Washington Square Park. The demonstrators, each wearing a black vest and white name band carrying the name and country of a human rights victim in Central America, then stepped into the park stage and recited the name and country of the deceased.

• The Nestle boycott is over. After seven years the Infant Formula Action Coalition has suspended the boycott against Nestle and affiliated products, including Stouffer's and Taster's Choice.

Nestle was under boycott for contributing to world hunger by marketing its products in such a way that poor women in developing countries stopped breast feeding their children. Recently the company began to follow the marketing codes of the World Health Organization. Ten nations participated in the boycott.

Science Magazine

• A group of women met February 11 to start a Women's Tax Resistance group. They feel they can't continue to demonstrate for peace and a feminist future while paying for war and destruction.

The money they withhold will be turned over to women's organizations, battered womens' shelters, clinics, daycare, etc., all those human services, so vital to women's lives, that have been cut.

All women are invited to resist with them in one of the following ways: refusing to pay telephone tax or some part of the federal income tax, or choosing to live simply below a taxable income. They said they are not opposed to paying taxes but can no longer pay for patriarchal violence either at home or around the world—helicopters over Nicaragua, the shelling of Lebanese villages—while school lunches and food stamps are cut, and decent housing is denied to the women, men and children of our city.

For more information about support meetings for Women's Tax Resistance call Margaret Jolly at 989-6615. There will be a general Tax Resistance workshop on March 25. Women from the women's group will be there.

Harriet Hirshorn

• A New York State ERA was opposed by leaders of National Women's Organizations at a recent meeting with Governor Mario Cuomo. Cuomo launched his attempt to pass a state Equal Rights Law in his second State of the State message. Women at the meeting warned Cuomo that his state proposal could damage chances for a federal Equal Rights Amendment. They explained that should ERA-NY lose, it would be a defeat from which women's organizations could not dissociate themselves whether or not they supported the campaign. Despite this opposition, Cuomo plans to ask the state legislature to pass the amendment this year and next.

The Guardian

• Eight Haitian women at the detention center of the Immigration and Naturalization Service (INS) started a hunger strike to protest policies toward refugees. The strike, which started on Jan. 19, has spread to one-third of the Krome detention center's prisoners. Detainees from Bangladesh, Lebanon, El Salvador, Guatemala, India, and Iran have joined the protest, which began when prisoners learned that three other Haitians just arriving from New Orleans were about to be deported after the Supreme Court turned down their appeal for political asylum.

The original strikers were joined by 62 Haitian men on Jan. 24 after an INS guard struck a Haitian refugee. Seventy more detainees joined the strike the next day. INS officials have barred the media and Haitian support group representatives from the camp since the hunger strike began.

The Guardian

• In January, the National Organization for Women sponsored its first Lesbian Rights Conference in Milwaukee, WI. The decision to hold the conference followed fierce internal struggles to realign the traditionally mainstream position of NOW, which has usually side-stepped lesbian issues.

In 1984, NOW made lesbian rights one of its four national priorities and began to plan the conference then. The 3-day conference, titled "Power and Politics in 84," focused on improving state laws on lesbian rights. In addition, the 350 delegates from across the nation chose New Jersey as a target state in which to pass a gay and lesbian civil rights bill.

The Guardian

• Over 400 pro-abortion forces in Washington state rallied on Jan. 22 against a crusade to close the Everett Feminist Women's Health Center. Since its opening in August, the center, which offers low-cost abortions, has been under attack by right-wing and fundamentalist Christian groups. These attacks included threatening phone calls and verbal and physical abuse of Center clients, and culminated in the firebombing of the clinic on Dec. 3, 1983.

Speakers at the rally insisted that abortion is an economic and not a moral issue. This was corroborated by a representative of the Whatcom County Labor Council, which passed a resolution noting that since women comprise 52% of the work force, women's right to safe and legal abortion is a labor issue.

• Following testimony by Nat'l Gay Task Force Executive Director Virginia M. Apuzzo on January 26, the Committee on Human Development of the U.S. Conference of Mayors endorsed legal protections for gay men and lesbians. The Committee unanimously approved a resolution stating that "recognizing the right of all citizens, regardless of sexual orientation, to full participation in American society, the Committee recommends that all levels of government adopt legal protections for the rights of gay and lesbian Americans. The Committee calls on its colleagues to consider executive and legislative remedies to guarantee equal opportunity and protection in the public and private sectors."

The full Conference of Mayors will consider the resolution at its June meeting in Philadelphia. Apuzzo outlined for the mayors a series of policy measures that localities should undertake to ban discrimination against lesbians and gay men. According to NGTF some forty cities already have at least some civil rights guarantees for lesbians and gay men, along with ten countries and seven states.

• 1,000 women marched to protest violence against women in San Juan, Puerto Rico on Nov. 29. Women shouted and carried banners, and a group of 30 women dressed up to present the different roles of women in society—all of whom are raped. Women dressed as nurses, secretaries, domestic workers, teachers, and one woman dressed as a bride. The marchers congregated around the Capitol Building where two women chanted a list of 118 women who have died at the hands of their husbands, boyfriends, and rapists.

Outwrite

• The case of a lesbian graduate teaching assistant who lost her position at Louisiana State University because of her involvement with an undergraduate is now pending in the Fifth Circuit Court of Appeals. Kristin Naragon challenged the termination of her teaching position, but the District Court upheld the University's position. In the appeal of the case, *Naragon vs. Wharton*, Lambda Legal Defense and Education Fund has filed a "friend of the court" brief. Lambda and the Louisiana Civil Liberties Union, which represents the plaintiff, argue that Naragon has been deprived not only of her right to professional training but of her constitutional rights to privacy, free association, and due process.

• Student doctors practicing vaginal examinations on unconscious women is a common and accepted practice in the teaching hospitals of England. In fact, according to a report on basic medical education "students on gynecology attachments find theatre sessions valuable for this reason."

The women—who have gone to the hospital as patients expecting health care—are not asked for their permission for these examinations.

Outwrite

Figure 3.2. Alison Bechdel's advertisement for *WomaNews* workshop as it appeared in the full page spread of the March 1984 issue of *WomaNews*. Courtesy of the Lesbian Herstory Archives. Reprinted with permission of author.

Community Announcements

"Black Women: Achievements Against the Odds," an exhibit which features 20 posters marking the contributions of Black women in American history, will run through March 31 at the Morris-Jumel Mansion, W. 160th Street and Edgecombe Ave. The exhibition is free with the museum admission of $1 and can be viewed from 10-4 p.m. (except Mondays). . Lambda Legal Defense has an opening for a Public Information Director. Strong writing & editing skills and working knowledge of the media helpful. Call 944-9488. Resume with references to Lambda Legal Defense, 132 West 43 St., NY, NY 10036. Minority and women candidates encouraged to apply. . Entries are now being accepted for the third annual San Francisco Gay Video Festival 1984, which is part of San Francisco's Lesbian/Gay Freedom Celebration. The festival brings together the best in professional, avant-garde, and short features by independent lesbian and gay producers around the country. Deadline for entries is May 31. Accepted formats are 3/4" and 1/2" VHS. For information and entry forms, contact: John Canaly, FRAMELINE, 182-B Castro St., San Francisco, CA 94114 or call (415) 861-0843. . "Work and Families in the '80's," a conference on changing roles and expectations, will be sponsored by the Yale Undergraduate Women's Caucus. Topics will range from workplace innovations and childcare to men and families and decision making on parenting. The conference will take place on Friday, March 2 and Saturday, March 3 at Dwight Hall, Yale. For more info contact Debra Schwartz, (203) 776-7704 or the Yale Women's Center (203) 432-3813. . The Second Annual Black Women's History Conference will take place on Saturday, March 24 and Sunday, March 25 on the Douglass College Campus of Rutgers University in New Brunswick. Cost for the conference is $41.50 and the deadline for registration is March 7th. Included in the weekend's events will be a concert on Saturday evening featuring Sweet Honey in the Rock. For more info, contact Viola Van Jones (201) 932-9603 or (201) 932-9729. . The Women's Coalition to stop U.S. Intervention in Central America and the Caribbean encourages membership of national organizations with differences in racial/ethnic makeup, age, experience, and faith traditions to work towards peace in this hemisphere. Annual membership for organizations is $25, for individuals in local chapters, $5. Contact: St. Marjorie Tuite, 475 Riverside Dr., Room 812, NY 10115 . A writer/editor seeks women who have given children up for adoption—either legal or covert—and are willing to write or talk about their experiences for an anthology bringing together women's voices and historical, cross-cultural, legal, and feminist perspectives on the institutions, customs and attitudes surrounding adoption. If you wish to participate, contact K. Kaufmann, c/o Plexus, 545 Athol Ave., Oakland, CA 94606. . Need a place to display your artwork? The Gay Women's Alternative's Lesbian Feminist Art Show will include the works of painters, weavers, photographers, potters, etc. Call Linda Grishman at (212) 989-2958 for more information. . Tuesday, March 20, will be Gay/Lesbian Lobby Day in Albany. The Lobby Day is being sponsored by the New York State Lesbian and Gay Lobby (NYSLGL). Topics range from funding for the AIDS Institute to the eventual passage of a gay and lesbian civil rights bill. All registered voters are eligible to participate. For further info, contact Richard Gottlieb—(212) 867-7500 (day) and (212) 757-7434 (night). . The week of April 29-May 5 will be "Women's Week" at Virginia Polytechnic Institute and State University. Lectures, workshops, entertainment and celebration with focus on women's lives, history, culture and accomplishments. Send your complimentary books, copies of periodicals & promotional material for display to: Evelyn Newlyn, Chair Women's Studies Committee, Virginia Polytechnic Institute & State University, Blacksburg, VA 24061. . Yenga Productions is looking for original half hour and hour-long radio plays by women of color or adaptations of such works for summer production. Deadline: March 30. Send a SASE for returns. Please include brief biographical sketch and send to: Yenga Productions, P.O. Box 25216-0, Durham, NC 27702. . International Women's Day on WBAI (99.5 FM) takes place on March 8 from 7:30am-11:30pm. The program will include documentaries, panels, news, interviews & music on women's issues. Detailed description of program available March 1 from WBAI-FM, 505 8th Ave., New York, NY 10018, tel. (212) 279-0707. . Lesbian Health workers are available for services at Community Health Project on Thursday nights, beginning March 8, from 7-9 pm. Call for appointment (212) 691-8282. Volunteers are welcomed and will be trained by the staff. . St. Mark's Women's Health Collective, New York's lesbian clinic will hold an orientation and training for new members on Friday, March 23 at 7:30pm. The clinic is located at 9 Second Ave. between Houston and East First St., tele. 228-7482, Tuesday evenings 5-9pm. ■

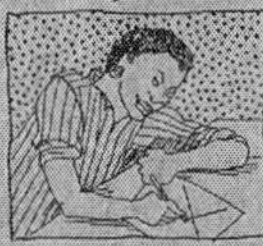

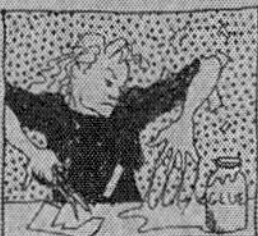

work explicitly served as the foundation for later work. Such was the case with a series of images of lesbians writing that Bechdel debuted in the October 1983 issue (Figure 3.3).[51] These graphics accompanied readers' letters. Bechdel consolidated these individual panels into a *DTWOF* comic in September 1984 (Figure 3.4) and substantially revised this strip for the first collection of her comics that Firebrand Books released in October 1986 (Figure 3.5).[52] This three-year period of intense refinement preceded her creation in early 1987 of the iteration of *DTWOF* that most readers are familiar with, which follows a dedicated cast of characters. By tracking her revisions for these letter-writing lesbians, it is possible to untangle Bechdel's process of making new lesbian subjectivities visible alongside her development as a politically informed comics artist. Moreover, her choices to represent a racially diverse grouping of women within these comics as well as in other graphics created for the collective echoes her commitment to women of color feminism that was ascendant within the feminist movement in the 1980s, as previous chapters have touched on and as the following chapter will delve into in further depth through the drawings of celebrated Chicana lesbian feminist Gloria Anzaldúa.

Bechdel's literary lesbians evoke the range of opinions that surround them on the letters page. The first image in the October 1983 issue of *WomaNews* shows an agitated woman, biting the tip of her pen while mulling over the next words to add to two pages of vigorously scrawled handwriting.[53] She sits in a simple, square panel at the beginning of the letters page, in the top left of three columns, right next to the staff box.[54] Her punchy persona and penmanship tap into the unsettled energies on the letters page. The extreme color contrast deployed in representation—only scratchy, intense blacks or negative white space, no shades of crosshatched gray—visually underscores the raw nerves.

The correspondence that surrounds this image has the same level of fierce passion to it—maybe even more. In one of the dispatches on the page, for instance, Gloria Anzaldúa and Cherríe Moraga issue a public call, asking *WomaNews* readers to donate money to help get *This Bridge Called My Back* (1981) back into print with Kitchen Table: Women of Color Press after the dissolution of Persephone Press, reported in the pages of *WomaNews* two months previous.[55] This much-lauded anthology of woman of color feminism launches the next chapter's focus on

Anzaldúa's own visual production. Having this letter share page space with Bechdel's figure underscores how interconnected the artists surveyed across this book were, even as they occupied distinct spaces within the feminist and gay and lesbian movements for social justice.

The women that Bechdel drew for the letters page in the following months similarly conveyed an intensity of feeling. All told, during her tenure at *WomaNews* she created six letter-writing lesbians who were freely repurposed in the same section in subsequent issues. In all these images, the women are actively putting words on the page. The last of these figures first appeared in the July/August 1984 issue of *WomaNews*, a year after Bechdel's first contributions to the collective.[56] This focused dyke, in a jumper and with an apparent mullet, crunches on M&Ms, which are spilled across the selfsame page where she is composing. This woman and those who precede her embody a wide variety of writerly affects—from those who smoke while writing[57] to those who contort their bodies to write[58] to those who stare out into the distance for inspiration.[59] In each iteration, the words of the letters surrounding these images supply the context, connecting the women to the voices on the page commenting about *WomaNews* and sharing about larger happenings in the feminist movement—like the publication troubles of *This Bridge*.

When Bechdel further developed these writerly affects in the "Literary *Dykes to Watch Out For*" comic strip in the September 1984 issue of *WomaNews* (Figure 3.4), she reframed these figures through her own words.[60] In this short strip, a narratorial voice, identified as "Heloise C. Bland" in the strip's subtitle, proposes, in the first, text-only panel, "to provide a brief psychological catalogue of the more common types of lesbians who write."[61] In the following panels, we encounter six distinct women, represented not just as "types" but more specifically as species: Bland gives each of them a pseudoscientific name in the accompanying boxes that describe each woman. These six species do not generally map one-to-one with their six *WomaNews* letters-page predecessors; rather, their evolutions are more complex.

Although the letters-page lesbians show a range of affects, their association with the opinions page of a feminist periodical restricts their representation. In fact, their framing bespeaks these limitations—they are seen, more or less, in medium close-up, focusing their attention on

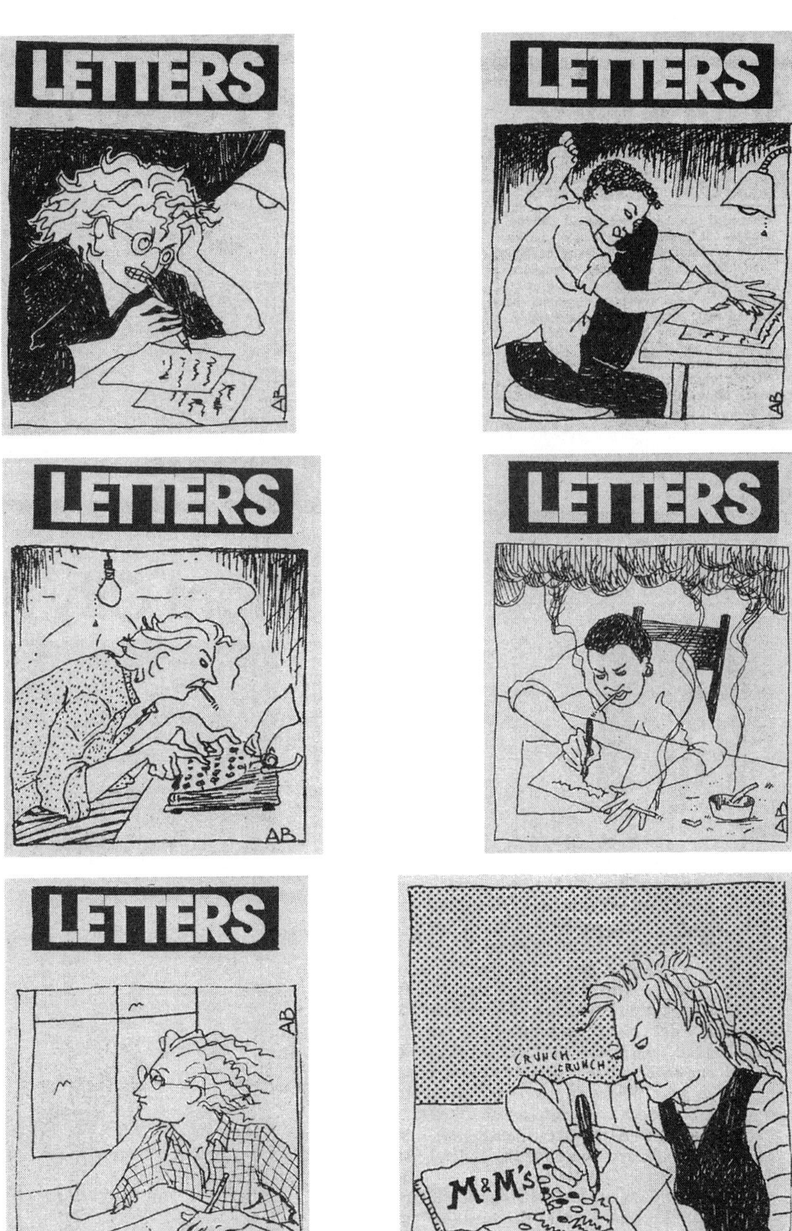

Figure 3.3. Six letter-writing lesbian cartoon illustrations by Alison Bechdel that appeared on the letters page of *WomaNews* over the course of several months from October 1983 to July/August 1984. Courtesy of the Lesbian Herstory Archives. Reprinted with permission of author.

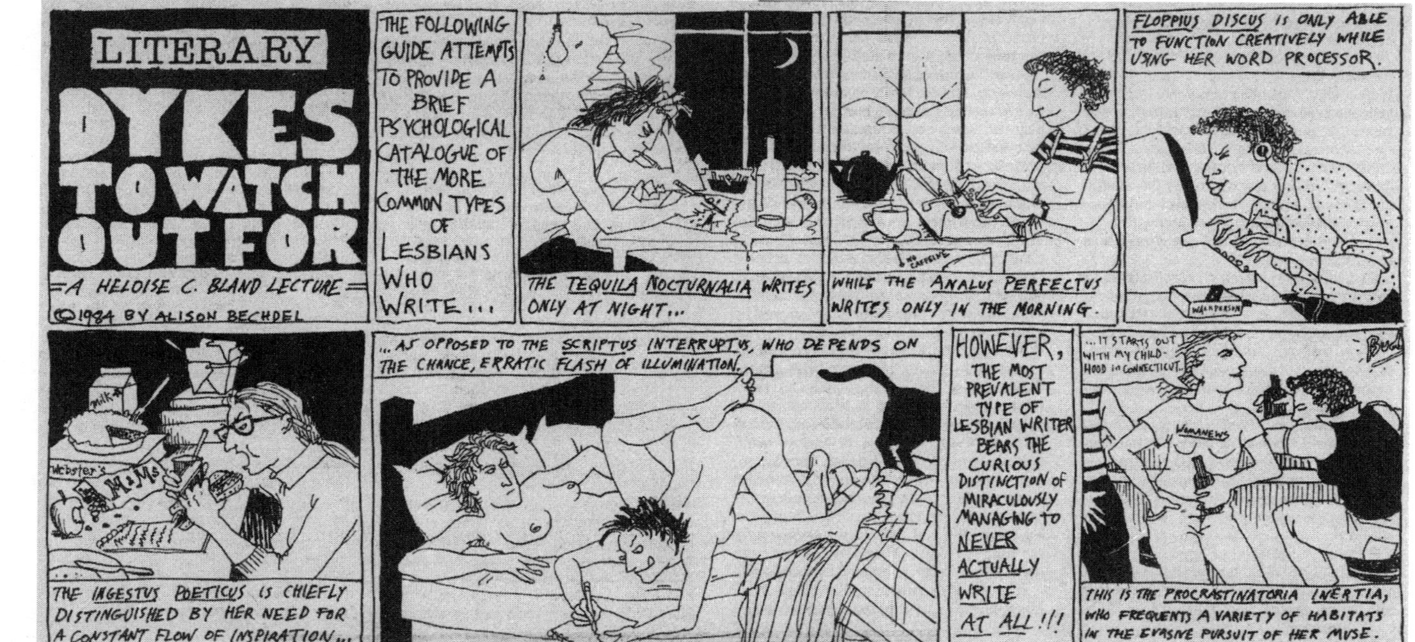

Figure 3.4. Alison Bechdel's "Literary *Dykes to Watch Out For*: A Heloise C. Bland Lecture" comic strip, which gathered together and poked fun at six types of literary lesbians and originally was published in the September 1984 issue of *WomaNews*. Courtesy of the Lesbian Herstory Archives. Reprinted with permission of author.

the act of composition. We know relatively little about the worlds of these characters. They universally evoke collectivity by remaining open for identification with the varied letter writers of *WomaNews*. In her strip, Bechdel retains the universal quality of these women by transforming them into literary species.

To understand these species, we must grasp their natural habitat and behaviors, so we are treated to these dykes in medium to medium-long shot, connected to their physical surroundings and the fullness of their bodies. In all the panels, we are told a story about the woman in association with her environment that shapes and is shaped by her writerly affect. The first four species are solitary, but the final two open up species of writers who are sexual (*Scriptus interruptus*) and social (*Procrastinatoria inertia*), and Bechdel increases the size of these panels in order to show these women engaged in composition through avenues of relation to other bodies. All these writerly species, however, have something, animate or otherwise, that inspires them to write.

The most newly evolved of the species in the strip is the one on the technological forefront, *Floppius discus*, who stares intently into a computer screen while jamming to tunes on her portable audio cassette player, the "Walkperson." Both of these technologies were newly available in the 1980s, with the personal computer highlighted in the American cultural zeitgeist in 1984 following an unprecedentedly popular Apple commercial during that year's Super Bowl.[62] This new, hip writerly persona exists alongside the orderly *Analus perfectus*, diligently at her typewriter with a cup of tea as day breaks. In the structure of the comic, this picture of perfection is formally contrasted with *Tequila nocturnalia*, the tortured writer—both smoker and alcoholic in this rendition—scribbling out words in the dead of night. But what about *Analus perfectus* vis-à-vis *Floppius discus*? We are in a moment of coexisting writerly technologies, but there is the future pull to the computer, borne out over time, further bolstering the forward motion of this woman. It is interesting, then, that in this strip Bechdel portrays *Floppius discus* as a Black woman and the only overtly raced character. The future is more multicultural and complex than the white and tidy world of *Analus perfectus*, soon to be obsolete.

When Bechdel published this strip in her first *DTWOF* collection in 1986, she made further changes, forecasting the developing politics of her representations (Figure 3.5). Indeed, looking from the version of

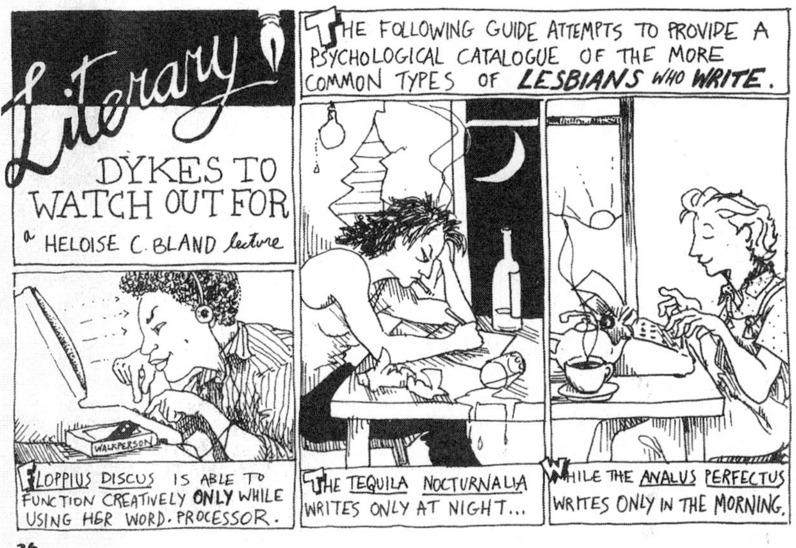

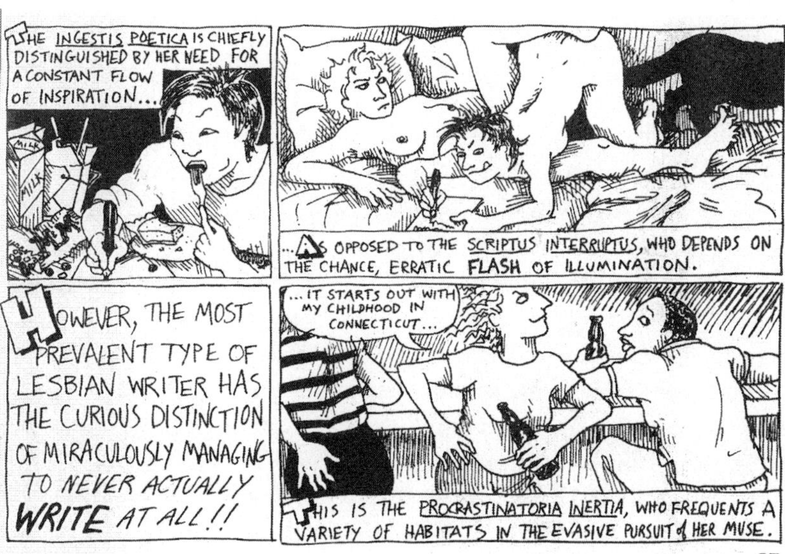

Figure 3.5. Alison Bechdel's revised "Literary *Dykes to Watch Out For*: A Heloise C. Bland Lecture" comic strip as it appeared in her first *Dykes to Watch Out For* (1986) collection. Reprinted with permission of author.

"Literary *Dykes to Watch Out For*" in *WomaNews* to the one in her first published collection is akin to a lesbian spoof of the childhood "spot the differences" game in any *Highlights* magazine. If *Floppius discus* were the multicultural future foretold in the first iteration, then this future is building steam in the second version, where two more dykes are visually reworked as women of color. These reworkings of *Ingestis poetica* and the woman listening to *Procrastinatoria inertia* do more than simply acknowledge the rising prominence of feminist women of color. These personages also foretell Bechdel's embrace of lesbian feminist representational diversity within her comics, which becomes further evident when she relaunched *DTWOF* with a multiracial cast of recurring characters in 1987. It's hardly a coincidence that these two revised figures resemble two of her *DTWOF* characters, Sparrow and Ginger, respectively.

Overall, the collected version of this comic is more polished—from the neater styling of the typeface to the amount of detail lavished in representing each woman. In the revision process, some background elements were omitted to streamline the drawing—from the missing ashtray in *Tequila nocturnalia*'s frame to the reduction of the food items represented in *Ingestis poetica*'s workspace. In the revision of *Procrastinatoria inertia*, the "most prevalent type of lesbian writer," Bechdel changed the panel in numerous subtle ways that culminate in altering its meaning and its relationship to the reader. In both iterations, *Procrastinatoria inertia* has vaguely the same look—her T-shirt-and-jeans torso faces forward while she gazes semi-wistfully off to the left in recounting her Connecticut childhood. In its first version, Bechdel directly aligned this dyke with the readers of *WomaNews* by portraying her in a *WomaNews* T-shirt. This *WomaNews Procrastinatoria inertia* tells her tale at the bar to no one in particular—there is a couple getting handsy off frame to her right, and on her left, her one potential listener dozes while clenching a bottle of alcohol. With this T-shirt, Bechdel suggests that all readers are likely this woman at one point or another. In her revision and with her addition of a Black proto-Ginger in the frame, *Procrastinatoria inertia* takes on new meaning. By depicting the woman in a plain white T-shirt, Bechdel removed the associational ties to *WomaNews*, but we know, by the framing of the comic, that she is still not only a lesbian but also ostensibly a dyke to watch out for, in the many valences of the phrase. Though the couple off frame to the right are still getting handsy in this version, this new *Procrastinatoria inertia*, in telling her tale, provokes a response—namely, proto-Ginger's apparent exasperation. Her annoyed expression isn't just about an irritating bar patron but gestures toward an exhaustion with this kind of white lesbian feminist, obliviously grandstanding about her privilege with no sense of the varied experiences of the feminists around her. For Bechdel, reflecting her engagement in the evolving feminist movement around her, intersectional politics became an even more overt discourse in *DTWOF* in future years, evident through the women of color characters she created for the strip and stories that often referenced prominent feminists of color like Audre Lorde and Barbara Smith.

Queer Comics–Adjacent Material

More than just comics, Bechdel's image–text contributions to *WomaNews* included covers, advertisements, and graphics accompanying articles—all of which were innovative in how they communicated feminist ideas in a distilled manner. Her visual language, which was heavily informed by the grassroots publication networks in which she operated, had enormous impact on the feminist and queer political communities who read her works, and who would in turn influence the broader discourse around gender and sexuality in feminism. In fact, by the 1990s, Bechdel would report in numerous interviews that women had learned about lesbian culture through her comics.[63] Her early and diverse image–text work in *WomaNews* allowed her to experiment with different ways to create more visible lesbian experiences.

Across Bechdel's many advertisements, including those promoting social events and collective-building workshops, we can see her nascent visual politics, where she is thinking about how to portray a range of characters that represent collective experience. Her advertisement for the *WomaNews* Fifth Anniversary Variety Show! embraced diversity by featuring five very different women locked arm in arm doing high kicks (Figure 3.6).[64] Unlike the Rockettes, the famous New York City all-female precision dance troupe known for both high kicks and a similitude of appearance among its members, the five women here differ from each other in every attribute: age, race, weight, cup size, height, shoe taste, hairstyle.[65] Bechdel's visual reference radiates particularly forcefully as the

December date of this event—and thus the publication of the advertisement in the November and December/January issues of *WomaNews*—coincided with the Rockettes' performative mainstay, the annual Christmas Spectacular.[66] For Bechdel to copy the Rockettes' signature high kick but radically depart from the accompanying display of only one sort of woman is especially progressive given that the Radio City Music Hall mainstays were not yet a racially integrated troupe.[67]

Bechdel's image suggests the unified movement of her dancers' high kick—other visual signifiers of similarity be damned. These women are linked together in political movement that builds strength from their diversity. Unlike the Rockettes, who pride themselves on uniformity, success here is judged by difference—how many kinds of women can come together in coalition, high-kicking (literally or metaphorically), arm in arm? This visual collectivity echoes artistic approaches discussed in chapters 1 and 2 that showed diverse groupings of women celebrating differences in feminist settings: in the comic printed in the Barnard *Diary* (1982), multiple Black and white women emerged out from under the bed in the final panel to talk with one another about sex, and in Lee Marrs's *Pudge* #1 (1973), the protagonist encountered a packed room of diverse women looking at their cervixes together and excitedly commenting on their differences.[68] The artists in the following chapters, Gloria Anzaldúa and Nan Goldin, also represent collectivity in their chosen visual media.

The wording of Bechdel's ad suggests further coalitional broadening beyond the visual register. The text framing the image is hand-drawn by Bechdel as well, suggesting that she was involved in the nitty-gritty details of the event. In the November version of the advertisement, the text beneath the image exclaims, "Singers! Dancers! Musicians! Surprises!" A number of possible expressions are enthusiastically encouraged; spectacles that fall outside the expected triptych are celebrated as "Surprises!" Further, prominently under the event information and taking up the same width as the image and its adjacent text, a line announces, "Performance space wheelchair accessible," welcoming sisters with physical disabilities. The text extends the range of expressions and bodies that can participate in both this variety show and this collective. Moreover, this advertisement, in both the November and December/January issues, is embedded on the bottom right of the two-page calendar of events

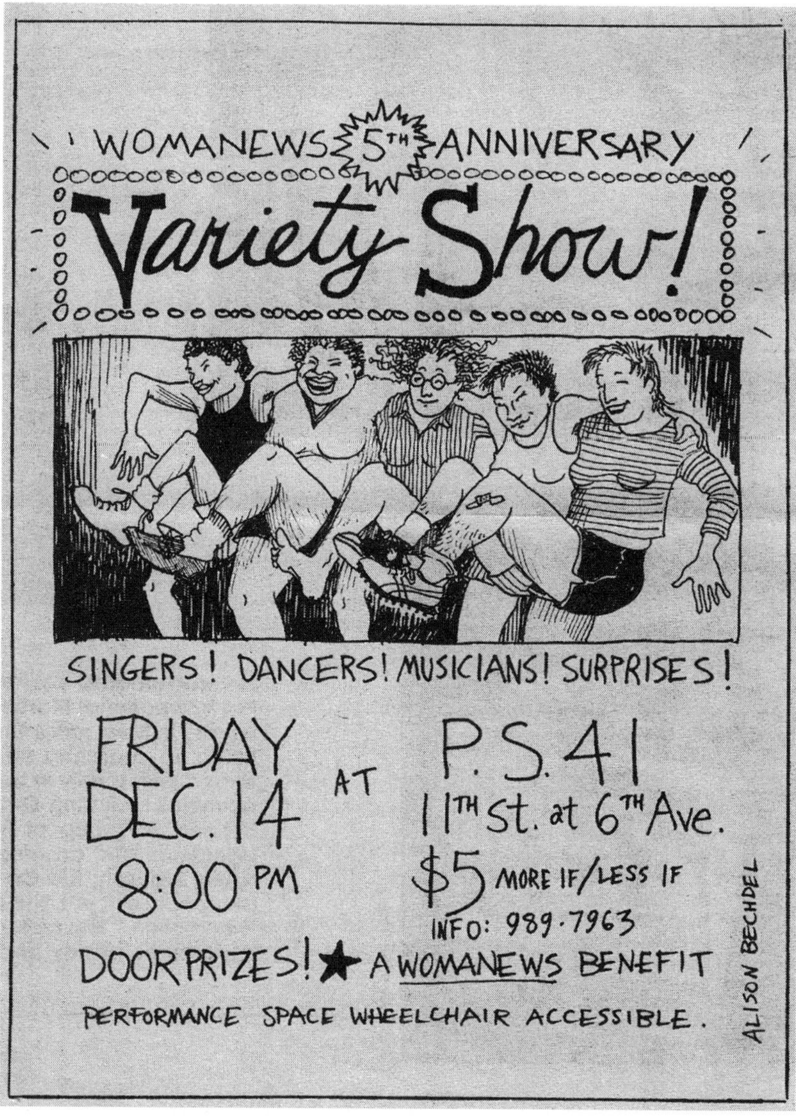

Figure 3.6. Alison Bechdel's advertisement for *WomanNews*'s fifth-anniversary variety show that depicts five very different women high-kicking together amid text describing the event as it appeared in the November 1984 issue of *WomaNews.* Courtesy of the Lesbian Herstory Archives. Reprinted with permission of author.

potentially of interest to those in the *WomaNews* community. Beyond the borders of this ad, we are immersed in a wide range of upcoming events for women of all sorts of dispositions.

In other advertisements, Bechdel showcased more ways that readers could support the collective. For the April 1984 issue, she devised a new advertisement for the sale of *WomaNews* T-shirts (Figure 3.7).[69] In seeking to draw women into the collective by celebrating its politics as an active, fun, engaged endeavor, Bechdel employed multiple panels. In its arrangement of panels into a two-by-two grid, this advertisement reads as a comic. The narrative does not follow one woman in her *WomaNews* T-shirt but potentially four different women with diverse approaches. In each panel, cropping or perspective obscures the face of each woman, but contrasting visual cues—background texture, T-shirt, and hairstyle—suggest that we are looking at four different lived experiences. The illustrations encourage various uses for the T-shirt, definitively echoed in exclamatory text in the space below each panel. In the top row of panels, Bechdel portrays two women altering the T-shirt to fit their daily lifestyles—the first woman rips off the collar, sleeves, and bottom hem of the shirt to create a punk look, while the second keeps a pack of cigarettes rolled in her right sleeve. By recommending alterations to the T-shirts in the very advertisement selling them, Bechdel and the *WomaNews* collective imagine a whole host of gender presentations in this garb. The *WomaNews* T-shirt and *WomaNews* itself are open for reinterpretation and negotiation on a regular basis.

The bottom row juxtaposes these diurnal activities by suggesting two nocturnal approaches to the garment. In these panels, both women are getting ready for bed while wearing their *WomaNews* T-shirts, but their shared experience diverges from there. Above a caption that intones, "Wear it to bed!" the first woman dons the T-shirt as her nightie while diligently brushing her teeth, an action that suggests a quiet end to the evening. This speculation is supported by both the content of the second panel and its negating caption, "Don't wear it to bed!" Here, a woman removes her T-shirt in order to join an already naked partner awaiting her under the covers; her evening is likely far from over. While this image is fairly innocuous in its portrayal of an imminent intimate encounter, the inclusion of lesbian sexuality as something that can be playfully tackled in a T-shirt advertisement gestures toward a feminist

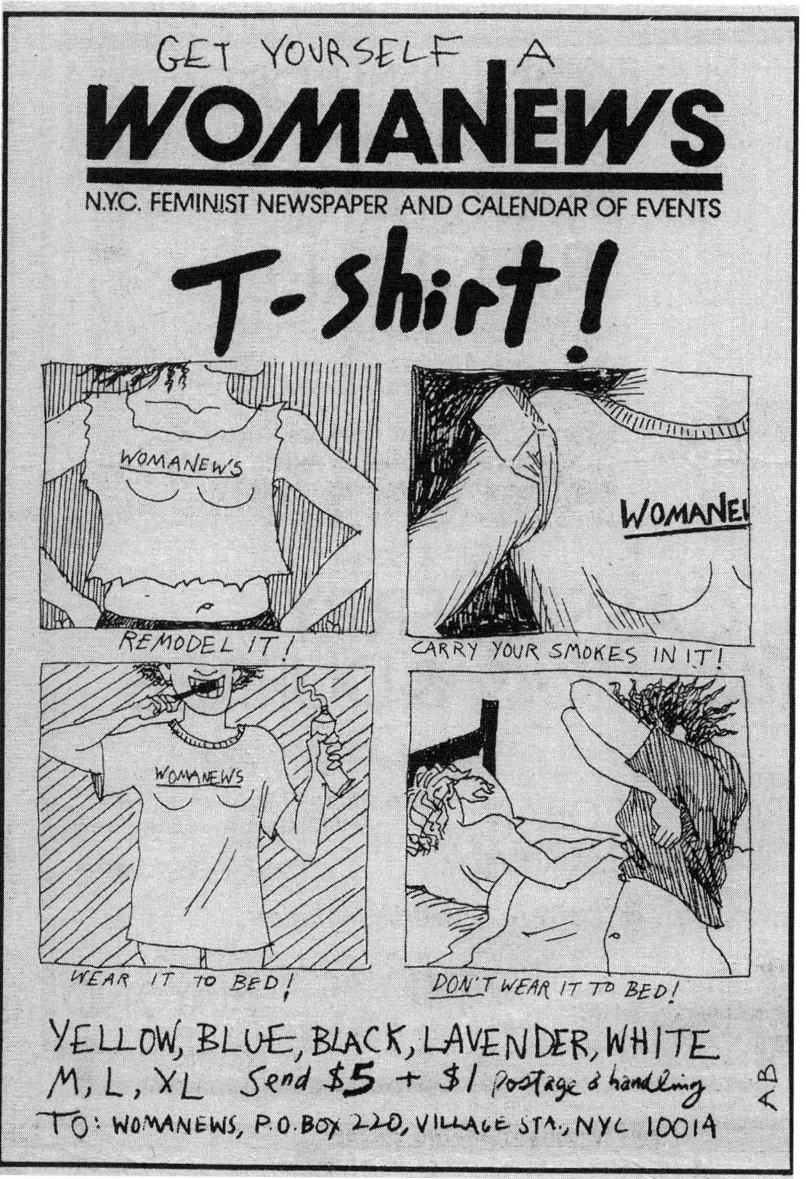

Figure 3.7. Alison Bechdel's advertisement for *WomaNews* T-shirts that includes a short comic of four women in different scenarios as it appeared in the April 1984 issue of *WomaNews*. Courtesy of the Lesbian Herstory Archives. Reprinted with permission of author.

politics that embraces a wide range of sexual expression, just as the first row validates a gamut of gender presentation. Taken together, these panels celebrate a variety of sartorial choices, reflecting the array of political coverage but injecting it with humor through the comics medium. In this and other advertisements, *WomaNews* is explicitly evoked at the top, framing these representations. The *WomaNews* collective nurtured Bechdel's visual politics and gave her the space to experiment with the comics form. Over the course of her career, grassroots spaces have continued to support Bechdel's growth. Similarly, for all the artists in this book, collective spaces foster creative experimentation and new mergings of image and text.

Archives and Afterlives: Networking Dykes *Online*

Eight years after ending *DTWOF* in 2008, Bechdel released a Thanksgiving strip in November 2016 that responded to the presidential election of Donald Trump. She published the comic both in her local Burlington, Vermont, paper, *Seven Days,* as well as on her personal blog, where she briefly prefaced it with the following: "Since I stopped drawing *Dykes to Watch Out For* at the tail end of the Bush administration, people have asked me many times if I thought about my characters, and if so, what they were up to. And I would have to be honest. No, I didn't think about them, and I had no idea what they were doing. But last week they all started flooding back."[70] She has since circulated two more strips in *Seven Days* and through her online outlets, the second coinciding with the Ides of Trump postcard-writing campaign in March 2017 and the third in July 2017 following the characters as they celebrate the Fourth of July. As she wrote on the release of this second strip, "I plan to continue doing these on an occasional basis as a way of staying sane."[71] The commenters on her website and Facebook post thanked her for this strip and agreed with her sentiment about maintaining sanity. Even though Bechdel had not published a strip in nearly a decade, her community continues to affectively relate to *DTWOF*—evident in these responses and in Bechdel's statement that people asked after her characters.

These moments of interaction evidence how the transformation of grassroots infrastructure in the digital era facilitates community connection. Bechdel herself cites this direct interaction with her "strong community of readers" as a reason to start releasing her strips on her blog when she began the practice in early 2006.[72] Though common Internet wisdom advises against reading the comments, in queer communities this space facilitates an engagement that shapes future work. This dialogue echoes the correspondence with individual periodicals that I discussed at the outset of this chapter. In both instances, those who love her work communicate their support and discuss the future trajectory of her plot. In digital space, she often directly responds to these suggestions in the comment stream or by penning response posts on her blog.[73] If you didn't engage these comment streams, you would miss how much of Bechdel's work is informed by and formed through dialogue with her readers. One of the hallmarks of comics is how they circulate among many publication venues, and I have argued throughout this chapter that we must centralize grassroots periodical networks as an important space that fosters feminist and queer visual cultures while simultaneously underlining how archives preserve these networks. The next chapters will look to how Gloria Anzaldúa and Nan Goldin also developed their visual practice through close connections with grassroots communities they represented in their artwork.

By turning to the digital in closing, I urge us to pay attention to how the electronic infrastructure of these spaces further facilitates "queerness as collectivity."[74] In digital spaces, we must regard both those new artists who have innovated the form of webcomics and those artists, like Bechdel, who take up the digital to supplement existing careers and how they re-create their physical communities in these new spaces. For Bechdel, this new infrastructure supports her identity as "the lesbian Norman Rockwell" as she connects more closely with readers while making lesbian experience visible in multiple forms.[75] On her blog, she not only distributes her comics but also shares sketches, textual reflections alongside accompanying photos, homemade videos, and various other new media image–text creations. This platform allows her to get back in touch with her grassroots beginnings at *WomaNews* and *Equal Time*, where she created comics-adjacent work in close proximity to her more formally legible comics. By embracing queer comics archives and affiliated spaces, we come to regard the role of queer community and transgress the borders of what constitutes comics in ways that better reflect and serve shifting queer activisms.

In the following chapters, I further push on those formal boundaries by highlighting the comicity of Anzaldúa's drawings and Goldin's photographs as both artists engaged sequence and multiplicity to build community. Like Bechdel, Anzaldúa and Goldin both challenged the visual formats they embraced, and they continue to be celebrated and supported in emerging digital networks when activists share their work on networks like Tumblr and create new work in their style on image-creation platforms like Instagram.[76] The next two chapters will look to how they created their innovative visual work through collective spaces and how the archives make visible their artistic activism in working to create visibility for diverse sexual experiences.

4

THE EDITOR AND PEDAGOGUE

Gloria E. Anzaldúa's Public Drawing

Building Bridges through Many Forms

In 1981 Persephone Press, a feminist press, published *This Bridge Called My Back: Writings by Radical Women of Color*. This anthology, co-edited by Gloria Anzaldúa and Cherríe Moraga, received near instant acclaim, and since its publication over four decades ago it has been reissued in four additional editions and sold over one hundred thousand copies.[1] The collection is widely celebrated for how it brought together women of color from diverse backgrounds to write openly about their identities and life experience—particularly as shaped by the intersection of their race, gender, sexuality, and class. In 2017, Cassius Adair and Lisa Nakamura called *This Bridge* "a cornerstone of our feminist consciousness," highlighting its publication history—including its official editions as well as its countless pirated versions—as evidence of its continuing influence.[2] The book's enduring relevance is due both to the variety of authorial perspectives it includes and to the range of forms the contributors used. Authors combined autobiographical, dialogic, poetic, discursive, epistolary, and other textual forms to describe their experiences as women of color. In their introduction to the first edition in 1981, Anzaldúa and Moraga celebrated this constellation of approaches: "The works combined reflect a diversity of perspectives, linguistic styles, and cultural tongues."[3] Pointing to the impact of the anthology's formal diversity, AnaLouise Keating, who edited *The Gloria Anzaldúa Reader* in 2009, described *This Bridge* as "demonstrat[ing] the transformative possibilities that arise when we theorize in multiple genres and modes."[4]

143

In her own work that she published alongside and following *This Bridge*, Anzaldúa was known for employing a variety of forms in order to theorize and figure out different ways of welcoming folks into thinking alongside her. In *This Bridge*, Anzaldúa contributed a multifaceted letter to "third world women writers" that incorporated epigraphs of other writers and her own journal entries, highlighting her collaborative mindset. At the outset of her letter, she describes herself and other women of color who "[lament] the lack of time to weave writing into your life" as she describes her choice of the epistolary format, since it allows her to "approximate the intimacy and immediacy [that she] want[ed]" to these women, as neither an essay nor a poem could do.[5] Further, *Borderlands / La Frontera* (1987), her acclaimed critical volume that followed *This Bridge*, also highlighted her interest in moving beyond traditional textual forms and incorporating multiple textual registers in a single space. In this book, she divided the manuscript in half between prose and poetry (although the actual styles of those forms varied widely, ten women described them as "hybrid, inclusive, many-voiced" in a group introduction to the third edition of the book).[6] Anzaldúa's embrace of a range of forms is evident throughout her published writings, and it is also strongly present in her unpublished work, particularly her drawings. This chapter, which looks specifically at how she deployed her visual creations to welcome others into her thought, underscores the crucial ways that Anzaldúa—like the artists discussed in prior chapters—used images to develop communities around groundbreaking new ideas.

In the previous chapters, I have traced the way that visual culture, particularly in the context of grassroots publishing, has centrally participated in feminist discourse during the 1970s and 1980s. This chapter builds on those discussions, specifically highlighting how visuality played a role in the work of Chicana lesbian feminist Gloria Anzaldúa. As an influential feminist theorist, Anzaldúa called for a greater engagement with how race, sexuality, and class affected a woman's life, developing intersectional feminism before Kimberlé Crenshaw coined the term in 1989.[7] Her drawings, which were rarely published, were fundamentally intertwined with her theoretical and community-building work. This chapter opens by looking again at Anzaldúa's well-known editing and how her building of community through this role echoed her little-known visual work and its collective praxis. Both of these forms were central to

Anzaldúa's reshaping of feminism through intersectional thinking in the 1970s and 1980s.

Across her career, Anzaldúa built coalitional networks through editing anthologies, making use of their capacity to contain many forms and voices. In two anthologies that followed *This Bridge* and *Borderlands / La Frontera*—*Making Face, Making Soul / Haciendo Caras: Creative and Critical Perspectives by Feminists of Color* (1990) and *this bridge we call home: radical visions for transformation* (2002)—Anzaldúa worked to expand the conversation that *This Bridge* had started, welcoming in people to reflect on their experiences from a diversity of social, economic, ethnic, and racial backgrounds. As with *This Bridge*, Anzaldúa saw her editorial work as one of mentorship, dedicating space to cultivate new writers and encouraging all contributors to experiment in order to find the form necessary to convey their experiences.[8] Unlike other multiauthored collections of writing where editors may encourage consistency of voices among the various contributors, Anzaldúa saw difference of expression as central to both volumes.

As she organized the pieces into sections, Anzaldúa intentionally juxtaposed and highlighted the multiplicity of forms to spur readers to action: "As the perspective and focus shift, as the topics shift, the listener/reader is forced into participating in the making of meaning—she is forced to connect the dots, to connect the fragments."[9] Just as Anzaldúa mentored each contributor to dig deep and find their own individual voice and form, so also did she mentor the readers into finding the community among all of these voices. With her anthologies, Anzaldúa thereby forges relationships with both her contributors and her readers that prompt them to pay attention to shifting forms in thinking through their own investments and connections with others.

Anzaldúa drew on the dynamic nature of multiple forms to build community when she used her own drawings to illustrate concepts in public lectures she gave. Across her career, she gave hundreds of talks, as she detailed in a 1994 interview: "Since 1981 I've been doing gigs. Some years I do twenty. This year I only did thirteen because I'm getting older and I'm diabetic. I can't do as much."[10] Early in her career, she animated her words and ideas through live drawings on chalkboards. Later on, she projected drawings on transparencies to welcome the audience into her thought and would reanimate the images during the talk by tracing her finger over her drawings and text as she moved through an idea. These images, which she called "glifos," were integral to her speaking presentation: "The images I place on overhead projectors 'contain' or 'illustrate' my ideas and theories."[11] No matter the format, Anzaldúa actively used drawings to bring the audience inside her thinking. Her use of these image–text combinations introduced her listeners to her process, since she began conceptualizing her theories through images.[12]

She filled her calendar with numerous speaking engagements because she saw them as vital community-building actions. Through incorporating drawings into her talks, she encouraged listeners to join her in cocreating their own understanding of her concepts alongside her. That is, the drawings spurred her listeners to action. This work is similar to her work of editorship as she mentored her audience in how to see and theorize on their own. Also like her editorship, her engagement in image making is something that evolved across the course of her career, as can be seen in her drawings from her early teaching and seminar notes in graduate school. Her image making is community-building mentorship in action, and it points to the collective nature of visual culture and the vital role it played in redefining the focus within feminist thought throughout the 1980s.[13]

A number of scholars have written about Anzaldúa's training in the visual arts and recognized the importance of her drawings to her written work. However, her visual production has not yet been fully theorized as important in its own right and as a crucial method of community building. In her scholarship, Diana Bowen examines how Anzaldúa would draw at the outset of her writing and then translate these images into words, which explains why her text is so often filled with "vivid imagery."[14] Other scholars have recognized her actual visual output—Keating reproduced some of her transparencies in the vital *Gloria Anzaldúa Reader* (2009), and Suzanne Bost in a recent *PMLA* article discussed how doodles were part of Anzaldúa's writing process.[15] However, when these scholars explore the visuality of Anzaldúa's work, they focus mostly on how she used the visual in service of her writing, often training their attention on how she first created her ideas through drawings. That is, they understand the visual as part of the drafting process, rather than as separate and significant work in its own right. By contrast, this chapter tracks how she created images throughout her career. In particular, it pays attention to how visuals operated at the opposite end of the writing process when she shared her ideas with an audience and how they served her larger project of network building. In her preface to the third edition of *This Bridge*, Anzaldúa acknowledges the pivotal role of images by centering visual language in her description of her work: "For positive social change to happen we need to envision a different reality, dream new blueprints for it, formulate new strategies for coping in it."[16] This sentiment expresses the need for multiple forms to achieve collective action, and her own work foregrounds how the visual plays a key role in facilitating social change at every stage of her thinking.

Just as the previous chapter showed how Bechdel's visual work was shaped by grassroots networks, this chapter demonstrates how Anzaldúa shapes networks through her visual production. Inevitably, the relationship between the networks and the artwork is reciprocal. By examining it from both angles, however, it's possible to see how this visual work is indebted to and linked to these networks. Anzaldúa's embrace of many forms, including the visual, exists in a rich ecosystem of women of color deploying multiple tactics to welcome more voices to the table and to recognize experiences that heretofore had not been articulated in writing.

The network building that Anzaldúa developed in her visual work overlaps in important ways with how Anzaldúa and Moraga developed feminist communities as editors of *This Bridge*. The feminist community building they did as editors for the anthology is well documented, and that work fostered further support for women of color through projects associated with the volume. Meredith Benjamin has closely examined the important community development that occurred through written correspondence during the creation of *This Bridge*, as well as in the public performances that took place around the launch of the book. As she writes, "*This Bridge Called My Back* is not an isolated intervention confined to one publication but rather a product of movements and networks that would inspire further networks and movements."[17] Anzaldúa and Moraga did all of this work embedded in and alongside *This Bridge* because they saw the volume as a "revolutionary tool" and "catalyst" that would uplift women of color in the present and the future.[18]

Because the contributors themselves represented only a small percentage of the women invested in the project of the book, Anzaldúa capitalized on that interest by simultaneously developing the Third World

Women Speakers List, gathering the names and credentials of women of color willing to serve as speakers on a number of issues. Anzaldúa worked on this project with Merlin Stone, a white woman who had encouraged Anzaldúa to move forward in creating *This Bridge*, and together they solicited names from colleagues and people in their networks that they could send to "Women's Studies Departments at over 300 colleges and universities" in the United States.[19] Correspondence in Anzaldúa's archives includes numerous responses to and excitement about this list, which aimed to push universities to expand the pool of potential speakers invited to present at any given event. Its goal was to "confront the situation of all white or token Third World representation among speakers chosen for Women's Conferences and individual speaking engagements for Women's Studies Programs."[20] They hoped this list would counter racial tokenization and ensure that the same small group of women of color wouldn't be called on repeatedly, and that, ultimately, a greater number of women of color of diverse perspectives would be more consistently asked to contribute to projects and events. Although the list was not published in *This Bridge*, it extended the anthology's project by making visible an exponentially larger community of women of color.

As part of the anthology, however, Anzaldúa and Moraga did include another list they compiled—a bibliography of work by and about women of color—which they added as an appendix in *This Bridge*. This bibliography illuminated the rich critical and fictional writing that had preceded *This Bridge* and helped circulate awareness of that important work to additional readers who might not know about it.[21] The list was broken out into categories that focused on racial groups represented in the anthology—"Afro-American," "Asian/Pacific American," "Latina," and "Native American women"—and included at the end a list of more than thirty small presses that published this kind of work. Both the bibliography that Anzaldúa and Moraga assembled and the list of speakers that Anzaldúa and Stone compiled demonstrated the depth and breadth of the community of women of color involved in social justice, and both lists represent important examples of how Anzaldúa's network building helped propel feminist discourse in new directions by connecting histories of women of color literary activism and providing the opportunity for new voices to contribute to scholarly discourse.[22] Moreover, like the artists in the previous chapters, Anzaldúa and her collaborators mobilized their individual work as a platform in the service of making a larger community visible.

Anzaldúa's visual praxis, which she developed alongside her better-known editorial and written work, illustrates how Anzaldúa—a key participant in the development of intersectional feminism—sought to welcome people to engage in the lineage of feminist organizing among women of color. As I explain in the chapter, Anzaldúa's drawings were associated with and transformative of her classroom praxis and published writing. While the drawings she made in classroom notes synthesized specific course material, her drawings created on transparencies for public talks had extended use. She would save these transparencies and repurpose them in future talks across many years. This practice paralleled her writing where her theories would build explicitly on past ideas, so that even older ideas would remain open for discussion. These drawings thus kept her theories in circulation and also opened them up for continual renegotiation. Upon her untimely death in 2004, her personal papers, including her drawings, became part of the Nettie Lee Benson Latin American Collection at the University of Texas at Austin, where they are a highlight and focal point of the archives. I center her visual work as a core component of her life as a thinker and a method that she used to connect with her public, much as Bechdel cultivated a national presence through her savvy self-syndication of her comic. Whereas previous chapters have looked across multiple archives, this chapter demonstrates how Anzaldúa's own archives and the images preserved therein are community-building endeavors, and how her collection exists within an ecosystem of similar collections from other women of color who often felt excluded from such official systems of history and memory.[23]

This Bridge Called My Archives

While Anzaldúa is a well-known literary figure, her image making is not widely recognized, likely due to the fact that she never published her visual works. However, Anzaldúa's archived papers neatly demonstrate her long-standing engagement with visual expression, and visual materials that she created are present all across her files. As scholars Keating and Bost have noted, Anzaldúa's archives contain a wealth of unpublished material and encourage us to reassess her legacy and her contributions to many critical conversations.[24] While stored in the archives, her drawings can continue to formulate connections as an "archival genre," a term that Kate Eichhorn develops to describe forms that mimic the sprawl of archives in "resist[ing] categorization" and thereby "offer a textual and social space where new genres can develop."[25] In this way, the archives not only make Anzaldúa's images visible, but the images themselves remain actively open for new interpretation and meaning.

Consequently, similar to the way these archives allow us to see and engage Anzaldúa's visual praxis, so do her images and their community-building work allow us to understand the function of archives anew. Her archives are the space where, ultimately, her many forms all sit together, and Keating has discussed how "she intentionally saved" "everything related to her writing process and career," "document[ing] her life as she lived (or should I say wrote?) it."[26] Keating even goes so far as to call Anzaldúa an "archival author," saying that her "papers represent her final, and most complex text."[27] For the purposes of this chapter, I am interested in how she saved her images, and also how these images and her process of building an archives as a whole are both processes deeply invested in cultivating community. Anzaldúa's embrace of both image-making and archives-building practices allows us to understand her calls to action in a new light. She synthesized some of her advice to women of color in a preface to a 1991 interview: "I use the idea of outlawed knowledge to encourage Chicanas and other women and people of color to produce our own forms, to originate our own theories for how the world works. I think those who produce new conocimientos have to shift the frame of reference, reframe the issue or situation being looked at, connect the disparate parts of information in new ways or from a perspective that's new."[28] In this quote, Anzaldúa emphasizes how important it is for "Chicanas and other women and people of color" to adopt new practices to articulate what's been overlooked about their experiences. The evocation of "outlawed knowledge" underlines the stakes of this work, resonating with how Anzaldúa was not allowed to choose Chicano literature as an area of focus when she was pursuing a doctorate at the University of Texas at Austin, which ultimately prompted her to leave the program and pursue a literary career in which she centered the voices of women of color, creating space and visibility for their work.[29] Her image making was one of a multiplicity of forms that Anzaldúa engaged in order to "produce new conocimientos," and it was the most public form she used to "reframe the issue or situation being looked at." In her classroom notes from UT Austin, her drawings allowed her to connect to and find her way into community with the materials themselves. In her public talks, her images did that same work for her audience, "encourag[ing]" them to "originate [their] own theories for how the world works." The connective quality of the images, themselves an archival genre that allows space "where new genres can develop," outlines the work of her archives as well and how she consciously built her collection as a space that contained these sets of "outlawed knowledge" and the tools to facilitate further community development.[30]

In this sense, archives can operate as bridges, to evoke the term that Anzaldúa used in the titles of two of her anthologies and also theorized in her writings as one way that women of color can make their experiences known to a larger community. Anzaldúa acted as a bridge in her own career, and her work continues to operate as a bridge, as she describes: "Being a bridge means being mediator between yourself and your community and white people, lesbians, feminists, white men."[31] In enacting this mediation, the archives and the materials therein function as bridges by speaking through their hybrid forms to encompass the experiences of women of color. In her foreword to the third edition of *This Bridge Called My Back*, Anzaldúa calls for women of color to do this bridging because "we do not inhabit un mundo but many, and we need to allow these other worlds and people to join in the feminist-of-color dialogue. . . . We must become nepantleras and build bridges between all these worlds as we traffic back and forth between them, detribalizing and retribalizing in different and various communities."[32] At the same time that Anzaldúa articulates how women of color are well positioned to act as bridges and form "communities" that uplift and center "feminist-of-color dialogue," she acknowledges that bridging can be difficult, thankless, and even painful work. Because Anzaldúa did her bridging through written and visual work, her work holds traces of that bridging and can continue to facilitate community.

Throughout her career, Anzaldúa carefully saved both her own manuscripts and also documents pertaining to her community-building practices, like her drawings, that she used for developing her lectures and writing and for explaining her ideas to others during presentations. She also preserved primary documents from the larger movements of women of color engaged in social justice. Considering how archives can function as bridges uncovers how individual archives can be collective endeavors, both in containing the work of other people and in containing forms that are collective in their composition. In this way, personal archives by women of color can effect this bridging; by acting as an "archival genre"—in Eichhorn's definition—Anzaldúa's images are able to facilitate the creation of "new genres" in the minds and hearts of her audience.

Recent scholarship focusing on the recovery of marginalized histories has underlined how grassroots archives provide critical mechanisms for preserving and making accessible works of marginalized populations whose histories would not be saved otherwise.[33] Indeed, this whole book relies upon the vital work of these spaces. Women of color incorporated the spirit of collectivity that we celebrate in grassroots archives within their own personal collections, and by doing so, built archives as bridges to preserve the social movements in which they were engaged. They did so because, as María Cotera documents in her scholarship on the creation of the Chicana por mi Raza Digital Memory Project and Archive, women of color couldn't trust that their materials would be saved otherwise.[34]

In addition to constructing bridges when creating her own archives, Anzaldúa's archives also exist in a rich ecosystem of individual collections by other women of color. The Chicana por mi Raza project provides a useful illustration of this point, particularly in relation to Chicana activists and artists. The Chicana por mi Raza digital archives is a project aimed at documenting Chicana history and activism from the 1960s to the 1980s. Cotera, who has been working on the archives since 2009, has built this collection along with a number of collaborators by going into the homes of over eighty women involved in activism and interviewing them about their lives and digitizing materials from their personal collections. Though their materials become part of the digital project, their individual collections remain intact in their homes.[35] Cotera has produced a number of articles about the importance of this project, including one that recently appeared in *Chicana Movidas* (2018), a collection she coedited with Maylei Blackwell and Dionne Espinoza, which strives to recuperate the work of Chicana activists across the last several decades.[36] Many of the essays therein are indebted to the work of the Chicana por mi Raza digital archives, and the editors begin their introduction by discussing how "Anzaldúa's attentiveness to the minor and the provisional, to the small acts of *rebeldía* that reshape movement discourses from the inside out," frames their approach to minor histories in the volume.[37]

Cotera's own essay in the volume thinks through the collecting processes of the women she has worked with on the project, beginning with her own mother, Martha P. Cotera, a well-known activist in the 1960s and 1970s who penned the influential *Diosa y Hembra: The History and Heritage of Chicanas in the U.S.* (1976) and *The Chicana Feminist* (1977), both of which appear in *This Bridge*'s bibliography. She begins by describing the physical space of her mother's library and how it is filled with decades of movement materials in various formats that intermix with her own writings. She asserts that this kind of dedicated space for a collection is typical of the women she has worked with for Chicana por mi Raza and then goes on to theorize about the role of these collections in the women's lives and living spaces:

> More than simply archives, these collections suggest modes of critical documentation and memory that bridge multiple polarities. Constituted through both practice and theory, they are intensely personal but also invested in collective transformation. While they carefully document the past, they are also deeply engaged with the present and even the future. And while they represent the traces of a particular intellectual and political development, they are also an active and disruptive space of collective remembrance and identity formation. If my years of labor in the libraries, offices, and garages of Chicana feminists have taught me anything, it is that these practices of collecting and remembrance are a central feature of Chicana feminist thought, and yet they remain largely unexplored in the historiography of the social movement era.[38]

By highlighting the way collections become "bridge[s]" through the women's actions, Cotera outlines the "collective" nature of these personal collections, and how the women critically document their work within a larger movement. Even though the bulk of the materials that the women hold in these spaces are often decades old, Cotera posits that such collections are "active and disruptive space[s]" that "are also deeply engaged with the present and even the future." The movements for social justice that these women were involved in continue to be relevant today. Moreover, there is a power inherent in such spaces that Cotera and her collaborators feel as they process each woman's materials,[39] and which the women themselves access through building, preserving, and actively sitting with their collections.

Such personal collections sustain the women who keep them active in their dwellings, as both scholars and activists involved in these kinds of collections have noted. For example, Celia Herrera Rodríguez, who curated artwork for inclusion in the third edition of *This Bridge* (2001), wrote about this subject in her essay published in that edition: "Although some of us read the books written by women of color in rooms covered with images produced by women of color, our words and images, have been distanced from each other conceptually and historically."[40] Herrera Rodríguez's words indicate the need for collaborative archival projects associated with women of color activism that bridge the "distance" and bring the "words and images" back together—projects such as *This Bridge*. She also acknowledges that such spaces, like archives, that bring these materials together—though rare—are vital to making movement history legible, since they reveal the connective bridges between activists and artworks that may not be visible outside these "rooms." As Herrera Rodríguez notes of the artworks that she chose to include in the third edition of *This Bridge*, "the majority of these images cannot be found in art history books, they are absent from the classroom, library, and museum."[41] Similarly, Cotera sees her Chicana por mi Raza project as important given "the relative invisibility of Chicanas in institutional archives."[42] As Cotera notes, the archives needs to be reimagined "not as a static repository but as an active site of knowledge production," further underlining how archives can serve as bridges wherein the collected materials remain active.[43]

Anzaldúa's archives—and her images in particular—depict how collected materials can remain active and act as bridges that will continually facilitate community. Today, as noted above, Anzaldúa's archives are part of an institutional archives at the Nettie Lee Benson Latin American Collection at the University of Texas at Austin. These archives, as a whole, document her commitment to collectivity. Her collaboration with an expansive community of individuals—and how she was influenced by these associations—is evident across her archives in her twenty-six boxes of correspondence, nine boxes of audio recordings of others' talks and tarot readings, and fifty-plus boxes of clippings that make evident the many fields and women of color who touched her work. Together, these elements focusing on her collaborations and collective work outnumber the seventy-three boxes devoted to Anzaldúa's own notably voluminous output of writings and published texts, which underscores the centrality and importance of community to her work. Moreover, as mentioned above, most of her writing projects were collaborative endeavors, and she built additional collective projects into their frameworks, as her archives bear out.

Further, Anzaldúa's drawings illustrate another kind of collectivity in the archives, as they indicate moments where her ideas engaged external publics more directly than in her written texts. Images exist all across Anzaldúa's papers as they are archived as part of the Benson Collection. There are also parts of the collection where images congregate, like the transparencies, which provide another map into Anzaldúa's intellectual work as a whole. Over one hundred transparencies are archived across seven folders. Most of these are not linked to any particular event, and video recordings of her talks saved in her archives indicate that she would reuse and rework these transparencies at will, shuffling them into new orders depending on the talk given. Her repeated repurposing of images echoes her visual style based on repetitions of imagery and line, and these modes parallel her connection to her material and to the community hailed by the work. Unlike other materials in her archives, the collective nature of the images is not always immediately apparent.

But tracing the way Anzaldúa evolved her use of images across her career—particularly the way she moved them from private use in early classroom notes to their public use in her talks—helps reveal how these images played a crucial role in her community-building work. In her early classroom notes, she was not only fine-tuning her visual style, but also formulating how images could embody complex concepts and prefiguring her later textual and visual theorizing. One particularly useful example of this is the way she visualizes her concept of mestiza identity. This conceptualization, which she articulated in *"La conciencia de la mestiza / Towards a New Consciousness"* (the final prose chapter of *Borderlands /*

La Frontera), is one of the theories that she is most known for, and the chapter itself "remains to this day her most anthologized and most widely read piece."[44] As Keating succinctly puts it, "For Anzaldúa, 'new mestizas' are people who inhabit multiple worlds because of their gender, sexuality, color, class, body, personality, spiritual beliefs, and/or other life experiences."[45] Because Anzaldúa uses this idea in her writing to describe her own and others' experiences, we can trace how she wielded this concept to connect people together and build coalition, particularly through her visual work.[46]

Prefiguring the Mestiza in Anzaldúa's Early Classroom Notes

In 1974, Anzaldúa set herself on her career path when she began her doctoral studies in comparative literature at the University of Texas at Austin. Even though this decision meant she set aside prior training as a visual artist to prioritize her writing,[47] that visual way of thinking stuck with her—as Bowen says of her writing process, "One strategy [Anzaldúa] uses is not to think, but to draw. After the work has been created, she analyzes the image and applies terms to these experiences. If the terms do not exist in theoretical language, she adopts new words to help explain these experiences."[48] Her course notes from graduate school encapsulate how images often served as starting or pivot points as she drew images to build bridges from other thinkers to her ideas and to position her perspectives in relationship to theirs.

We see this visual work particularly in notes for two courses she taught and took in the 1976–77 academic year: "La Mujer Chicana," a course she taught in the Fall 1976 semester, and "Gay Fiction: East and West," a graduate seminar she took with Roy E. Teele in the Spring 1977 semester. Though visual moments do occupy the marginalia of notes for other courses, they are not as prolific as in these two instances, where the course material so formatively speaks to issues that will later become the core of Anzaldúa's theorizing. In various interviews over the years, Anzaldúa identified both of these courses as foundational to her development as a thinker: "I was . . . teaching . . . the Mujer Chicana course, and taking some courses. One of which was Homosexuality East and West, and there is where I started including a wide variety of cultures.

I started trying to find other women besides Chicanas who were interested in social justice for women and who were articulating points of view that were missing from the movement at the time."[49] In analyzing the visual production from both of these courses, I focus on how Anzaldúa juxtaposes course content with drawings of women. Her drawings of the female form, including explicitly Chicana women, prefigure her later theorizations of mestiza consciousness. These private drawings help her find the space in discourse that she will soon fill with her words inspired by such drawings. These formative early drawings set the stage for her later writing and stylistically echo her public visual praxis connected to that work.

As much as "La Mujer Chicana" and "Gay Fiction: East and West" courses were foundational for Anzaldúa and her later work, long-simmering tensions over her proposed course of study would prompt her to leave the program in the summer of 1977, having just completed these courses and all the requirements aside from her dissertation.[50] She wrote about this experience in *Borderlands* when she outlined her repeated attempts to incorporate Chicano literature into her research and teaching: "In graduate school, while working toward a Ph.D., I had to 'argue' with one advisor after the other, semester after semester, before I was allowed to make Chicano literature an area of focus."[51] In various interviews, she was even more candid about the multifaceted nature of the discrimination she faced: "I wanted to make feminism and women's studies [a] focus for the studies and for my dissertation. I was told no, I could not do that because it wasn't a legitimate area of study. At the same time, I wanted Chicano literature to be my focus, and I got the same thing, that it wasn't a legitimate literature. The third focus was Spanish literature and they okayed that."[52] In both of these anecdotes, Anzaldúa articulates how these continuing refusals took a toll through invalidating both her course of study as well as her own experiences.

While the two courses represented an outlet where Anzaldúa could examine some of these dismissed literatures and identities, they remained fraught, limited in their immediate impact since she was unable to further pursue these lines of inquiry in her dissertation research to complete her degree at the institution. In fact, UT Austin eventually removed "La Mujer Chicana" from the curriculum, an unrelated decision that further reinforced the unwelcome environment.[53] Still, looking back at these two courses and the visual work that Anzaldúa creates in them demonstrates their importance to her developing line of written thought and visual theorizing.

When Anzaldúa taught "La Mujer Chicana" in 1976, it linked her to other Chicana scholars and activists and deepened her understanding of her own work and identity. She was not the first person to teach the course, having taken it in a prior semester from Inés Hernández-Tovar (now Hernández-Ávila), a fellow scholar completing her PhD at the University of Houston, who served as a "mentor but also [a] colleague because we were helping each other."[54] In her iteration of the course, Anzaldúa brought in guest speakers from the feminist community, including Martha Cotera, and revised the syllabus to include homosexuality as a topic, facilitating the study of Chicana lesbians like herself.[55] Anzaldúa has called teaching this class "a turning point, because it connected [her] to [her] culture and to being queer, to the writing, and to the feminism."[56]

Her lecture notes that she kept and that are now preserved in the archives reflect this sense of purpose. Drawings are prominent throughout her notes, trading off with blocks of text in their placement across the center of the page. That is, these images are not marginal afterthoughts, but share space and pair with the text in communicating course content. Some of these sketches operate as visual schemata to explain individual concepts and could be replicated by Anzaldúa on a classroom chalkboard. Other, more detailed drawings synthesize course material and convey in their expressive renderings the subject matter's stakes.

In one of these images from her September 16, 1976, class session early in the semester, Anzaldúa anticipates mestiza consciousness in her drawing of a Chicana woman that occupies over half of the page (Figure 4.1).[57] This simply sketched woman tilts her head upward, her eyes shut tight as her open mouth expresses an emotional response, echoed by the gesture of her hands clasped to her heart. This drawing, which Anzaldúa captions, "Xicana Grito after Munch's 'The Scream' 9-16-1976," acts as a visual culmination of the sentiments that she's written in textual notes above the screaming figure. All of these notes, text and image alike, are done in neon pink pen, adding another layer of intensity, especially given that her notes for this class and others were most often in blue or black ink. Within a block of notes titled "Regeneración," Anzaldúa writes, "Woman has to liberate herself can't blame outside force anymore.

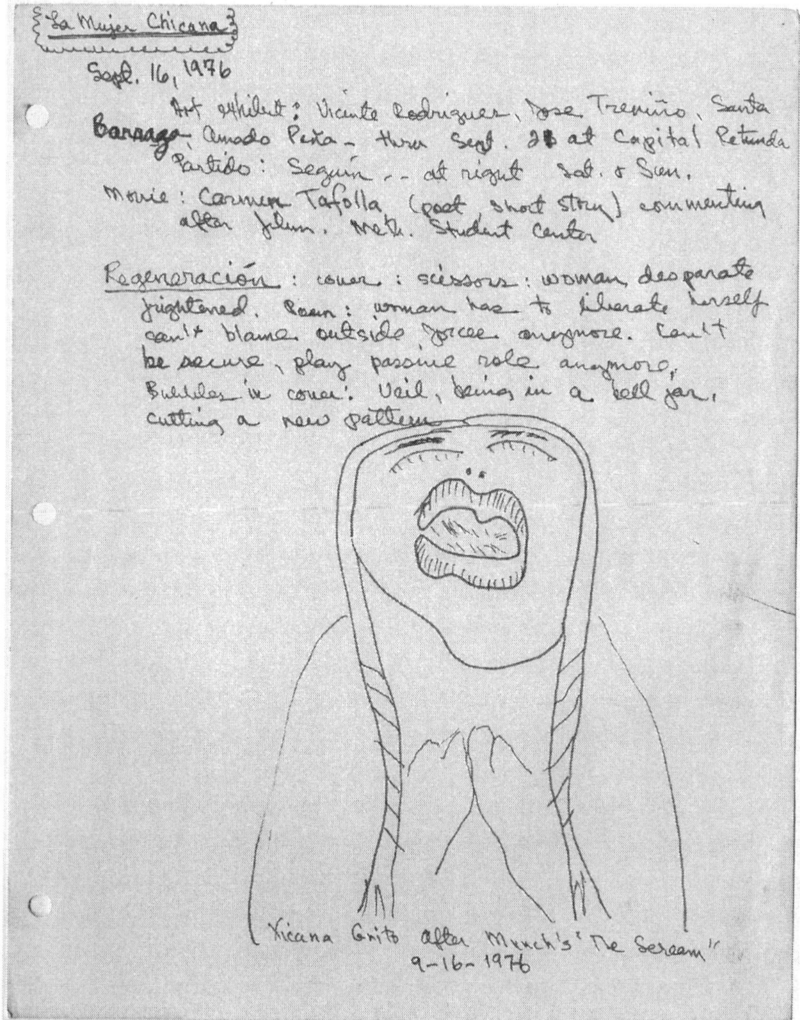

Figure 4.1. Gloria Anzaldúa's September 16, 1976, lecture notes for her "La Mujer Chicana" course where, under textual notes, she drew an image of a woman screaming from her heart and titled it "Xicana Grito after Munch's 'The Scream' 9-16-1976." Box 104, Folder 2, Collection on Gloria Evangelina Anzaldúa, Nettie Lee Benson Latin American Collection, University of Texas Libraries, The University of Texas at Austin. Copyright by the Gloria E. Anzaldúa Literary Trust. Benson Latin American Collection. University of Texas Libraries. By permission of Stuart Bernstein Representation for Artists, New York, and protected by the Copyright Laws of the United States. All rights reserved. The printing, copying, redistribution, or retransmission of this Content without express permission is prohibited.

Can't be secure, play passive role anymore." Both of these fragmentary statements end with the temporal marker "anymore," implying a coming change that's long overdue, underlined by the repetition of "anymore." At the boiling point of "anymore," the only possible response is a big one, letting loose a visceral scream that's been building inside. The sheer size of the drawing, which abuts and eclipses the text, makes this point especially well.

The deliberate caption adds another layer of meaning to the drawing, particularly given that she doesn't often caption her drawings. Her title suggests a way to read the image, as inspired by and paying homage to Edvard Munch's iconic and ceaselessly parodied painting *The Scream* (1893). Like Munch's painting, this woman is stylistically simple yet terrifically expressive, but she departs from Munch's figure in her posture, with hands clasped to the breast rather than to the sides of one's face, suggesting that the pain expressed emanates from the core of one's being. In identifying her drawing as a Chicana woman, Anzaldúa particularizes her, insisting on the importance of her individual experience through linking her to this universally known piece of art.

Moreover, the fact that Anzaldúa dated her drawing identifies it as a moment of catharsis happening right then on the page and in the classroom. The course provided the space for this emotional release. We can imagine how for Anzaldúa, in addition to the general conditions that provoked this outcry, her own experiences and frustrations with her doctoral program animated this Xicana. While she and her students could spend this semester studying Chicana experiences together, she was not allowed to pursue this line of research further at the university. The fact that she was compelled to make this drawing, and to preserve it in her notes, points to the way her drawings took on an important role in the development of her thought, and how visual work like this, which is strongly represented in her archives, would continue to underpin the theoretical explorations in her research and community development work for years to come. Just as the drawing refuses to remain silent and yells out from the space of the page about her life as a Chicana woman, so, too, would Anzaldúa carve out the space for herself and other women of color to relate their experiences in *This Bridge* and later theorize mestiza consciousness in *Borderlands / La Frontera,* her landmark monograph.

Another important early example of the way Anzaldúa used visual material as a central tool for expanding her ideas that would lead to future groundbreaking collaborative work are the drawings she created as she worked through the "Gay Fiction: East and West" graduate seminar. She had begun reading about lesbianism prior to graduate school in the writings of white feminists, but this course allowed her to expand the scope of this study and importantly build on the research she had done the semester prior in examining homosexuality in her "La Mujer Chicana" course with her students.[58] During this class she made a number of drawings in her notes, but many of her drawings respond to the course material less directly. Like her drawings in her lecture notes for "La Mujer Chicana," they remain central on the page, proving that they are not marginal embellishments but occupy the same plane as the course content. Many of these images are geometric and non-figural with a heavy use of spirals and parallel, radiating lines. These detailed images make clear that Anzaldúa spent a lot of time with each drawing, embedding her reaction to the course content in the time that she took to render each image during the seminar alongside the textual notes she took. When her drawings do take bodily form, they're overwhelmingly women, such that she's simultaneously investigating herself and the object of her desire in this context. Though she does not mark these drawings explicitly as Chicana, her aesthetic approach echoes that of "La Mujer Chicana" drawings and foreshadows how she will represent the bodily entanglements of mestiza identity in her future drawings for a public audience.

During that semester, for example, Anzaldúa made a drawing on a page of her class notes that would forecast the bodily actions and engagements she will later theorize as part of mestiza consciousness. On this page of notes from late February 1977, her drawing takes up nearly the whole page, aside from a single line of notes: "Movement statement:—Last wk. March Morgan—Rich" (Figure 4.2).[59] What we see here instead of a movement statement is a movement *image*: a mostly full-length, fantastical female figure, rendered in Anzaldúa's expressive streamlined hand. Three upward-tilted lines convey the expression of the face as a closed-eye smile. This simply rendered visage is accompanied by a bodily outline drawn in an almost unbroken line, with breasts and vulva marked out on the nude form. This woman, with radiating, halo-connoting lines for hair, takes action, dropping stars into a pail on a table with her right

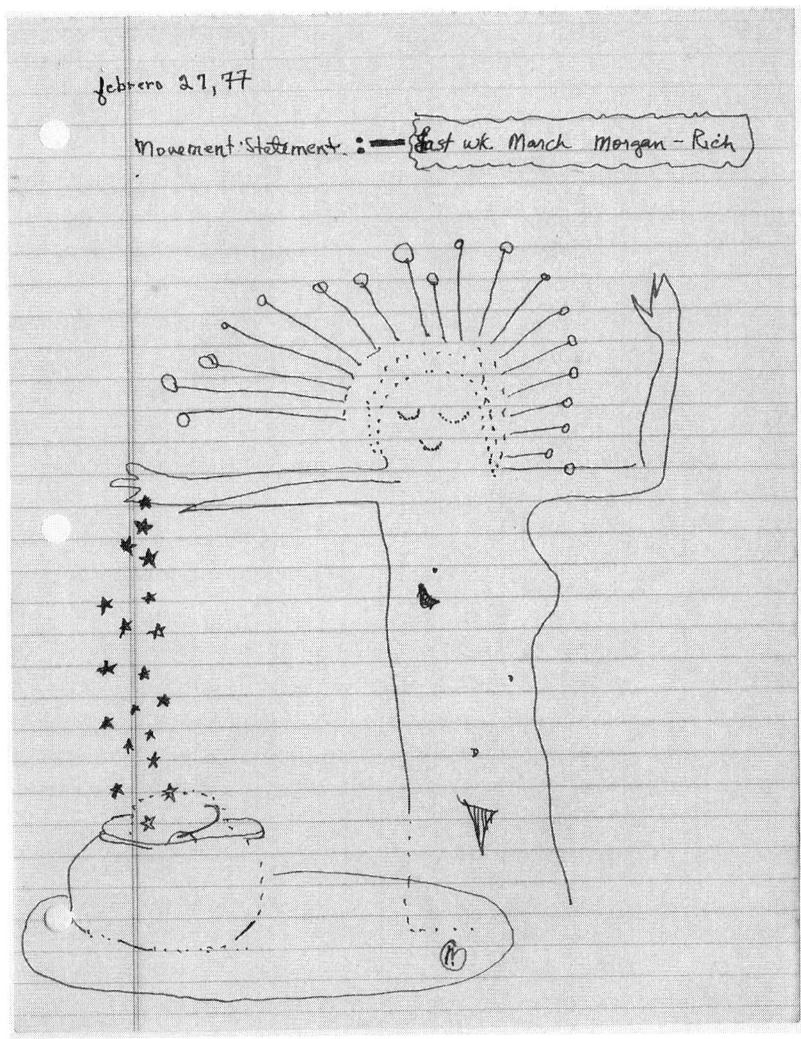

Figure 4.2. Gloria Anzaldúa's February 27, 1977, notes for Dr. Roy E. Teele's "Gay Fiction: East and West" graduate seminar where she drew an image of a radiant, fantastical woman who occupies most of the page. Box 230, Folder 6, Collection on Gloria Evangelina Anzaldúa, Nettie Lee Benson Latin American Collection, University of Texas Libraries, The University of Texas at Austin. Copyright by the Gloria E. Anzaldúa Literary Trust. Benson Latin American Collection. University of Texas Libraries. By permission of Stuart Bernstein Representation for Artists, New York, and protected by the Copyright Laws of the United States. All rights reserved. The printing, copying, redistribution, or retransmission of this Content without express permission is prohibited.

hand while her left hand is raised in blissful solidarity. This latter gesture evokes the feminist fist, which was emblazoned on the cover of *Sisterhood Is Powerful* (1970), Robin Morgan's feminist anthology, and is often associated with this earlier moment of women's liberation. Adrienne Rich, a celebrated poet, also represented the then-present of the feminist movement as she began to produce and publish explicitly feminist work in the late 1960s and early 1970s, including in pieces reprinted in the 1979 *On Lies, Secrets, and Silence* collection of essays.[60] Thus "Morgan—Rich" identifies an era of feminist organizing through the work of two white women, disregarding the vital work of many women of color in the same period.

This enigmatic woman responds by engaging in transcendent, mystical action. She takes up most of the page to make visible her body and her new action. This embodied response anticipates how Anzaldúa will later delineate in text and image that mestizas negotiate their positioning in multiple cultures through their bodies. Moreover, the spiritual feeling of the drawing underlines how Anzaldúa embraced mysticism as a vital facet of mestiza consciousness that played a role in social justice activism.[61] In drawing this movement image that juxtaposes with the white 1970s feminism that Anzaldúa engages in this course, she visualizes a new path forward that she will soon manifest with her efforts to amplify the voices of women of color in feminist discourses across the 1980s.

A few weeks later, in early March, Anzaldúa turned her attention to visualizing the psyche, another important component to her later theorizing of mestiza consciousness. In a sketch for a class session focused on consciousness, mental labor, and ideology, Anzaldúa focuses in on women's consciousness and visually interprets the subject matter by drawing a woman's head staked on top of a box and surrounded by parallel, swirling, geometric lines (Figure 4.3).[62] This closed-eye woman's head is a sparsely brutal figure, even in the absence of any accompanying gore. The multiplicity of lines surrounding this form do not simply radiate out from her but take on and embed spirals and other shapes. All these lines and the amount of space the resulting drawing occupies on the page emphasize the importance and the long reach of the psyche and anticipate later mestiza drawings by Anzaldúa where she overemphasizes the size of the head to show how many cultural positions and identities fill the mestiza's thoughts and form. Again, as with her other drawing for

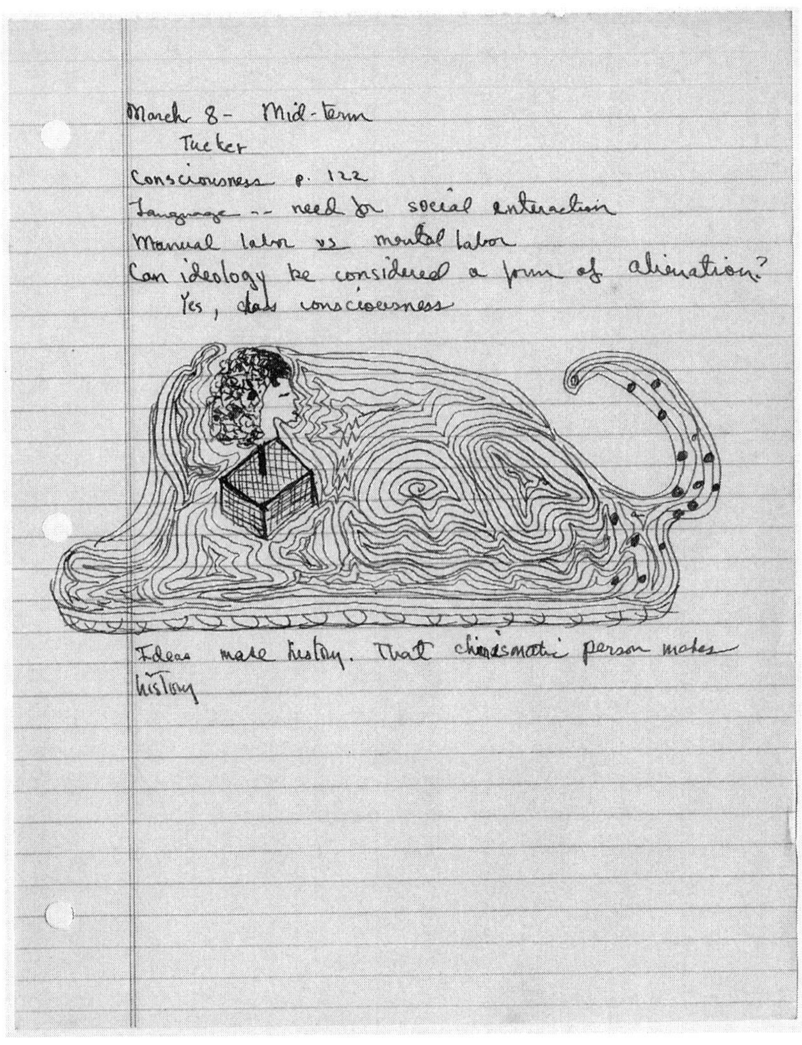

Figure 4.3. Gloria Anzaldúa's March 8, 1977, notes for Dr. Roy E. Teele's "Gay Fiction: East and West" graduate seminar where she drew a women's head staked on a box and surrounded by sets of wavy lines amid textual notes about consciousness. Box 230, Folder 6, Collection on Gloria Evangelina Anzaldúa, Nettie Lee Benson Latin American Collection, University of Texas Libraries, The University of Texas at Austin. Copyright by the Gloria E. Anzaldúa Literary Trust. Benson Latin American Collection. University of Texas Libraries. By permission of Stuart Bernstein Representation for Artists, New York, and protected by the Copyright Laws of the United States. All rights reserved. The printing, copying, redistribution, or retransmission of this Content without express permission is prohibited.

this course, the text surrounding this composition is minimal, suggesting that much of the session's content captured on this page has been encoded in this image. These radiating lines make visible how much is carried along with the psyche that remains invisible in real space.

These early experiences at the University of Texas at Austin set the stage for Anzaldúa's career, as the roadblocks she encountered there reshaped her work and career trajectory. After her departure from UT Austin in the summer of 1977, Anzaldúa pursued the kind of critical work that she was not allowed to research in her studies, including creating space for more women of color to write about their experiences. Following a writing workshop in February 1979 in which she was the only woman of color, Anzaldúa decided to put together a collection of new writings by women of color and invited Cherríe Moraga to collaborate with her. They sent out the initial call for what would become *This Bridge* in late April 1979. As alluded to above, the immediate success of *This Bridge* upon its publication in 1981 laid the foundation for Anzaldúa's future work, including her monograph *Borderlands / La Frontera*, which was also widely celebrated upon its release in 1987 and remains a critical touchstone she would return to as she continued to develop her theories over the course of her career. It is important to underline here how she intentionally completed this work outside the academic structures that had spurned her along with this subject matter. It would not be until after these two publications and a full decade following her departure from UT Austin that she would resume graduate studies at another institution, when she began study in the literature program at the University of California, Santa Cruz, in 1988.

Still, we can see in her evolving visual praxis how these early courses where she did encounter support shaped her career. She began to develop her theories in relationship to the writing of others in these classes and to sketch out visualizations for theories she would later articulate in her own writing. She was able to start to visualize who the mestiza was, what her experiences were, and how she related to the world around her. In both style and substance, these early drawings anticipate her later drawings that she used in public talks to visualize her own concepts. As much as her early drawings allowed her the space to be in conversation with other thinkers, her later drawings facilitate that relationship for her audience.

In a way, her drawing practice embodies her idea of la facultad that she outlined in *Borderlands / La Frontera*: "*La facultad* is the capacity to see in surface phenomena the meaning of deeper realities, to see the deep structure below the surface. It is an instant 'sensing,' a quick perception arrived at without conscious reasoning. It is an acute awareness mediated by the part of the psyche that does not speak, that communicates in images and symbols which are the faces of feelings, that is, behind which feelings reside/hide. The one possessing this sensitivity is excruciatingly alive to the world."[63] As a whole, this definition echoes how her drawings respond to and synthesize course content to pierce through "surface phenomena" and grasp at larger questions. As Anzaldúa delineates, la facultad can manifest in many ways, but her early drawings epitomize how one of the ways "that [it] communicates [is] in images and symbols." A couple of paragraphs later, Anzaldúa posits that la facultad is "a kind of survival tactic that people, caught between the worlds, unknowingly cultivate," which marks this ability as one that mestizas wield to navigate the world and a tactic that can then be used to understand their experience.[64] These drawings and others provide Anzaldúa access to this "deeper" knowledge and ultimately act as a starting point for her own theorizations, as Bowen notes in her description of Anzaldúa's writing process that begins this section.

Due to this deep and integral relationship to images as an access point to la facultad, it makes sense that Anzaldúa would employ drawings to communicate her own ideas to public audiences and encourage them to develop their own relationship to la facultad and their own internal visualizations. In the following section, I discuss how Anzaldúa used a wealth of drawings in public talks to visualize the different components of mestiza consciousness for her audience, linking her drawings back to her textual theorizations in *Borderlands / La Frontera*. In this way, these undated drawings also reveal how she continued to evolve ideas about mestiza identity and develop related concepts across the course of her career.

Making the Mestiza Transparencies for Public Talks

The previous chapters of this book showed the crucial ways that women artists produced visual material within grassroots communities that anticipated and shaped the future direction of feminist discourse in the final decades of the twentieth century. Anzaldúa's use of visual materials in her public talks provide another important example of this, as they were part of her career-long commitment to build new networks and forms for women of color, the impact of which has been acknowledged in the proliferation of scholarship assessing Anzaldúa's theoretical importance to feminist theory and other discourses. The archives make plain Anzaldúa's commitment through the documentation of her frequent public speaking, which shows up all over her papers. She kept extensive documentation and notes relating to her "gigs," as she called them, including a number of video recordings of some of her talks. Most valuable, perhaps, is that she kept the drawings that she did for her talks from the mid-1990s forward. More than anything written, these drawings provided the backbone for her speaking engagements. These works, created with multicolored dry-erase markers on transparencies, could be erased by a mere spritz of cleaning solution. The preservation of such ephemeral materials is made even more striking by the fact that Anzaldúa created and kept over one hundred of these drawings, which are stacked, one on top of the other, across seven folders in her archives. With every folder you open, you peer through an entire stack of drawings, gazing through coalesced constellations of concepts. The drawings show how she evolved her foundational and famous ideas, like mestiza consciousness, from their early articulations to connect with new ideas that she developed in the following decades. Her meticulous documentation demonstrates how central her talks were to her career—providing both financial and intellectual support for Anzaldúa, who developed her thinking in, with, and through dialogue with public audiences.

A photo of Anzaldúa in front of a chalkboard filled with her drawings depicts how she would use a profusion of images to illustrate her concepts (Figure 4.4).[65] Through a series of juxtaposed, diagrammatic images, we can see Anzaldúa depicting various types of struggles that people of color endure. Behind Anzaldúa on the board, we see shapes contrasting the roles of subject and object, people of color enclosed within the white frame of reference that contains mis/disinformation, and an outline of a body laid out and bisected, as if for study. This photograph, which is filed amid Anzaldúa's correspondence with the reputed lesbian feminist journal *Sinister Wisdom,* was published in *Sinister Wisdom* #56 (1995) in an issue focused on language. Lesbian photographer Cathy Cade, who

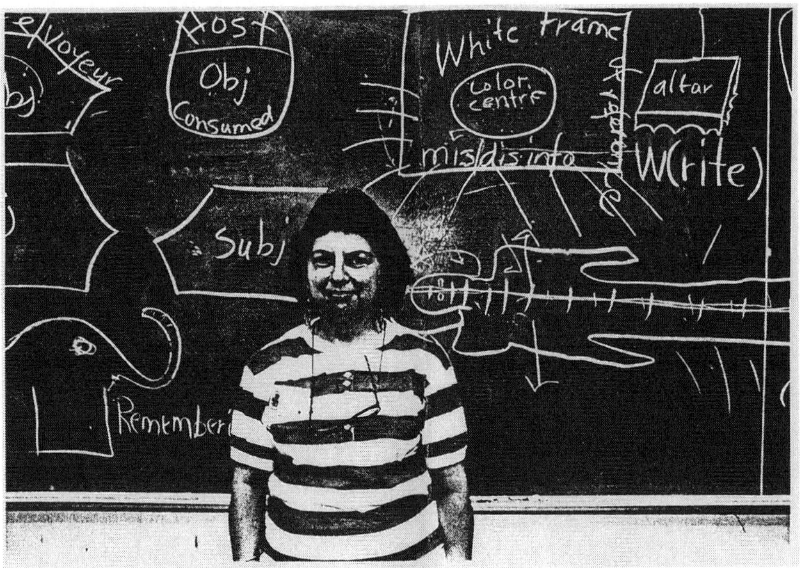

Figure 4.4. Cathy Cade's photograph "Gloria Anzaldúa in Front of Her Drawings Presenting Her Book: *Borderlands* at the Montréal Feminist Book Fair, 1988," which shows Anzaldúa in front of a chalkboard of drawings she made for a public talk. Cathy Cade photograph archive, BANC PIC 2012.054—PIC, box 1:2. Copyright by the Regents of the University of California, the Bancroft Library, University of California, Berkeley. Box 20, Folder 11, Collection on Gloria Evangelina Anzaldúa, Nettie Lee Benson Latin American Collection, University of Texas Libraries, The University of Texas at Austin.

took the photo, composed a caption and paragraph to appear with the photograph in print. Her caption identifies the presentation as one that Anzaldúa gave about *Borderlands / La Frontera* at the Montréal Feminist Book Fair in 1988. Cade's paragraph under the caption reflects on the power of Anzaldúa's multimodal way of presenting: "Writers who read their work aloud know the issue of translating the written word into the spoken word. To get a book of photographs published, I must translate the photographs into words so word-people feel comfortable. Imagine my great pleasure experiencing Gloria Anzaldúa presenting her book *Borderlands*—in which the issue of multiple languages is central—by talking, reading and drawing about the concepts in her book. With great energy, Gloria treated the audience to spoken words, printed page, and images as a continuous revelation."[66] Cade's reflection on how Anzaldúa presented her work through both verbal and visual language connects this practice to her own as a photographer who created books like *A Lesbian Photo Album: The Lives of Seven Lesbian Feminists* (1987) where text appeared alongside photos and provided an overarching narrative frame for the images. Cade sees this multipronged approach as echoing the hybrid nature of *Borderlands / La Frontera* itself and describes this experience delivered "with great energy" by Anzaldúa "as a continuous revelation," underlining this dynamic presentation as an active transmission from Anzaldúa to the audience.

As much as these images speak to concerns present in *Borderlands / La Frontera*, they more directly illustrate the ideas in an essay Anzaldúa published in *Sinister Wisdom* #33 (1987) around the same time the photo was taken, which was later reprinted in her anthology *Making Face, Making Soul / Haciendo Caras*.[67] In the middle of the piece, in a section titled "Breaking Out of the Frame," Anzaldúa observes, "Even those of us who don't want to buy in get sucked into the vortex of the dominant culture's fixed oppositions, the duality of superiority and inferiority, of subject and object. Some of us, to get out of the internalized neocolonial phase, make for the fringes, the Borderlands. And though we have not broken out of the white frame, we at least see it for what it is."[68] In this passage, Anzaldúa describes how the binary values of white, "dominant culture" have a negative impact on people of color, who struggle not to "internalize" these false and "fixed oppositions." The labels on her chalkboard drawings echo the language of the passage in visualizing the split between "subject and object" and how the "white frame" traps people of color. The drawings also go even further to visualize the impact of these pressures through her image of the bisected body, which is divided horizontally into many slices by perpendicular hash marks and torn open by arrows on either side of the chest cavity, as if to extract the heart. This body initially appears fixed in one place by the pervasive Lilliputian microaggressions of white culture. In the passage, Anzaldúa describes how "some of us" can escape and "make for the fringes, the Borderlands," and she visualized that action on the chalkboard by the lines radiating out from both the body and the nearby white frame of reference. Putting this photograph back into conversation with her published writing shows how her method of filling the board with many conceptual drawings, which she annotates as she talks, allows her to connect various ideas together.

She would continue to use this same presentation method and drawing style throughout her career, though her presentation tools shifted, as shown by the video recordings of her talks and as corroborated by Anzaldúa in various interviews.[69] Throughout the 1980s and into the early 1990s, Anzaldúa presented her work with chalkboard drawings. Then, in the mid-1990s, she switched to using a projector to show her drawings on transparencies. In a video recording from the year before her death, she was still using the transparency drawings, but they had been digitized into PowerPoint slides. Across all these presentation formats, Anzaldúa moved through many drawings in the course of a talk. When discussing the use of these images during her talks, Anzaldúa would tell the audience that the visuals' purpose was to help audiences remember the ideas afterward. In an interview from the early 1990s where Anzaldúa speaks about how she connects with and teaches others through her work, she posits, "My role is that of teacher, healer, translator, mediator. That's my job as a writer. People look to me for images, for ideas. They take these ideas, think about and expand on them. They think of me as a model."[70] Key here is how she equates "images" and "ideas" as what others "look to" her for. In her talks, not only does she herself serve "as a model," but the images themselves also play this role. Their streamlined simplicity made her ideas accessible to her audience, so that these ideas could be transported into their lives. In this way, Anzaldúa's adoption of the visual register echoes that of the other artists in this book, who worked to synthesize complex concepts and make them broadly accessible through visual frameworks.

Her drawings of mestiza identity work as models on multiple registers. The mestiza, a person who occupies multiple identity (race, class, etc.) categories, inhabits these many positions, and this multiplicity becomes the focus of Anzaldúa's renderings as she speaks to her own experience and awakens the audience to their own hybrid identities. Roughly a dozen of her transparencies reference mestiza identity and related concepts, and she would sometimes use multiple of these mestiza transparencies in a single talk to further underline the many ways this multiplicity manifested. In my analysis, I include groupings of multiple images to echo how Anzaldúa drew on many images in her talks, and I title each of these images according to prominent words present on the transparency. Patterns of representing mestiza identity emerge through these groupings, and it becomes clear how Anzaldúa connects this concept to other ideas in her larger network of thought.

One of these drawings, which Anzaldúa explicitly references as a "model," works particularly well in introducing both the concept of mestiza identity and also her process of welcoming the audience into her thinking (Figure 4.5).[71] With a bit of humility, Anzaldúa writes to the left of her drawing of the mestiza, "Model—just a representation of how I see reality, a reduction of the real. My fantasy." This piece of metacommentary, which would be the first thing viewers would read if they scanned the image from left to right and from top to bottom, facilitates audience participation. By emphasizing the autobiographical specificity of this image and how it only speaks for "how [she] see[s] reality," Anzaldúa encourages folks to reflect on their own experience while thinking with this "model." Her drawing distills the core elements of mestiza experience, but it isn't meant to be understood as the definitive diagram. Instead, it opens up the visual field to other representations of the hybrid mestiza experience—other people's "fantas[ies]." This text, in maintaining that this is only how Anzaldúa sees, asks her audience how they see and how they might theorize visually. Through her images, text, and presentation, Anzaldúa creates a relationship with her audience that prizes their potential contributions, embodying what feminist rhetoricians call "invitational rhetoric."[72]

Her declaration of this image as only one way of seeing explains why Anzaldúa redraws the mestiza in so many transparencies and why she keeps all these iterations: they open up new ways of seeing this hybrid figure. It takes an accumulation of two-dimensional drawings to embody this concept fully and make it three-dimensional for her audience. At the beginning of her *Borderlands* chapter on mestiza consciousness, Anzaldúa encapsulates many of the facets of mestiza identity in a short, eight-line poem that she expands on across the course of the chapter.[73] She identifies the mestiza by her perpetual motion through "cultures," articulating that experience as both a physical reality and an internal struggle. In the first half of the poem, she describes the mestiza as both walking through and standing in "all cultures at the same time." In the second half, she turns to the mestiza's psyche, depicting how her soul

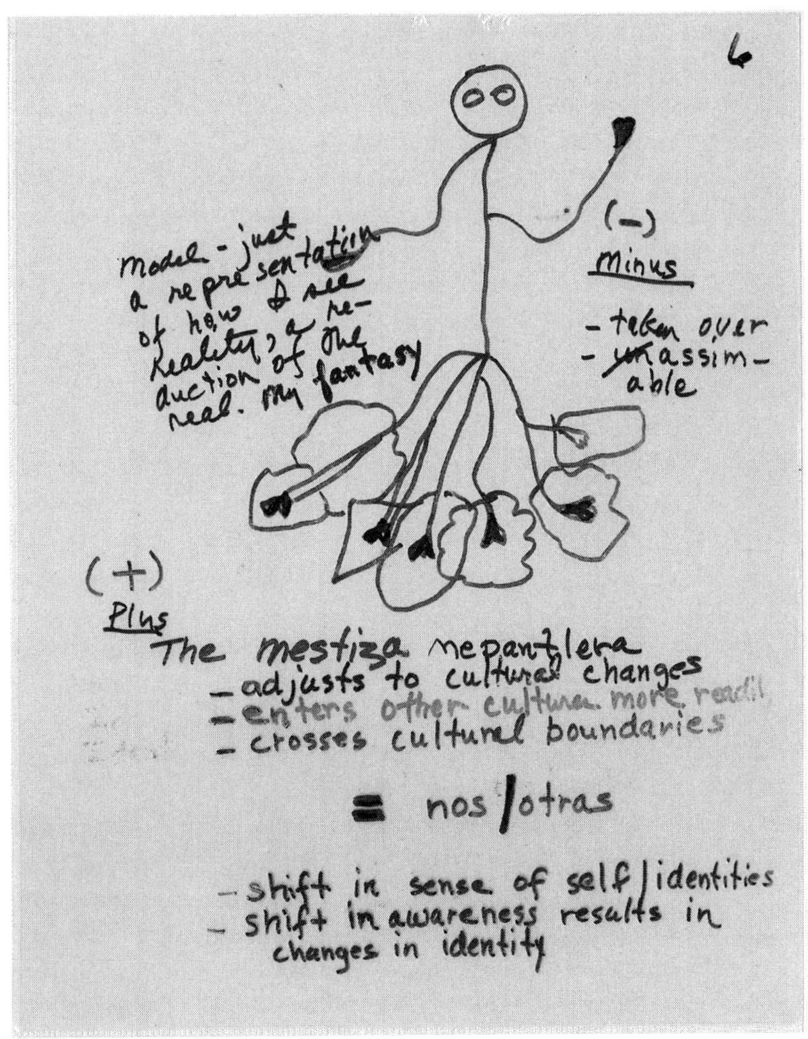

Figure 4.5. Multicolored transparency where Gloria Anzaldúa illustrates a mestiza stick figure with six legs that she annotates as a "model—just a representation of how I see reality." Box 131, Folder 15. Collection on Gloria Evangelina Anzaldúa, Nettie Lee Benson Latin American Collection, University of Texas Libraries, The University of Texas at Austin. Copyright by the Gloria E. Anzaldúa Literary Trust. Benson Latin American Collection. University of Texas Libraries. By permission of Stuart Bernstein Representation for Artists, New York, and protected by the Copyright Laws of the United States. All rights reserved. The printing, copying, redistribution, or retransmission of this Content without express permission is prohibited.

straddles multiple worlds and how she feels disoriented by "*todas las voces*" talking in her head "*simultáneamente.*" The visual language with which Anzaldúa theorizes in her written texts lends itself to these transparencies, which combine images and words together.[74] This particular drawing of the mestiza exemplifies that movement by giving the model six legs with which to navigate these multiple cultures. These multiple legs certainly represent the mestiza in motion, but they also gesture to her mental disorientation through their sheer numerical impossibility. In the other text surrounding her, Anzaldúa details the daily "adjust[ments]" and "shift[s]" that the mestiza has to negotiate because of this positioning "in all cultures." These words act as a postscript to the poem where, in a catalog under the drawing, Anzaldúa prioritizes the positive results that can come through embracing this identity. These positive attributes are ones that Anzaldúa further explores across her chapter in *Borderlands*, as well as throughout her career in the concepts of "nepantlera" and "nos/otras" that she names and associates with the mestiza on this transparency.

Mestiza models in other transparencies visually echo this one by also showing the figure enmeshed in many cultures underfoot (Figure 4.6).[75] In each rendering, Anzaldúa represents the additional sets of enmeshed feet in distinct ways, each of which emphasizes different effects of being positioned in multiple cultures. First, multiple feet of different lengths embedded in overlapping and multicolored shapes create visual chaos, depicting how the mestiza "disrupts neat categories," as Anzaldúa annotates to the right of the composition. By contrast, the body in the next image is orderly, with two feet firmly planted in one space labeled "artista" while other puzzle piece–like shapes fit together around her form, identified in annotations as the "interlocking communities" where she can act as an "activista." Labeled drawings to the right of the mestiza further reflect on the "imagin[ed]" and "[real]" possibilities for how such "communities" will provide support. The mestiza in the third image is the most visually similar to Figure 4.5 with the same green circles for eyes and a profusion of legs growing out of her form, like roots from a tree trunk. Across *Borderlands*, Anzaldúa discusses rootedness in different cultural positions as embodied phenomena, celebrating "where she can plumb the rich ancestral roots" while critiquing where "we were jerked out by the roots, truncated, disemboweled, dispossessed, and

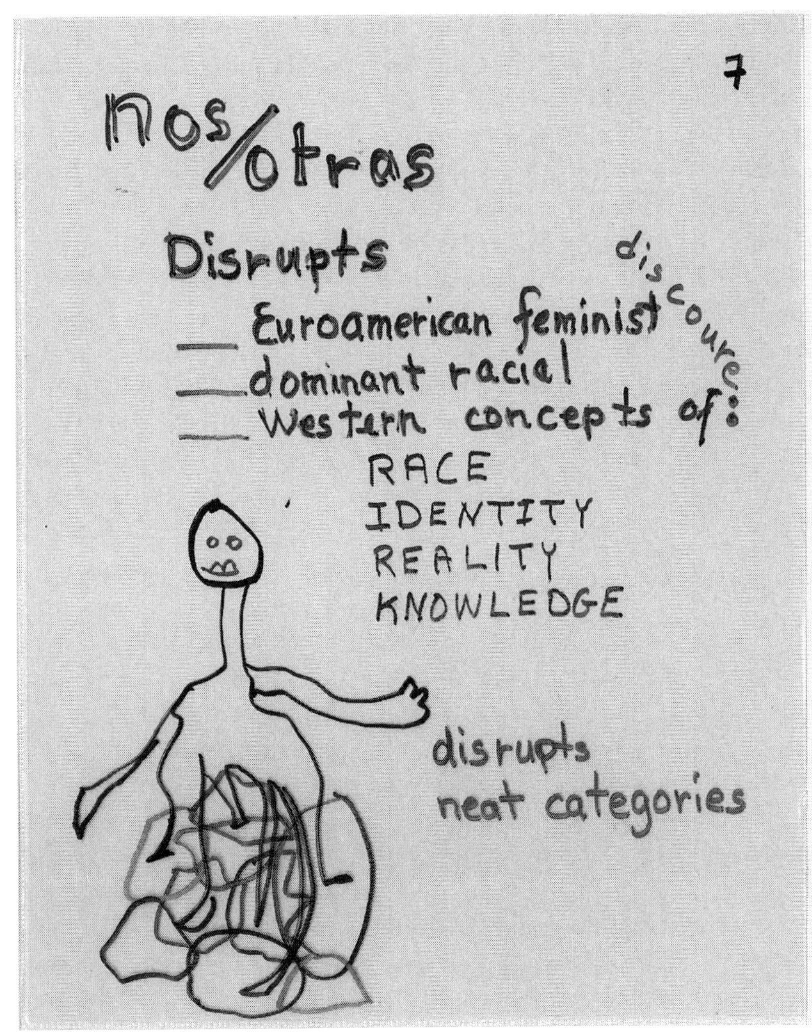

Figure 4.6. Three multicolored transparencies where Gloria Anzaldúa draws a stick figure with her feet in multiple positions and where each of these figures is annotated by surrounding text and drawings. Box 131, Folders 14–15, Collection on Gloria Evangelina Anzaldúa, Nettie Lee Benson Latin American Collection, University of Texas Libraries, The University of Texas at Austin. Copyright by the Gloria E. Anzaldúa Literary Trust. Benson Latin American Collection. University of Texas Libraries. By permission of Stuart Bernstein Representation for Artists, New York, and protected by the Copyright Laws of the United States. All rights reserved. The printing, copying, redistribution, or retransmission of this Content without express permission is prohibited.

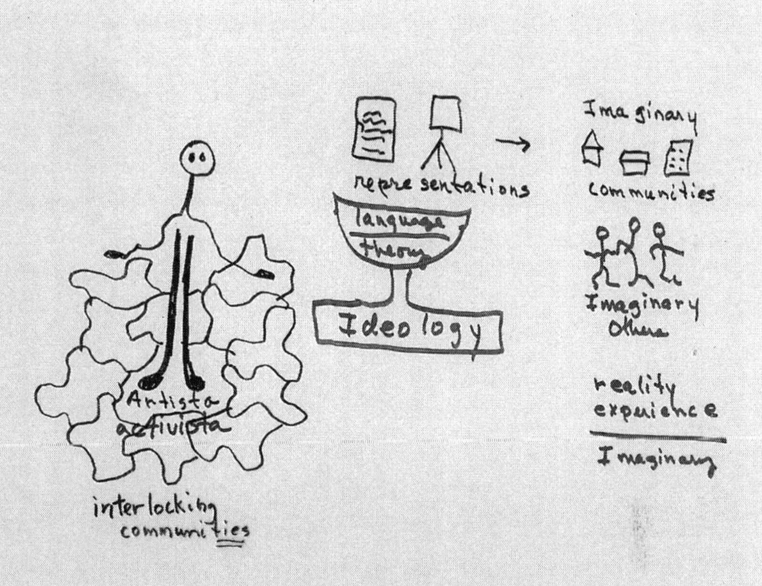

Artista
activista
interlocking
communities
representations
language
theory
Ideology
Imaginary
communities
Imaginary
Others
reality
experience
Imaginary

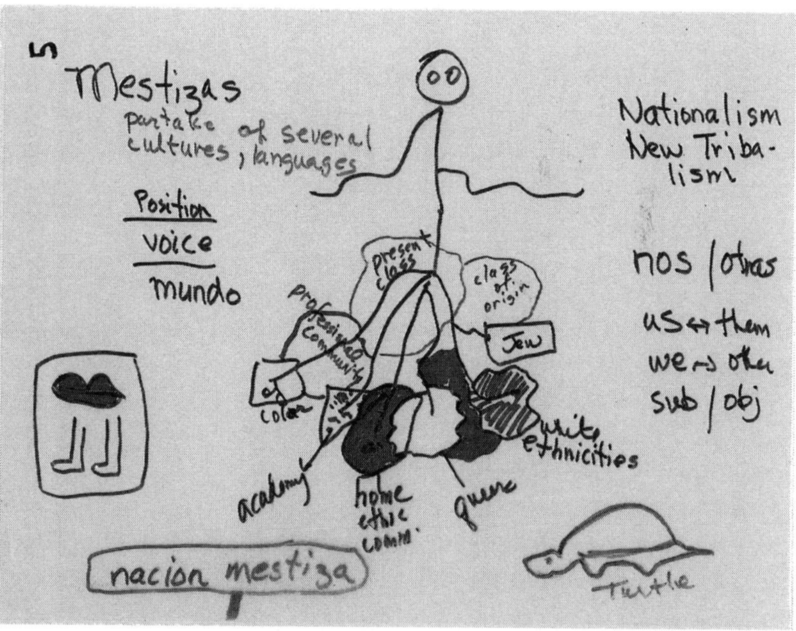

5
Mestizas
partake of several
cultures, languages
Position
voice
mundo
Nationalism
New Triba-
lism
nos / otras
us ↔ them
we ↔ other
sub / obj
present
class
class
of
origin
Jew
professional
Community
color
academy
home
ethic
comm.
queere
white
ethnicities
Turtle
nacion mestiza

separated from our identity and our history."[76] In this representation, Anzaldúa labels the cultural positions that occupy the spaces closing around her feet in different colors: "present class," "class of origin," "Jew," "white ethnicities," "queer," "home/ethnic community," "academy," "of color," "professional community."[77] These are the rooted and uprooting influences that she must navigate as she moves through space. Labeling them more directly demonstrates the complexities inherent in how a mestiza moves through her daily life while negotiating multiple identities. Anzaldúa fills in some of the spaces in solid red, suggesting the taxing energy required by moving through certain identities while broadly gesturing to the unique demands of being situated in any particular identity.

Looking at these three transparencies together with the first gives a sense of Anzaldúa's overall stylistic approach and reveals how small differences in the figure and its framing can emphasize different facets of mestiza identity and the connection of this concept to others. These drawings show how her visual theoretical style developed from her graduate school notes. Unlike those earlier drawings, these are composed with multiple colors and integrate words as part of the drawings. She has also streamlined her drawing of human forms, reducing them to outlines and stick figures. She specifies their identities further by the words that surround them. By simplifying the human forms, she can focus attention on modeling particular aspects of mestiza identity, which we see in these four transparencies through her attention to enmeshed feet. Her deployment of drawings to convey complex theories with striking simplicity underscores the capacity of visual artwork to communicate concisely, suggesting why she and the other artists in this book embodied their core ideas about identity in a visual format that their audiences could take in and viscerally feel as they identified with the body on the page. Whereas earlier artists like Marrs, Gregory, and Bechdel particularized their characters in order to make lesbian and bisexual women visible, Anzaldúa creates her mestizas in a nondescript manner in order to welcome all in to identify accordingly.

As Anzaldúa's opening poem in *Borderlands* details, the mestiza navigates multiple cultures both externally as well as internally in her daily life, and this duality also shows up in her transparencies. In these transparencies (Figure 4.7), Anzaldúa continues to show how the mestiza is standing in many multicolored cultural positions, but that multiplicity is also shown in the proliferation of shapes that occupy the headspace.[78] First, the head is replaced by an interlocking series of six circles, like a knockoff Olympics logo. As she did in labeling the positions underfoot with the third image of Figure 4.6, so does Anzaldúa label the mental positions crowding the mestiza's headspace in the second image of Figure 4.7. This psychological rendering illustrates how all these identities put pressure on personal identity—the "I, mi, yo" nestled near center—and epitomize Anzaldúa's textual representation of this state of affairs in *Borderlands / La Frontera*: "In perceiving conflicting information and points of view, she is subjected to a swamping of her psychological borders. She has discovered that she can't hold concepts or ideas in rigid boundaries."[79] In this drawn depiction, Anzaldúa makes use of ovals in order to demonstrate the mestiza's permeable boundaries. There's a generous oval inscribed for the head, but the labeled identities do not end there; additional identities "[swamp these] psychological borders." A second, larger circle labeled "white frame of reference" encompasses this figure, compressing all of these separate identities and creating strain as the mestiza is forced to take up and embody all these conflicting perspectives. This spatial coalescence in one representative mestiza drawing communicates not only this impossible, hyper-embodied strain, but also the affinities among the marginalized subjectivities named here. In *Borderlands*, Anzaldúa puts these identities together in a catalog where she weighs the psychological implications: "The struggle is inner: Chicano, *indio*, American Indian, *mojado*, *mexicano*, immigrant Latino, Anglo in power, working class Anglo, Black, Asian—our psyches resemble the bordertowns and are populated by the same people. The struggle has always been inner, and is played out in the outer terrains. Awareness of our situation must come before inner changes, which in turn come before changes in society. Nothing happens in the 'real' world unless it first happens in the images in our heads."[80] With this list, Anzaldúa expresses the possibilities of coalition among these identities marginalized by race or class, uniting them under the banner of "our psyches" and a shared "struggle" that begins in the crowded "inner" space. She insists on the close relationship between "inner" and "outer" by exploring the dynamics between these spaces in each of the three following sentences. The inner psyche reflects outward and can make "changes," but slowly. In her transparency,

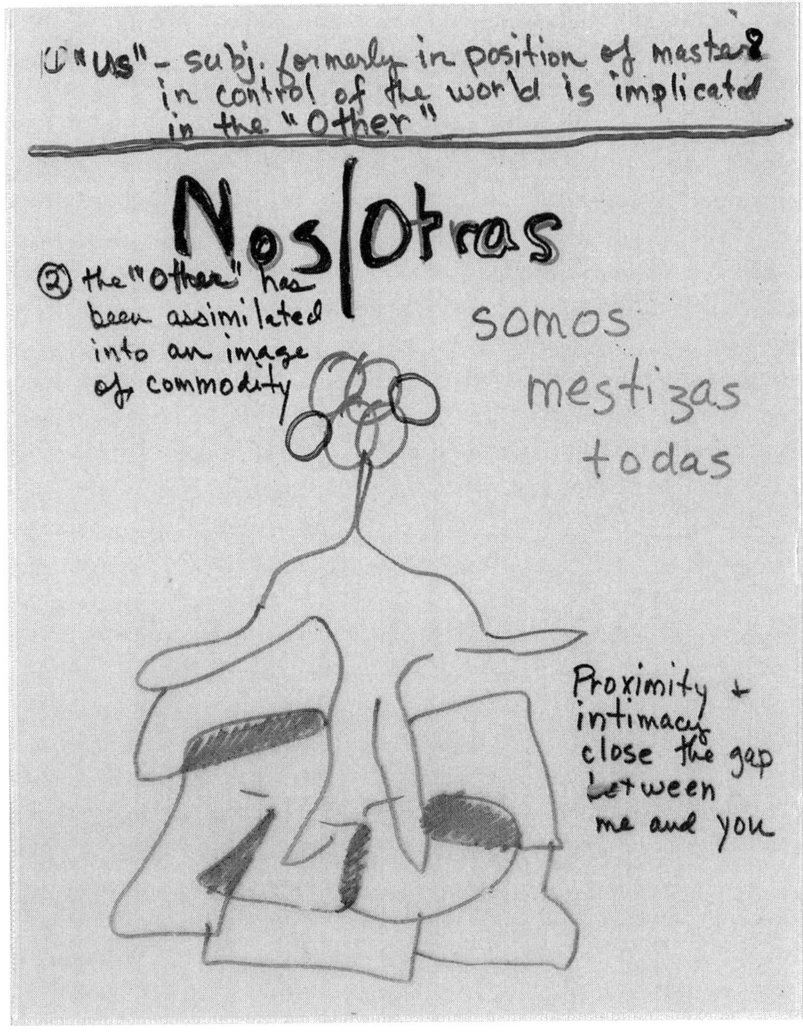

Figure 4.7. Two multicolored transparencies where Gloria Anzaldúa depicts figures with a lot occupying their headspace while their feet continue to traverse multiple positions. Box 131, Folder 15, Collection on Gloria Evangelina Anzaldúa, Nettie Lee Benson Latin American Collection, University of Texas Libraries, The University of Texas at Austin. Copyright by the Gloria E. Anzaldúa Literary Trust. Benson Latin American Collection. University of Texas Libraries. By permission of Stuart Bernstein Representation for Artists, New York, and protected by the Copyright Laws of the United States. All rights reserved. The printing, copying, redistribution, or retransmission of this Content without express permission is prohibited.

3

Other

Theorist
Native mind
mustache(?)
Feminist
activist
Woman
I
bee
Jew
artist
Poet
You
mi yo
political views
Lang
academic
Black
tu
Queen
Chicana
dyke
Intellectual

Cluster/Series of identities (keeps shifting) = person

Dominant culture
monoculture

White Frame of Reference

fish in white sea

Multi-cult

the "white frame of reference" represents this stumbling block to change, constraining possibilities. Her annotation of the space between the figure and this outline—"dominant culture monoculture"—shows how this white frame completely overwhelms her. Just like the small red "fish in [the] white sea" next to her, she is completely awash in white culture.

Anzaldúa fits nearly thirty written identities in and around the bounds of the mental headspace, tripling the number of identities from her written list in *Borderlands / La Frontera*. In addition to naming racial and ethnic subject positions in her transparency—"Chicana, Black, Asian, Native American, or Jewish"—she also adds sexual and social locations—"queer, patlache, feminist, activist, artist, theorist, dyke, intellectual, woman, poet, academic"—that integrate with these racial identities in order to connect or isolate these women from community. All these identities swirl in the psyche around the struggle for self—the "I, you, mi, tu, yo, mind, body" at the center of the crowded mestiza mental space. The nonlinear page space permits Anzaldúa to elaborate on what's happening within the mestiza's head. Whereas text allows for an ordered catalog and three-sentence exposition on the interactions between inner and outer, this illustration can encompass and interrelate multiple sets of identities, swirling them together to underline the ebb, flow, and chaos of this interaction. This transparency, with all these labeled identities, encourages her audience to locate themselves in this space and consider their own connections and what identities they navigate through on a daily basis.

While Anzaldúa's articulation of mestiza identity in *Borderlands / La Frontera* was so fundamental to critical conversations in future years, her drawings, which reached an overlapping but distinct group of people on the many occasions that Anzaldúa gave talks every year, touched her listeners with an even greater intimacy. These drawings, echoing Anzaldúa's own visually attuned words, not only helped her audience "envision a different reality" through these "new blueprints" of mestiza identity but went further in "formulat[ing] new strategies for coping" and enacting "positive social change" by showing the mestiza engaged in collective action.[81] With her transparencies, Anzaldúa connects theory to action by visualizing how mestizas could take action, given these constraints, thinking through the possibilities of both collective and individual actions (Figures 4.8 and 4.9).[82] In both of these transparencies, the mestiza body is reduced to a stick figure in order to focus on the environment that the mestiza finds herself enmeshed within. In Figure 4.8 that shows a number of mestizas gathered together, Anzaldúa represents the prospect for solidarity as the mestizas unite, acknowledging their "commonalities" and "differences" while standing together as "nos/otras" under an umbrella. The umbrella, itself labeled mestisaje, groups multiple identities under it and functions like the single mestiza figure by gathering many subjectivities. Together, they stand in coalition "under the sky of feminism," and the relationship they have with this environment can be understood in at least two directions. Within *Borderlands / La Frontera*, Anzaldúa argues that "the struggle of the *mestiza* is above all a feminist one," and this image depicts mestizas living in a world governed by feminism, which attains god(dess)ly presence in its skyward position.[83] However, the existence of raindrops from the sky onto the umbrella details a more complicated relationship between these two contingents—even if mestizas operate as feminists, they are also, simultaneously, embattled against some of the prevailing forces of feminism. In this vein, we can consider this feminism as synonymous to the "white frame of reference." In this manner, this transparency also tells the tale of *This Bridge Called My Back* where women of color feminists speak out against not only the dominant white culture but the dominant white feminist culture as well. In gathering the women together, the rain allows them to root themselves strongly and deeply, as signaled by the tree on the right of the transparency. Altogether, the image portrays how collective action allows the mestiza to remake herself and survive.

Anzaldúa's transparency drawings also show how her visual works resonated with feminist discourses surrounding the scale of political actions, demonstrating how a mestiza can engage her community when acting individually and encouraging members of the audience to feel empowered doing so. Figure 4.9 illustrates this point. In this transparency, a mestiza stands before an audience, much like Anzaldúa often found herself in front of a classroom or another space when giving a talk. She focuses her representation on all the influences outside of mestiza identity and separates these forces into multiple layers of pressure. At the center, we have the mestiza orating, thinking "words/images/theories." In *Borderlands / La Frontera*, Anzaldúa theorizes the responsibilities of the mestiza, positing, "Our role is to link people with each other—the Blacks with Jews with Indians with Asians with whites with extraterrestrials. It is to transfer ideas and information from one culture to another."[84] The mestiza performs this process of bridging by "transfer[ring] ideas and

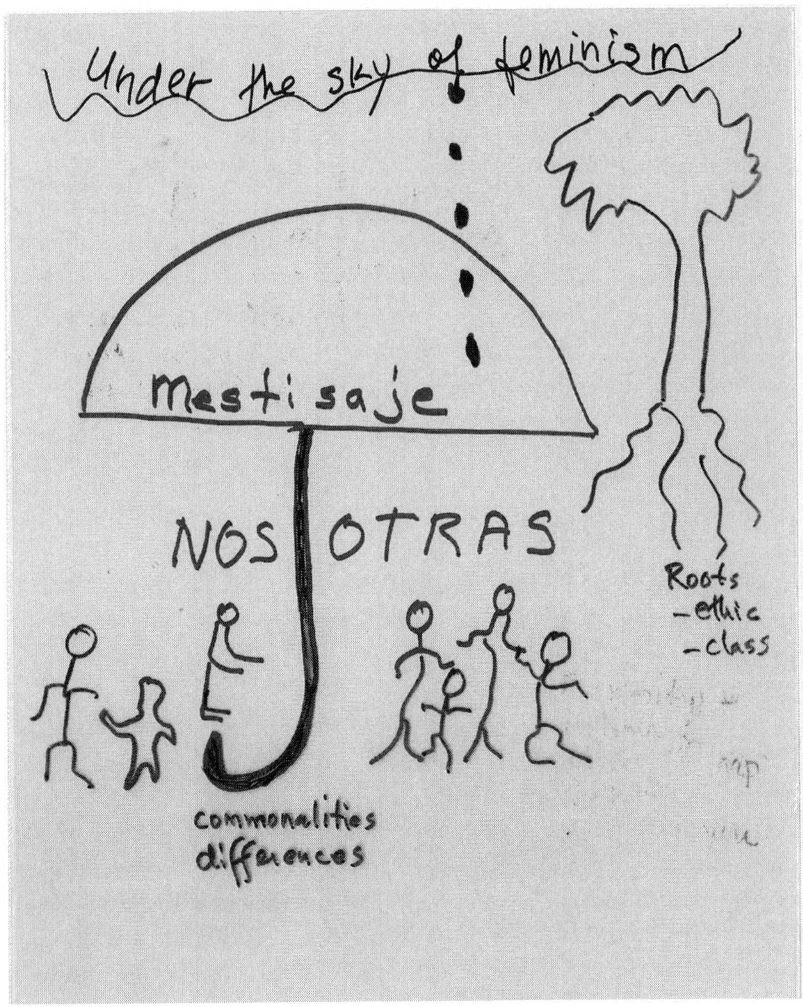

Figure 4.8. Black, red, and purple transparency where Gloria Anzaldúa represents a group of stick figures gathering together under a large "mestisaje" umbrella that keeps them dry "under the sky of feminism." Box 131, Folder 15, Collection on Gloria Evangelina Anzaldúa, Nettie Lee Benson Latin American Collection, University of Texas Libraries, The University of Texas at Austin. Copyright by the Gloria E. Anzaldúa Literary Trust. Benson Latin American Collection. University of Texas Libraries. By permission of Stuart Bernstein Representation for Artists, New York, and protected by the Copyright Laws of the United States. All rights reserved. The printing, copying, redistribution, or retransmission of this Content without express permission is prohibited.

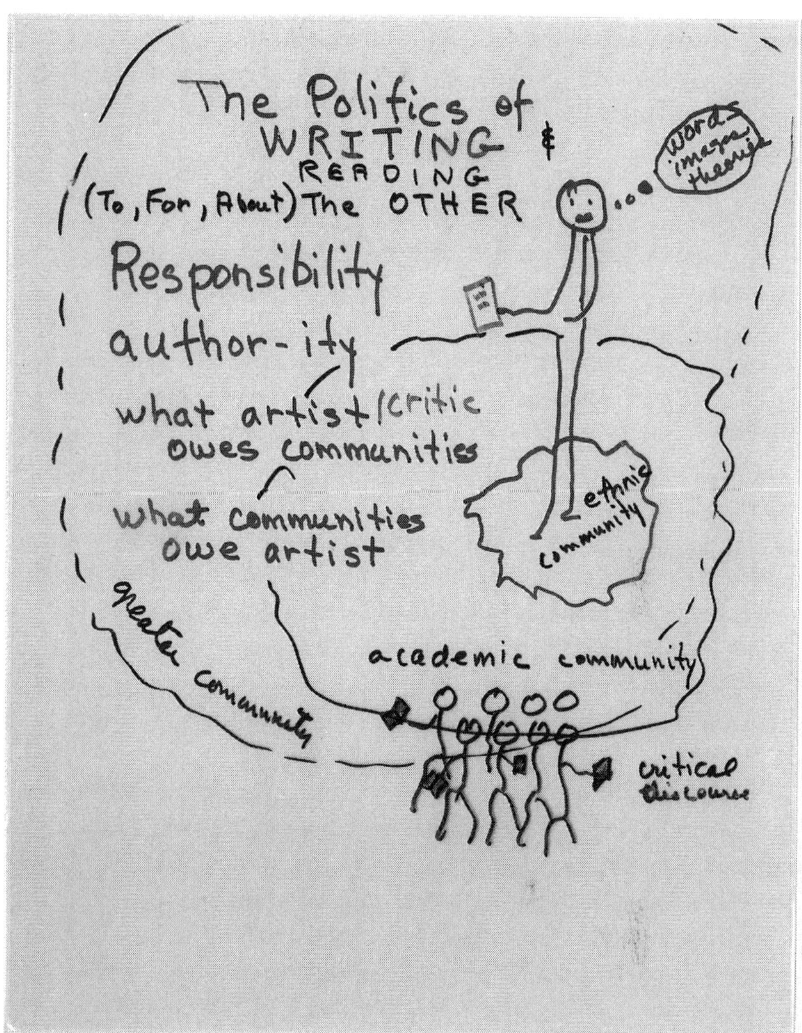

Figure 4.9. Red, purple, and green transparency where Gloria Anzaldúa portrays how a central stick figure is received by larger communities of individuals that encircle her. Box 131, Folder 16, Collection on Gloria Evangelina Anzaldúa, Nettie Lee Benson Latin American Collection, University of Texas Libraries, The University of Texas at Austin. Copyright by the Gloria E. Anzaldúa Literary Trust. Benson Latin American Collection. University of Texas Libraries. By permission of Stuart Bernstein Representation for Artists, New York, and protected by the Copyright Laws of the United States. All rights reserved. The printing, copying, redistribution, or retransmission of this Content without express permission is prohibited.

information," but the space of the transparency productively complicates Anzaldúa's notion of transmission "from one culture to another." In this transparency, when the mestiza speaks, she reaches from her "ethnic community" and projects outward to touch increasingly larger groups, both "academic" and "greater communit[ies]" as well as the embodied idea of "critical discourse." The word-filled paper she speaks from becomes a book that the group of stick figures—standing among the labels for and simultaneously representing "academic community," "greater community," and "critical discourse"—hold.

But this image does not simply show the outward dissemination of ideas, as Anzaldúa uses text ("what artist/critic owes community / what communities owe artist") to qualify that there exists or should ideally exist a reciprocal relationship. This text redefines how we read the spatiality of the diagram as dynamic and flowing continuously in multiple directions. Further, while the image itself and the textual labels encourage an understanding of the outward movement of ideas, these dynamic spatial descriptors pull us back to the mestiza at the center and ask us to consider again how the mestiza as creator operates from within and in relationship to her own community. She, like Anzaldúa, acts as a bridge, and this image itself also functions as a bridge for the audience in providing access to knowledge.

In their present location in the archives, Anzaldúa's drawings sit alongside many other materials that demonstrate her multifaceted focus on community building. Whereas some of these efforts, like the bibliography in *This Bridge* or her speakers list, were projects bounded in time, her images were her most public work that drew folks into movement with her. Anzaldúa brought her ideas to life through two-dimensional transparencies, giving them a body and form as they became three-dimensional live performances. These transparencies and her graduate school notes before them retain these public connections as they move into the archives, acting anew as bridges that reactivate Anzaldúa's ideas for those who encounter them.

Archives and Afterlives: Activating New Communities

It only took a year following Anzaldúa's unexpected death in 2004 for her collection to open as part of the Nettie Lee Benson Latin American

Collection in 2005. Though her journals remain closed to researchers for twenty years, this quick move meant that her ideas could continue to develop in dialogue with other scholars as they accessed her work and pored over her unpublished manuscripts, including her images. Keating has published some of her transparencies posthumously in two volumes she edited, *The Gloria Anzaldúa Reader* (2009) and *Light in the Dark / Luz en lo Oscuro: Rewriting Identity, Spirituality, Reality* (2015). The former collects writings from across Anzaldúa's career and includes the images as their own "gallery" section, while the latter, which is an edited version of Anzaldúa's dissertation she was completing at the time of her death, intersperses a number of transparencies throughout the text.

In addition to these projects, which introduced readers to Anzaldúa's visual production and gave them a chance to think about the interrelationships between these images and her text, the director of the Benson Collection, Julianne Gilland, curated an art exhibition of Anzaldúa's transparencies, "Between Word and Image: A Gloria Anzaldúa Thought Gallery."[85] The opening of this exhibition in May 2015 coincided with the meeting of the Society for the Study of Gloria Anzaldúa at the University of Texas at Austin that year, meaning that her images had another opportunity to speak with a large body of interested interlocutors. The exhibition has since traveled to multiple locations both nationally and internationally, giving these images further opportunity to reach audiences. Though Anzaldúa can no longer activate these images herself, lectures and events scheduled alongside the exhibit in addition to her body of work perform those connections. These new modes of circulating underline the power of images as an "archival genre" in that they are malleable to these transformations, which open up new "textual and social space[s]" for the audiences who encounter them.[86] Moreover, all these posthumous circulations both continued the bridging work that Anzaldúa did in her lifetime and foregrounded in real-world encounters how the archives can extend that bridging.

The following, final chapter will pick up on this thread of visual circulation in thinking through how images can be recontextualized in different formats and spaces to do specific political work by looking at Nan Goldin's photographic and curatorial work. As Anzaldúa's images allowed her to plumb the depths of her texts and open up new meanings for her audiences, Goldin achieves this aim as a primarily visual artist presenting her photographs in multiple ways across the 1980s. When the HIV/AIDS crisis devastated her larger artistic community, it propelled Goldin to reconceptualize her earlier photography and the activism it could do to bring visibility to this issue. The work of both of these artists and the archives demonstrates the openness of images to addressing political change.

5

THE PHOTOGRAPHER
AND CURATOR
Nan Goldin's Witness to HIV/AIDS

Building a Community amidst the HIV/AIDS Epidemic

The Ballad of Sexual Dependency is Nan Goldin's best-known work. She first started taking the photographs that make up the project in the 1970s, and it continues to be exhibited regularly in major museums worldwide, nearly fifty years since it was begun. In this work, Goldin extensively documented her artistic community of friends and lovers, foregrounding their lifestyles of sexual liberation. She exhibited the photographs in various venues across the 1980s as a slideshow set to a musical soundtrack that contained roughly seven hundred photos, revising and refining the order of photos for each viewing.[1] Many of the subjects of the photos in this work were members of the art scene in downtown Manhattan, who also composed her audience when she first exhibited the slideshow in the early 1980s in bars and nightclubs across New York City. But as the project began to develop a following, she started showing the work in gallery and museum spaces, including notably at the Whitney Biennial in 1985. Following that, she published a selection of 125 photographs as a book in 1986.[2]

Critics who review *The Ballad of Sexual Dependency* often focus on Goldin's troubled romantic relationship with a man named Brian that she threads through the work. Though the photographic work featuring Brian depicts scenes of violence and pain, particularly the images showing the effect of his domestic abuse on Goldin, she included the images of him and of the abuse in the slideshow and book version of the work because, as she later revealed, they reminded her never to go back to him.[3] In her subsequent work, Goldin continued to draw on *The Ballad of Sexual Dependency*, publishing additional photographs from that era while also creating new photographs of people within her artistic community, which had proven to be a sustaining force for her work. Her photographic projects in the 1990s showed how the HIV/AIDS epidemic affected many of Goldin's close confidantes who later died from AIDS-related illnesses. The cumulative losses in her community recast the meaning of her photographic record, whereby "pictures of friends seen in moments of joy or excitement unexpectedly became elegiac tributes, memorials to a lost generation."[4] How Goldin repeatedly returns to this era and revises its meaning demonstrates how the enduring acclaim for her work emerges from the fact that she is not simply a photographer, but also a curator.

Goldin, like all the artists featured across this book, was invested in representing diverse sexual identities, but this final chapter examines how she and other artists responded when the emergence of HIV/AIDS in the 1980s fractured their communities. Artists scrambled to preserve their queer worlds—not only through direct action on the street, but also through their own artwork. For example, Roberta Gregory and Alison Bechdel, cartoonists analyzed in earlier chapters, contributed comics to *Strip AIDS USA* (1988).[5] This collection featuring the work of 121 artists sought to destigmatize perceptions of HIV/AIDS and raised over $11,500 for the Shanti Project, an organization that supported people with AIDS.[6] Even more than the art forms analyzed earlier in the book, photography allowed Goldin to directly portray the individuals in her community whose lives were curtailed because of the virus. At the same time, her photography also remained vital to feminists rallying for explicit depictions of sexuality within the feminist sex wars and was featured in *Caught Looking* (1986), the volume discussed in the first chapter that Hannah Alderfer, Beth Jaker, and Marybeth Nelson visually designed to challenge legal efforts to restrict sexual expression.[7]

Goldin's photographic and curatorial praxis show how these two arenas of social justice—pro-sex feminism and HIV/AIDS activism—were interlinked. She had to struggle to preserve both her artistic community and artwork in the face of conservative forces who wanted to erase deviant individuals and welcomed the convenient lethality of HIV/AIDS. This chapter reflects on how artists, their artwork, and the archives work together to preserve communities of individuals. The two previous chapters, on Bechdel and Gloria Anzaldúa, have shown the deliberateness with which both artists gathered a larger community with their artwork and preserved it in their papers. This final chapter examines how Goldin first brought her sexually liberated community together through her evolving *Ballad of Sexual Dependency* photo series and how she later remobilized them to raise awareness about the HIV/AIDS epidemic through her curation of *Witnesses: Against Our Vanishing*. Goldin's work documents collective change and how discourses around sexual liberation adapted to respond to the HIV/AIDS epidemic as she underlined the vital significance of the community her earlier photographs made visible.

In the 1980s, particularly in New York where Goldin worked, the AIDS crisis tore rapidly through artistic communities. At the time, the disease was not understood, which led to extraordinary suffering, confusion, and death whose effects continue to reverberate to this day. During this time, Goldin began to rethink her early photographic work. Particularly through the act of curation, she focused on bringing to light and detailing the impact that HIV/AIDS had on her community.[8] When Susan Wyatt, who was director of Artists Space, a downtown Manhattan gallery, asked Goldin to curate an art exhibit in the late 1980s, Goldin "quickly decided to spotlight AIDS because of her firsthand experience of the impact of the disease. Goldin left New York in 1988 to enter a drug treatment program in Boston. By the time she returned, many friends and acquaintances had died."[9] Goldin's Artists Space exhibit, *Witnesses: Against Our Vanishing*, the first art show about HIV/AIDS in New York City, ran from November 1989 through January 1990.[10] In the exhibit, Goldin brought together the visual artwork of roughly two dozen artists she counted as members of her community, including many whom she had previously photographed.[11] She also curated a catalog that contained a handful of original essays that described how HIV/AIDS had devastated this community, including one in which she articulated the rationale for the exhibit through her own personal experiences of HIV/AIDS, which were shifting her understanding of her own life and artwork. As I discuss later in this chapter, Goldin's curation of this catalog and exhibit underscores how *Witnesses* acted as a personal turning point that changed her relationship to her community, highlighting how the disease's devastation among her chosen family of friends and fellow artists began to determine the course of her future work, including how she drew on

The Ballad of Sexual Dependency going forward. Like the other artists discussed in this book, activism and artwork were intertwined for Goldin, with each shaping the other.

In the years after *Witnesses*, Goldin would even more directly examine how HIV/AIDS had affected her community by recontextualizing her earlier photos within the framework of HIV/AIDS.[12] In 1990, she exhibited *The Cookie Portfolio, 1976–89*, which brought together her photos of Cookie Mueller from across the entirety of their close friendship, beginning in the mid-1970s when Mueller was already a subcultural icon for having starred in a number of John Waters films like *Pink Flamingos* (1972) and *Female Trouble* (1974). This collection included many images strongly associated with *The Ballad* and Mueller's iconic status more broadly, but it also documented her decline and untimely death from HIV/AIDS in 1989 at the age of forty. In 1992, Goldin exhibited and published *The Other Side*, which featured her photographs of drag queens and trans women from the 1970s through the 1990s, opening with the community of these women with whom she had lived in Boston in the early 1970s. In her textual preface to the printed volume, she recognizes AIDS as a presence across these photos: "The plague of AIDS has affected this community. One of my closest friends in the pictures from the 70s died a few years ago and one of the beauties in the recent pictures, a few weeks ago."[13] Similarly, she has linked her *Ballad* photos to the HIV/AIDS crisis through textual afterwords she wrote in 1996, 2012, and 2021 for new editions of the book version of *The Ballad*.[14] In 1996, concurrent with a huge retrospective of her work at the Whitney Museum of Art, the *I'll Be Your Mirror* documentary surveying her work devoted over half the film to discussing the impact of HIV/AIDS on her community, including in the continued declines and deaths of loved ones in the 1990s.

Like the creators in previous chapters, Goldin made deliberate artistic choices that underlined her collective ethos and her commitment to documenting her community and their diverse sexual and gender expressions in order to make these groups of people visible. Goldin's practice of exhibiting her photographs as a slideshow to share it with a public audience echoes Anzaldúa's embrace of image making in public talks to make her written ideas accessible to a larger community. Just as

Anzaldúa's published books allowed her ideas to travel even further and get her invited to give the very talks where she deployed her community-building imagery, so did Goldin's publishing of a selection of her *Ballad* photography as a book make her work accessible to an even larger audience. Because the book couldn't replicate the dynamic experience of the slideshow, many scholars and critics have downplayed its role. However, the book succeeds in introducing her community and framing them through her vision that she articulates in a textual introduction and afterword to the photographs. Both she and Anzaldúa demonstrated across their careers a dedication to preserving their community in their work because there was the very real possibility that their worlds wouldn't be recorded otherwise.

In this chapter, I centralize the book version of *The Ballad of Sexual Dependency* to ask how Goldin builds her community through this format. Other critics focus on what is lost in the transition from slideshow to book, with Chris Townsend positing, "[The photograph] was reduced to an individual, static object of contemplation that could be considered for a protracted period, outside the context of the images that surrounded it and also outside the context of the audience that surrounded the spectator in live screenings. . . . Publication also separated the images from the music that accompanied live performance."[15] Like others, Townsend casts the book as a reductive format that decontextualizes the photographs by removing the bulk of the photographs as well as aspects of the live performance, including the audience and the soundtrack. In the analysis that follows, I instead read the book as a distillation of her project and examine how the added elements, like photo captions and textual paratexts, make her work of community formation legible to a larger public and account for the shifting meaning of the photographs as HIV/AIDS affects her community. I then focus my analysis on the *Witnesses* catalog as the central site of Goldin's curation, examining how she mobilizes this document to frame the exhibit and the community and articulate their experiences with HIV/AIDS. As discussed above, this catalog provides a blueprint for Goldin's work in the following years, including in how she reframes *The Ballad* to speak to the epidemic. Because both of these print volumes combine visual and textual elements, they allow Goldin to directly weigh in on and further curate the meaning of the visual artwork through text, thus making her editing legible. Together, the book and the catalog give us two complementary snapshots of Goldin's community: one in formation and the other in action as the community was under threat.

Curating Cultural Memory in Photographs and Archives

When Goldin published *The Ballad of Sexual Dependency* as a book in 1986, she wrote a preface that not only theorized the project but also described the personal circumstances behind why she became a photographer in the first place and how they informed her artistic process going forward. Goldin discussed how her older sister, Barbara, died by suicide at eighteen due to feeling sexually repressed and trapped in her life and how that trauma spurred an eleven-year-old Nan to pursue a different life path, running away from home at fourteen and attending the Satya Community School where she learned to photograph at eighteen.[16] Goldin has repeated this anecdote throughout her career as her origin story. More than the specific details that Goldin narrates, it is crucial to note how she wields them to articulate an artistic ethos, pairing her words in *The Ballad* with a photograph of Barbara in the last year of her life (Figure 5.1). Her discussion of how she photographs to guard against loss speaks more broadly to her artistic process as photographer and curator. Goldin's process is a notable departure from how other critics and photographers have conceived of photography, and her approach links her to the modus operandi behind contemporary archives that preserve the cultural memory of LGBTQ individuals, particularly those living with HIV/AIDS in this period.

Goldin includes the photograph as the final element of her preface, directly below a dedication to her sister. Goldin did not include the image just to honor her sister's memory—its inclusion allowed Goldin to make a broader critique of the oppressive conditions that led to Barbara's death, which Goldin strives against both in her own life and her photographic career. In the text, Goldin discloses that she "lost the real memory of [her] sister," a sentiment she echoes in her dedication as well as when she encapsulates her drive to photograph: "I don't ever want to lose the real memory of anyone again."[17] Though the photograph depicts

This book is dedicated to the real memory of my sister, Barbara Holly Goldin. closer to the experience of memory, a story without end.

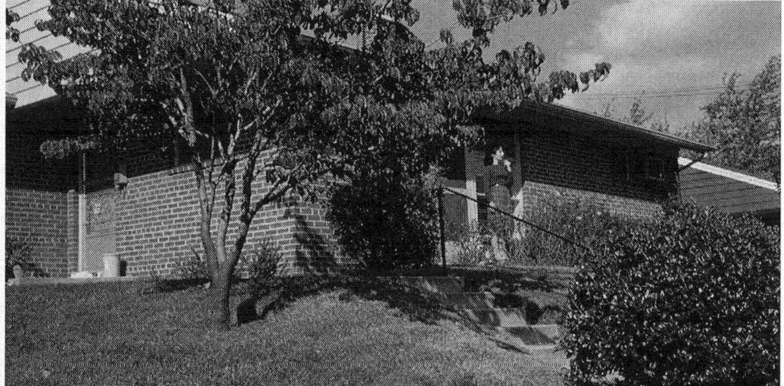

Barbara in front of family house, Silver Spring, Md. 1964

9

Figure 5.1. Photograph of Nan Goldin's older sister, Barbara, included at the end of Nan Goldin's textual preface to *The Ballad.* Copyright by Nan Goldin. Reprinted with permission of Nan Goldin, *Barbara in front of family house, Silver Spring, Md. 1964.*

Barbara, Goldin effectively argues that it doesn't preserve her "real memory"—in text she posits, "I remember my version of her, of the things she said, of the things she meant to me. But I don't remember the tangible sense of who she was, her presence, what her eyes looked like, what her voice sounded like."[18] Goldin thereby infers that her own photographs aim to capture these personal details that are absent from the photo of Barbara she includes, which depicts her standing just outside the family home. Because Goldin had not begun photographing until years after Barbara's death, we know that this image is not Goldin's own and likely one her parents took of Barbara as they would've liked to see her.

What we see in this photograph is how Barbara was trapped by the social norms of where she was raised, communicated through the family home, which dominates the frame and dwarfs her figure. Because of her small size in the image and because she looks away from the camera, her gaze is inscrutable—we cannot see "what her eyes looked like." Rather than the real Barbara who attempted to rebel against the strictures of home, we see her confined to this space—a tiny, perfect paper-doll rather than a real person. We don't see Barbara as Nan saw her or likely how she would have wanted to be seen. We see her alone and lacking a like-minded community of support that proved so vital for Goldin's own survival and livelihood.

We can see these things about this photo not simply in the context of Goldin's words, but also in how this photo provides a stark contrast with Goldin's own, which portray her chosen community. That is, Goldin's curatorial eye is at play in making her argument about how her photography both connects to and departs from this familial midcentury tradition. Goldin's own photographs are printed roughly twice as large in size and often center bodies in the frame, sometimes in close-up. As a result, the members of Goldin's community are many magnitudes larger than Barbara, and we come to know their "real memory" through the proliferation of photos that Goldin takes of each individual and later on through Goldin's curation of their artwork in exhibits like *Witnesses.* Even more fundamental than that, Goldin and her subjects are able to express themselves freely and embody the sexual liberation that Barbara could not attain. Goldin photographs these freedoms openly, which is one of the reasons why her work speaks so powerfully in making visible representations that had previously been taboo.

How Goldin juxtaposes this photo with her own reveals her aesthetic genius as an editor and curator. As Tahneer Oksman has noted, Goldin's own photos begin on the following page, so this curatorial placement puts the photo into sequence with hers, heightening the aforementioned differences.[19] Though we can see little of Barbara in this photo, her posture of peering out and away to the right suggests that she is looking ahead to Goldin's photos and the community that her younger sister was able to make for herself. A number of Goldin's subjects echo Barbara's gaze, evoking the possibility that these lives could have been Barbara's own, had she survived. Goldin's selection of this particular photo of Barbara allows for these interpretations.

In contrast to this singular and distant photo of Barbara, Goldin shows us with *The Ballad* how she preserves the "real memory" of other people by photographing them repeatedly over a number of years, including and especially in intimate moments. She visualizes what she lost of Barbara and what Barbara was never able to have for herself. Though she had to select a smaller grouping of photos for the book version of *The Ballad,* there are still numerous individuals we see multiple times over the course of the work. All these individuals and how she sequences them together for emotional impact speaks to the power of her editing. Through these photographs, Goldin made hyper visible an expansive community brimming with LGBTQ individuals by photographing them again and again, so that you could not miss them. Whereas many of the earlier artists were creating through collage, comics, and drawings multiple models or characters for their audiences to relate to and welcome into the movement, Goldin was staunchly determined to directly document the movement itself through photography, creating instead a visual index that spoke to the size of this community and its vibrant artistic and sexual practices.

Just as Goldin contrasts Barbara's isolation with her community's connectivity, so also does she make her photographic praxis communal—collaborating with her community in the making of her artwork as did each of the artists discussed in the earlier chapters. All the artists in this book used visual culture to nurture and make community visible. Throughout their careers, their artwork made the lives, experiences, and bodies of feminist and queer people more broadly legible to an increasingly larger public. Goldin created, exhibited, and edited her photos in such a way as to allow for dynamic feedback from the subjects of her work. She discusses how she encouraged those she photographed to give her input—whether while sharing photos of her roommates with them and having them nix the ones they didn't like[20] or from feedback gathered at viewings of *The Ballad* as a slideshow in its first years when the audience members were mainly the subjects of her photos who would audibly vocalize their assessments, "screaming when they [saw] themselves on-screen."[21] These iterative, public viewings of the slideshows shaped the form of the work, and they provided a space for community input that Goldin took into account while editing. For example, after Goldin exhibited an early version of the slideshow at the *Times Square Show* in 1980, Maggie Smith, who employed Goldin and other women artists at her Tin Pan Alley bar, told Goldin she was "a very political artist" and "helped [her] see the work is about gender politics."[22] This support and these remarks profoundly influenced the project and how Goldin sequenced her subsequent slideshows to examine the relationships between genders.

Other individuals like art curator Marvin Heiferman participated more closely in helping her find venues for her artwork, stage many of her slideshows, and ultimately select the photos for the book version of *The Ballad*—a process that also involved *Aperture* editor Mark Holborn and Suzanne Fletcher, an old friend who featured prominently in Goldin's photos.

Her curatorial process with *Witnesses* was similarly a collective endeavor, foregrounding how such a collaborative mode underlies much of her work. With *Witnesses*, Artists Space director Susan Wyatt invited Goldin to serve as a guest curator, and Goldin decided to focus the exhibit on the impact of the HIV/AIDS epidemic on her community of fellow artists—many of whom she had photographed previously. By welcoming her community to participate, she invited them to shape the meaning of the exhibit in a manner similar to how they had shaped her photographic work. The exhibit itself ended up courting controversy as John Frohnmayer, the new director of the National Endowment for the Arts, threatened to revoke funds for the show based on the inflammatory political critique that artist David Wojnarowicz made in his essay for the exhibit catalog. The Artists Space records for *Witnesses*, which are archived as part of the Downtown Collection at New York University's Fales Library, document how the exhibit made front-page news nationwide as a result of this dispute, which was eventually resolved with funding restored when Frohnmayer visited the exhibit and Artists Space found another source of financial support for the catalog. Steven C. Dubin analyzes the conflict in his scholarship, describing how the collaboration between Wyatt, Goldin, and Wojnarowicz inflamed the situation as each acted from a different position in response to the crisis—with Wyatt seeking to preserve Artists Space and the funding relationship with the NEA while Goldin and Wojnarowicz were upholding artistic integrity by communicating hard truths about the real impact of HIV/AIDS.[23] Beyond the controversy, in both the catalog and on the walls of the exhibit, it was clear how the artists were interconnected in a larger network and how their work was shaped from being in conversation with each other, underlining the impact of each loss. Goldin herself lost dear friends who had been sources of inspiration in the months and days leading up to the exhibit and in the years thereafter.

The collaborative nature of Goldin's photographic process, where both her individual photos and their larger sequence were shaped collectively, sets her apart from how other photographers and critics conceived of the artform. Across her career, she has positioned herself in distinction from Henri Cartier-Bresson, one of the first street photographers who was accepted as a high-art photographer at the time when she was establishing her craft.[24] On numerous occasions, she has described her process with reference to his concept of the "decisive moment," recently alluding to his notion again in an interview included in an issue of *Aperture* devoted to *The Ballad*: "I never believed in the decisive moment. I never believed that one photograph encapsulates the whole of one person. Of course, published, there are single images on a page, but the whole way that I frame my work is in multiple images."[25] Cartier-Bresson's concept communicates the idea that a good photographer can capture a scene at just the right moment, which Goldin pushes back against in this quotation but also in her process, wherein she takes many photos of an individual at any one moment, akin to the process of fashion photographers, and later decides on an image. Her critique goes further in suggesting, however, that there's no single decisive moment where a photograph can reveal the essential nature of a subject, but that multiple images, over time, can impart their presence.

The work is not finished when the photographer clicks the shutter; her process foregrounds collaborative editing and sequencing individual photos into a larger whole. In discussing her own process over the years, Goldin has insisted her artwork emerged through how she worked with the photographs after she took them, recently saying, "I would say that my work is editing. I've always said that primarily the art is not photography, the art is editing. . . . The point is about making cinematic work out of still images, and the editing is where I feel my intelligence lies."[26] In identifying her work as editing, Goldin is crucially not referring to the technical capacity to perfect an individual photo but instead her ability to see each image as part of a larger whole, place them into conversation with each other, and have them speak to a larger cultural context. For Goldin, that process invites in the participation of her larger artistic community and, thus, her artwork makes visible the ethos of that community as a whole as it portrays their bodies and lifestyles. In this manner, her praxis articulates a different method to understand the nature of photography than Susan Sontag and Roland Barthes theorized in their contemporaneous volumes of critique that are often cited in scholarship.[27] For both critics, they theorize through individual photos and auteurs, while meaning accumulates for Goldin through multiplicity—both of images and of collaborators.

The ethos of Goldin's drive to guard against loss by taking multiple images at any one time and over time aligns her process with the other artists discussed in the book, who preserved their communities by documenting them in their work. Her methods also parallel not only the work of archivists acquiring and processing LGBTQ material just like the artists discussed in prior chapters, they also specifically resonate with those collections focused on preserving the work of individuals who died of HIV/AIDS. There are countless tales of lives forgotten because homophobic families destroyed the ephemeral traces of an individual after death or, as Goldin's example of Barbara shows, of individuals whose identities were denied expression during their lives. The first and third chapters focus on the role of grassroots archives in preserving LGBTQ material because those works weren't being preserved elsewhere, but this chapter considers how more official repositories started to preserve such lives, like the numerous Gay and Lesbian and HIV/AIDS Collections at the New York Public Library, which began when the grassroots International Gay Information Center donated their collection to the library in 1988; and the Downtown Collection, which Marvin Taylor founded at New York University's Fales Library in 1994.[28] As Marika Cifor relates, such archival collections were built out of the extensive documentation that HIV/AIDS activists explicitly created in order to preserve their culture: "In the accelerated registers of 'epidemic time' during the 1980s and early 1990s, AIDS activists responded by enacting the care work that Ben Alexander and Andrew Flinn call 'activist archiving' at a furious pace, creating documentation, and collecting, preserving, curating, and making these records accessible. They accumulated rich, extensive archives that they mobilized for contemporaneous social change."[29] As this chapter documents, Goldin participated in this same "care work" as she photographed numerous friends who were HIV positive and memorialized friends who had died from AIDS-related illnesses, including in exhibits like *Witnesses*.

The Downtown Collection is of particular interest for this chapter since the Artists Space Records contain documentation of the *Witnesses* exhibit (although the collection as a whole is also important since it chronicles the downtown New York City art scene that Goldin and her fellow artists participated in). The scope of the collection is bigger than the subject of HIV/AIDS, but the virus and the devastation it wrought is a central part of the story, since the decimation of New York City's artistic community and the way that threatened the preservation of artistic legacies played an important role in spurring Taylor to create the archives. As Olivia Laing writes of the impetus behind the Downtown Collection:

> Like many archives, the Downtown Collection was created out of a state of peril. When Marvin Taylor founded Fales in 1994, many of the possessions belonging to artists who were dying of AIDS in New York were literally being thrown into the trash by indifferent landlords or antagonistic families. The combination of homophobia and AIDS stigma meant an entire world was at risk of being destroyed twice over, since without documentation or abiding relics, no one will be remembered long.
>
> The Downtown Collection is a witness to the monumental losses of the AIDS crisis, and it also exists to counteract that loss, to ensure that the people who died are not forgotten, to keep some essence of their lives secure.[30]

This description of the founding and purpose of the Downtown Collection echoes Goldin's photographic ethos in capturing people in images to guard against their loss. Just as the archives remember the artists by preserving their work and the documentation surrounding it in exhibits, correspondence, posters, et cetera, so also does Goldin remember these individuals and how they formed a community, made visible through her editing and sequencing of her own photos in *The Ballad* and in her curating of their artwork in *Witnesses*. Especially when HIV/AIDS started to affect her community, which inspired both the *Witnesses* exhibit as well as her photographic focus in the following years, her motive directly parallels that of the Downtown Collection. Indeed, if you replaced the Downtown Collection with Goldin's name in Laing's final sentence excerpted here, you would have a fair summary of the principles of Goldin's work. While the Downtown Collection achieves this goal through gathering collections from artists and galleries, Goldin photographs and curates her community, preserving them in photographic projects and exhibits. Just as the archives continue to acquire materials from this period, so does Goldin continue to publish and circulate new photos from this time, keeping these individuals alive in the present moment and in dialogue with contemporary photographs she takes.

The following two sections examine how Goldin edits, sequences, and curates her community by analyzing the book version of *The Ballad* and the catalog of *Witnesses*, both of which combine image and text and communicate Goldin's motives through these hybrid means. Many scholars focus on the documentary aspect in how and what Goldin photographs, but by close reading these books, I aim to dig a level deeper in examining the actions Goldin takes after she photographs, which are similar to an archivist processing a collection and striving to make the material accessible to a larger public.[31] As this section establishes, the work Goldin does is necessarily collaborative and her ethos in guarding against loss echoes that of contemporaneous archives seeking to preserve the same communities that Goldin herself is a part of and records in her artwork.

Editing and Sequencing Community through The Ballad

On its surface, *The Ballad of Sexual Dependency* is about the fraught relationships between men and women. The focus on Goldin's own troubled history with Brian may make the project seem heteronormative in nature. However, Goldin herself is not straight, nor is her community. A number of them aren't cisgender, either. When you look through the photos with these facts in mind, you can see how she's examining the toxicity of gender roles at the same time that she and those around her are actively deconstructing them. Goldin's identity as bisexual, which she has often foregrounded in discussing her work, shaped not only how she engaged her subjects in the taking of the photos but also how she edited the work and understood people from multiple angles.[32] While Goldin does include a number of her lovers in *The Ballad*, the bulk of the project documents her wide-ranging community of friends, who were often also aspiring artists and close like family. In recollecting his experience with Goldin in the 1980s, novelist Darryl Pinckney recalls how she navigated multiple social circles with ease: "What amazed me then—and still amazes me—was how many people Nan knew and knew well. She has a gift for friendship."[33] In reviewing the book form of *The Ballad*, this section focuses on how Goldin structures her community through these often-homosocial friendships that fill her photos and shape her career. These are the sustaining individuals who continue to support Goldin and whose memories Goldin keeps alive, by curating *Witnesses* and with her photographic work across the 1990s, when many of them died from HIV/AIDS.

The earliest photo Goldin includes as part of the book version of *The Ballad of Sexual Dependency* demonstrates how this project was founded in queer community and how this support structure shaped her life and work. The 1973 image shows a group of women sharing cake and laughter at an Easter picnic (Figure 5.2).[34] The five women are from the social circle of drag queens and trans women that Goldin lived with in Boston for a few years before she went to the School of the Museum of Fine Arts in Boston to pursue her bachelor's degree. It is a rare early

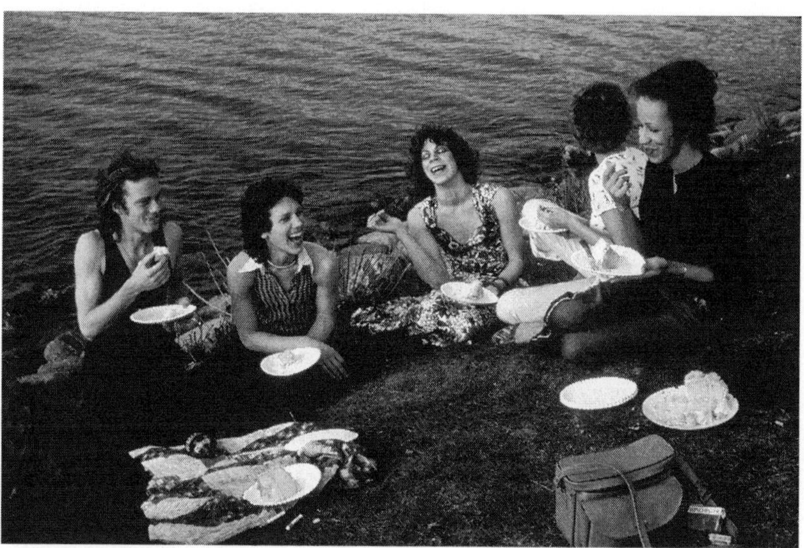

Figure 5.2. The earliest photograph included in *The Ballad* depicts Nan Goldin's trans women and drag queen friends picnicking together in a park along the Charles River. Copyright by Nan Goldin. Reprinted with permission of Nan Goldin, *Picnic on the Esplanade, Boston 1973.*

color photo from Goldin, who was mostly photographing in black and white at the time; and, partly due to the fact the image is in color, it is the only photograph from this period in Goldin's life to appear in *The Ballad* (*The Ballad* is composed solely of color photographs). After this photograph, the next earliest photos are from 1976. In the context of *The Ballad*, this photo is the initial image in a section of photos featuring gatherings of Goldin's community, and these evidence how much her community departs from normative gender roles. These trans women and drag queens each have their own individual relationship to the female gender (Goldin explores this subject directly in her book *The Other Side*), but here they're together, relaxing in these identities and completely at ease with one another.[35]

Across the book version of *The Ballad*, Goldin pairs two photos from different times and places. The two photos typically feature different people across the page spreads, suggesting a relationship between images and individuals. However, at a handful of section breaks in the book—such as the section that opens with this picnic photograph—Goldin includes a white page on the left-hand side, thus leaving the initial photo on the right-hand side unpaired. This artistic choice has implications for the way one understands the photographs. In the case of this photo of the picnic, without a paired photo, Goldin suggests that the community is unparalleled. Ivy, centered in this photo, whom Goldin would photograph extensively over time, was her roommate for many years, including when Goldin later moved to New York City. We also see her in a number of other photos in *The Ballad* outside of her drag identity, as Kenny. By the time Goldin curated *Witnesses*, Ivy was among those Goldin had lost to HIV/AIDS.[36] When Goldin released an expanded edition of *The Other Side* in 2019, she lamented how, aside from a couple of the drag queens and trans women she associated with in the early 1970s, "AIDS and violence have wiped out our tribe, a whole generation of pioneers gone."[37] We don't encounter the picnic photograph until relatively late in *The Ballad*, but the image and the community it depicts represented an undeniably important influence on her life and work. In the years to come, she would continue to use photography to build queer community for herself in Boston and New York City. When she exhibited and published her work, she made her queer community visible to an even larger public, making a loud argument for the vibrant universality of this community perhaps even more so than the previous artists in this book since she showed and named specific individuals.

Just as Anzaldúa's visual public talks forged a community who joined her in dialogue about intersectional feminism, so does Goldin make use of the book format to welcome individuals to see and feel a part of a larger queer community. She translates aspects of the slideshow for the book version, making her project more readily accessible, since it doesn't depend on the handful of museums who own copies screening it. To account for the musical soundtrack that accompanied live viewings of the slideshows, Goldin includes a table of contents where the section titles are named for the songs that she paired those images with, such that a savvy reader could construct their own playlist. This eclectic mix of "songs from opera, Top 40, downtown New Wave dance clubs, and obscure blues records" included titles like Maria Callas's "Casta Diva," Dean Martin's "Memories Are Made of This," Ennio Morricone's "The Good, the Bad and the Ugly" theme, the Velvet Underground's "I'll Be Your Mirror," and Dionne Warwick's "Don't Make Me Over."[38] In interviews, Goldin has described the music as "the narrative voice" of the slideshow where she could "make more political points about sexual politics, about gender, about relationships. That comes from the juxtaposition of images with narrative, with lyrics."[39] With the book, image–music becomes image–text, as Goldin trades the lyrics of popular music for her own words in the form of a textual preface. Moreover, the textual afterwords Goldin pens, which she has revised in each newer edition, has allowed her to keep the project open to new interpretations—as mentioned above, these afterwords are where Goldin has discussed how she lost many of the individuals depicted in the photos to HIV/AIDS in the intervening years. To her, the community is a living one, so its meaning changes over time, echoing how history has affected and shaped broader queer communities.

Along with these paratexts that introduce the project and the community to the reader, descriptive titles below each photograph welcome outsiders into the distilled version of the community that the book portrays. The format of the slideshow, where each photo flashes on screen "for three or four seconds," does not allow for such text, so this addition provides book readers further insight into the community.[40] The photos occupy most of the available space on the page, with small italic text tucked neatly underneath them. These captions follow a general pattern in giving the viewer factual information about the photographs: first, the people in the photograph are identified, most often by their first name; then, a few words about the action or space being photographed are included; last, the geographic location and year when the photograph was taken are listed. For example, *Suzanne on the train, Wuppertal, West Germany 1984* or *Roommate as Napoleon, New Year's Eve, New York City 1980*.[41] This practice of titling photographs in this descriptive manner is one that Goldin would continue throughout her career. These titles allow viewers another avenue for reading the photographs and understanding the relationships that emerge between depicted individuals that Goldin creates through sequencing, especially since a viewer can linger at length with each spread and make meaning from their juxtaposition. This ability for the audience to sit with the images and sort out their relationship is akin to the comicitous action of closure that Scott McCloud defines in *Understanding Comics* (1993), where he differentiates how comics allow for greater audience participation because readers actively engage in making meaning from one image to the next.[42] The captions also grant viewers the ability to trace new pathways through the photos, tracking the appearance of one subject or one location, for example, and considering their role throughout the project.

The photographs of women Goldin included throughout *The Ballad* often illuminated homosocial intimacy between women, underscoring how crucial female friendships are to the success of feminist community. While this book most often focuses on lesbian and bisexual women's sexuality, it is important to note that the power of each artist's depictions of women lies not only in how they depict women who are lovers, but also in their portrayals of women's intimate friendships, which are made stronger by their investment in a shared community. For example, one of the individuals who emerges quite prominently across *The Ballad of Sexual Dependency* is Suzanne Fletcher, who is the most photographed woman in the volume and whose presence dominates the photos in the first third of the book in particular, illustrating her close friendship with Goldin.[43] Their friendship dates back to adolescence when they both were students at the Satya Community School.[44] Their friendship continued even when Fletcher moved to New York City in the 1970s to attend Columbia University while Goldin remained in Boston for her degree.[45]

Fletcher connected Goldin to Manhattan life and social scenes during these years and served as a point of connection when Goldin moved there herself in 1978 after she had completed her degree in Boston.[46] As mentioned in the previous section, Fletcher was also one of the individuals who helped Goldin edit and sequence the book version of *The Ballad*.[47] The eleven photos of Fletcher in the book depict her both in her daily life in New York City[48] and traveling the world with Goldin. They journey across Mexico[49] and Germany[50] together, and Goldin also brings her on a visit home to her parents.[51]

The photos Goldin takes of Fletcher subtly demonstrate how community works and what emotional support it can provide. Whereas other photos document the vibrant sexualities and lives of the community, Goldin's photos of Fletcher go deeper in showing the many levels of informal support that women in community together can provide for each other, just as Marrs's and Gregory's comics visualized the different kinds of feminist support groups that existed within the broader community. Goldin's photo of Suzanne from the trip home to her parents exemplifies the intimacy of their friendship, especially given that Goldin had a notably strained relationship with her parents. In a page spread, Goldin juxtaposes two photographs of Fletcher lying in bed—the left-hand photo from their Mexico trip in 1981 and the right-hand photo from their visit to Goldin's parents in 1985 (Figure 5.3). In the Mexico image, Goldin reveals their somewhat spare hotel room in Mérida. She shoots the image while standing near the end of Fletcher's bed, positioning her full body on the mattress near the center of the photo, while also capturing much of the atmosphere of their spartan accommodations. The focus on the room obscures Fletcher's individuality in this photo, but the facing photo provides a stark contrast, showing Fletcher in close-up as she lies in bed with no representation of the room around her. The proximity suggests their long-time friendship, since Goldin photographs her so closely in an unfiltered moment where Fletcher appears somewhat ill at ease as she rests her head on the pillow. The photo's title adds additional context that deepens the sense of their relationship: *Suzanne in The Parents' Bed, Swampscott, Mass. 1985*. Not only do we closely encounter Fletcher in a private moment, but she's also lying in one of the most intimate of locations: Goldin's parents' bed. While much of *The Ballad* shows Goldin's community in more revealing

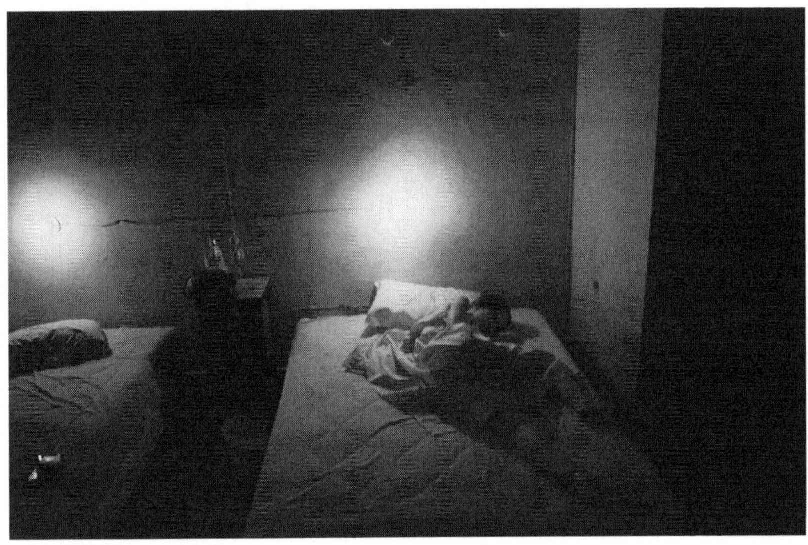

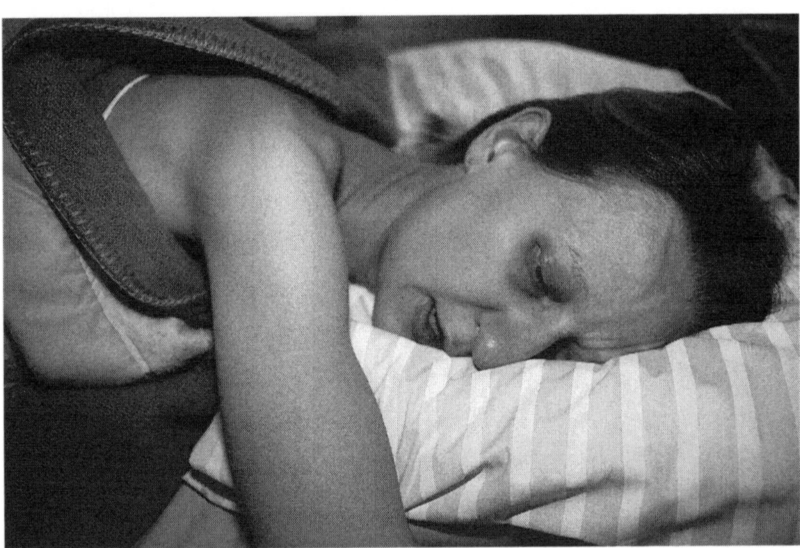

Figure 5.3. Two photographs of Nan Goldin's close friend, Suzanne Fletcher, one at a distance and one in close-up, appear on facing pages in *The Ballad*. Copyright by Nan Goldin. Reprinted with permission of Nan Goldin, *Suzanne in yellow hotel room, Hotel Seville, Merida, Mexico 1981* and *Suzanne in The Parents' Bed, Swampscott, Mass. 1985*.

and sexual encounters in bed, the significance of this particular bed foregrounds the level of trust that exists between the two women.

While these photos evidence the intimacy and care that exists between the two women, Fletcher's indispensable support of Goldin in her troubled relationship with Brian is only subtly reflected in the photo record. Besides Goldin, Fletcher is the only named individual to appear in a photo with Brian when Goldin photographs the two of them sitting at the opposite ends of a bench on the boardwalk at Coney Island in Brooklyn, New York, in 1982.[52] She occupies the same narrative timespace as Brian, offering Goldin the support of sustaining friendship in the face of his violent destruction. After Brian brutally beat Goldin in 1984, it was "Fletcher [who] helped get [Goldin] to a hospital so that her eye could be saved."[53] As briefly mentioned at the outset of the chapter, his violence gets discussed often in part because of the iconic photo Goldin makes of herself that shows the aftermath one month after he beat her.[54] What's absent from these discussions is the fact that Fletcher took this photo; Goldin thanks Fletcher for her "hands on the shutter" in her acknowledgments for the 1996 version of *The Ballad*.[55] These two details indicate Fletcher's crucial presence during a difficult period in Goldin's life and how what we see of her in the photo record is only the tip of the iceberg. The fullness with which Goldin attempts to represent her subjects echoes the work of all the artists across the book, who strove to create fully fleshed subjectivities to counter narrow stereotypes and provide portrayals of diverse sexualities. All the artists depicted women in community with each other, but it is Goldin who really theorizes and visualizes the succor that a feminist friendship can provide.

For all the support that Fletcher provided to Goldin, we can also see Goldin's care for her in another photo of Fletcher that Goldin structurally links to her iconic photo documenting the aftermath of Brian's domestic abuse. In the "Sweet Blood Call" section of *The Ballad* that features photos of women suffering physical and emotional pain, Goldin begins with the iconic photo of herself and ends with a photo that depicts a distraught Fletcher in tears (Figure 5.4).[56] Just like the photo of Fletcher in Goldin's parents' bed, we encounter Fletcher again in close-up, such that we can intimately read the distress on her face through every furrow of her brow as a single tear rolls down her cheek. A critic said that this was "the closest a human being could get to another."[57]

Because this photo is paired in sequence with Goldin's, it foregrounds the reciprocity in their relationship—Fletcher was there for Goldin and now, in the timespace of the photo, Goldin is there for Fletcher. Not all of Goldin's photos capture her subjects at such close proximity, but these photos provide an especially jarring contrast to the Barbara photo she curated in the preface, underlining the level of emotional vulnerability she is able to develop with her chosen family as they open themselves up to her and vice versa.

Focusing on Fletcher illuminates both the close connections that Goldin had with the subjects of her photos and how she amplified that rapport through how she arranged the photos in *The Ballad of Sexual Dependency*. My reading shows how the descriptive titles play a role in the book version in further contextualizing the photos, identifying individuals and providing information that shapes the meaning of each image. As the exhibition of Goldin's project moved further away from her community who attended many of the slideshows in the early years, the additional information that Goldin provides in the book version through

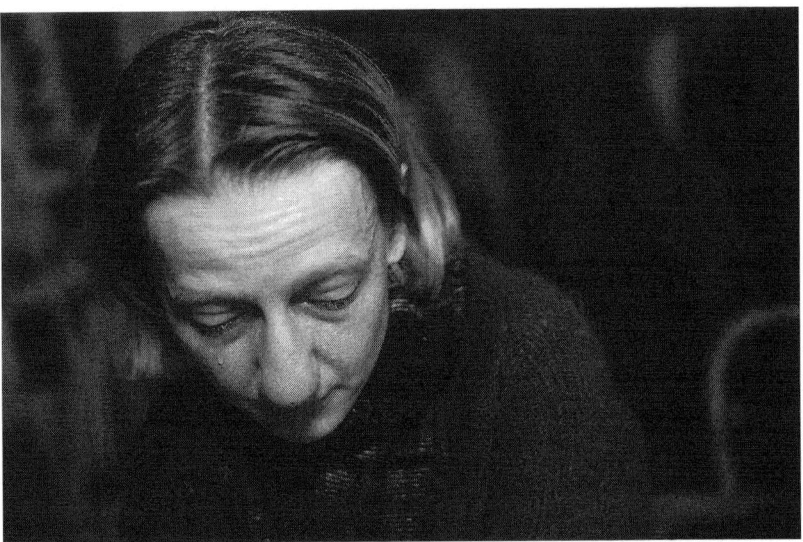

Figure 5.4. Close-up photograph of Suzanne Fletcher crying with one tear rolling down her cheek that ends a section of photos titled "Sweet Blood Call" in *The Ballad.* Copyright by Nan Goldin. Reprinted with permission of Nan Goldin, *Suzanne crying, New York City 1985.*

captions and paratexts allows her new audience to become acquainted with her community. Along with the afterwords in which Goldin names those who have passed away—many of them from HIV/AIDS—the photo titles allow the viewer to identify these individuals and hold them in memory. Like Goldin herself, Fletcher is still alive, but many members of Goldin's community, like those trans women and drag queens making merry at the picnic, are not.

The most recent photo that Goldin includes in *The Ballad* subconsciously anticipates those losses. Juxtaposed with an image of her parents' wedding photo sitting on a dresser in a yellow bedroom, Goldin brings us to the wedding of Cookie Mueller and Vittorio Scarpati, who were both HIV positive when they married in 1986 (Figure 5.5).[58] She shows the couple in medium close-up, as Scarpati smiles and gazes on the tearful Mueller. Despite their diagnoses, these are tears of joyous celebration, for both were determined to keep living.[59] By pairing this photo with her parents, Goldin insists on the distance between these two modes of marriage—while Mueller and Scarpati's marriage might seem straight,

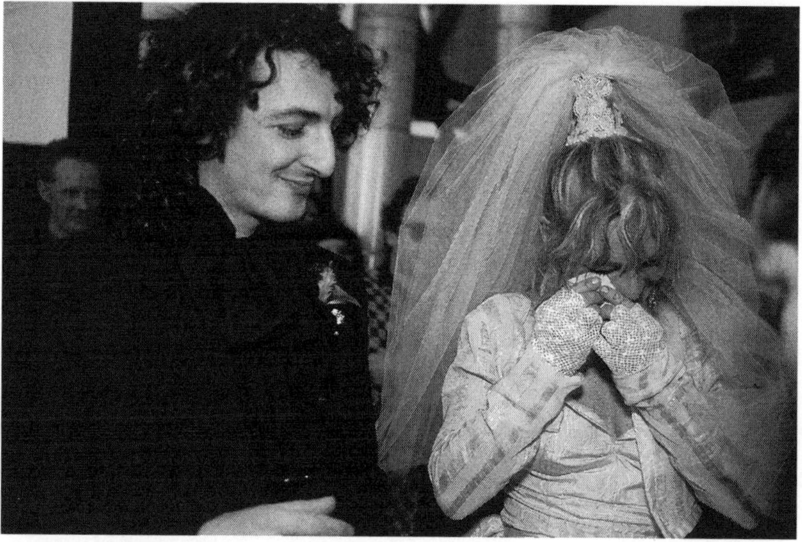

Figure 5.5. The most recent photograph included in *The Ballad,* which shows Cookie Mueller and Vittorio Scarpati getting married. Copyright by Nan Goldin. Reprinted with permission of Nan Goldin, *Cookie and Vittorio's wedding, New York City 1986.*

Mueller was avowedly bisexual and previously in a long-term relationship with Sharon Niesp. Her relationship with Scarpati was one they both came to in their thirties, and each accepted the other's artistic lifestyle of sexual liberation.

When Goldin turns to curate *Witnesses*, she does it in honor of those in the community who were living with and had died from HIV/AIDS, naming several individuals who were a part of *The Ballad*: Kenny Angelico (Ivy), Max diCorcia, Mark Morrisroe, and Vittorio Scarpati.[60] Mueller, whom she didn't name, would die from AIDS-related complications on the eve of the exhibit's opening, two months following the death of Scarpati.[61] The following section, in examining Goldin's curating of *Witnesses* through the catalog, demonstrates how Goldin continues to wield images to make her community visible and, together with text, mobilize them for action. The increasing political tenor of Goldin's work at decade's end echoes that of Alderfer, Jaker, and Nelson in chapter 1, whose *Caught Looking* took a more strident and explicit approach in advocating for sexual expression in response to the feminists who were joining up with conservative politicians to try to enact anti-pornography ordinances. For all these women, the conservative political backdrop exacerbated existing problems, especially when it came to the HIV/AIDS crisis, which President Reagan rarely acknowledged in public statements.

The Witnesses *Catalog: Curating Loss, Theorizing Response*

Between the release of *The Ballad of Sexual Dependency* as a book in 1986 and her curation of *Witnesses: Against Our Vanishing* in 1989, Goldin went to rehab for drug use, having spiraled into deep addiction following the end of her relationship with Brian. In an interview, Goldin recounts how the presence of the HIV/AIDS epidemic in her community influenced her decision to enter rehab: "In 1987, a friend of mine said, 'It's ridiculous watching you trying to kill yourself on drugs when all our friends are trying to stay alive with AIDS.' It took me a while, but that had a big effect on me."[62] In 1988, she left New York City to start rehab in Boston, and it was while she was there that Artists Space invited her to curate a show, which Steven C. Dubin describes that "she conceived of . . . as a memorial, a therapeutic experience for sick and/or grieving artists, and a way to increase public awareness about the disease. *Witnesses* was a logical extension of the type of work Goldin has done throughout her own career. She has continuously photographed herself and her friends in the most intimate situations."[63] This sense that Dubin articulates of how *Witnesses* is connected to Goldin's previous work through its "intimate" focus on her own community is one that Elisabeth Sussman echoes in her essay on Goldin's career, written for a major retrospective of Goldin's work that she curated with photographer David Armstrong at the Whitney Museum in 1996: "In a period of much political art, this exhibition stood out. Like Goldin's work, it had a simple directness and was a product of a community."[64] In looking again at *Witnesses* and Goldin's curation of the exhibit, this section focuses on how she politically activates her community and their losses through image and text in the exhibit catalog itself. By making HIV/AIDS visible through her community, Goldin refused to allow HIV/AIDS to remain a shameful, private matter. She began her own catalog essay by openly discussing her experience with rehab and how "when [she] came back to life, [she] realized how much had changed, how many of those [she] most admired were sick or had been killed by AIDS."[65]

Goldin's own essay and the four others in the *Witnesses* catalog connected the exhibit to larger conversations about social justice work around HIV/AIDS, which was furthered through associated actions that transpired during the exhibit's run from November 1989 to January 1990. For example, on November 28–29, just after the exhibit opened, a group of literary artists held a two-night reading in the exhibit space, contributing the proceeds from the event to the activist AIDS group ACT UP.[66] On December 1, the *Witnesses* exhibit also participated in the first Day Without Art action that the AIDS art organization Visual AIDS called for, joining over eight hundred other galleries, museums, and art institutions by closing for the day to acknowledge how HIV/AIDS was ravaging the artistic community.[67] Wojnarowicz's essay, with its damning critique of the homophobic actions and remarks of Cardinal John O'Connor, an archbishop in the Catholic Church, foreshadowed ACT UP's major Stop the Church demonstration on December 10 where members staged a die-in in St. Patrick's Cathedral while O'Connor was holding mass for his congregants.[68]

In the thirty-two-page catalog for *Witnesses*, about half the catalog is devoted to the essays, while the other half focuses on introducing the twenty-three contributing visual artists by pairing a featured image with a short biographical statement. Artists Space director Susan Wyatt's acknowledgments at the outset of the catalog introduce the exhibit as a whole and the sources of funding that supported the show. Each of the following essays, including Goldin's own, personally grapple with the HIV/AIDS epidemic in different ways, outlining the range of emotional responses present in this hard-hit community, which the exhibit artwork also echoed.

Goldin explains her goal for curating an emotional diversity of work in her own essay, asserting, "I want to empower others by providing them a forum to voice their grief and anger in the hope that this public ritual of mourning can be cathartic in the process of recovery, both for those among us who are now ill and those survivors who are left behind." Crucial here is how her approach empowers not only attendees but also the contributors themselves, by giving them this space to "voice their grief and anger" and join with others to create "this public ritual of mourning." Such a gathering is very different in tone from but overlaps in attendance with Goldin's early slideshows. Her curatorial latitude reveals how Goldin's collaborative spirit in her photographic process gets translated into curatorship; because Goldin allows each contributor autonomy in "select[ing] work that represents their personal responses to AIDS," most opt to make "new work especially for this exhibit."[69] Like Anzaldúa's supportive mentorship, Goldin's personal approach encouraged her contributors to dig deep and produce work that freshly articulated the continuing toll of HIV/AIDS in their immediate lives, a vision for the show that only gained in gravity as contributors and intimates died, or their health worsened, in the months leading up to the opening.

Goldin's essay, penned in October 1989, accounts for this ever-growing number of losses not only through her autobiographically informed text but also through two devices that deepen her statements and make visible the personal losses within this community: a fatalities roll call and a funeral photograph (Figure 5.6). These paratextual elements visually frame Goldin's essay in personal reminders of loss. In the column below her title, Goldin dedicates *Witnesses* to seven people whose deaths from HIV/AIDS touch, shape, and personally inform the exhibit: Kenny Angelico, Keith Davis, Max diCorcia, Peter Hujar, Mark

Morrisroe, Vittorio Scarpati, and Bibi Smith. At the end of this list, she adds to the dedication—connecting these local deaths to the broader expanses of HIV/AIDS losses—"and everyone else we have lost to AIDS." This larger invocation was added to a fairly final draft of the essay kept in Artists Space's records, suggesting that the list is necessarily partial and the real count is continuing.[70] The October 1989 timestamp at the end of her essay and others, which was added in final page proofs, further underlines how this list would continue to grow. As Goldin's essay mentions, two of the exhibit artists had died in the months leading up to the exhibit: Morrisroe in July, followed by Scarpati in September. Goldin also refers in her essay to the decline of Cookie Mueller, whose earlier writing she includes in the catalog and who would die as the exhibit opened in November. In addition to Scarpati and Morrisroe, the other five people that Goldin dedicated the exhibit to were friends and family of the exhibit artists. Kenny Angelico was a close friend and roommate of Goldin whom she also photographed in drag as Ivy (as discussed in the previous section); and Peter Hujar, whose photographs she included in the exhibit, was Goldin's professional mentor and David Wojnarowicz's lover. Keith Davis was Wojnarowicz's close friend, and Max diCorcia and Bibi Smith were the siblings of *Witnesses* artists Philip-Lorca diCorcia and Kiki Smith, respectively. This brief list demonstrates the intimate devastation within this interconnected artistic community, which the exhibit as a whole would lay bare. Also, the fact that this list is one of collective loss echoes the collaborative nature of Goldin's curation, which resonates not only with Anzaldúa's collaborations with fellow artists and audiences in her edited collections and talks as I discussed in the previous chapter, but also gestures back to how Alderfer, Jaker, and Nelson visually incorporated the conference organizers and presenters into the Barnard *Diary* as I examined in the first chapter.

As she does in *The Ballad* where she gestures to a larger community while also depicting her own individual experience, Goldin juxtaposes this list of collective grief with her own local loss. In the space below the end of her essay, Goldin includes a new photo of her own from the month before, "Vittorio Scarpati and Cookie Mueller, 1989," which makes the losses from HIV/AIDS freshly visible. This photo depicts essay–contributor Mueller standing in front of the open casket of her husband and *Witnesses* contributor, Scarpati. It provides a stark contrast

IN
THE
VALLEY
OF
THE
SHADOW

Against Our Vanishing
is dedicated
with love to:
Kenny Angelico,
Keith Davis,
Max diCorcia,
Peter Hujar,
Mark Morrisroe,
Vittorio Scarpati,
Bibi Smith
and everyone else
we have lost
to AIDS.

In the summer of 1988 I left New York for the weekend. Now, one and a half years later, I'm on my way home. In the process of withdrawl from addiction I suffered a kind of amnesia, a profound loss of identity. During early recovery I picked up my camera again. Through my work I began to reconstruct myself, to fit back into my own skin. I discovered the light after years in the dark. I wanted to live. Most of all I wanted to reconnect with my family of friends with whom I'd lost contact in my last few years of isolation and destruction. I was full of a new hope that I wanted to share.

During this period ARTISTS SPACE invited me to curate a show. I wanted to produce an exhibition by, for and about this community of friends, whose lives and work have inspired my life and my work. But when I came back to life, I realized how much had changed, how many of those I most admired were sick or had been killed by AIDS. I have had to face that there could not be all the joyous reunions I'd envisioned when I resurfaced from my own hell. My priority became to formulate an exhibition that would include the whole community, that those who have died would be as much a part of those who still survive, and that would serve to both keep their spirit with us and allow us to formally say goodbye.

Originally I conceived of a show entitled *Sexuality, Spirituality and Recovery in the age of AIDS*. Its primary purpose was to celebrate the indomitable spirit of our community; to prove that our way of life still exists, that we are being killed by AIDS but our sensibility could not be killed-off. To show how hard we have been hit and at the same time to affirm all that is left.

I feel my own recent recovery from addiction, and that of many of my friends, is directly related to AIDS. With the advent of a fatal illness in our midst, the glorification of self destruction wore thin. We were no longer playing with death -- it was real and among us, and not at all glamorous. We have been forced to make survival, recovery and healing our priorities as individuals and as a community. We realize that we can live the same lifestyle, but in the light. That we can still live fully in the moment but with an awareness of consequences. That we can take pride in the legacy of our past without contrition, regret, or revision, but with a new belief in the possibility of future.

I have intended all along to exhibit work that deals explicitly with sex and sexuality. The outbreak of the Helms controversy and

4

Figure 5.6. Page spread of Nan Goldin's curatorial text for the *Witnesses: Against Our Vanishing* catalog (1989). Courtesy of Artists Space, New York, and Artists Space Archive. MSS 291, Box 32, Folder 5, Fales Library and Special Collections, New York University Libraries. Copyright by Nan Goldin. Reprinted with permission of Nan Goldin.

the new success of government censorship of art in
this country has only
strengthened my resolve.
The influence of the New
Morality and the effective
use of AIDS as the most
powerful tool for sexual repression makes it even more
imperative to continue to
create and exhibit art that
portrays sexuality as a
positive force. To prove that
a gay aesthetic continues to
flourish. To prove that
sex=death is a false equa-
tion. To show that homo-
eroticism cannot be disap-
peared. To show that the
strictly demarcated lines
between homo and hetero-
sexual cultures can be
seamlessly crossed. That
the public and private mani-
festations of all forms of
sexuality can still be
positive and liberating. That
the sexual liberation movement need not become
extinct but requires a new
responsibility.

Over the past year four more
of my most beloved friends
have died of AIDS. Two
were artists I had selected
for this exhibit. One of the
writers for this catalogue
has become too sick to
write. And so the tone of the
exhibition has become less
theoretical and more per-
sonal, from a show about
AIDS as an issue to more of
a collective memorial.

I am often filled with rage at
my sense of powerlessness
in the face of this plague. I
want to empower others by
providing them a forum to
voice their grief and anger
in the hope that this public
ritual of mourning can be
cathartic in the process of
recovery, both for those
among us who are now ill
and those survivors who are
left behind.

I have asked each artist to
select work that represents
their personal responses to
AIDS. Most have created
new work especially for this
exhibit. The focus of the
responses vary: out of loss
come memory pieces,
tributes to friends and lovers
who have died; out of anger
come explorations of the
political cause and effects of
this disease. Some work
concentrates on the continuum of daily life, relationships and sexuality under
the shadow of AIDS, other
on the physicality of the
disease through the effects
on the body and the individual construction of identity.
And some respond with work
pertaining to death and
reclamation of the spirit.

This is not a show for or
about the art market. I am
not at all concerned here
with art as a commodity but
as an articulation, as an
outcry, and as a mechanism
for survival. This is not
intended to be a definitive
statement about the state of
art in the era of AIDS but as
a vehicle to explore the
effects of this plague on one
group of artists in a way that

hopefully will speak to all
survivors of this crisis. By
its very existence and its
volume, this show proves its
own premise -- that AIDS
has not and will not eliminate our community, or
succeed in wiping out our
sensibility or silencing our
voice.

I have sometimes experi-
enced survivors in these
times criticizing themselves
or one another about appro-
priate or inappropriate ways
of mourning. We are all
clumsy in dealing with grief.
I do not believe we need to
develop a correct etiquette.
Every one of our responses
is valid, passivity and
silence are the gravest
dangers. It is not the time to
distract ourselves with
divisiveness.

I have also witnessed this
community take care of its
own, nurse its sick, bury its
dead, mourn its losses, and
continue to fight for each
others' lives. We will not
vanish.

NAN GOLDIN
Boston, October 1989

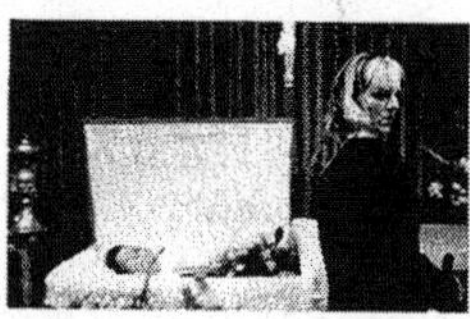

Vittorio Scarpati and Cookie Mueller,
1989; photo by Nan Goldin

to the photo of their wedding that Goldin included in *The Ballad*. Though this photo is reproduced in black and white and at about an inch high, it clearly communicates an experience all too familiar in their community as deaths stacked up. Rather than another paragraph of words, this photograph forcefully and ironically speaks, for it depicts a moment in which both Scarpati and Mueller could no longer speak themselves (AIDS took away Mueller's power of speech in her final weeks). This photograph would be the first piece of artwork that viewers would encounter inside the catalog. And, notwithstanding the high attendance rates for the exhibit, Artists Space's records document a number of people mailing in requests to purchase the catalog, suggesting that, for some, it may have been their only physical encounter with the exhibit.[71] In this manner, the photograph frames not only Goldin's words but also the rest of the exhibit.

Goldin's inclusion of this photo and placement of it at the end of her essay also echoes her curation of Barbara's photo at the end of her preface in *The Ballad*. Like that photo, this one reflects the textual content but speaks to a deeper emotional reality. This juxtaposition is especially striking given that her close friendship with Mueller was a sort of sisterhood; as Hilton Als remarks of their relationship, "Looking at the warm, playful, and wrenching photographs of Mueller in *The Ballad* is like seeing a ghost—the woman Barbara Goldin never got to be. Mueller survived girlhood in postwar Maryland and became herself. Barbara didn't. (Mueller died, of AIDS, in 1989.)"[72] Both images foretell Goldin's loss of these women, but Mueller was able to craft a life on her own terms, even if it was one cut short by illness at the age of forty. Paired with her dedication list, this photograph visualizes those losses, and, through the inclusion of Mueller in the frame, foreshadows the imminent and additional losses to come, including other *Witnesses* contributors in the coming years.

The tonal diversity of the other essays in the catalog by Wojnarowicz, Linda Yablonsky, and Mueller reflected Goldin's curatorial aim: "The focus of the responses vary: out of loss comes memory pieces, tributes to friends and lovers who have died; out of anger come explorations of the political cause and effects of this disease."[73] Goldin traces how loss and anger coalesce a number of the responses, which these essays exemplify. Wojnarowicz—in the longest essay in the catalog—excoriates how HIV and AIDS have been handled politically and socially. Mueller laments her earliest HIV/AIDS loss in 1982 and all those that have followed, and Yablonsky speaks poetically about the ghosts gathering around her and explicitly discusses Mueller's decline and imminent death. Together, they set the tone for the artwork to follow.

Goldin's curation of Wojnarowicz's essay deserves special mention—not just because the essay precipitated the aforementioned NEA funding crisis, but because it also became iconic in AIDS activist circles in the coming years. During the dispute with NEA, Goldin stood firmly beside Wojnarowicz and his words, evidencing her support of his fury.[74] His essay foreshadowed the aforementioned Stop the Church demonstration in December 1989 and also inspired the October 11, 1992, Ashes Action where ACT UP activists threw the ashes of dead lovers, friends, and family onto the White House lawn. Two recent ACT UP documentaries, in describing the orchestration of this action, cite the word of Wojnarowicz, who writes near the end of the essay:

> I imagine what it would be like if friends had a demonstration each time a lover or friend or stranger died of AIDS. I imagine what it would be like if, each time a lover, friend or stranger died of this disease, their friends, lovers, or neighbors would take their dead body and drive with it in a car a hundred miles to washington dc and blast through the gates of the white house and come to a screeching halt before the entrance and then dump their lifeless forms on the front steps. It would be comforting to see those friends, neighbors, lovers and strangers mark time and place and history in such a public way.[75]

While his anger here fuels an impossible fantasy of busting through the White House gates to "dump . . . lifeless forms on the front steps," it suggests a very public action in the face of death. ACT UP embraced such tactics as HIV/AIDS deaths grew exponentially with little public health response from the federal government. While Wojnarowicz died three months before the Ashes Action, his own death was recognized in the manner that he details at the outset of this passage, as activists marched his casket in a procession that wound through the East Village on July 29, 1992, a week after his death.[76] In interviews, Goldin describes Wojnarowicz as her "moral litmus test," and by encouraging him to write this essay and giving it ample space in the catalog she links her exhibit to this living history of activist approaches.[77]

Goldin's personal approach to introducing each of the show's twenty-three visual artists in the second half of the catalog echoes that of Alderfer, Jaker, and Nelson's process in the *Diary* that they put together for the Barnard Sex Conference in 1982. In that case, they wanted to represent the diversity of feminist perspectives by incorporating as many women in the *Diary* as possible, evident in the conference presentation section through collaging in postcards that the workshop leaders sent with handwritten annotations. With *Witnesses,* Goldin also wanted to emphasize the range of perspectives on HIV/AIDS, but her collaborative approach to sharing the artwork and words of others goes further in that she is working to memorialize explicitly the three contributing artists who had passed—Hujar, Morrisroe, and Scarpati (Figure 5.7). Along with an image of an artwork and a brief artist biography, personal details under each artist's name note the year of their birth and their current city or the city and year in which they died. Where the living contributors described their artistic vision for their work in this space, Goldin included artist biographies for these men that described their physical presence and their artwork, viscerally connecting them to the attendees. These entries echo the obituaries that were a common and countless phenomenon at this time, particularly in the gay press. Goldin wrote elegiac biographical statements for Hujar and Scarpati, while she excerpted Morrisroe's own words, from earlier that year in January, for his entry about actions he imagines taking in response to being ignored by his nurses while hospitalized for HIV/AIDS. In her final sentence for both Hujar and Scarpati, she insists on their continuing presence in their artwork: "AIDS robbed us of Peter's vitality, but not of his vision"; "[Scarpati] has left behind an indelible record of his fight for life and given us a gift of wit and wisdom." As the curator of an exhibit on AIDS, Goldin tasked herself with building a bridge between the living and the dead so that we might remember their contributions and participate, alongside her, in being active witnesses against our own vanishing.

To further this goal, it is likely no coincidence that Goldin features a self-portrait of these three men in the catalog alongside their biographies. As these artists could no longer represent themselves in new words or works, their autobiographical artworks let us know who they were via their own hand. Morrisroe's photograph and Scarpati's drawing show them in the last year of their lives, while Hujar's photograph depicts him in 1975, over a decade before his diagnosis and death in 1987, gesturing to the length of an artistic career that began in the 1950s.[78] Again, in this small sample of work, we see the range of representation that echoes the diversity implicit in Goldin's curatorial vision of the exhibit. Similar to the range of her photography, her curatorial work insists that there are many modes of representation, many registers of witnessing. This representational multiplicity used in the service of HIV/AIDS activism is of a piece with the other artists in this book, who visualized their communities to advocate for sex-positive, intersectional feminism. Moreover, Goldin's participation in HIV/AIDS activism echoes that of numerous other queer women in the late 1980s, and her work provides one artistic way of contributing that seeks to guard against loss.

Archives and Afterlives: Continuing Activism

Goldin's work with both *Witnesses: Against Our Vanishing* and *The Ballad of Sexual Dependency* makes visible a grouping of artists who defy traditional heteronormative tenets and embrace sexual liberation in their lives and artwork, even before the AIDS crisis. Goldin's work honing the political angle of *Witnesses* and connecting it to the direct action of groups like ACT UP not only evidences her own personal consciousness-raising but also points to a broader societal shift that was underway in the late 1980s and early 1990s, particularly a tightening conservatism that Goldin fought with deliberate radicalism. As she wrote in her catalog essay, "The influence of the New Morality and the effective use of AIDS as the most powerful tool for sexual repression makes it even more imperative to continue to create and exhibit art that portrays sexuality as a positive force."[79] As *Witnesses* makes visible, such a response was necessary, for people were dying and would continue to die. In a long review of *Witnesses* published in the *Washington Post*, Goldin explained the loss in personal terms, contrasting it with what the media reported about HIV/AIDS: "I'm 36 . . . and I've lost half my friends. It's important for people to know what they're losing. A lot of people have told me that the *Witnesses* show gave AIDS a human face for them. Reading the statistics, reading the medical costs, seeing the news—that doesn't really show people what is being lost."[80] In this sound bite, Goldin argues that *Witnesses* makes visible "a human face" not apparent in other public sources,

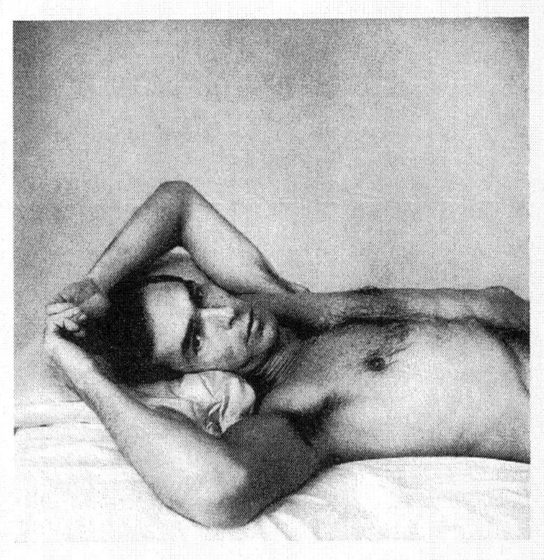

Figure 5.7. Biographical statements and accompanying self-portraits of Peter Hujar, Mark Morrisroe, and Vittorio Scarpati—who all died of complications from AIDS—that show the men on their own terms in the *Witnesses* (1989) catalog. Courtesy of Artists Space, New York, and Artists Space Archive. MSS 291, Box 32, Folder 5, Fales Library and Special Collections, New York University Libraries. Copyright by Nan Goldin. Reprinted with permission of Nan Goldin.

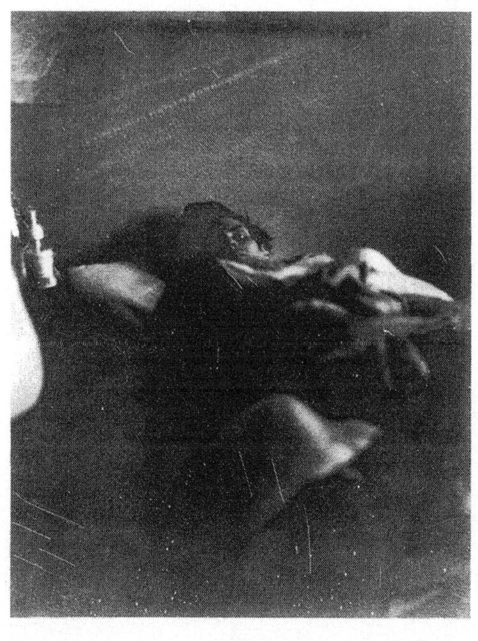

MARK MORRISROE
1959-1989
Died in Jersey City, NJ

Self-portrait 1989
Polaroid
10x8 inches
Courtesy: Pat Hearn Gallery

They have stopped listening to me,
so I wrote everything down in a note;
who was trying to murder me and
how, and then smashed the vase of
flowers Pat Hearn sent me so I would
have something to mutilate myself
with by carving in my leg, 'evening
nurses murdered me'; and I took the
phone receiver and pummeled my
face over and over and sprayed blood
all over the walls and on this book;
and then I took the butter pat from my
dinner tray and greased up the note
and stuffed it up my asshole so they
would find it during my
autopsy....
--Mark Morrisroe
January, 1989
(as excerpted from
Mark Morrisroe's biography
by Ramsey McPhillips)

VITTORIO SCARPATI
1955-1989
Died in New York City

What Happened to My Lungs?
ink on paper
6x8 inches
Courtesy: 56 Bleeker Gallery

Vittorio Scarpati made these drawings while living in the hospital for months hooked up to machines to keep breathing after his lungs had collapsed from AIDS- related pneumonia. Drawing became his outlet and his weapon for survival-- a way to help bear terrible pain and to sustain his sense of humor. These drawings are a visual diary of his days living in suspension, full of the mundane realities of illness and hospitalization and his memories, fantasies, and dreams. He has left behind an indelible record of his fight for life and given us a gift of wit and wisdom.
--Nan Goldin

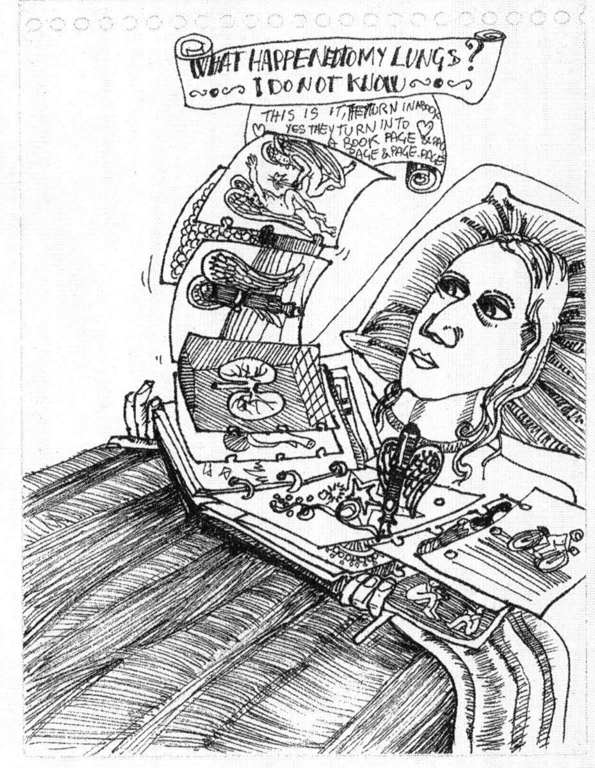

which remain impersonal. The exhibit as a whole performs this action, but it is most poignantly apparent with the biographical entries for Hujar, Morrisroe, and Scarpati in the catalog. For Goldin, this visibility was a matter of witnessing against a vanishing not only of physical death but also of social death. In her work as photographer and curator, she makes people visible in the frame or on the gallery wall, preserving their lives and memories in a manner akin to the archives mentioned throughout this book.

As discussed at the outset of this chapter, Goldin would focus on HIV/AIDS in her subsequent photography, memorializing those who had already died and documenting those who were still living with HIV/AIDS. The way she mobilized her community for activism by making their personal struggles public with *Witnesses* is a tactic she has again embraced in recent years as she formed PAIN (Prescription Addiction Intervention Now) in 2018 to address the opioid crisis and target the Sackler family, major funders of the arts who profited off the crisis by producing and aggressively marketing OxyContin. In a recent interview, she linked her work with PAIN to that of *Witnesses*, averring, "The opioid crisis is the epidemic of our times, like AIDS was, and it's also related to government malfunction and to the lack of medical practices and lack of prescriptions that are used to help people. They also share the same stigma, and so a lot of our work is to try to destigmatize addiction, and to educate people on that. Our battles are similar."[81] As with *Witnesses*, her work with PAIN draws from what her personal community is facing, making visible and "destigmatiz[ing]" their lives. These activist projects align with and draw energy from her photography, all pushing for openness and honesty against the secrecy of her upbringing. Together with the other artists in this book, Goldin makes visible the sexual lives of women freed from repression. All these media align with the sex-positive politics of the coming third wave of feminism in the 1990s. By returning to these works now and considering how they intersect with archives, we can ask how these and similar women will be remembered in the future and what capacity archives of different sorts have to remember and structure the memory of such diverse visual media.

EPILOGUE

Whenever Gloria Anzaldúa gave a public talk illustrated by her drawings or Nan Goldin shared her slideshow of photographs in a neighborhood bar or Alison Bechdel self-syndicated her comic in someone's local newspaper, innumerable people were influenced in ways that we cannot fully trace. The works of all the artists featured in this book continue to reverberate in the present moment and touch contemporary discourses around identity and sexual expression, though they remain unevenly remembered outside the archives. The archives and afterlives sections across this book trace some of these connections to the present, but each artist's embrace of communal modes of creation and distribution defies neat and tidy lines of transmission.

All the women in this book contributed to feminist and queer discourse in underacknowledged ways and laid the foundation for later critical work—whether that be through the evolution of new visual styles or through the development of new theory inspired by their imagistic interventions. Artistically, their focus on fluid representations of sexuality that embraced the multivalence of identity and foregrounded intersectional portrayals was echoed in the third and subsequent waves of feminism, including in the DIY self-published zines that young girls produced in connection to the riot grrrl movement in the early 1990s. Their once avant-garde approaches are now often subsumed into the mainstream. For instance, art critic Craig Hubert sees "an appropriation of [Goldin's] work by the current snapshot-obsessed generation" who share their photos on social media platforms like Instagram.[1] The ideas and critiques of these artists remain relevant today.

Much of the artwork discussed in this book remains difficult to access, filed away in visible archives and on the edges of our collective memory. Physical archives rather than the bookstore, library, or internet were how I first encountered most of these materials during grant-funded research trips over the course of a decade.[2] Much of the research in this book relies on archival collections processed in the past two decades. In the last ten years, there has been a resurgence of interest in prominent lesbian feminists from the 1980s, including Gloria Anzaldúa, Gayle Rubin, and Barbara Smith, as newly released anthologies of their writing have made their theoretical contributions available again.[3] At the same time, increasing numbers of scholars have been deftly recovering the print histories of feminist and LGBTQ activism across the 1970s and 1980s.[4] This book contributes to this body of work by centralizing the importance of visuality to these movements, which has received relatively little attention.

The rise of digitization has begun to transform access as more and more feminist as well as gay and lesbian activist sources have been put online in proprietary, open-access, and grassroots spaces.[5] Some of the very work I cite in this book can now be found online and sometimes in multiple repositories, like Bechdel's early comics that can be located in digitized copies of *WomaNews* on Reveal Digital's open-access Independent Voices project and in Gale's proprietary Archives of Sexuality and Gender. If you looked for her comics as they began to appear in other grassroots periodicals, the field of relevant digital archives widens even further. However, just because something is preserved in visible archives, whether physical or digital, does not mean that it has been safeguarded against being forgotten. Digitization doesn't always go far enough to contextualize artwork within its time or communities, and visual materials are not always easy to find in digital archives, especially in collections that rely on optical character recognition technologies that make searchable the embedded text but none of the images. Yes, Bechdel's early comics are online, but you would need to know how and where to look for them, and the work of countless lesser-known artists remains further submerged, despite digitization.

We need to consider how we can bring the vibrant worlds of these artists and their surrounding communities to public knowledge so that they can influence future generations. As a quick illustration of this point,

I always ask: Who can't you google? Who isn't on Wikipedia? For example, despite the impact of their sex-positive collages on the feminist sex wars, Hannah Alderfer, Beth Jaker, and Marybeth Nelson are virtually invisible online. None of these artists is easy to google and none of them have a Wikipedia page, nor are they mentioned on the Wikipedia pages dedicated to the 1982 Barnard Sex Conference for which they designed the *Diary* (1982) or the collaborative artist collective they helped form in the late 1970s, Group Material.

To counter such gaps, in comics courses I've taught I've had students recover the legacy of cartoonists underrepresented on Wikipedia. In recent iterations of this project, I had students focus on LGBTQ cartoonists from the 1980s and 1990s, most of whom had participated in the long-running *Gay Comix* (1980–98) series where Roberta Gregory and Lee Marrs had pioneered representations of queer women. Across two semesters of this project, students had improved twenty-nine biographies and created twenty-one new entries. Even so, roughly half of the hundred-plus artists who participated in the *Gay Comix* series still do not have biographies on Wikipedia, so the work continues.[6]

More than one specific approach to recovery, however, it is my hope that the archival sections present in each chapter of this book, built from the experiences of researching these women across many archives and engaging relevant discourses around archives, will provide useful methods and context for thinking through how to approach research and how to engage the infrastructure of archives in order to recover the memory not only of individual artists but also of the larger milieux that supported them. Such support does not end with the creation of the artwork, but continues as these works find residence in the archives. After all, what I've encountered in the archives is there because of communities of individuals who valued, saved, and deposited it and the archivists who welcomed, cataloged, and made it accessible. As the critical conversations around archives across this book underline, the lives of women, people of color, and queer folks have historically been seen as disposable and unworthy of preservation, so this book is indebted to the creation of all those grassroots archives that welcomed and upheld difference and to all the folks who went to work within more established archives and began to imagine who and what to collect differently. Thank you.

ACKNOWLEDGMENTS

This book, which is about how women's artwork has been supported by and generative of community, would not be possible without the attentive care, generosity, and brilliance of many folks across the years. The seeds of this project were planted in Nancy K. Miller's "Experimental Selves" seminar in Fall 2009 during the second year of my PhD in English at the CUNY Graduate Center. In that course, we discussed how women and men narrated their lives in textual, visual, and multimodal memoirs. Professor Miller encouraged us to pay special attention to the importance of relationships between women that disrupted the patriarchal norms of vertical inheritance that often limit women's lives. It was in this course that I first encountered and wrote about Nan Goldin's photography, which I later expanded and revised heavily for both my dissertation and then again for this book. It was also in this course that I first read comics in a scholarly context and learned about the field of comics studies when we read proofs from Hillary Chute's *Graphic Women*, which was published in 2010 by Columbia University Press's Gender and Culture Series that Miller coedited. How Chute centered women and their lives in comics—often stereotypically seen as an artform dominated by male artists—profoundly shaped the field of comics studies and my own scholarship in the years to come. It was also in this seminar that I met Meredith Benjamin and Melina Moore, who would later become vital interlocutors and writing partners.

This course was the first of several that I took with Professor Miller, each of which helped me develop a feminist attentiveness to the small and meaningful details of how women developed careers as artists, and how they did so with the support of others while working around societal constraints. Miller eventually became my dissertation director, and I fondly remember when we went to see Goldin's new "Scopophilia" art exhibit at the Matthew Marks Gallery in December 2011 and then mapped out what would become my dissertation project as we walked along the High Line and ate grilled cheese at a diner in Lower Manhattan.

Other courses and professors in my program at the Graduate Center—which I often referred to as the top-ranked quirky school because of its embrace of noncanonical literatures and cutting-edge methods—were key to my scholarly formation. In David Gerstner's Film History II course in Spring 2011, I first engaged and became enthralled with archives as I researched and wrote a seminar paper about how the production of *The Philadelphia Story* (1940) reshaped Katharine Hepburn's career, utilizing archival collections at both the New York Public Library for the Performing Arts as well as the Margaret Herrick Library that holds the collections of the Academy of Motion Picture Arts and Sciences in Beverly Hills, California. Following that initial research experience, I realized that archives were going to be integral to my developing interest in women's visual–textual artwork that had so often been overlooked. In her introduction to *Graphic Women* (2010), Chute outlined the vibrant world of women producing comics in the countercultural underground scene in the 1970s; these comics, by and large, did not exist outside of archives in the present day, though that has been changing in the past several years with the digitization of some comics and the republication of others, including the Fantagraphics rerelease of underground series, including *Wimmen's Comix* in 2016 and *Tits & Clits* in 2023.

Meeting Jonathan W. Gray, a professor of race and comics, was also transformative, as he provided a model for a scholar successfully centering his research on comics and questions of identity and social justice. Conversations with Gray were formative in making comics a key part of my scholarly agenda, and he has remained a champion of my scholarship throughout my career. Alongside Gray, Miller was also instrumental in my development as a comics scholar; she had long included graphic memoirs in her teaching and her own scholarship in the fields of autobiography and women's and gender studies and actively encouraged students who wanted to research comics. Tahneer Oksman, another student of Miller's a few years ahead of me in the program who wrote her entire dissertation on comics—which became the fantastic *"How Come Boys Get to Keep Their Noses?": Women and Jewish American Identity in Contemporary Graphic Memoirs* (2016)—was another important role model for me.

Grants from my doctoral institution—through two Doctoral Student Research Grants (2012, 2014) and three Advanced Research Collaborative (ARC) Knickerbocker Awards for Archival Research in American Studies (2013, 2014, 2015)—funded my initial visits to archives across the United States. I am particularly thankful to Duncan Faherty, who was one of the initiators of the ARC awards and who also supported my archival endeavors in coursework and dissertation workshops. Grants from archives—the Gloria Anzaldúa CMAS-Benson Latin American Collection Short-Term Research Fellow at the University of Texas at Austin (2013), the Mary Lily Research Grant from the Sallie Bingham Center for Women's History and Culture at Duke University (2016), the Travel-to-Collections Grant from the Sophia Smith Collection at Smith College (2016), and the Queer Zine Archive Project summer residency project in Milwaukee, Wisconsin (2017)—and other external organizations—New York City Digital Humanities Graduate Student Digital Project Award (2015)—allowed me to expand my archival research. When the Society for the Study of Gloria Anzaldúa invited me back to UT Austin in 2015 to present on my research in Anzaldúa's papers, I was able to extend my trip and conduct new research on Anzaldúa that reshaped my eventual analysis of her visual artwork.

All told, across my years of research, the following archives and the archivists therein were critical to the research conducted for this book: ONE National Gay and Lesbian Archives at the University of Southern California; Special Collections and University Archives at Cal State University, Long Beach; Paul Brians and Lynn R. Hansen comics collections at Washington State University; Nettie Lee Benson Latin American Collection at the University of Texas at Austin; Queer Zine Archive Project in Milwaukee, Wisconsin; the Comic Art Collection of the Russel B. Nye Popular Culture Collection at Michigan State University; Sallie Bingham Center for Women's History and Culture at Duke University; Sophia Smith Collection at Smith College; Human Sexuality Collection at Cornell University; Fales Library at New York University; Barnard Center for Research on Women Records in Barnard Archives and Special Collections, Barnard College; various research divisions at the New

York Public Library; and Lesbian Herstory Archives in Brooklyn, New York. Living within a short walk of the Lesbian Herstory Archives for five years had a special influence on this project, in ways both manifest and subtle. Digital archival collections, including the Alexander Street Press Underground and Independent Comics Collection; Independent Voices Collection at Reveal Digital; and Gale Archives of Sexuality and Gender helped contextualize the research conducted in physical archives. Karen Green, the extraordinary comics curator at Columbia University who has built impressive circulating and archival comics collections, introduced me to the Alexander Street Press collection shortly after it was launched, and it was here that I read my first feminist underground comics before later researching them in collections at WSU and MSU in the summer of 2012.

An inimitable team of brilliant and inspiring scholars—Nancy K. Miller, Jonathan W. Gray, David Gerstner, Kandice Chuh, and Hillary Chute—helped shepherd the project through exams and the dissertation defense, each one leaving a mark that shaped my revision and eventual book. For Chute to agree to serve on my dissertation committee as an outside reader was particularly meaningful as *Graphic Women* remains such an important touchstone. Chute's support of my scholarship has been integral to my professional success throughout my career, and I wouldn't be in the field—at least not in the same way—if I hadn't encountered her research, which sparked and undergirded my own.

As I was beginning to write my dissertation, the writing group I formed with Meredith Benjamin and Melina Moore, two fellow graduate students who also worked with Miller as their primary adviser, was indispensable in helping me finish my dissertation and find my scholarly voice. Since our first formal meeting on June 22, 2015, and ongoing to the present day, our group, self-styled as M3, has supported one another. We've exchanged hundreds of emails, likely thousands of texts, and innumerable pages, talking about all aspects of professionalization. It is so special to have readers who deeply understand your writing process and can help cheer you on to completion when writing feels nearly impossible. Their brilliant insights are present in nearly every page of this manuscript, and I am a profoundly better writer and thinker thanks to our group. I could not ask for better colleagues and friends. Earlier writing groups during grad school with other English Program students

Christopher Ian Foster and Velina Manolova as well as with J. Ashley Foster, Angela Francis, Tracy Riley, and Leah Souffrant influenced my scholarly trajectory and provided lasting colleagues.

Other groups during grad school also helped me flourish as a scholar. In my educational technology work as coordinator of Open-CUNY, an open-source digital platform where graduate students could build websites and develop public digital scholarship, and as an Instructional Technology Fellow in the Macaulay Honors College program, I worked alongside an interdisciplinary cohort of scholars who were capacious in their thinking. A number of them—including Gregory Donovan, Jen Jack Gieseking, Laurie Hurson, Amanda Licastro, and Christina Nadler—became quick and enduring friends who challenged me to think about how my scholarship moved across disciplines.

The comics studies panels at the Modern Language Association conference, both those organized by the Comics and Graphic Narratives Forum as well as those put together independently, were my first foray into the field and were key to my scholarly development. Jonathan W. Gray, who served on the Forum at its inception, made me feel welcome in the field and at MLA—no easy feat for such a huge conference—introducing me to countless scholars and making me feel like my contribution was important. As I started presenting on and organizing panels at the MLA, befriending Leah Misemer, a fellow graduate student in the field, at the conference in 2014 was a turning point in my scholarly development. We became collaborators and champions of each other's research, putting together panels at the MLA and other comics conferences as well as coediting a special issue of *INKS: The Journal of the Comics Studies Society* based on one of those panels. Through my friendship with Misemer and further participation in comics studies panels and conferences, the whole field opened up, and I made close connections with emerging and established scholars. This community proved crucial as I stepped into the profession and includes Michelle Abate, Colin Beineke, Jenny Blenk, Scott Bukatman, Jeremy M. Carnes, andré carrington, Julian Chambliss, Hillary Chute, Brannon Costello, Anthony Michael D'Agostino, Fernanda Díaz-Basteris, Lan Dong, Ramzi Fawaz, Kristen Gay, Erica Gillingham, Karen Green, Justin Hall, Charles Hatfield, Jason Helms, Yetta Howard, Bill Kartalopoulos, Aaron Kashtan, Katherine Kelp-Stebbins, Susan E. Kirtley, Joshua Abraham Kopin,

Frederik Byrn Køhlert, Zack Kruse, Martha Kuhlman, Rachel Kunert-Graf, Andrew J. Kunka, Sarah Lightman, Francesca Lyn, Keith McCleary, Sam Meier, Nicholas E. Miller, Rachel R. Miller, Elizabeth "Biz" Nijdam, William Orchard, Osvaldo Oyola, Anna Peppard, Christopher Pizzino, Alexander Ponomareff, Roger Sabin, Lara Saguisag, Nicholas Sammond, Joe Sutliff Sanders, Jeremy Stoll, Gwen Athene Tarbox, Janine Utell, Emmy Waldman, Rebecca Wanzo, Qiana Whitted, Justin Wigard, and Daniel Worden. A special thanks to Carnes and N. E. Miller for our seltzer weekend writing retreats where I revised portions of this manuscript; to Kopin, McCleary, and Oyola who offered informal writing support and friendship through our prolific Housewives Cat Popcorn group chat; and to Kirtley and Kunka who read the full manuscript as I prepared the final version for the press.

As I was finishing my dissertation in the spring of 2015, I was over the moon to receive an email from Jason Weidemann, the editorial director at the University of Minnesota Press, expressing interest in my research after having heard about it from my dear friend Jen Jack Gieseking. When Jason and I met at the following MLA conference in January 2016 after I had defended my dissertation, we had a deeply warm and engaging conversation about the importance of uplifting queer history. The level of engagement he brought to the conversation let me know that Minnesota would be the right home for the project, and it has been lovely to work with him throughout the years to transform the dissertation into a book. His unwavering enthusiasm helped me see the way forward in revising my newly defended dissertation, particularly as I crafted the book proposal in the spring of 2016 and finalized the advance contract that September. I am thankful to the anonymous peer reviewers and faculty board who approved the project in its early and revised forms as well as to Zenyse Miller, the editorial assistant at the Press who made preparing the manuscript seamless thanks to her detail-oriented attention. Countless individuals at the Press were instrumental in the production and preliminary promotion process, including Shelby Connelly, Eric Lundgren, Rachel Moeller, Caitlin O'Neil, Maggie Sattler, Mike Stoffel, Nicholas Taylor, and all the other great folks at the Press I will meet as the book makes its way into the world. Thanks also to Jeff Clark and his design firm, Crisis, for the gorgeous cover design,

Neil West of BN Typographics West for typesetting, and Sean Grattan for a wonderfully comprehensive and subtly amusing index.

Many thanks are due to the generosity of the artists and executors of the artists involved in this book for allowing the art to be reprinted. Thanks as well to Gayle Rubin, Carole S. Vance, and Nancy K. Miller who shared additional insights about the feminist sex wars and the Barnard Sex Conference, reading and responding to my first chapter with detailed remarks that helped strengthen the final version.

Imagining how to tackle the revision and incorporate an explicit discussion of archives into every single chapter and have the different topics speak to each other was no easy feat, but it was made possible both thanks to Jason Weidemann as well as to the support of my M3 writing group as well as other editors at crucial points in the process. Notably, as I heavily revised my chapter on Alison Bechdel for the "Queer about Comics" special issue of *American Literature*, the issue editors, Ramzi Fawaz and Darieck Scott, spent ample time discussing with me how I might better foreground my claims and articulate the intertwined role of archives and grassroots networks. Fawaz made time for one-on-one conversations with me about the research, enacting the critical generosity of editorship as mentorship, and it shows in the essay, which was completely transformed from the dissertation chapter and gave me the critical apparatus and vision for how I would reshape the rest of the book. The three honors that the Bechdel essay in *American Literature* received let me know that I was on the right path. Moreover, being invited by Fawaz, Tori Yonker, and other individuals at the Department of English at the University of Madison, Wisconsin, to speak as part of the Americanist Lecture Series in 2019 gave me a chance to share my newly revised chapter on Lee Marrs and Roberta Gregory and receive invaluable feedback from the community.

Another key figure was Chris Lura, who worked with me as a developmental editor on the project, helping me focus on the nuts and bolts and zero in on the small details of how to revise the dissertation into a book. Lura spent a lot of detailed time with me on my writing, extensively marking up chapters and writing out multiple pages of overall feedback where he took time to explain specific principles to follow to strengthen both my writing and the connective tissue across the chapters of the book. We also spent hours on the phone and video chat reviewing his notes and discussing the process of revision. What I learned from Lura's feedback helped me improve my writing across the board.

In 2016–17, the same academic year I secured the book contract, I had the extremely good fortune of landing a tenure-track job in visual rhetoric in the English department at the University of Florida (after three years of applying to nearly two hundred jobs) where I was hired to support the long-standing comics studies program that the late Don Ault started after he came to the university in the 1980s. I immediately felt welcome and at home in the department—another quirky school that embraces noncanonical literatures, foregrounds cutting-edge theoretical approaches, and prioritizes a diversity of intersectional representation. Getting a job where I could put comics front and center in my research and teaching heavily influenced my approach to the book and my research trajectory. In that first year at UF, I applied for and received the Humanities Scholarship Enhancement Fund, which supported a monthlong research trip to New York City as well as my developmental editing work with Chris Lura. In New York, I researched and wrote in the Shoichi Noma Reading Room at the New York Public Library after having found it wonderful to research and write in the Wertheim Study while I was first conceiving of the dissertation project as a graduate student. It was during that stay in New York in the summer of 2018 that I constructed a new outline for the book and reimagined how the project would need to grow and change. This funding from UF was fundamental in jump-starting the revisions on the book, and I have felt even further supported by my very warm and collegial department where not only am I encouraged to teach comics as I see fit but other faculty also regularly include comics in their curricula and advise grad students who research comics.

Over the years, my chair, Sid Dobrin, has been a champion of my research and a constant source of advice. Barbara Mennel, who directed the Center for the Humanities and the Public Sphere, has been instrumental in helping me secure research funding both inside and outside the university, and Sophia Acord, who used to work alongside Barbara at the Center, has been similarly wonderful. The University of Florida College of Liberal Arts and Sciences and Center for the Humanities and Public Sphere (Rothman Endowment) also provided a publication subvention to support this book's production. Kenneth Kidd and Anastasia Ulano-wicz, my colleagues in children's literature who also support the comics research in the department, have been invaluable mentors and friends. I serve often with Kenneth and Anastasia on dissertation committees, and it has been gratifying to learn from both of them about their approaches to the field as scholars of children's literature. Marsha Bryant and Jodi Schorb have both been huge founts of feminist and queer wisdom in helping me navigate the profession and the university. Over the past few years, it's been lovely to be in a writing group with Kenneth and my colleagues Rae X. Yan, Delia Steverson, and Suzan Alteri. Their energy and enthusiasm for their research was always motivating, especially in the moments where the book project felt insurmountable. More recently, I also joined with my colleagues Marsha Bryant and Leah Rosenberg in a writing accountability check-in as we all worked to complete major projects, which was so useful as I completed portions of the manuscript. I have been extremely lucky to be in a department with a thriving community of junior faculty. I have also met wonderful colleagues in other departments, including Rachel Gordan, Ariel Pomputius, and Dillon Vrana. It has been particularly amazing to find so many scholars across the university who are enthusiastic about the importance of comics in a research setting. A long-standing local cartooning school in Gainesville, the Sequential Artists Workshop, has been another important space of community.

The engagement of my students at UF as well as at NYU Gallatin—where I taught first-year writing and research courses from 2013 to 2017 as I was writing my dissertation—has been a sustaining force as I composed this book. In my graphic archives course that I've taught in many iterations at both NYU and UF, students learn how to research visual print culture in archives while immersing themselves in recent theoretical conversations around radical archives and materials. Watching how these younger generations embraced visual cultures from generations past and how their archival encounters were transformative demonstrated to me how important it was to put discussions of archives at the heart of the manuscript. Teaching comics, especially now that I can center comics in my curricula at UF, has allowed me to consider the particular ways of looking at image and text together that comics encourage.

Throughout this process, friends have provided crucial moral support and helped me see the path to completion. These are the folks with whom I've bantered about ideas and passionately shared research findings, but also those who listened to me vent over the difficulties of the writing process. Their friendships have provided the sustenance necessary to finish the book. My friend Matt Glass has read much of what I've written and has even driven me to archives when I did research in his hometown of Atlanta. He's been a vital sounding board helping ensure that my writing made sense to a lay audience.

Over the past few years, Melissa Iuliano and I have shared a weekly meetup at a local coffee shop where we drank caffeine, enjoyed baked goods, and worked on creative projects. The redrafting of several chapters of the book happened during our meetings, in which our mutual friends Roxanne Palmer and Maxine Worthy sometimes participated. The cadence and continuity of our meetings helped me make steady progress and feel like things were moving forward, even when I was struggling with the manuscript. At our meetings, Melissa was often prototyping art projects for the students she teaches—it was illuminating to sit alongside an artist and watch her work through her process at the same time that I wrote about other visual artists and their artmaking practices. Becoming friends with Maxine, Melissa, and Roxanne—the Meow Brigade—when I moved to Gainesville has been a major bright point in my life. All of them are visual artists in a variety of media; watching how they move between the different forms and adapt processes informed my understanding of how many of the artists in this book drew on many forms in their own careers.

The culinary and crafty companionship of Leah Souffrant has influenced this project in many ways. In the years when I lived in New York City we often gathered together to cook and chat, talking about and sometimes making art. As an academic, multimedia artist, and poet, Leah has been both an inspiration and a role model; her constant belief in the significance of my research has kept me going. Over the years, cooking and sharing a meal together has been something that I've done with a number of people whose friendship has been integral for this book. Amanda Licastro and Joanna Tsai are two of those folks with whom I've cooked many a meal and whose fierce friendship has sustained me. Some other key individuals who've been there throughout this long process include Joan Brady, Ivy Chang, Mia Chen, Rachel Corbman, Gregory Donovan, Jen Jack Gieseking, Sean Grattan, Velina Manolova,

Edie Nugent, Heath Pennington, Tracy Riley, Sasha Terris-Maes, Christie Troy, Lora Webb, Mary Zaborskis, and Carolyn Zola.

During the first year of the pandemic, Dillon Vrana organized the neighbors in our cul-de-sac to socialize safely every Friday outside. We were academics in different departments at the university, so our conversations were a fun and dizzying cross section of ideas. My partner, Tyler, and I looked forward every week to our Friday gatherings with Dillon, Natalie A. Cooper, Heidi Jensen, and Jason Mullen, and we all celebrated our birthdays and major holidays (Fourth of July, Halloween, Thanksgiving, Christmas) with one another. This space of friendship and joy at a difficult moment gave me the energy to keep working on and believing in the book.

Thanks to my family, who are always there at the end of the phone line or cross-country plane trip, for their support. Thanks to my mom for driving me to various archives in the Los Angeles area and helping me select the camera that's been invaluable to my research process. There's also something about the all-consuming, detail-driven way in which I research that very much comes from Mom. Thanks to my dad, the computer scientist, for his engineering ethos that practically grounds my work and for his spot-on software conversations. Early in life, Dad gave me a book on how to make art with Microsoft Word, which I took to with particular alacrity, learning the ins and outs of formatting precisely with a word processor. The spreadsheets I made over the course of my research for this book to help me organize my ideas were definitely inspired by Dad. My older sister, Tina, has always been someone I've looked up to and who's provided me level-headed advice for any life situation. In her many years together with her husband, Terrell, it has filled my heart to see our family grow. Becoming an aunt to Liyah, Maya, and Ayla has been a delight. Though my grandparents have all been gone for many years now, I carry them forward with me, drawing on their work ethic and unceasing love. I hope I've done them and our family proud.

And last but certainly not least, much credit is due to my partner, Tyler Stalbaum, and our two cats, Champ and Jagger. We've become a fearsome foursome over the past three years as the pandemic raged and we mutually supported one another amid stressors both large and small. Champ and Jagger are very different cats, but each is incredibly loving in his own way and spent ample time with me as I worked on or worried over the book. The Covid-19 pandemic ramped up soon after Tyler and I first met in February 2020, fast-tracking the emotional depth of our budding relationship and commitment to each other. Not only did Tyler help keep me sane during Covid, cooking me good food and concocting delicious cocktails, he also took to learning about my area of research with enthusiasm and has been a sounding board and source of advice as I was striving to complete a book manuscript amid a global pandemic. Not only has Tyler been a strong emotional support, but he has also actively participated in the book's completion, helping me make scans of a number of images and driving me to archives for research and also piloting our U-Haul steadily and safely during a cross-country move as I proofed my book in the front passenger seat. My writing is even stronger and more polished thanks to this family of mine who helped me drag this book across the finish line.

NOTES

Introduction

1. Wilshire, "More Nasty Women's Humor," 39.

2. Sherman, "Sex and the 60-Second Warning," 110.

3. Fawaz, "Queer Sequence," 589.

4. Beineke, "On Comicity."

5. This approach echoes how Bart Beaty puts comics in dialogue with the high art world in *Comics versus Art* and examines how these art worlds, which are sometimes considered disparate, connect. In this book, I am pointing out how all these various art forms belong to and were produced within the social world of grassroots activism.

6. Beins, *Liberation in Print*, 11.

7. Chute, *Graphic Women*; Fawaz, *New Mutants*; Fawaz, "Stripped to the Bone"; Scott and Fawaz, "Introduction."

8. Beirne, *Lesbians in Television and Text*; carrington, *Speculative Blackness*; Howard, *Ugly Differences*; Scott, *Keeping It Unreal*.

9. Scott and Fawaz, "Queer about Comics"; Abate, Grice, and Stamper, "Lesbian Content and Queer Female Characters"; Halsall and Warren, *LGBTQ+ Comics Studies Reader*.

10. Eisner, *Comics and Sequential Art*; McCloud, *Understanding Comics*, 9.

11. Chute, *Graphic Women*, 7, 221n20. In *Comics versus Art*, Bart Beaty also discusses McCloud's decision to claim these ancient forms as comics, focusing his discussion on the Bayeux Tapestry: "The question of whether the Bayeux Tapestry can meaningfully be considered to be a comic is dependent upon the definition that one chooses to employ. From the standpoint of the Americanists with their emphasis on recurrent characters and word balloons, the Tapestry is self-evidently not a comic. Nonetheless, from more generous perspectives the seventy-metre-long embroidery, which tells the tale of the Norman Conquest of England of 1066 through a combination of words and sequential images, could indeed be meaningfully regarded as a comic" (31).

12. Fawaz, "Stripped to the Bone," 338, 362.

13. Sedgwick, *Epistemology of the Closet*, 22.

14. Gregory, *Dynamite Damsels*.

15. Gregory, 4.

16. Chute, *Graphic Women*, 11.

17. Piepmeier, *Girl Zines*, 18.

18. Cvetkovich, *Archive of Feelings*; Eichhorn, *Archival Turn in Feminism*.

19. Caswell, "'Archive' Is Not an Archives," par. 3.

20. Sellie et al., "Interference Archive," 461.

21. Heresies Collective, "Editorial," 3.

22. Eichhorn, *Archival Turn in Feminism*, 3.

23. Eichhorn, x.

24. I have had a chance to learn from all these individuals about the development of their collections during in-person events, classroom visits, and archival research sessions. Their discussion and careful thinking through of the challenges that accompany trying to collect and preserve comics and zines in both institutional and independent spaces has been hugely influential in my thinking. Freedman, Miller, Wilde, and Wooten have been active in considering the difficulties of cataloging and preserving zines in libraries and archives, creating zines, and curating digital spaces and projects like https://www.zinelibraries.info/ and https://zinecat.org/. Beyond Eichhorn's book, which treats Darms, Freedman, and Wooten, Nick Sousanis's "Life in Comics" profiles Green's career in comics, and Alana Kumbier has a chapter about the Queer Zine Archive Project in their book *Ephemeral Material*. Darms also has a book, *The Riot Grrrl Collection*, that showcases some of the zines in the Riot Grrrl Collection she initiated as part of the Downtown Collection at NYU Fales, and Wooten has coedited a collection with Liz Bly, *Make Your Own History*.

25. Caswell, Punzalan, and Sangwand, "Critical Archival Studies," 2. In addition to this essay, another piece by Caswell, "'The Archive' Is Not an Archives," provides an overview of some of the trends that animate the research of archivists and information studies scholars who engage the archives in a critical fashion.

26. DiVeglia, "Accessibility, Accountability, and Activism," 72.

27. Keating, "Archival Alchemy and Allure"; Bost, "Messy Archives and Materials That Matter."

28. I further discuss the rise of LGBTQ archives during the 1970s and 1980s in chapter 1.

29. I further discuss how institutional and university archives started to collect HIV/AIDS materials in chapter 5, but Marika Cifor's recent *Viral Cultures* is a must-read deep dive on this topic.

30. Rich, "Compulsory Heterosexuality and Lesbian Existence," 648.

31. DeCrescenzo, "Alison Bechdel Celebrates 20 Years," 25.

32. Als, "Nan Goldin's Life in Progress."

1. The Collage Activists

1. Vance, "Epilogue," 431.

2. Alderfer et al., *Diary of a Conference on Sexuality*, 2, 38, 44–67. The scholars and activists who participated as part of the conference planning committee

were Julie Abraham, Hannah Alderfer, Meryl Altman, Jan Boney, Frances Doughty, Ellen DuBois, Kate Ellis, Judith Friedlander, Julie German, Faye Ginsburg, Diane Harriford, Beth Jaker, Mary Clare Lennon, Sherry Manasse, Nancy K. Miller, Marybeth Nelson, Esther Newton, Claire Riley, Susan R. Sacks, Ann Snitow, Quandra P. Stadler, Judy R. Walkowitz, Ellen Willis, and Patsy Yaeger.

3. Coalition for a Feminist Sexuality and Against Sadomasochism, "We Protest."

4. Vance, "Epilogue," 432. For a comprehensive overview of the conference planning and aftermath, see Corbman, "Scholars and the Feminists."

5. Vance, "Epilogue," 433; Coalition for a Feminist Sexuality and Against Sadomasochism, "We Protest." As Carole S. Vance alludes to in her epilogue to *Pleasure and Danger* and Rachel Corbman and Lorna Norman Bracewell confirm in their retrospective research on the conference, the leaflet was largely composed by the Women Against Pornography and the other two groups were mere signatories. See Corbman, "Scholars and the Feminists," 60; and Bracewell, "Beyond Barnard," 24.

6. Vance, "Epilogue," 434.

7. Vance, "More Danger, More Pleasure," 295. As Vance recounts in her epilogue to *Pleasure and Danger*: "'Friends' and colleagues decided they were too controversial to associate with; anonymous calls were made to their employers; they were disinvited to feminist panels and conferences; projects in which they were even marginally involved were blacklisted. Personal attacks made at the conference disrupted their lives for months" (434).

8. As Vance recounts in her epilogue to *Pleasure and Danger*, "The *Diary* was eventually reprinted and distributed, but not without the intervention of a lawyer, and plans for a 1983 conference handbook were scuttled" (434).

9. Women's Center, "Women's Center Annual Report."

10. Abelove, Barale, and Halperin, *Lesbian and Gay Studies Reader*; de Lauretis, "Queer Theory."

11. The print run of the original, uncensored *Diary*, which the Barnard administration confiscated, was 1,500. Vance, "Epilogue," 431.

12. Vance, "Epilogue"; Echols, "Retrospective"; Rubin, "Blood under the Bridge"; Corbman, "Scholars and the Feminists"; Bracewell, "Beyond Barnard"; Duggan and Hunter, *Sex Wars*; Bronstein, *Battling Pornography*.

13. Ault, *Show and Tell*, 7–8.

14. Ault, 37, 49.

15. Ault, 48.

16. Heresies Collective, "Heresies #12."

17. Heresies Collective, 36–37.

18. These details about the creation of the cover for *Pleasure and Danger* come from an email in which Alderfer and Nelson shared, "The cover of *Pleasure and Danger* was actually collaged in black and white, then color Xeroxed. Those are photos of Hannah's legs, Beth's stairwell, the handbag was cut from an ad, and the ledger drawn in." Nelson and Alderfer, "Re: Caught Looking Etc."

19. Nan D. Hunter creates a timeline that chronicles the growing debate, tracing the movement from an anti-pornography ordinance that was first drafted in 1983 by Dworkin and MacKinnon for use in Minneapolis, then adapted in 1984 for Indianapolis following Minneapolis's rejection of the measure. FACT and other groups then fought the ordinance in court, which the U.S. Court of Appeals ruled unconstitutional in 1985. The Supreme Court finally confirmed it as unconstitutional when it refused to hear the case in February 1986. Hunter, "Pornography Debate in Context."

20. Hunter and Law, "Brief Amici Curiae," 70.

21. Alderfer, Jaker, and Nelson, "Designers' Statement," 5.

22. Ellis, O'Dair, and Tallmer, "Introduction," 8.

23. Nestle, "Will to Remember," 86–87; Nestle, "Who Were We?," 240.

24. Alderfer, Jaker, and Nelson, "Designers' Statement," 5. Later in their statement in *Caught Looking*, they note, "Most of the images were donated by private collectors, photographers, models and artists, rather than drawn from generally available commercial photography."

25. The artists' approach to the research for these images, like the method of combining images on the page, is one of collage. This process is distinct from historical research in that these materials are transferred from their original contexts and connected with images from other contexts in order to create a broader argument about sexuality.

26. The conclusion to this chapter outlines some of the renewed attention the feminist sex wars have received in recent years.

27. As Marika Cifor puts it, "The community archives movement exploded in the wake of upheaval prompted by 1960s' to 1970s' social movements. In the 1980s, a gay and lesbian archives movement began to flourish, offering a means to locate and remember queer lived experiences and to evade and contest social subordination" (*Viral Cultures*, 19).

28. Marika Cifor and Stacy Wood review the connections between social movements and archives building more broadly in the postwar era ("Critical Feminism in the Archives," 3–7).

29. DiVeglia, "Accessibility, Accountability, and Activism," 73.

30. Cvetkovich, *Archive of Feelings*, 252.

31. Ellis et al., *Caught Looking* (1986 ed.), 96.

32. In thinking through how records never remain static in the archives, Ketelaar writes, "Every interaction, intervention, interrogation, and interpretation by creator, user, and archivist is an activation of the record. The archive is an infinite activation of the record. Each activation leaves fingerprints which are attributes to the archive's infinite meanings" ("Tacit Narratives," 137).

33. Eichhorn, *Archival Turn in Feminism*, 3.

34. The *Diary* was produced for the roughly 750 conference participants, while *Caught Looking* was produced in four editions in 1986, 1988, 1992, and 1995, with the first and second editions each printed in runs of five thousand copies. Many of the visual materials across this book, though rare, exist in multiple copies and are organized in different collections at various archives, as the

following chapter will explore. Because they are not physically fragile, many of the archives allow relatively unfettered use, adopting the "preservation through use" attitude of the Interference Archive, a grassroots institution that makes social movement documents available to the general public. Sellie et al., "Interference Archive."

35. Alderfer et al., *Diary of a Conference on Sexuality*, 70.

36. Alderfer et al., 43, 48–49, 54–55, 60–61, 69.

37. The start of the next chapter discusses the beginnings of the feminist sex wars before the Barnard Sex Conference.

38. In a chronological account of key events of "the pornography debate," Nan D. Hunter traces how the anti-pornography ordinance was introduced in a variety of U.S. locations between 1983 and 1985: Minneapolis; Indianapolis; Suffolk County, New York; Los Angeles; Cambridge, Massachusetts. In most of these places it was soundly defeated, though it initially gained some traction in Indianapolis until the U.S. Court of Appeals and the Supreme Court declared it unconstitutional. Hunter, "Pornography Debate in Context," 29.

39. Vance, "Epilogue," 431.

40. Snitow, *Feminism of Uncertainty*, 77–78.

41. Ellis et al., *Caught Looking* (1986 ed.), 94–96.

42. Barry, *One Hundred Demons*; Barry, *What It Is*; Barry, *Picture This*; Barry, *Blabber Blabber Blabber*; Barry, *Syllabus*; Lopez, *Lap Dancing for Mommy*; Lopez, *Flaming Iguanas*; Lopez, *Girl Must Die*. Alderfer, Jaker, and Nelson even incorporated some of Barry's work from NAKED LADIES! NAKED LADIES! NAKED LADIES! into *Caught Looking*.

43. Alderfer et al., *Diary of a Conference on Sexuality*, 9.

44. By contrast, many of the academics in the conference planning group here and in subsequent pages opt for printed text that would allow them the space for a mini treatise on sexuality. Both Jaker and Nelson also choose to handwrite in plain block letters to convey their remarks and focus their words on the form of the diary in their entries printed later in the volume. The fact that all three artists wrote about the form of a diary in their own handwriting and how it can reveal truths makes sense since they were primarily responsible for the *Diary's* visual conceptualization. Alderfer et al., 9, 25, 41, 71–72.

45. The conference planning committee continued to meet through April, but these initial meetings were especially important to share as they established the framework and guiding principles for the event. Alderfer et al., 72.

46. Piepmeier, *Girl Zines*, 79.

47. Butler, "Politics, Pleasure, Pain," par. 1.

48. Corbman, "Scholars and the Feminists," 59.

49. Barnard's archives reveal the starkness of this difference, as the *Diary* stands out among the minimal, four-page pamphlets of conferences from the years prior and following. There was also a similar four-page pamphlet produced for the 1982 conference to accompany the *Diary*.

50. Alderfer et al., *Diary of a Conference on Sexuality*, 1.

51. Alderfer et al., 2.

52. Alderfer et al., 4–34.

53. Alderfer et al., 6–8, 10–11; Butler, "Politics, Pleasure, Pain."

54. Alderfer et al., *Diary of a Conference on Sexuality*, 26–29.

55. In addition to the photos in the comic itself, the inclusion of text in a thin space below each panel transforms each one into a Polaroid.

56. Alderfer et al., 3.

57. Alderfer et al., 73.

58. Alderfer et al., 40.

59. Bronstein, *Battling Pornography*, 215.

60. Hunter, "Pornography Debate in Context," 27–28. In Paula Webster's account of a Women Against Pornography slideshow, she recounts the array of explicitly and implicitly pornographic images that the group included in its presentation: "I remember seeing a slide show with about 30 images of predominantly heterosexual couples engaged in intercourse (genital and anal), bondage, and sadomasochism. There were shots of individual women, bound and gagged, pictures of female dominatrices, assorted album covers, posters, clothing advertisements, as well as a handful of very jarring images of self-mutilation and the now-infamous *Hustler* photos of women arranged as food on a platter or put through a meat grinder" ("Pornography and Pleasure," 31).

61. Bronstein, *Battling Pornography*, 217.

62. Hunter, "Pornography Debate in Context," 28.

63. Elinor Fuchs, "Staging the Obscene Body," 35, 55.

64. Beth Jaker and Nan D. Hunter were also involved in editing *Caught Looking*.

65. Ellis, O'Dair, and Tallmer, "Introduction," 4.

66. Alderfer, Jaker, and Nelson, "Designers' Statement," 5.

67. Ellis et al., *Caught Looking*, 1986, 60–61.

68. Ellis et al., 3.

69. Duggan, "Censorship in the Name of Feminism," 65.

70. Heresies Collective, "Heresies #12," 48–51. Webster also participated as a member of the Heresies Collective who edited the "Sex Issue."

71. Webster, "Pornography and Pleasure," 34.

72. Webster, 32–33.

73. This pairing is remembered today in how the word *cougar* is used to describe an alluring older woman who preys on younger men.

74. Duggan and Hunter, *Sex Wars*, 26; "American Booksellers Association, Inc. v. Hudnut."

75. Ellis, O'Dair, and Tallmer, "Introduction," 8.

76. Ellis, O'Dair, and Tallmer, 8.

77. There was a print run of five thousand copies for the first and second editions of the book, while the print run for the other editions remains unknown.

78. Ellis et al., *Caught Looking* (1988 ed.).

79. Ellis et al., *Caught Looking* (1992 ed.).

80. Stein, "Introduction to Barnard Special Issue"; Love, "Introduction"; Walters, "Introduction."

81. "About the Journal." As editor Heather K. Love acknowledges in the text prefacing the *Diary*'s reprinting, "Despite subsequent reprinting, the *Diary* remains exceedingly rare" ("Diary of a Conference on Sexuality," 50).

82. Abelove, Barale, and Halperin, *Lesbian and Gay Studies Reader*.

83. Love, "Diary of a Conference on Sexuality," 54–61.

84. Love, 50.

85. The print run of the original, uncensored *Diary*, which the Barnard administration confiscated, was 1,500. Vance, "Epilogue," 431.

2. The Comics Visionaries

1. Hunter, "Contextualizing the Sexuality Debates."

2. Hunter, 22–23; Rich, "Feminism and Sexuality in the 1980s," 526.

3. Visual artist Tee Corinne, in the opening lines of an article where she recovers these works for the feminist audience of the *Country Women* periodical, recounts the reasons that feminists reject comics: "One of the reasons I wanted to write about women's comics is that most women's bookstores do not carry them because: 'They are too dirty,' 'They are too violent,' 'They do not further the revolution,' 'They don't uplift women's ideals,' etc. Or, as one East Coast Women's Bookstore owner put it: 'Women have better things to spend their money on than that trash'" ("Comics by Women," 25). I discuss this article and Corinne's research binder of women's comics that she archived at the Lesbian Herstory Archives throughout a piece tracing lesbian comics networks through archives ("Archiving Grassroots Comics").

4. Kirtley, "'Word to You Feminist Women'"; Cook, "Underground and Alternative Comics."

5. In this chapter, I am broadly using the general spelling of *comics* rather than adopting *comix*, in order to emphasize and foreground the connections of these feminist works with other comics by women, past and present. Comics within the underground were often called comix, for as Roger Sabin explains, "Instead of pandering to a kids' market, these [underground] titles spoke to the counter-culture on its own terms, which meant dealing with subjects like drugs, anti-Vietnam protest, rock music and, above all, sex" (*Comics, Comix and Graphic Novels*, 92). Further, as Nicholas Sammond relates in an entry on "comix" for *Keywords in Comics Studies*, "Robert Crumb is usually given credit for swapping the second *c* in comics to the *x* in comix. . . . First and foremost, the new spelling was a rejection of the North American comics industry and its restrictive and prudish Comics Code. . . . A potent signifier, the *x* invoked a rejection of the code in favor of unbridled, libidinous, and uncensored expression. It foreshadowed the X rating for movies" (58).

6. Marrs, *Wimmen's Comix* #2. Marrs contributed front covers to Rudahl, *Wimmen's Comix* #3, and Leschen and Dinegar, *Wimmen's Comix* #9, and the back cover for Robbins and Richards, *Wimmen's Comix* #5.

7. While many scholars describe Gregory as the first openly lesbian contributor to *Wimmen's Comix*, it is important to note that she identifies as bisexual.

In her scholarship on *Wimmen's Comix*, Leah Misemer discusses the import of Gregory's comics to the series and how she was in dialogue with other creators on the matter of sexuality. Gregory, "Modern Romance"; Gomez, "She Changed Comics"; Misemer, "Serial Critique."

8. Robbins, "Wimmen's Studies," 31.

9. Marrs, *Pudge, Girl Blimp* #1; Marrs, *Pudge, Girl Blimp* #2; Marrs, *Pudge, Girl Blimp* #3; Gregory, *Dynamite Damsels.*

10. Chute, "Introduction"; Kirtley, "'Word to You Feminist Women'"; Meier, "On Teenage Abortions"; Meier, "Forgotten History"; Misemer, "Hands across the Ocean"; Misemer, "Serial Critique"; Sammond, "Meeting in the Archive."

11. Sherman, "Interview with Trina Robbins," 54.

12. "Interviews with Women Comic Artists: Lee Marrs," 24.

13. Nicholas Sammond has written about the distribution troubles of women's and queer underground comics, honing his insights through interviews with underground cartoonists and publishers. He notes how the underground publishers who welcomed women and gay perspectives were founded on publishing straight men, so the established distribution networks were not entirely welcoming to these titles. He also observes that women's bookstores were hospitable to some titles, "but those outlets were limited and the network unreliable" ("Meeting in the Archive," 106). Rachel R. Miller has discussed how feminist titles also encountered difficulty getting shelved, noting that "comic-book shops often marginalized comics by women by bagging and shelving them alongside pornographic or erotic comic books because of their explicit depictions of sex, queerness, and women's bodies" ("When Feminism Went to Market," 430).

14. "Interviews with Women Comic Artists: Lee Marrs," 24.

15. These remarks come not only at a time of transition in the movement at large, but also for the women creating feminist comics in the underground movement. Both *Wimmen's Comix* and *Tits & Clits* stopped publishing for seven years near the end of the 1970s, amplifying these sentiments. Their feelings of dismissal were also heightened by fractures within the *Wimmen's Comix* collective. Both scholars and the cartoonists themselves often individualize this rift, focusing on a select group of specific women—Trina Robbins on one side and Aline Kominsky-Crumb and Diane Noomin on the other—who disagreed about what constituted feminist art. Kominsky-Crumb and Noomin ultimately separated from the collective in the late 1970s and published their own comic book, *Twisted Sisters* (1976), which featured solely their own comics. However, the movement was bigger than just these women: none of them was particularly central to *Tits & Clits* and nearly each issue of both series contained a different constellation of contributors with their own particular viewpoints, who numbered over a hundred for both series over the course of their run. While the seven-year publishing drought contributed to the ill feelings captured in these interviews, its cessation motivated artists to branch out and pursue other publishing opportunities and also welcomed in new energy and new artists when the comics continued, reinvigorating both series in ways that are not often discussed.

Moreover, when *Wimmen's Comix* returned in the 1980s, Robbins, Kominsky-Crumb, and Noomin all contributed to the series, often within the same issue. Still, this moment of pause in the late 1970s when the artists weigh in about their collective project and its struggles embodies the critique of the movement at large and their local version of the movement that Marrs and Gregory unwind in comics form in order to theorize new future possibilities. See Gebbie and Bucher, *Wimmen's Comix* #7; LeMieux and Binswanger, *Wimmen's Comix* #8; Farmer and Fleener, *Tits & Clits* #7; Kominsky and Noomin, *Twisted Sisters*; Chute, "Introduction"; Dueben, "Oral History of *Wimmen's Comix*"; Robbins, "Babes & Women"; Noomin, "Wimmin and Comix"; "Interviews with Women Comic Artists: Aline Kominsky"; Kirtley, "'Word to You Feminist Women'"; Galvan, "Archiving *Wimmen*."

16. Marrs, *Pudge, Girl Blimp* #1; Marrs, *Pudge, Girl Blimp* #2; Marrs, *Pudge, Girl Blimp* #3; Gregory, *Dynamite Damsels*.

17. Sammond, "Meeting in the Archive," 107; Gomez, "She Changed Comics."

18. Hesford, *Feeling Women's Liberation*, 4.

19. "Interviews with Women Comic Artists: Lee Marrs"; Marrs, "Interview with Lee Marrs"; House, Cowan, and Gregory, "Criticism, Feedback and Changes"; Aldama, "Roberta Gregory."

20. Beins, *Liberation in Print*, 15.

21. Beins, 91–114.

22. Stoler, *Along the Archival Grain*.

23. Kirtley, "'Word to You Feminist Women,'" 275.

24. Chute, "Introduction," 20–24. For more on the importance of Chute's creation of a genealogy of modern women cartoonists amid a discussion of other similar contemporary projects, see Galvan, "From Julie Doucet to Gabrielle Bell."

25. Underground cartoonist Trina Robbins has been doing recovery work of women cartoonists since the mid-1980s and has published numerous volumes attempting a full history of women producing in the comics form alongside a number of volumes focused on recovering the work and history of specific women producing comics during different eras of the twentieth century. See Robbins and yronwode, *Women and the Comics*; Robbins, *Century of Women Cartoonists*; Robbins, *From Girls to Grrrlz*; Robbins, *Nell Brinkley and the New Woman*; Robbins, *Great Women Cartoonists*; Robbins, "Wimmen's Studies"; Robbins, *Brinkley Girls*; Robbins, *Pretty in Ink*; Robbins, "Babes & Women"; Robbins, *Babes in Arms*; Robbins, *Flapper Queens*.

26. Sammond, "Meeting in the Archive," 110. Jean Bessette further meditates on how archives are shaped by various implicit and explicit ideologies across her monograph *Retroactivism in the Lesbian Archives*: "The evidence housed and highlighted in archives can be shaped by the archive itself. The organization, mediation, and even production of archival records and artifacts occur in specific rhetorical situations in response to historically located exigencies. The implications of this point should prompt rhetoricians and historians alike to attend critically to the circumstances of the production and preservation of historical

evidence. When and through what means was the record produced, mediated, selected and arranged?" (135–36).

27. "Steve Willis Underground Comics Collection"; "Lynn R. Hansen Underground Comics Collection."

28. Rosenkranz, *Rebel Visions*. I discuss how the typical periodization marginalizes comics by women and LGBTQ folks in Galvan, "Adjacent Genealogies, Alternate Geographies."

29. Galvan, "Archiving Grassroots Comics"; Galvan, "Finding Feminist Comics Histories."

30. Eichhorn, *Archival Turn in Feminism*; Beins and Enszer, "'We Couldn't Get Them Printed'"; Meagher, "'Difficult, Messy, Nasty, and Sensational'"; Enszer, "'Fighting to Create and Maintain'"; Enszer, "Night Heron Press"; McKinney, "Newsletter Networks"; Groeneveld, *Making Feminist Media*; Hogan, *Feminist Bookstore Movement*; Beins, *Liberation in Print*; Bessette, *Retroactivism in the Lesbian Archives*; Meagher and Runyon, "Backward Glances." There have also been numerous special issues of academic journals focused on the recovery of contemporary feminist history, including Adkins and Dever, "Archives and New Modes of Feminist Research"; Groeneveld and Thrift, "Thinking beyond Backlash"; and Jordan and Meagher, "Feminist Periodical Studies."

31. Agatha Beins's canny reading of the periodical page at the outset of *Liberation in Print* is relevant for discussing comics as I discuss in the introduction to this book, though she does not address comics within her monograph.

32. Marrs, *Pudge, Girl Blimp* #1, 3, 5–6.

33. Marrs, 6.

34. Marrs, 10.

35. Warren, "Consciousness-Raising and Difference," 3; Allan et al., *Self-Health*.

36. Kaplan, *Erotics of Talk*, 155.

37. Marrs, *Pudge, Girl Blimp* #1, 10–11.

38. Murphy, "Immodest Witnessing"; Caruana, "Great Yogurt Conspiracy."

39. Caruana, "Great Yogurt Conspiracy."

40. Murphy, "Immodest Witnessing," 136.

41. Caruana, "Great Yogurt Conspiracy."

42. Marrs, *Pudge, Girl Blimp* #1, 11.

43. Marrs, 25.

44. Marrs, *Pudge, Girl Blimp* #2, 42.

45. Some of the most outwardly psychedelic women's comics can be seen in the work of Willy Mendes, who edited a psychedelic collection of comics titled *Illuminations* and published "Wiley Willy's Realm of Karma Comix" and other pieces that integrate high concentrations of patterning and geometric repetition in *All Girl Thrills*. While Marrs's comics are more subtle and conventionally cartoony in their design, she also had connections to psychedelia, as evidenced by her editing of *Spit in the Ocean* #4, a literary series initiated by Ken Kesey, whose writing appeared in every issue.

46. Cixous, "Laugh of the Medusa," 887–88.

47. Cixous.

48. Marrs, *Pudge, Girl Blimp* #2, 4.

49. Marrs, *Pudge, Girl Blimp* #3, 5–6.

50. Marrs, 6.

51. Marrs, 16–19, 40–42.

52. Marrs, 48.

53. This opening up of narrative possibilities echoes the theoretical writings of Joanna Russ, a science fiction author and feminist whose 1972 essay "What Can a Heroine Do? or Why Women Can't Write" discussed how women characters were often constrained by patriarchal narrative structures and theorized how science fiction could offer more narrative possibilities for women that broke with these limitations.

54. This group, who soon named themselves the Radicalesbians, also distributed the now-iconic "Woman-Identified Woman" statement at this action. Gallo, *Different Daughters*, 173–74; Mankiller et al., *Reader's Companion to U.S. Women's History*, 330–31; Stein, *Rethinking the Gay and Lesbian Movement*, 92.

55. Davies, "Lavender Menace Members Hold Signs."

56. "Lavender Menace Action."

57. There are a couple of independent prefatory comics at the outset and one at the conclusion that, in addition to the usual paratexts, frame the main narrative and contribute to the thirty-six-page comic.

58. Gregory, *Dynamite Damsels*, 4.

59. Although the story line follows Frieda and her sexual evolution, race does return in a later vignette, "Nothing Remains Constant," that also features the character of Edie. Here, a Black male challenges her commitment to her race by denigrating her involvement with "that white women's lib." While this confrontation forces her to consider if she "[has] to decide whether [she's] more black or more woman?" and quit that particular consciousness-raising group, she affirms her commitment to feminism by participating in a "black sisters C.R. group" that's "plan[ning] the constitution for [a] new black women's liberation group." Her movement out of the overwhelmingly white group and into her own space echoes contemporaneous moves by Black feminists like Barbara Smith, who helped start the Black lesbian feminist Combahee River Collective in 1974 and coedited with Lorraine Bethel *Conditions Five: The Black Women's Issue.* There is a moment of possible reconciliation later when Frieda says that Edie's planning a shared potluck for the two groups, but we never see this potluck made manifest. Gregory, 21, 23; Combahee River Collective, "Combahee River Collective Statement."

60. Gregory, *Dynamite Damsels*, 4.

61. Gregory, 4.

62. Gregory, 7.

63. Gregory, 9, 17.

64. Gregory, 9.

65. Gregory, 17.

66. Gregory, 17.

67. Gregory, 9.

68. Gregory, 14–16.

69. Her exuberant outcry "Sisterhood is beautiful" echoes *Sisterhood Is Powerful*, and this repetition is confirmed by her T-shirt, which has the woman's symbol with a fist on it, also recalling the feminist warrior of *Dynamite Damsel*'s cover. Gregory, 14.

70. Gregory, *Dynamite Damsels*, 14.

71. Gregory, 15.

72. Gregory, 15.

73. Gregory, 16.

74. Gregory, 24.

75. Gregory, 28.

76. Gregory, 28–29.

77. Gregory, 29.

78. Galvan, "Archiving Grassroots Comics."

79. To read about the complexity of romance comics genre, see Nolan, *Love on the Racks*; Heifler, "Teen Age Temptations"; and "PanelxPanel #36—Romance."

80. Mangels, *Gay Comics* #21.

81. Cruse, *Gay Comix* #2.

82. Mangels, *Gay Comix* #14.

83. Mangels, *Gay Comics* #25.

84. Camper, *Rude Girls and Dangerous Women*.

85. Camper, *Juicy Mother*; Camper, *Juicy Mother 2*. I further trace the contours of Camper's career and her community-building ethos in an article about her work which appeared in an issue of *Journal of Lesbian Studies* dedicated to lesbian comics; see Galvan, "Making Space."

86. Mangels, "History of Contributors," 75; Warren, *Dyke Strippers*, 67; Ewing, "Longtime Pacific Center Executive Director."

87. Mangels, "History of Contributors," 76; Beirne, "Image, Sex, and Politics," 54.

88. Warren, *Dyke Strippers*, 157.

89. Natalie, *Stonewall Riots*; Natalie, *Night Audrey's Vibrator Spoke*; Natalie, *Rubyfruit Mountain*.

90. Warren, *Dyke Strippers*.

91. Warren, 7.

92. Cruse, *Gay Comix* #1, n.p.

93. Eichhorn, *Archival Turn in Feminism*.

94. Sammond, "Meeting in the Archive," 110.

95. Galvan, "Archiving Grassroots Comics."

96. Some duplicates of certain comics also exist within the zines collection upstairs at the Lesbian Herstory Archives, suggesting the possibility for how these comics play a role within multiple histories.

3. The Newspaper Cartoonist

1. Bechdel, *Fun Home*; Lacayo and Grossman, "10 Best Books"; "John Simon Guggenheim Foundation"; "MacArthur Fellows Program"; Playbill Staff,

"*Fun Home* Breaks Box Office Record." Hillary Chute also sums up the many accolades that Bechdel has received since *Fun Home*'s publication in her preface to interviews with Bechdel that she published in *Outside the Box* and in her account of Bechdel's influence in her chapter about queer comics in *Why Comics?* See Chute, "Alison Bechdel"; and Chute, "Why Queer?"

2. Bechdel, *Indelible Alison Bechdel*, 9; Rubenstein and Bechdel, "Alison Bechdel Interview," 115–16.

3. Bechdel, *Indelible Alison Bechdel*, 27; Bechdel, "*Dykes to Watch Out For*, Plate No. 19."

4. Bechdel, *Dykes to Watch Out For*; Bechdel, *Indelible Alison Bechdel*, 28.

5. Bechdel, *Dykes to Watch Out For*; Bechdel, *More "Dykes to Watch Out For.*"

6. Bechdel, *Essential "Dykes to Watch Out For.*" For some scholars, like Judith Kegan Gardiner, this collection becomes the space through which to analyze the overarching series; see "Queering Genre." Bechdel's publication of her first collection with Firebrand Books in 1986 combined with her success at self-syndicating the strip and developing a stable readership that she could count on may have contributed to her choice to redevelop the strip with recurring characters, which launched in February 1987. Bechdel, "*Dykes to Watch Out For*: One Enchanted Evening."

7. Bechdel, "Cartoonist's Introduction," xiv.

8. In a 1995 interview with Anne Rubenstein, Bechdel explains how she got started at *WomaNews*: "And I started volunteering at a feminist newspaper called *WomaNews* where I did paste-up and production and wrote an occasional review" ("Alison Bechdel Interview," 116). In a 1990 interview with Chris Dodge, Bechdel describes her work at *Equal Time*: "*Equal Time* comes out every two weeks and it's a community newspaper for lesbians and gay men. And my job is doing all the key lining and layout production and doing the physical part of the paper" ("Interview with Alison Bechdel," 5).

9. I analyze how Bechdel uses this strip to participate in and theorize queer subjectivity and difference at the time in a chapter within a collection of essays on Bechdel; see Galvan, "*Servants to* What *Cause.*"

10. In designating certain archives as queer-adjacent, I identify spaces that aren't explicitly queer but that contain a lot of materials relevant to queer experience, like the Sophia Smith Collection. This use of *adjacent* resonates with Eve Kosofsky Sedgwick's discussion of the non-dualistic nature of *beside* in *Touching Feeling* and how the spaciousness of that preposition allows "a wide range of desiring, identifying, representing, repelling, paralleling, differentiating, rivaling, leaning, twisting, mimicking, withdrawing, attracting, aggressing, warping, and other relations" (8).

11. These special issues and edited collection have been central locations mapping out the emerging scholarly conversation around queer comics: Scott and Fawaz, "Queer about Comics"; Abate, Grice, and Stamper, "Lesbian Content and Queer Female Characters in Comics"; Halsall and Warren, *LGBTQ+ Comics Studies Reader*.

12. *Gay Comix* was a comics series that ran for twenty-five issues between 1980 and 1998 under three successive editors: Howard Cruse (#1–4), Robert Triptow (#5–13), and Andy Mangels (#14–25). In issue #15 (1992), Mangels renamed the series *Gay Comics*, acknowledging the changing times and diminished presence of the underground comix scene that initially birthed the series. When discussing the series collectively, I refer to it by its initial title as that appears to be the general convention.

13. Cruse, Triptow, and Mangels, *Gay Comix* #1–25; Melia and Gracey-Whitman, *Strip AIDS*; Robbins, Sienkiewicz, and Triptow, *Strip AIDS USA*; Triptow, *Gay Comics*; Warren, *Dyke Strippers*; Camper, *Juicy Mother*; Camper, *Juicy Mother 2*; Murphy, *Gay Genius*; Hall, *No Straight Lines*; Christensen, *Anything That Loves*; Kirby, *QU33R*; Macy and Avery, ALPHABET; Jesanis, Lorenz, and Glass, *Being True*; Thornton and Avery, *We're Still Here*; Joy, Gauvin, and Lee, *Rainbow Reflections*; Bors, *Be Gay, Do Comics!*; Greenwood, Assan, and Eaton, *When I Was Me*.

14. Mangels, "Alison Bechdel." This is the same series that inspired Bechdel to start cartooning in the early 1980s after she encountered it in the Oscar Wilde Memorial Bookshop, a gay bookstore in Greenwich Village in New York City. Bechdel, *Indelible Alison Bechdel*, 9.

15. Hall, "No Straight Lines," n.p.

16. Rubenstein and Bechdel, "Alison Bechdel Interview," 114.

17. Robbins and Bechdel, "Watch Out for Alison Bechdel," 82.

18. Bechdel, *Fun Home*; Bechdel, "United States."

19. Hilty, "Joan Hilty Letter to Alison Bechdel."

20. Bechdel, "Questions for Syndicate."

21. In both the Rubenstein and Robbins interviews Bechdel referenced turning down UPS's offer due, in part, to not wanting to have to alter her politics for a mainstream audience. She discussed her decision at length in the Rubenstein interview, saying, "The woman I talked to said they were thinking of a strip that had both men and women in it, and that was 'less political' than *Dykes to Watch Out For*. . . . But eventually I came to my senses and told them I didn't want to pursue it. I'm really happy doing what I'm doing. And I have less than no interest in speaking to the mainstream." Rubenstein and Bechdel, "Alison Bechdel Interview," 121; Robbins and Bechdel, "Watch Out for Alison Bechdel," 85.

22. She eventually stopped the side business in the mid-1990s because it was very labor-intensive but not very profitable. As she described in the 2001 Robbins interview, "It was exhausting and I realized that I was barely breaking even. It did help me to support myself for years but it just got to be too much work. It might have been OK if I was just creating the designs and someone else was running the business. I was doing almost everything myself. Writing clever copy for the catalog, doing the layout, dealing with T-shirt wholesalers, taking orders from people over the phone—I'd pretend I wasn't me when I answered so people wouldn't know it was this pathetic one-person operation. It was all fun for a while, but eventually it became clear that this was a sad misallocation of my skills." Robbins and Bechdel, "Watch Out for Alison Bechdel," 83–84.

23. Bechdel, "*Dykes to Watch Out For:* Groves of Academe."

24. Sheklow, "Letter to Alison Bechdel."

25. While researching in Bechdel's papers, I encountered numerous letters of this sort among her correspondence with specific periodicals. In a chapter dedicated to her readership in *The Indelible Alison Bechdel,* Bechdel shows how thoroughly readers engage with her strip by reprinting numerous excerpts from letters she's received over the years, prefacing them by saying, "Serial episodes appear in newspapers every two weeks, and thus I have the dubious privilege of receiving constant feedback about the progress of the narrative. Being an assertive, egalitarian lot, my audience does not scruple to let me know what's wrong (or right, for that matter) with the strip, or to inform me of directions and issues that they think I should be exploring" (207–8). For more on the community of readers who wrote letters to Bechdel, see Kirsten Leng's article in *Feminist Media Studies.*

26. In her 1995 Rubenstein interview, Bechdel discusses how she drew on these periodicals when creating her strip: "Should I tell you how I create a strip? First, I procrastinate until the last possible minute. Then I go to the huge stack of magazines and newspapers I get every month and skim through them, making notes about what's going on in the world, and in the community, what the latest issue is, what people are wearing. . . . I just feed all this stuff into the hopper. Then I get out my big chart. I have all my episodes listed on one axis, and all my characters on the other so I can track what's happening to whom and whose story needs attention. . . . I get a foot-high stack of queer papers every month. And 'zines. And I get *The Nation,* and *Ms.,* and miscellaneous newsletters and magazines. *On Our Backs*—rather, *off our backs.* Well, actually I read them both. And the daily paper, of course. It all goes into the hopper." Rubenstein and Bechdel, "Alison Bechdel Interview," 119–20.

27. Bechdel, *Indelible Alison Bechdel,* 71–83.

28. De Lauretis, "Imaging," 67–68.

29. Stephenson, "Alison Bechdel."

30. Bechdel, "Cartoonist's Introduction," xiv. With this pledge, Bechdel is also referencing an Adrienne Rich passage that she shows herself and an early lesbian lover reading a few pages earlier: "Whatever is unnamed, undepicted in images, whatever is omitted from biography, censored in collections of letters, whatever is misnamed as something else, made difficult-to-come-by, whatever is buried in the memory by the collapse of meaning under an inadequate or lying language—this will become, not merely unspoken, but unspeakable." Rich, *On Lies, Secrets, and Silence* (1995 ed.), 199; Bechdel, "Cartoonist's Introduction," x.

31. Bechdel, "*Dykes to Watch Out For* 1994 Calendar."

32. Stephenson, "Alison Bechdel," 6.

33. Cvetkovich, *Archive of Feelings*; Cvetkovich, "Drawing the Archive"; Chute, "Animating an Archive"; Eichhorn, *Archival Turn in Feminism*; Kumbier, *Ephemeral Material.*

34. Chute, "Animating an Archive."

35. Bechdel, "Memoirist's Lament."

36. Bechdel, "From the Archives"; Bechdel, "Ithaca."

37. Bechdel, "Cartoonist's Introduction," vii.

38. Bechdel, viii.

39. Bechdel, "From the Archives."

40. Cvetkovich, *Archive of Feelings*, 268.

41. De Lauretis, "Imaging," 67–68.

42. DiVeglia, "Accessibility, Accountability, and Activism," 88.

43. Muñoz, *Cruising Utopia*, 11.

44. Galvan, "Archiving Grassroots Comics," par. 9.

45. As I examine through this chapter, the relationship between all these elements of an individual page matters, building off of how Agatha Beins conceptualizes the space of the periodical page, as I discuss in the introduction to this book. See Beins, *Liberation in Print*.

46. Anzaldúa, *Borderlands / La Frontera* (2007 ed.).

47. Beins and Enszer, "'We Couldn't Get Them Printed'"; Beins, *Liberation in Print*; Beins, "Publishing Assemblage"; Enszer, "Night Heron Press"; Enszer, "'Fighting to Create and Maintain'"; Enszer, "Lesbian Books"; McKinney, "Newsletter Networks"; Groeneveld, "Letters to the Editor"; Blackwell, "Engendering Print Cultures"; Korinek, "*voices* of Gay, Lesbian, and Feminist Activists"; Meagher, "'Difficult, Messy, Nasty, and Sensational'"; Springer, "Soul of Women's Lib." A number of the most recent articles here come from "Feminist Periodical Studies," a special issue of *American Periodicals* edited by Tessa Jordan and Michelle Meagher.

48. Bechdel, "Advertisement: *WomaNews* Workshops."

49. Muñoz, *Cruising Utopia*, 11.

50. Two months after first publishing in *WomaNews*, Bechdel joined the staff box (masthead) as a named contributor; two months later, in the December 1983/January 1984 issue, she appeared as a full member of the collective's staff, a position she continued to hold for a year and a half until the July/August 1985 issue.

51. Bechdel, "Letters Page Caricature Graphic: Pen-Biting Agitated Female"; Bechdel, "Letters Page Caricature Graphic: Contortionist Letter-Writer"; Bechdel, "Letters Page Caricature Graphic: Intent, Typewriting Female"; Bechdel, "Letters Page Caricature Graphic: Chainsmoking Letter-Writer"; Bechdel, "Letters Page Caricature Graphic: Pensive Letter-Writer"; Bechdel, "Letters Page Caricature Graphic: M&M Letter-Writer."

52. Bechdel, "Literary *Dykes to Watch Out For*" (1984 ed.); Bechdel, "Literary *Dykes to Watch Out For*" (1986 ed.).

53. Bechdel, "Letters Page Caricature Graphic: Pen-Biting Agitated Female."

54. Coincidentally, the October 1983 issue was the first in which Bechdel was listed in the staff box as a contributor to the collective.

55. Anzaldúa and Moraga, "Bring Bridge Back!"; WomaNews Collective, "Persephone Press Passes."

56. Bechdel, "Letters Page Caricature Graphic: M&M Letter-Writer."

57. Bechdel, "Letters Page Caricature Graphic: Intent, Typewriting Female"; Bechdel, "Letters Page Caricature Graphic: Chainsmoking Letter-Writer."

58. Bechdel, "Letters Page Caricature Graphic: Contortionist Letter-Writer."

59. Bechdel, "Letters Page Caricature Graphic: Pensive Letter-Writer."

60. Bechdel, "Literary *Dykes to Watch Out For*" (1984 ed.).

61. Heloise C. Bland, an anagram of Bechdel's first and last name, is one of a few anagram avatars she deploys in *DTWOF*.

62. Linda M. Scott describes the huge public response following the advertisement in January 1984, which translated into big sales for Apple in the following months. See "'For the Rest of Us,'" 67–68.

63. In an interview with *Circles*, a lesbian publication based in Colorado, Bechdel discusses how she had encountered many young women in recent years who first learned about lesbian culture through her *Dykes to Watch Out For* comic strip: "And one of these young women said—and this is some feedback that I've heard quite frequently—that her first exposure to the lesbian community was through my cartoon. That before she was out she had access to the cartoons and this was what she thought it was going to be like! [*laughing*] And in some ways it was and some ways it wasn't like that when she finally got out into the world. But I think it's really bizarre that the strip is some people's first glimpse of [lesbian life]. That puts a lot of pressure on me" (McChesney, "Hot Throbs," 42).

64. Bechdel, "Advertisement: *WomaNews* 5th Anniversary! Variety Show!," November 1984; Bechdel, "Advertisement: *WomaNews* 5th Anniversary! Variety Show!," December 1984 / January 1985.

65. Lambert, "Rockettes and Race," par. 11.

66. Lambert, par. 18.

67. Peterson, "Rockettes."

68. Alderfer et al., *Diary of a Conference on Sexuality*; Marrs, *Pudge, Girl Blimp* #1.

69. Bechdel, "Advertisement: Get Yourself a *WomaNews* T-Shirt!"

70. Bechdel, "Same as It Ever Was."

71. Bechdel, "Postcards from the Edge."

72. Bechdel, "Mo' Mo."

73. Bechdel, "What Is Real?"

74. Muñoz, *Cruising Utopia*, 11.

75. Stephenson, "Alison Bechdel."

76. Adair and Nakamura, "Digital Afterlives"; Eckardt, "Photographer Nan Goldin"; Miller, "Why Nan Goldin."

4. The Editor and Pedagogue

1. Moraga, "Catching Fire," xxi.

2. Adair and Nakamura, "Digital Afterlives," 255.

3. Moraga and Anzaldúa, "Introduction, 1981," xlv. In this section of the introduction, Anzaldúa and Moraga reflect at length on the importance of this

textual range: "The selections in this anthology range from extemporaneous stream of consciousness journal entries to well thought-out theoretical statements; from intimate letters to friends to full-scale public addresses. In addition, the book includes poems and transcripts, personal conversations and interviews. The works combined reflect a diversity of perspectives, linguistic styles, and cultural tongues. In editing the anthology, our primary commitment was to retaining this diversity, as well as each writer's especial voice and style. The book is intended to reflect our color loud and clear, not tone it down. As editors we sought out, and believe we found, non-rhetorical, highly personal chronicles that present a political analysis in everyday terms" (xliv–xlv).

4. Keating, "Introduction," 9.

5. Anzaldúa, "Speaking in Tongues," 163.

6. "Introduction to the Third Edition." The ten women who penned short essays for this introduction were Norma Alarcón, Julia Alvarez, Paola Bacchetta, Rusty Barcelo, Norma Ella Cantú, Ana Castillo, Sandra Cisneros, T. Jackie Cuevas, Claire Joysmith, and AnaLouise Keating.

7. Crenshaw, "Demarginalizing the Intersection of Race and Sex."

8. In her introduction to *Making Face, Making Soul*, Anzaldúa writes, "Because there is little publication support for our writings, I've made a special effort to work with women who do not consider themselves writers, or at least not yet. The book provides space for some ethnic mestizas who have been silenced before uttering a word, or, having spoken, have not been heard" ("Haciendo Caras, Una Entrada," xvii).

9. Anzaldúa, xvii–xviii.

10. Anzaldúa, *Interviews/Entrevistas*, 232.

11. Anzaldúa, *Light in the Dark*, 60.

12. Diana Bowen discusses the role of the visual within Anzaldúa's system of theorizing: "When describing her process, Anzaldúa explains that she starts with a feeling, an experience for which she may not have the language to describe. She might then employ an artistic medium such as drawing a picture or writing poetry or fiction. Once this item is created, she may go back and name the experience using academic language" ("Gloria Anzaldúa").

13. Anzaldúa's approach in creating images and in presenting them in many ways reflects Sonja K. Foss and Cindy L. Griffin's feminist concept of "invitational rhetoric" whereby "invitational rhetoric constitutes an invitation to the audience to enter the rhetor's world and to see it as the rhetor does. . . . Rhetors recognize the valuable contributions audience members can make to the rhetors' own thinking and understanding" ("Beyond Persuasion," 5–6). Since Foss and Griffin articulated the concept in 1995, it has remained important in the discourse. Anzaldúa's writings often get cited by rhetorical scholars engaging ideas of invitational rhetoric, including in Foss and Griffin's recent volume *Inviting Understanding*, so it might be worthwhile asking how her images can be read as embodying invitational rhetoric as well.

14. Bowen, "Gloria Anzaldúa."

15. Anzaldúa, *Gloria Anzaldúa Reader*; Bost, "Messy Archives and Materials That Matter." Bost later transformed her essay into a chapter on Anzaldúa in her most recent book, *Shared Selves*.

16. Anzaldúa, "Counsels from the Firing," 265.

17. Benjamin, "'Archive of Accounts,'" 48.

18. Moraga and Anzaldúa, "Introduction, 1981," xlvi.

19. "Third World Feminist Speakers List."

20. "Third World Feminist Speakers List."

21. Bibliographies have historically been a vital tool for marginalized people to gather and make visible writings that represent their experiences, as recent critical conversations in Black bibliography have illuminated. See McHenry, *To Make Negro Literature*; and Goldsby and McGill, "Black Bibliography."

22. Although Anzaldúa and Moraga did attempt to highlight prior work in these areas with the inclusion of the bibliography, some scholars have critiqued the level of attention given to the anthology. For example, Norma Alarcón has been critical of how white feminists have lavished attention on *This Bridge* while ignoring the rich history of writing and activism among women of color, both those connected to the book and preceding its publication ("Theoretical Subject[s]"). In her introduction to *The Gloria Anzaldúa Reader*, AnaLouise Keating reflects on the legacy of *This Bridge*: "Although some scholars describe *This Bridge* as women of color's entry into the feminist movement, I see the book somewhat differently, as a crucial reminder that feminism was not and never had been a 'white'-raced women's movement with a single-issue, middle-class agenda. Anzaldúa and the other contributors self-identified as feminists, and most had done so for many years before *This Bridge*'s publication. In *This Bridge Called My Back*, they remind readers that feminism, defined broadly and flexibly, offers crucial points of connection for social-justice workers of diverse backgrounds" (8). Additionally, Cynthia G. Franklin has done research "resituating *This Bridge* in relation to [its] historical contexts," detailing how a rich ecosystem of lesbian and feminist work, particularly by women of color, influenced *This Bridge* ("Another 1981," 32).

In response to this and other erasures, recent scholars of color have been working to recuperate and acknowledge the vital work of women of color in this period. Erica Townsend-Bell has shown how the profusion of work by women of color in the 1980s was preceded and made possible by women of color in the 1960s and 1970s ("Writing the Way to Feminism"). María Cotera has done similar work recuperating forgotten Chicana activists from those decades through her Chicana por mi Raza Digital Memory Project and Archive that interviews these women and digitizes their personal libraries and records of activism ("'Invisibility Is an Unnatural Disaster'"). The recent anthology *Chicana Movidas*, which Cotera edited with Maylei Blackwell and Dionne Espinoza, further broadened that work.

Simply put, women of color were active in building networks preceding and contemporaneous to *This Bridge*. Across the women's movement in the 1970s, women of color were actively building spaces that would foster their creative works. This work was vital because they felt their needs were ignored, as illustrated in an earlier chapter by the Black female character of Edie featured in Roberta Gregory's *Dynamite Damsels* who was quickly sidelined when she asked about the whiteness of the feminist movement in her consciousness-raising group. Indeed, essays like the "Combahee River Collective Statement" identified the needs of Black women that had been ignored and were created in dialogue with newly formed groups designed to address these needs. Such works and the groups they were created within continued to inspire the women involved and others to create publications and networks to voice the needs of a larger coalition of women of color. Barbara Smith, a member of the Combahee River Collective, kept working and advocating for Black women and women of color more broadly through collective endeavors like coediting *Conditions Five: The Black Women's Issue* with Lorraine Bethel and founding Kitchen Table: Women of Color Press in 1980, which published a number of significant books centering the voices of women of color, including her own, *Home Girls: A Black Feminist Anthology*, a revised and updated version of *Conditions Five*. *This Bridge* would go on to reprint the "Combahee River Collective Statement," as well as publishing a dialogue between Smith and her twin sister Beverly about "their experiences as Black feminists in the Women's Movement" (111).

More broadly, across the intertwined worlds of art and activism, women of color were engaged in network building across the 1970s and into the 1980s. In the visual arts, women of color were forming groups like Where We At (formed in 1971), Las Mujeres Muralistas (formed early 1970s), the Indigenous Women's Network and Artistas Indigenas (both founded in 1983), and the Asian American Women Artists Association (founded in 1989), which created communities for Black, Chicana, Indigenous, and Asian American female artists to help facilitate their art and provide mutual support, while groups like the Guerrilla Girls (formed in 1985) famously advocated against sexism and racism in the art world and worked for the inclusion of such art in gallery and museum spaces. In the literary arts, women of color presses—like Third Woman Press (founded 1979), Kitchen Table, and Aunt Lute (founded 1982)—were formed as a response to the need for these spaces outside the mainstream and in distinction from the almost completely white feminist presses. The failure of feminist presses to support women of color was epitomized by the literal bankruptcy of Persephone Press, which threatened the survival and distribution of the newly published *This Bridge Called My Back* in 1981 and canceled plans to publish *Home Girls*, galvanizing the newly formed Kitchen Table, which would release a second edition of *This Bridge* in 1983, the same year *Home Girls* was eventually published.

23. This chapter comes at a moment when scholars are calling for a reassessment of Anzaldúa's work, given that so much scholarship focuses narrowly on parts of her oeuvre and that her archives, with their plethora of unpublished materials, open up new avenues for consideration. In her work reassessing Anzaldúa's legacy through her archives, Suzanne Bost writes, "The Anzaldúa that most people know is limited to a few famous essays, but the poems, stories,

pictures, revisions, and other materials in the archive overturn some of the conclusions of those essays. I found in the archive a very different body of work, one that thematizes urban dwelling, spirituality, science fiction, shape-shifting, illness, and the author's reluctance to share her sexuality with others" ("Messy Archives and Materials That Matter," 627). There have been many reassessments of Anzaldúa's contributions following her death, including in edited collections and special issues of journals. Moreover, the Society for the Study of Gloria Anzaldúa was founded after Anzaldúa's passing, and its conferences provide the material for the "El Mundo Zurdo" series of volumes containing new assessments of Anzaldúa's import. See Keating, *Entre Mundos*; Keating and González-López, *Bridging*; Cantú, "Comparative Perspectives Symposium"; Cantú et al., *El Mundo Zurdo*; Saldívar-Hull et al., *El Mundo Zurdo 2*; Mercado-López, Saldívar-Hull, and Castañeda, *El Mundo Zurdo 3*; Cuevas, Mercado-López, and Saldívar-Hull, *El Mundo Zurdo 4*; Perez, Mercado-López, and Saldívar-Hull, *El Mundo Zurdo 5*; Ramírez, Mercado-López, and Saldívar-Hull, *El Mundo Zurdo 6*; Ramírez, Mercado-López, and Saldívar-Hull, *El Mundo Zurdo 7*; and Zaytoun, *Shapeshifting Subjects*.

24. Bost, "Messy Archives and Materials That Matter"; Keating, "Archival Alchemy and Allure."

25. Eichhorn, "Archival Genres."

26. Keating, "Archival Alchemy and Allure," 161.

27. Keating, 160–61.

28. Anzaldúa, *Interviews/Entrevistas*, 178.

29. Anzaldúa, *Borderlands / La Frontera* (2007 ed.), 82; Anzaldúa, *Interviews/Entrevistas*, 52–54; Anzaldúa and Torres, "The Author Never Existed," 122; Blackwell and Anzaldúa, "Many Roads, One Path," 113–15.

30. Eichhorn, "Archival Genres"; Anzaldúa, *Interviews/Entrevistas*, 178.

31. Anzaldúa, "Bridge, Drawbridge, Sandbar, or Island," 147.

32. Anzaldúa, "Counsels from the Firing," 264. Contemporaneous to this piece, Anzaldúa also defines being a bridge in similar terms in her preface to *this bridge we call home*, saying, "To bridge means loosening our borders, not closing off to others. Bridging is the work of opening the gate to the stranger, within and without. To step across the threshold is to be stripped of the illusion of safety because it moves us into unfamiliar territory and does not grant safe passage. To bridge is to attempt community, and for that we must risk being open to personal, political, and spiritual intimacy, to risk being wounded" (3).

33. See chapter 1, in particular, on how grassroots archives preserve marginalized histories and the conversation that has arisen about this function, including Rebecka Taves Sheffield's intensive study of four LGBTQ grassroots archives, *Documenting Rebellions*, which reveals previously unknown historical details about these institutions.

34. Cotera, "'Invisibility Is an Unnatural Disaster'"; Cotera, "Unpacking Our Mothers' Libraries"; Cotera, "Nuestra Autohistoria."

35. Cotera, "'Invisibility Is an Unnatural Disaster,'" 787; Cotera, "Nuestra Autohistoria," 489–90.

36. Cotera, "Unpacking Our Mothers' Libraries."

37. Cotera, Blackwell, and Espinoza, "Introduction," 2.

38. Cotera, "Unpacking Our Mothers' Libraries," 300.

39. Cotera, "'Invisibility Is an Unnatural Disaster,'" 796–98.

40. Herrera Rodríguez, "Sacred Thing That Takes Us Home," 280.

41. Herrera Rodríguez, 280.

42. Cotera, "Unpacking Our Mothers' Libraries," 300.

43. Cotera, "'Invisibility Is an Unnatural Disaster,'" 783. Kate Eichhorn makes a similar statement about the archives as a site of "knowledge production" when she writes, "Rather than a destination for knowledges already produced or a place to recover histories and ideas placed under erasure, the making of archives is frequently where knowledge production begins" (*Archival Turn in Feminism*, 3).

44. Koegeler-Abdi, "Shifting Subjectivities," 74.

45. Keating, "Introduction," 10.

46. This concept is one that she continued to evolve across her career: "Her later theories transform the Borderlands into nepantla, new mestizas into nepantlera and nos/otras, and mestiza consciousness into conocimiento" (Keating, 10).

47. In a 1995 interview with María Henríquez Betancor, Anzaldúa explains her decision to give up on being a visual artist when she opted instead to pursue her writing: "When I decided to become a writer I had to give up the idea of doing visual art—not enough time to practice and be good in two art forms, to buy oil paints, brushes, and other art materials. At that time I looked around to see what other Chicanas were writing and I found very little" (Anzaldúa, *Interviews/Entrevistas*, 236).

48. Bowen, "Gloria Anzaldúa." Granted, thinking and drawing are also often linked and not separate processes for Anzaldúa, as this chapter bears out.

49. Blackwell and Anzaldúa, "Many Roads, One Path," 111. In her 2001 foreword to *This Bridge*, Anzaldúa discusses how the "seed" for the collection came out of her coursework and teaching at UT Austin ("Counsels from the Firing," 262), and she also affirms how this period inspired the work of *Borderlands / La Frontera* in a 1990 interview with Hector A. Torres ("Author Never Existed," 135).

50. Blackwell and Anzaldúa, "Many Roads, One Path," 115.

51. Anzaldúa, *Borderlands / La Frontera* (2007 ed.), 82.

52. Blackwell and Anzaldúa, "Many Roads, One Path," 113. See also her discussion of leaving the doctoral program at UT Austin in Anzaldúa, *Interviews/Entrevistas*, 52–54; and Anzaldúa and Torres, "Author Never Existed," 122.

53. Anzaldúa recounts in a 1982 interview with Linda Smuckler, "I used to teach 'The Mujer Chicana' at UT Austin. They banned that course a few years after I left because they said it was divisive of men and women in the Chicano movement" (Anzaldúa, *Interviews/Entrevistas*, 54).

54. Blackwell and Anzaldúa, "Many Roads, One Path," 115.

55. Blackwell and Anzaldúa, 111; Anzaldúa, *Interviews/Entrevistas*, 54.

56. Anzaldúa, 54.

57. Anzaldúa, "Notebook and Journal on La Mujer Xicana: September 16, 1976."

58. In a 1995 telephone interview with Ann E. Reuman, Anzaldua describes reading the work of white feminists like Kate Millet, Robin Morgan, and Judy Grahn in the mid-1970s before she started graduate school, saying, "I had the experience but I didn't have the vocabulary to articulate it, and these white feminists gave me the vocabulary. And once I had the vocabulary, then I had to start thinking of, developing my own, using my own cultural words and symbols and images." This moment in the interview follows her discussion of the need for *This Bridge*, and she then goes on to discuss the literature by women of color, and Black women in particular, that had an influence on her later thought. Reuman and Anzaldúa, "Coming into Play," 37–40.

59. Anzaldúa, "Gay Fiction, East and West, Prof Teele, Spring 1977: February 27, 1977."

60. It is important to note that Rich later became an advocate and supporter of Anzaldúa's work and the work of other women of color, as many scholars have examined.

61. This mysticism is present across Anzaldúa's work, but take a look at the "Tlilli, Tlapalli: The Path of the Red and Black Ink" chapter in *Borderlands* (2007 ed.), in which she talks at length about the vital and spiritual role of images.

62. Anzaldúa, "Gay Fiction, East and West, Prof Teele, Spring 1977: March 8, 1977."

63. Anzaldúa, *Borderlands / La Frontera* (2007 ed.), 60.

64. Anzaldúa, 61.

65. Cade, "Gloria Anzaldúa in Front of Her Drawings."

66. Cade, "Gloria Anzaldúa," 25.

67. Anzaldúa, "En Rapport, in Opposition" (1987 ed.); Anzaldúa, "En Rapport, in Opposition" (1990 ed.).

68. Anzaldúa, "En Rapport, in Opposition" (1987 ed.), 14.

69. In discussing her use of images in various interviews, Anzaldúa often describes them in great detail. Here are some of her evocations of images related to mestiza identity that she developed across her career, even before she began preserving them on transparencies and reusing them. In a 1990 interview with Hector A. Torres, Anzaldúa describes the mestiza figure as we later see it replicated across her transparencies: "In my lectures, I always insist on having a blackboard because I like to make what I call my hieroglyphics or these little pictures out of which I can explicate my theory. For *Borderlands*, I had the figure of a woman with all these little squares that were the plots that she was standing on. One plot was being a lesbian. Another plot was being in the academy. Another was being a working campesina, working-class. Another was feminist. Another one was the writing profession. As many worlds as there are and the mestiza has to operate in all these little plots, in all these little worlds. So, in crossing from one to the other, in this constant traveling back and forth, her subjectivity, her identity becomes multiple, moving, movable subjectivity or

identity" ("Author Never Existed," 130–31). In a 1999 interview with Karin Ikas reprinted in the back of the third edition of *Borderlands / La Frontera,* Anzaldúa describes how her "little drawings" serve to help her articulate her thinking in writing. She lists some of these images, which show up across her transparencies, demonstrating how she reproduces the images for her audience that also help her articulate her written concepts in the first place: "The way that I originate my ideas is the following: First there has to be something that is bothering me, something emotional so that I will be upset, angry or conflicted. Then I start meditating on it, sometimes I do that while I am walking. Usually I come up with something visual of what I am feeling. So then I have a visual that sometimes is like a bridge, sometimes like a person with fifty legs, one in each world; sometimes la mano izquierda, the left-handed world; the rebollino, et cetera, and I try to put that into words. So behind this feeling there is this image, this visual, and I have to figure out what the articulation of this image is. That's how I get into the theory. I start theorizing about it. But it always comes from a feeling" ("Interview with Gloria Anzaldúa," 235–36).

70. Anzaldúa, *Interviews/Entrevistas,* 200.

71. Anzaldúa, "Transparency: Model."

72. I briefly discuss the concept of invitational rhetoric in an earlier note in this chapter. See also Foss and Griffin, "Beyond Persuasion"; Foss and Griffin, *Inviting Understanding.*

73. Anzaldúa, *Borderlands / La Frontera* (2007 ed.), 99.

74. Diana Isabel Bowen has written about Anzaldúa's visual language in her scholarship, asserting, "Anzaldúa's theory of the borderlands contains imagistic elements, that is, she uses vivid imagery and examples to describe her concepts" ("Gloria Anzaldúa"). Laura E. Pérez has further written about the visual elements in the text of *Borderlands / La Frontera,* positing, "In Anzaldúa's *Borderlands,* image and written or spoken word are inseparably linked, as image and spoken word are in the functioning of the Mesoamerican glyph (pictograph/ideogram). . . . From Anzaldúa's cultural perspective, writing is an image-making practice, that as such can indeed shape and transform what we imagine, are able to perceive, and are able to give material embodiment. Understood, therefore, is the great responsibility and sacredness of the very real and consequential 'transformative power' wielded by the image-makers, which literally 'makes face, makes soul' in a reading process understood to be part of a larger performance" ("Spirit Glyphs," 50).

75. Anzaldúa, "Transparency: Nos/Otras Disrupts"; Anzaldúa, "Transparency: Artista Activista"; Anzaldúa, "Transparency: Mestizas Partake."

76. Anzaldúa, *Borderlands / La Frontera* (2007 ed.), 30, 45. In some of her transparencies, Anzaldúa further focuses on these ethnic roots through visualizing this tree, echoing the moment in *Borderlands,* as well, where the mestiza is "digging her way along the roots of trees" to find her cultural inheritance (104).

77. Emphasizing the strain of this negotiation is a labeled turtle at the front of her path. Like the turtle, she carries around her identity, but she drags it at her feet instead. This animal is not simply evocative in this transparency, but

also in *Borderlands / La Frontera* in an earlier section of the text where Anzaldúa discusses the "native cultural roots" of Chicanas and encapsulates her point by stating, "I am a turtle, wherever I go I carry 'home' on my back" (43). In the transparency, too, the turtle echoes and evokes the mestiza in a tidy, compact form, all the tangled, conflicting identities that the mestiza wades through here bundled up under the shell.

78. Anzaldúa, "Transparency: Nos/Otras Somos Mestizas Todas"; Anzaldúa, "Transparency: White Frame of Reference."

79. Anzaldúa, *Borderlands / La Frontera* (2007 ed.), 101.

80. Anzaldúa, 109.

81. Anzaldúa, "Counsels from the Firing," 265.

82. Anzaldúa, "Transparency: Under the Sky of Feminism"; Anzaldúa, "Transparency: The Politics of Writing & Reading."

83. Anzaldúa, *Borderlands / La Frontera* (2007 ed.), 106.

84. Anzaldúa, 106–7.

85. Sharpe, "Anzaldúa across Borders."

86. Eichhorn, "Archival Genres."

5. The Photographer and Curator

1. The slide count of *The Ballad* ranges slightly across various sources, which attests to the shifting nature of the slideshow itself. Darsie Alexander lists the Whitney Museum of American Art's copy of the work as containing "approximately seven hundred color slides" ("Nan Goldin," 107), Greil Marcus brings the tally up to "more than seven hundred color photographs" ("Songs Left Out," 76), and Goldin herself accounts for "750 images shown in 45 minutes" (Westfall, "Ballad of Nan Goldin," 31). Further, it is important to note that although *The Ballad* became a printed text in 1986, it continued as a living, growing slideshow in the years after although the general construct remained the same. See Holert, "Nan Goldin Talks to Tom Holert," 232.

2. Marvin Heiferman, one of her editorial collaborators on the book and in her early career, notes the count as 127, which includes her paratextual photos of Greer Lankton and Robert Vitale with the title page and the photo of her sister Barbara in the introductory text. Pérez and Heiferman, "Original Ballad," 55.

3. In the 1996 afterword to *The Ballad*, she writes, "I realize I took the picture of myself battered so I wouldn't go back to the man who beat me up" ("Afterword," 1996 ed., 145).

4. Editors, "Editors' Note," 21.

5. Robbins, Sienkiewicz, and Triptow, *Strip AIDS USA*.

6. Robbins, Sienkiewicz, and Triptow; Robbins, *Last Girl Standing*, 184.

7. Ellis et al., *Caught Looking* (1986 ed.). Goldin's photography also appeared in Vance, *Pleasure and Danger*, a volume of essays that originated in the Barnard Sex Conference as discussed in the first chapter.

8. In retrospective accounts, Goldin remembers reading the first major newspaper article about HIV/AIDS—by Lawrence K. Altman, published in the

New York Times in July 1981—with her artist friends Cookie Mueller and David Armstrong while they were spending the July Fourth holiday on Fire Island, a famed gay and lesbian New York beach destination. They "laughed it off" at the time but soon realized its severity as their loved ones started to die, with Goldin marking the death of one of Armstrong's lovers in 1982 as the "first friend" to be lost. Goldin, "'Nan Goldin on Cookie Mueller'"; Altman, "Rare Cancer Seen in 41 Homosexuals."

9. Dubin, "AIDS," 210.

10. Junge, *Art about AIDS*, 38; O'Neill-Butler, "Out of Sheer Rage," 98.

11. A number of artists in *Witnesses* also appear in the book version of *The Ballad*, including Jane Dickson, Greer Lankton, Mark Morrisroe, Vittorio Scarpati, and Kiki Smith. Cookie Mueller's writing appears in the exhibit catalog. Additionally, some of the artists, including David Armstrong, Siobhan Liddell, Stephen Tashjian, Shellburne Thurber, and David Wojnarowicz, appear in other photographs by Goldin from the period, including in the slideshow version of *The Ballad*. Goldin, *Ballad of Sexual Dependency* (1986 ed.), 29, 41, 60, 92–93, 99, 102, 123; Goldin and Armstrong, *Double Life*, 105, 110, 122–23, 128–29; Goldin, *Couples and Loneliness*, 59–64.

12. She would also produce new photographs on HIV/AIDS by documenting the decline of friends who were HIV positive and contribute to and curate other focused exhibits on the topic. Perlson, "Nan Goldin."

13. Goldin, *Other Side*, 7. These remarks from 1992 are reprinted in a new and expanded 2019 edition of the project and precede a new preface where AIDS and the losses of many people in her photos and community loom even larger across the whole of her remarks. See also Goldin, 8–9.

14. Goldin, "Afterword" (1996 ed.); Goldin, "Afterword" (2012 ed.); Goldin, "Afterword" (2021 ed.).

15. Townsend, "Nan Goldin," 109.

16. Goldin, *Ballad of Sexual Dependency* (1996 ed.), 8–9.

17. Goldin, 9.

18. Goldin, 9.

19. Oksman, "Mourning the Family Album," 238.

20. Goldin, *Other Side*, 5; Coulthard and Goldin, *I'll Be Your Mirror*.

21. Pérez and Heiferman, "Original Ballad," 56.

22. Pinckney and Goldin, "Ballad of Nan Goldin," 25; Bengal, "Conversation with Nan Goldin."

23. Dubin, "AIDS."

24. Lubow, *Diane Arbus*, 120.

25. Pinckney and Goldin, "Ballad of Nan Goldin," 31; Coulthard and Goldin, *I'll Be Your Mirror*.

26. Pinckney and Goldin, "Ballad of Nan Goldin," 30.

27. Sontag, *On Photography*; Barthes, *Camera Lucida*.

28. Baumann, "Introduction," xx; Laing, "Fold in Time," 94. To read more on HIV/AIDS archives, check out Marika Cifor's *Viral Cultures: Activist Archiving in the Age of AIDS*, where she deftly examines the major archives, including

Fales and the New York Public Library, that have preserved the HIV/AIDS epidemic and its activisms.

29. Cifor, 4.

30. Laing, "Fold in Time," 94.

31. Precup, "Wound Which Speaks"; Oksman, "Mourning the Family Album"; Prosser, "Testimonies in Light"; Raymond, "Performances"; Ruddy, "'Radiant Eye Yearns from Me'"; Townsend, "Nan Goldin."

32. In her 1992 preface reprinted in the new edition of *The Other Side*, Goldin says, "As a bisexual person, for me the third gender seems to be the ideal," as she discusses her transgender friends (7). In an overview of her career, she further expounds on how the social circle of drag queens resonated with feeling in-between as a bisexual woman: "Drag queens in the early 1970's in Boston were totally alienated from both the homosexual and the heterosexual communities and lived a real underground existence. I lived with them for a few years and I wanted to be a queen. I love queens because they're the most beautiful people in the world. And they're perfect for a bisexual person" (*Couples and Loneliness*, 20). In the preface to *The Ballad*, she discusses how her inclinations toward both genders often seem paradoxical: "I often feel that I am better suited to be with a woman; my long-term friendships with women are bonds that have the intensity of a marriage, or the closeness of sisters. But a part of me is challenged by the opacity of men's emotional makeup and is stimulated by the conflict inherent in relationships between men and women" (1996 ed., 8).

33. Pinckney, "Nan's Manhattan," 204. Writer Lucy Sante also reflected on Goldin's capacity for making a large network of friends in her essay in *I'll Be Your Mirror*: "Nan was a social evangelist; she introduced whole crowds to each other. She seemed to have met more people in a few months than most of us had managed over the course of years" ("All Yesterday's Parties," 99).

34. Goldin, *Ballad of Sexual Dependency* (1996 ed.), 109; Costa and Goldin, *Nan Goldin*, 16. Goldin also includes this image in the middle of the section of her photographs from this period that she publishes in *The Other Side*, which features her photographs of drag queens and trans women from across her career (26–27).

35. Goldin, *Other Side*, 10–39.

36. Wyatt et al., "Catalog."

37. Goldin, *Other Side*, 8.

38. Marcus, "Songs Left Out," 76, 79.

39. Westfall, "Ballad of Nan Goldin," 31.

40. Marcus, "Songs Left Out," 76.

41. Goldin, *Ballad of Sexual Dependency* (1996 ed.), 19, 53.

42. McCloud, *Understanding Comics*, 65–69.

43. The most photographed person in the book version of *The Ballad* is Brian, with fourteen photos. Fletcher follows with eleven, then Goldin with eight.

44. Als, "Nan Goldin's Life in Progress."

45. Sante, "All Yesterday's Parties," 99; Pinckney, "Nan's Manhattan," 203.

46. Sante, "All Yesterday's Parties," 99; Pinckney, "Nan's Manhattan," 203–4.

47. Pérez and Heiferman, "Original Ballad," 55; Als, "Nan Goldin's Life in Progress."

48. Goldin, *Ballad of Sexual Dependency* (1996 ed.), 16, 17, 33, 87, 121.

49. Goldin, 23, 35, 42.

50. Goldin, 19, 25.

51. Goldin, 43.

52. Goldin, 16.

53. Als, "Nan Goldin's Life in Progress."

54. Goldin, *Ballad of Sexual Dependency* (1996 ed.), 83; Costa and Goldin, *Nan Goldin*, 46–47. A number of scholars spend time discussing this photograph, including Claire Raymond, who takes a number of paragraphs to excavate its significance to Goldin's oeuvre. Raymond, "Performances," 125–27; Dean, "Intimacy at Work"; Kaplan, "Photography and the Exposure of Community"; Prosser, "Testimonies in Light."

55. Goldin, *Ballad of Sexual Dependency* (1996 ed.), 147.

56. Goldin, 87.

57. Guido Costa provides this quote from a review without an attribution in his short analysis of the photo. Costa and Goldin, *Nan Goldin*, 48–49.

58. Goldin, *Ballad of Sexual Dependency* (1996 ed.), 99; Avena and Goldin, "Interview with Nan Goldin," 155.

59. In an interview, Goldin discusses Mueller's diagnosis and how she coped by "medicat[ing] herself with various herbs" and "writ[ing] a column called 'Ask Dr. Mueller' for *High Times* magazine as a home-remedy doctor." Avena and Goldin, 155.

60. Wyatt et al., "Catalog."

61. Goldin, *Couples and Loneliness*, 76.

62. Avena and Goldin, "Interview with Nan Goldin," 154.

63. Dubin, "AIDS," 210.

64. Sussman, "In/of Her Time," 38.

65. Wyatt et al., "Catalog," 4.

66. "Flyer"; "Visual AIDS."

67. Wyatt et al., "Catalog," 3; "Visual AIDS."

68. Wyatt et al., "Catalog," 7; Deparle, "111 Held in St. Patrick's AIDS Protest."

69. Wyatt et al., "Catalog," 6.

70. Wyatt et al., "Catalogue Drafts."

71. Wyatt, "Attendance Records."

72. Als, "Nan Goldin's Life in Progress."

73. Wyatt et al., "Catalog," 5.

74. Avena and Goldin, "Interview with Nan Goldin," 151–52.

75. Wyatt et al., "Catalog," 11. See also Hubbard, *United in Anger*; and France, *How to Survive a Plague*.

76. Fellow downtown artists James Romberger and Marguerite Van Cook also memorialized Wojnarowicz in the coming decade in *Seven Miles a Second,* a richly vibrant comic that draws heavily on his written memoirs and visual artwork in recounting his life. Wojnarowicz, Romberger, and Van Cook, *Seven Miles a Second.*

77. Avena and Goldin, "Interview with Nan Goldin," 151.

78. In the exhibit itself, Wojnarowicz included a series of three black-and-white photographs that showed Hujar just after his death in 1987. See "Artists Checklist."

79. Wyatt et al., "Catalog," 5.

80. Kastor, "Content."

81. O'Neill-Butler, "Out of Sheer Rage," 98.

Epilogue

1. Hubert, "Behind the Camera."

2. I touch on my archival research process in the acknowledgments.

3. Rubin, *Deviations*; Smith, *Ain't Gonna Let Nobody*; Moraga and Anzaldúa, *This Bridge Called My Back* (2015 ed.); Moraga and Anzaldúa, *This Bridge Called My Back* (2021 ed.); Anzaldúa, *Light in the Dark*; Anzaldúa, *Borderlands / La Frontera* (2021 ed.).

4. Murray, *Mixed Media*; Springer, *Living for the Revolution*; Blackwell, *¡Chicana Power!*; Harker and Konchar Farr, *This Book Is an Action*; Hogan, *Feminist Bookstore Movement*; Beins, *Liberation in Print*; Groeneveld and Thrift, "Thinking beyond Backlash"; Jordan and Meagher, "Feminist Periodical Studies"; Harker, *Lesbian South*; McKinney, *Information Activism*.

5. During the COVID-19 pandemic, I compiled a list of open-access digitized media for my students learning about archival research and grassroots media; see Galvan, "Resource."

6. Some students also encountered difficulties where other Wikipedians flagged their entries for deletion, saying that the figures were not notable enough, continuing the marginalization of these important subcultural artists.

BIBLIOGRAPHY

Abate, Michelle Ann, Karly Marie Grice, and Christine N. Stamper, eds. "Lesbian Content and Queer Female Characters in Comics." Special issue, *Journal of Lesbian Studies* 22, no. 4 (2018).

Abelove, Henry, Michèle Aina Barale, and David M. Halperin, eds. *The Lesbian and Gay Studies Reader*. New York: Routledge, 1993.

"About the Journal *GLQ: A Journal of Lesbian and Gay Studies*." Duke University Press. Accessed January 11, 2021. https://read.dukeupress.edu/glq/pages/About.

Adair, Cassius, and Lisa Nakamura. "The Digital Afterlives of *This Bridge Called My Back*: Woman of Color Feminism, Digital Labor, and Networked Pedagogy." *American Literature* 89, no. 2 (June 2017): 255–78.

Adkins, Lisa, and Maryanne Dever, eds. "Archives and New Modes of Feminist Research." Special issue, *Australian Feminist Studies* 32, nos. 91/92 (2017).

Alarcón, Norma. "The Theoretical Subject(s) of *This Bridge Called My Back* and Anglo-American Feminism." In *Criticism in the Borderlands: Studies in Chicano Literature, Culture, and Ideology*, edited by Héctor Calderón and José David Saldívar, 28–39. Durham, N.C.: Duke University Press, 1991.

Aldama, Frederick Luis. "Roberta Gregory." In *Your Brain on Latino Comics: From Gus Arriola to Los Bros Hernandez*, 166–70. Austin: University of Texas Press, 2009.

Alderfer, Hannah, Meryl Altman, Kate Ellis, Beth Jaker, Marybeth Nelson, Esther Newton, Ann Snitow, and Carole S. Vance, eds. *Diary of a Conference on Sexuality*. New York: Faculty Press, 1982. Box 5, Folder 10, Barnard Archives and Special Collections, Barnard Library, Barnard College.

Alderfer, Hannah, Beth Jaker, and Marybeth Nelson. "Designers' Statement." In *Caught Looking: Feminism, Pornography and Censorship*, edited by Kate Ellis, Beth Jaker, Nan D. Hunter, Barbara O'Dair, and Abby Tallmer, 5. East Haven, Conn.: Long River Books, 1986.

Alexander, Darsie. "Nan Goldin." In *Slideshow*, 107–8. University Park: Penn State University Press, 2005.

Allan, Catherine, Judy Irola, Allie Light, and Joan Musante, dirs. *Self-Health*. San Francisco: San Francisco Women's Health Center, 1974.

Als, Hilton. "Nan Goldin's Life in Progress." *New Yorker*, June 27, 2016. https://www.newyorker.com/magazine/2016/07/04/nan-goldins-the-ballad-of-sexual-dependency.

Altman, Lawrence K. "Rare Cancer Seen in 41 Homosexuals." *New York Times*, July 3, 1981. http://www.nytimes.com/1981/07/03/us/rare-cancer-seen-in-41-homosexuals.html.

"American Booksellers Association, Inc. v. Hudnut." CaseBriefs. Accessed January 11, 2021. https://www.casebriefs.com/blog/law/constitutional-law/constitutional-law-keyed-to-cohen/governmental-control-of-the-content-of-expression/american-booksellers-association-inc-v-hudnut/.

Anzaldúa, Gloria E. *Borderlands / La Frontera, The New Mestiza: Third Edition*. San Francisco: Aunt Lute Books, 2007.

Anzaldúa, Gloria E. *Borderlands / La Frontera, The New Mestiza: The Critical Edition*. San Francisco: Aunt Lute Books, 2021.

Anzaldúa, Gloria E. "Bridge, Drawbridge, Sandbar, or Island: Lesbians-of-Color Hacienda Alianzas." In *The Gloria Anzaldúa Reader*, edited by AnaLouise Keating, 140–56. Durham, N.C.: Duke University Press, 2009.

Anzaldúa, Gloria E. "Counsels from the Firing . . . Past, Present, Future: Foreword to the Third Edition, 2001." In *This Bridge Called My Back: Writings by Radical Women of Color*, edited by Cherríe Moraga and Gloria E. Anzaldúa, 4th ed., 261–66. Albany: SUNY Press, 2015.

Anzaldúa, Gloria E. "En Rapport, in Opposition: Cobrando cuentas a las nuestras." *Sinister Wisdom*, no. 33 (Fall 1987): 11–17.

Anzaldúa, Gloria E. "En Rapport, in Opposition: Cobrando cuentas a las nuestras." In *Making Face, Making Soul / Haciendo Caras: Creative and Critical Perspectives by Feminists of Color*, edited by Gloria E. Anzaldúa, 142–48. San Francisco: Aunt Lute Books, 1990.

Anzaldúa, Gloria E. "Gay Fiction, East and West, Prof Teele, Spring 1977: February 27, 1977," February 27, 1977. Box 230, Folder 6: Gay Fiction, East and West, Prof Teele, Spring 1977, Collection on Gloria Evangelina Anzaldúa, Nettie Lee Benson Latin American Collection, University of Texas Libraries, University of Texas at Austin.

Anzaldúa, Gloria E. "Gay Fiction, East and West, Prof Teele, Spring 1977: March 8, 1977," March 8, 1977. Box 230, Folder 6: Gay Fiction, East and West, Prof Teele, Spring 1977, Collection on Gloria Evangelina Anzaldúa, Nettie Lee Benson Latin American Collection, University of Texas Libraries, University of Texas at Austin.

Anzaldúa, Gloria E. *The Gloria Anzaldúa Reader*. Edited by AnaLouise Keating. Durham, N.C.: Duke University Press, 2009.

Anzaldúa, Gloria E. "Haciendo Caras, Una Entrada." In *Making Face, Making Soul / Haciendo Caras: Creative and Critical Perspectives by Feminists of Color*, edited by Gloria E. Anzaldúa, xv–xxviii. San Francisco: Aunt Lute Books, 1990.

Anzaldúa, Gloria E. *Interviews/Entrevistas*. Edited by AnaLouise Keating. New York: Routledge, 2000.

Anzaldúa, Gloria E. *Light in the Dark / Luz En Lo Oscuro: Rewriting Identity, Spirituality, Reality*. Edited by AnaLouise Keating. Durham, N.C.: Duke University Press, 2015.

Anzaldúa, Gloria E, ed. *Making Face, Making Soul / Haciendo Caras: Creative and Critical Perspectives by Feminists of Color*. San Francisco: Aunt Lute Books, 1990.

Anzaldúa, Gloria E. "Notebook and Journal on La Mujer Xicana: September 16, 1976," September 16, 1976. Box 104, Folder 2: Notebook and Journal on La Mujer Xicana, 1976, Collection on Gloria Evangelina Anzaldúa, Nettie Lee Benson Latin American Collection, University of Texas Libraries, University of Texas at Austin.

Anzaldúa, Gloria E. "Preface: (Un)natural Bridges, (Un)safe Spaces." In *this bridge we call home: radical visions for transformation*, edited by Gloria E. Anzaldúa and AnaLouise Keating, 1–5. New York: Routledge, 2002.

Anzaldúa, Gloria E. "Speaking in Tongues: A Letter to Third World Women Writers." In *This Bridge Called My Back: Writings by Radical Women of Color*, edited by Cherríe Moraga and Gloria E. Anzaldúa, 4th ed., 163–72. Albany: SUNY Press, 2015.

Anzaldúa, Gloria E. "Transparency: Artista Activista," n.d. Box 131, Folder 14: Transparencies for Gigs, n.d., Collection on Gloria Evangelina Anzaldúa, Nettie Lee Benson Latin American Collection, University of Texas Libraries, University of Texas at Austin.

Anzaldúa, Gloria E. "Transparency: Mestizas Partake," n.d. Box 131, Folder 15: Transparencies for Gigs, n.d., Collection on Gloria Evangelina Anzaldúa, Nettie Lee Benson Latin American Collection, University of Texas Libraries, University of Texas at Austin.

Anzaldúa, Gloria E. "Transparency: Model: Just a Representation," n.d. Box 131, Folder 15: Transparencies for Gigs, n.d., Collection on Gloria Evangelina Anzaldúa, Nettie Lee Benson Latin American Collection, University of Texas Libraries, University of Texas at Austin.

Anzaldúa, Gloria E. "Transparency: Nos/Otras Disrupts," n.d. Box 131, Folder 15: Transparencies for Gigs, n.d., Collection on Gloria Evangelina Anzaldúa, Nettie Lee Benson Latin American Collection, University of Texas Libraries, University of Texas at Austin.

Anzaldúa, Gloria E. "Transparency: Nos/Otras Somos Mestizas Todas," n.d. Box 131, Folder 15: Transparencies for Gigs, n.d., Collection on Gloria Evangelina Anzaldúa, Nettie Lee Benson Latin American Collection, University of Texas Libraries, University of Texas at Austin.

Anzaldúa, Gloria E. "Transparency: The Politics of Writing & Reading (to, for, about) the Other," n.d. Box 131, Folder 16: Transparencies for Gigs, n.d., Collection on Gloria Evangelina Anzaldúa, Nettie Lee Benson Latin American Collection, University of Texas Libraries, University of Texas at Austin.

Anzaldúa, Gloria E. "Transparency: Under the Sky of Feminism," n.d. Box 131, Folder 15: Transparencies for Gigs, n.d., Collection on Gloria Evangelina

Anzaldúa, Nettie Lee Benson Latin American Collection, University of Texas Libraries, University of Texas at Austin.

Anzaldúa, Gloria E. "Transparency: White Frame of Reference," n.d. Box 131, Folder 15: Transparencies for Gigs, n.d., Collection on Gloria Evangelina Anzaldúa, Nettie Lee Benson Latin American Collection, University of Texas Libraries, University of Texas at Austin.

Anzaldúa, Gloria, and Cherríe Moraga. "Bring Bridge Back!" *WomaNews*, October 1983. Newsprint Collection, *WomaNews*. Lesbian Herstory Archives.

Anzaldúa, Gloria E., and Karin Ikas. "Interview with Gloria Anzaldúa." In *Borderlands / La Frontera: The New Mestiza, Third Edition*, by Gloria E. Anzaldúa, 227–46. San Francisco: Aunt Lute Books, 2007.

Anzaldúa, Gloria E., and AnaLouise Keating, eds. *this bridge we call home: radical visions for transformation*. New York: Routledge, 2002.

Anzaldúa, Gloria E., and Hector A. Torres. "The Author Never Existed." In *Conversations with Contemporary Chicana and Chicano Writers*, by Hector A. Torres, 115–45. Albuquerque: University of New Mexico Press, 2007.

"Artists Checklist: Witnesses: Against Our Vanishing," 1989. MSS 291, Box 31, Folder 4, Artists Space Archive, Fales Library and Special Collections, New York University Libraries.

Ault, Julie, ed. *Show and Tell: A Chronicle of Group Material*. London: Four Corners Books, 2010.

Avena, Thomas, and Nan Goldin. "Interview with Nan Goldin." In *Life Sentences: Writers, Artists, and AIDS*, edited by Thomas Avena, 148–60. San Francisco: Mercury House, 1994.

Avery, Tara Madison, and Jeanne Thornton, eds. *We're Still Here: An All-Trans Comics Anthology*. Dana Point, Calif.: Stacked Deck Press, 2018.

Barry, Lynda. *Blabber Blabber Blabber: Volume 1 of Everything*. Montreal: Drawn and Quarterly, 2011.

Barry, Lynda. NAKED LADIES! NAKED LADIES! NAKED LADIES! Seattle: Real Comet Press, 1984.

Barry, Lynda. *One Hundred Demons*. Seattle: Sasquatch Books, 2005.

Barry, Lynda. *Picture This: The Near-Sighted Monkey Book*. Montreal: Drawn and Quarterly, 2010.

Barry, Lynda. *Syllabus: Notes from an Accidental Professor*. Montreal: Drawn and Quarterly, 2014.

Barry, Lynda. *What It Is*. Montreal: Drawn and Quarterly, 2008.

Barthes, Roland. *Camera Lucida: Reflections on Photography*. Translated by Richard Howard. New York: Hill and Wang, 1981.

Baumann, Jason. "Introduction." In *The Stonewall Reader*, edited by Jason Baumann, xiii–xxi. New York: Penguin Classics, 2019.

Beaty, Bart. *Comics versus Art*. Toronto: University of Toronto Press, 2012.

Bechdel, Alison. "Advertisement: Get Yourself a *WomaNews* T-Shirt!" *WomaNews*, April 1984. Newsprint Collection, *WomaNews*, Lesbian Herstory Archives.

Bechdel, Alison. "Advertisement: *WomaNews* 5th Anniversary! Variety Show!" *WomaNews*, November 1984. Newsprint Collection, *WomaNews*, Lesbian Herstory Archives.

Bechdel, Alison. "Advertisement: *WomaNews* 5th Anniversary! Variety Show!" *WomaNews*, December 1984/January 1985. Newsprint Collection, *WomaNews*, Lesbian Herstory Archives.

Bechdel, Alison. "Advertisement: *WomaNews* Workshops." *WomaNews*, March 1984. Newsprint Collection, *WomaNews*, Lesbian Herstory Archives.

Bechdel, Alison. *Are You My Mother? A Comic Drama*. New York: Houghton Mifflin Harcourt, 2012.

Bechdel, Alison. "Cartoonist's Introduction." In *The Essential "Dykes to Watch Out For,"* vii–xviii. New York: Houghton Mifflin Harcourt, 2008.

Bechdel, Alison. *Dykes to Watch Out For*. Ithaca, N.Y.: Firebrand Books, 1986.

Bechdel, Alison. "*Dykes to Watch Out For* 1994 Calendar," 1994. Box 66, Folder 17: *DTWOF* 1994 Calendar: Review Copies (1993–1994), Firebrand Books records, #7670, Division of Rare and Manuscript Collections, Cornell University Library.

Bechdel, Alison. "*Dykes to Watch Out For*: Groves of Academe." *Valley Women's Voice*, July 1988. Newsprint Collection, *Valley Women's Voice*. Lesbian Herstory Archives.

Bechdel, Alison. "*Dykes to Watch Out For*: One Enchanted Evening." *off our backs* 17, no. 2 (1987): 27.

Bechdel, Alison. "*Dykes to Watch Out For*, Plate No. 19: Twyla Is Appalled to Learn That Irene Is a Morning Person." *WomaNews*, August 1983. Newsprint Collection, *WomaNews*. Lesbian Herstory Archives.

Bechdel, Alison. *The Essential "Dykes to Watch Out For."* New York: Houghton Mifflin Harcourt, 2008.

Bechdel, Alison. "From the Archives." *Dykes to Watch Out For* (blog), March 12, 2008. http://dykestowatchoutfor.com/from-the-archives.

Bechdel, Alison. *Fun Home: A Family Tragicomic*. New York: Mariner Books, 2006.

Bechdel, Alison. *The Indelible Alison Bechdel: Confessions, Comix, and Miscellaneous "Dykes to Watch Out For."* Ithaca, N.Y.: Firebrand Books, 1998.

Bechdel, Alison. "Ithaca: Archival Kisses, Drunken Birds, Firebrand." *Dykes to Watch Out For* (blog), April 13, 2008. http://dykestowatchoutfor.com/catching-up.

Bechdel, Alison. "Letters Page Caricature Graphic: Chainsmoking Letter-Writer." *WomaNews*, February 1984. Newsprint Collection, *WomaNews*, Lesbian Herstory Archives.

Bechdel, Alison. "Letters Page Caricature Graphic: Contortionist Letter-Writer." *WomaNews*, November 1983. Newsprint Collection, *WomaNews*, Lesbian Herstory Archives.

Bechdel, Alison. "Letters Page Baricature Graphic: Intent, Typewriting Female." *WomaNews*, December 1983/January 1984. Newsprint Collection, *WomaNews*, Lesbian Herstory Archives.

Bechdel, Alison. "Letters Page Caricature Graphic: M&M Letter-Writer." *WomaNews*, July/August 1984. Newsprint Collection, *WomaNews*, Lesbian Herstory Archives.

Bechdel, Alison. "Letters Page Caricature Graphic: Pen-Biting Agitated Female." *WomaNews*, October 1983. Newsprint Collection, *WomaNews*, Lesbian Herstory Archives.

Bechdel, Alison. "Letters Page Caricature Graphic: Pensive Letter-Writer." *WomaNews*, April 1984. Newsprint Collection, *WomaNews*, Lesbian Herstory Archives.

Bechdel, Alison. "Literary *Dykes to Watch Out For*: A Heloise C. Bland Lecture." *WomaNews*, September 1984. Newsprint Collection, *WomaNews*, Lesbian Herstory Archives.

Bechdel, Alison. "Literary *Dykes to Watch Out For*: A Heloise C. Bland Lecture." In *Dykes to Watch Out For*, 36–37. Ithaca, N.Y.: Firebrand Books, 1986.

Bechdel, Alison. "The Memoirist's Lament." YouTube, July 16, 2008. https://youtu.be/cCuSglq5IAc.

Bechdel, Alison. "Mo' Mo." *Dykes to Watch Out For* (blog), March 1, 2006. https://dykestowatchoutfor.com/mo-mo/.

Bechdel, Alison. *More "Dykes to Watch Out For."* Ithaca, N.Y.: Firebrand Books, 1988.

Bechdel, Alison. "Postcards from the Edge." *Dykes to Watch Out For* (blog), April 13, 2017. https://dykestowatchoutfor.com/postcards-from-the-edge/.

Bechdel, Alison. "Questions for Syndicate," 1993. SSC-MS-00633, Alison Bechdel Papers, Sophia Smith Collection, Smith College Special Collections.

Bechdel, Alison. "Same as It Ever Was, Only Much Worse." *Dykes to Watch Out For* (blog), November 23, 2016. https://dykestowatchoutfor.com/same-as-it-ever-was-only-much-worse/.

Bechdel, Alison. *The Secret to Superhuman Strength*. Boston: Mariner Books, 2021.

Bechdel, Alison. "The United States: March 2006," March 2006. Alison Bechdel Papers, Sophia Smith Collection, SSC-MS-00633, Smith College Special Collections.

Bechdel, Alison. "What Is Real? A Short Disquisition." *Dykes to Watch Out For* (blog), August 25, 2006. https://dykestowatchoutfor.com/what-is-real-a-short-disquisition/.

Beineke, Colin. "On Comicity." INKS: *The Journal of the Comics Studies Society* 1, no. 2 (Summer 2017): 226–53.

Beins, Agatha. *Liberation in Print: Feminist Periodicals and Social Movement Identity*. Athens: University of Georgia Press, 2017.

Beins, Agatha. "A Publishing Assemblage: Building Book History Methodology through Feminist Periodicals." *American Periodicals* 28, no. 2 (2018): 105–22.

Beins, Agatha, and Julie R. Enszer. "'We Couldn't Get Them Printed,' So We Learned to Print: *Ain't I a Woman?* and the Iowa City Women's Press." *Frontiers: A Journal of Women Studies* 34, no. 2 (2013): 186–221.

Beirne, Rebecca. "Image, Sex, and Politics: Cultural, Political, and Theoretical Contexts." In *Lesbians in Television and Text after the Millennium*, 21–60. New York: Palgrave Macmillan, 2008.

Beirne, Rebecca. *Lesbians in Television and Text after the Millennium*. New York: Palgrave Macmillan, 2008.

Bengal, Rebecca. "A Conversation with Nan Goldin on the 30th Anniversary of *The Ballad of Sexual Dependency*." *Vogue*, October 26, 2015. http://www .vogue.com/13364942/nan-goldin-interview-ballad-of-sexual-dependency -30th-anniversary/.

Benjamin, Meredith. "'An Archive of Accounts': *This Bridge Called My Back* in Feminist Movement." *Tulsa Studies in Women's Literature* 40, no. 1 (Spring 2021): 45–68.

Bessette, Jean. *Retroactivism in the Lesbian Archives: Composing Pasts and Futures*. Carbondale: Southern Illinois University Press, 2017.

Bethel, Lorraine, and Barbara Smith, eds. *Conditions Five: The Black Women's Issue*. Brooklyn: Conditions, 1979.

Blackwell, Maylei. *¡Chicana Power! Contested Histories of Feminism in the Chicano Movement*. Austin: University of Texas Press, 2011.

Blackwell, Maylei. "Engendering Print Cultures and Chicana Feminist Counterpublics in the Chicano Movement." In *¡Chicana Power! Contested Histories of Feminism in the Chicano Movement*, 133–59. Austin: University of Texas Press, 2011.

Blackwell, Maylei, and Gloria E. Anzaldúa. "Many Roads, One Path: A Testimonio of Gloria E. Anzaldúa." In *Chicana Movidas: New Narratives of Activism and Feminism in the Movement Era*, edited by Dionne Espinoza, María Eugenia Cotera, and Maylei Blackwell, 110–19. Austin: University of Texas Press, 2018.

Bly, Lyz, and Kelly Wooten, eds. *Make Your Own History: Documenting Feminist and Queer Activism in the 21st Century*. Los Angeles: Litwin Books, 2012.

Bors, Matt, ed. *Be Gay, Do Comics! Queer History, Memoir, and Satire from "The Nib."* San Diego: IDW Publishing, 2020.

Bost, Suzanne. "Messy Archives and Materials That Matter: Making Knowledge with the Gloria Evangelina Anzaldúa Papers." *PMLA* 130, no. 3 (2015): 615–30.

Bost, Suzanne. *Shared Selves: Latinx Memoir and Ethical Alternatives to Humanism*. Urbana: University of Illinois Press, 2019.

Bowen, Diana Isabel. "Gloria Anzaldúa: From Borderlands to *Nepantla*." *Oxford Research Encyclopedia of Communication*, November 20, 2018. https://doi.org/ 10.1093/acrefore/9780190228613.013.606.

Bracewell, Lorna Norman. "Beyond Barnard: Liberalism, Antipornography Feminism, and the Sex Wars." *Signs: Journal of Women in Culture and Society* 42, no. 1 (2016): 23–48.

Bronstein, Carolyn. *Battling Pornography: The American Feminist Anti-Pornography Movement, 1976–1986*. Cambridge: Cambridge University Press, 2011.

Butler, Judith. "Politics, Pleasure, Pain: The Controversy Continues; *Diary of a Conference on Sexuality*." *Gay Community News* 10, no. 20 (December 4, 1982): 1.

Cade, Cathy. "Gloria Anzaldúa." In "On Language" special issue, edited by Akiba Ona'da-Sikwoia, *Sinister Wisdom*, no. 56 (Summer/Fall 1995): 25.

Cade, Cathy. "Gloria Anzaldúa in Front of Her Drawings Presenting Her Book: *Borderlands* at the Montréal Feminist Book Fair, 1988." Box 20, Folder 11, *Sinister Wisdom*, 1983–1998, Collection on Gloria Evangelina Anzaldúa, Nettie Lee Benson Latin American Collection, University of Texas Libraries, University of Texas at Austin.

Cade, Cathy. *A Lesbian Photo Album: The Lives of Seven Lesbian Feminists*. Oakland, Calif.: Waterwomen Books, 1987.

Camper, Jennifer, ed. *Juicy Mother: Celebration*. New York: Soft Skull Press, 2005.

Camper, Jennifer, ed. *Juicy Mother 2: How They Met*. San Francisco: Manic D Press, 2007.

Camper, Jennifer. *Rude Girls and Dangerous Women*. Bala Cynwyd, Penn.: Laugh Lines Press, 1994.

Cantú, Norma. "Comparative Perspectives Symposium: Gloria E. Anzaldúa, an International Perspective." *Signs: Journal of Women in Culture and Society* 37, no. 1 (Autumn 2011): 1–5.

Cantú, Norma E., Christina L. Gutiérrez, Norma Alarcón, and Rita E. Urquijo-Ruiz, eds. *El Mundo Zurdo: Selected Works from the Meetings of the Society for the Study of Gloria Anzaldúa, 2007 and 2009*. San Francisco: Aunt Lute Books, 2010.

carrington, andré m. *Speculative Blackness: The Future of Race in Science Fiction*. Minneapolis: University of Minnesota Press, 2016.

Caruana, Stephanie. "Great Yogurt Conspiracy." *off our backs* 3, no. 5 (January 1973): 7.

Caswell, Michelle. "'The Archive' Is Not an Archives: Acknowledging the Intellectual Contributions of Archival Studies." *Reconstruction* 16, no. 1 (2016). http://reconstruction.digitalodu.com/Issues/161/Caswell.shtml.

Caswell, Michelle, Ricardo Punzalan, and T-Kay Sangwand. "Critical Archival Studies: An Introduction." *Journal of Critical Library and Information Studies* 1, no. 2 (2017): 1–8.

Christensen, Charles "Zan," ed. *Anything That Loves*. Seattle: Northwest Press, 2013.

Chute, Hillary L. "Alison Bechdel." In *Outside the Box: Interviews with Contemporary Cartoonists*, 155–75. Chicago: University of Chicago Press, 2014.

Chute, Hillary L. "Animating an Archive: Repetition and Regeneration in Alison Bechdel's *Fun Home*." In *Graphic Women: Life Narrative and Contemporary Comics*, 175–217. New York: Columbia University Press, 2010.

Chute, Hillary L. *Graphic Women: Life Narrative and Contemporary Comics*. New York: Columbia University Press, 2010.

Chute, Hillary L. "Introduction: Women, Comics, and the Risk of Representation." In *Graphic Women: Life Narrative and Contemporary Comics*, 1–28. New York: Columbia University Press, 2010.

Chute, Hillary L. "Why Queer?" In *Why Comics? From Underground to Everywhere*, 349–88. New York: Harper, 2017.

Cifor, Marika. *Viral Cultures: Activist Archiving in the Age of AIDS*. Minneapolis: University of Minnesota Press, 2022.

Cifor, Marika, and Stacy Wood. "Critical Feminism in the Archives." *Journal of Critical Library and Information Studies* 1, no. 2 (2017): 1–27.

Cixous, Hélène. "The Laugh of the Medusa." Translated by Keith Cohen and Paula Cohen. *Signs: Journal of Women in Culture and Society* 1, no. 4 (July 1976): 875–93.

Coalition for a Feminist Sexuality and Against Sadomasochism. "We Protest," April 1982. Box 5, Folder 10, Barnard Center for Research on Women records, 1962–2019, Barnard Archives and Special Collections, Barnard Library, Barnard College.

Combahee River Collective. "The Combahee River Collective Statement." In *Home Girls: A Black Feminist Anthology*, edited by Barbara Smith, 272–82. New York: Kitchen Table: Women of Color Press, 1983.

Cook, Roy T. "Underground and Alternative Comics." In *The Routledge Companion to Comics*, edited by Frank Bramlett, Roy T. Cook, and Aaron Meskin, 34–43. New York: Routledge, 2016.

Corbman, Rachel. "The Scholars and the Feminists: The Barnard Sex Conference and the History of the Institutionalization of Feminism." *Feminist Formations* 27, no. 3 (Winter 2015): 49–80.

Corinne, Tee. "Comics by Women." *Country Women*, no. 29 (June 1978): 25–27.

Costa, Guido, and Nan Goldin. *Nan Goldin*. Phaidon 55s. New York: Phaidon Press, 2001.

Cotera, María. "'Invisibility Is an Unnatural Disaster': Feminist Archival Praxis after the Digital Turn." *South Atlantic Quarterly* 114, no. 4 (October 2015): 781–801.

Cotera, María. "Nuestra Autohistoria: Toward a Chicana Digital Praxis." *American Quarterly* 70, no. 3 (September 2018): 483–504.

Cotera, María. "Unpacking Our Mothers' Libraries: Practices of Chicana Memory before and after the Digital Turn." In *Chicana Movidas: New Narratives of Activism and Feminism in the Movement Era*, edited by Dionne Espinoza, María Eugenia Cotera, and Maylei Blackwell, 299–316. Austin: University of Texas Press, 2018.

Cotera, María, Maylei Blackwell, and Dionne Espinoza. "Introduction: Movements, Movimientos, and Movidas." In *Chicana Movidas: New Narratives of Activism and Feminism in the Movement Era*, edited by Dionne Espinoza, María Eugenia Cotera, and Maylei Blackwell, 1–30. Austin: University of Texas Press, 2018.

Cotera, Martha P. *The Chicana Feminist*. Austin: Information Systems Development, 1977.

Cotera, Martha P. *Diosa y Hembra: The History and Heritage of Chicanas in the U.S.* Austin: Information Systems Development, 1976.

Coulthard, Edmund, and Nan Goldin, dirs. *I'll Be Your Mirror*. London: BBC, 1996.

Crenshaw, Kimberlé. "Demarginalizing the Intersection of Race and Sex: A Black Feminist Critique of Antidiscrimination Doctrine, Feminist Theory, and Antiracist Politics." *University of Chicago Legal Forum* 140 (1989): 139–67.

Cruse, Howard, ed. *Gay Comix* #1. Princeton, Wis.: Kitchen Sink Press, 1980.

Cruse, Howard, ed. *Gay Comix* #2. Princeton, Wis.: Kitchen Sink Press, 1981.

Cruse, Howard, Robert Triptow, and Andy Mangels, eds. *Gay Comix* #1–25. Princeton, Wis.: Kitchen Sink Press; San Francisco: Bob Ross, 1980–98.

Cuevas, T. Jackie, Larissa M. Mercado-López, and Sonia Saldívar-Hull, eds. *El Mundo Zurdo 4: Selected Works From the 2013 Meeting of the Society for the Study of Gloria Anzaldúa*. San Francisco: Aunt Lute Books, 2015.

Cvetkovich, Ann. *An Archive of Feelings: Trauma, Sexuality, and Lesbian Public Cultures*. Durham, N.C.: Duke University Press, 2003.

Cvetkovich, Ann. "Drawing the Archive in Alison Bechdel's *Fun Home*." *WSQ: Women's Studies Quarterly* 36, nos. 1/2 (Spring/Summer 2008): 111–28.

Darms, Lisa, ed. *The Riot Grrrl Collection*. New York: Feminist Press at CUNY, 2013.

Davies, Diana. "Lavender Menace Members Hold Signs Reading 'The Women's Movement Is a Lesbian Plot,'" May 1970. Manuscripts and Archives Division, New York Public Library Digital Collections. http://digitalcollec tions.nypl.org/items/510d47e3-57fc-a3d9-e040-e00a18064a99.

Dean, Alison. "Intimacy at Work: Nan Goldin and Rineke Dijkstra." *History of Photography* 39, no. 2 (2015): 177–93.

DeCrescenzo, Teresa. "Alison Bechdel Celebrates 20 Years of Queer Comic Genius." *Lesbian News* 29, no. 2 (September 2003): 24–25.

de Lauretis, Teresa. "Imaging." In *Alice Doesn't: Feminism, Semiotics, Cinema*, 37–69. Bloomington: Indiana University Press, 1984.

de Lauretis, Teresa. "Queer Theory: Lesbian and Gay Sexualities: An Introduction." *Differences* 3, no. 2 (Summer 1991): iii–xviii.

Deparle, Jason. "111 Held in St. Patrick's AIDS Protest." *New York Times*, December 11, 1989. https://www.nytimes.com/1989/12/11/nyregion/111 -held-in-st-patrick-s-aids-protest.html.

Derrida, Jacques. *Archive Fever: A Freudian Impression*. Translated by Eric Prenowitz. Chicago: University of Chicago Press, 1995.

DiVeglia, Angela L. "Accessibility, Accountability, and Activism: Models for LGBT Archives." In *Make Your Own History: Documenting Feminist and Queer Activism in the 21st Century*, edited by Lyz Bly and Kelly Wooten, 69–88. Los Angeles: Litwin Books, 2012.

Dodge, Chris, and Alison Bechdel. "Interview with Alison Bechdel: Writer and Lesbian Cartoonist." In *Alison Bechdel: Conversations*, edited by Rachel R. Martin. 3–15. Jackson: University Press of Mississippi, 2018.

Dubin, Steven C. "AIDS: Bearing Witness." In *Arresting Images: Impolitic Art and Uncivil Actions*, 197–225. London: Routledge, 1992.

Dueben, Alex. "An Oral History of *Wimmen's Comix* Part 2." *The Comics Journal* (blog), April 6, 2016. http://www.tcj.com/an-oral-history-of-wimmens -comix-part-2/.

Duggan, Lisa. "Censorship in the Name of Feminism." In *Caught Looking: Feminism, Pornography and Censorship*, edited by Kate Ellis, Beth Jaker, Nan D. Hunter, Barbara O'Dair, and Abby Tallmer, 62–69. East Haven, Conn.: Long River Books, 1986.

Duggan, Lisa, and Nan D. Hunter. *Sex Wars: Sexual Dissent and Political Culture*. New York: Routledge, 2006.

Echols, Alice. "Retrospective: Tangled Up in Pleasure and Danger." *Signs: Journal of Women in Culture and Society* 42, no. 1 (September 2016): 11–22.

Eckardt, Stephanie. "The Photographer Nan Goldin Has Finally Joined Instagram, the App She's Been Credited with Creating." *W Magazine*, December 21, 2017. https://www.wmagazine.com/story/nan-goldin-joins-instagram/.

The Editors. "Editors' Note: Ballads." *Aperture*, no. 239 (Spring 2020): 20–21.

Eichhorn, Kate. "Archival Genres: Gathering Texts and Reading Spaces." *Invisible Culture*, no. 12 (Spring 2008). https://www.rochester.edu/in_visible_cul ture/Issue_12/eichhorn/.

Eichhorn, Kate. *The Archival Turn in Feminism: Outrage in Order*. Philadelphia: Temple University Press, 2013.

Eisner, Will. *Comics and Sequential Art*. Tamarac, Fla.: Poorhouse Press, 1985.

Ellis, Kate, Beth Jaker, Nan D. Hunter, Barbara O'Dair, and Abby Tallmer, eds. *Caught Looking: Feminism, Pornography and Censorship*. East Haven, Conn.: Long River Books, 1986.

Ellis, Kate, Beth Jaker, Nan D. Hunter, Barbara O'Dair, and Abby Tallmer, eds. *Caught Looking: Feminism, Pornography and Censorship*. 2nd ed. Seattle: Real Comet Press, 1988.

Ellis, Kate, Beth Jaker, Nan D. Hunter, Barbara O'Dair, and Abby Tallmer, eds. *Caught Looking: Feminism, Pornography and Censorship*. 3rd ed. East Haven, Conn.: Long River Books, 1992.

Ellis, Kate, Beth Jaker, Nan D. Hunter, Barbara O'Dair, and Abby Tallmer, eds. *Caught Looking: Feminism, Pornography and Censorship*. 4th ed. East Haven, Conn.: Long River Books, 1995.

Ellis, Kate, Barbara O'Dair, and Abby Tallmer. "Introduction." In *Caught Looking: Feminism, Pornography and Censorship*, edited by Kate Ellis, Beth Jaker, Nan D. Hunter, Barbara O'Dair, and Abby Tallmer, 4, 6, 8. East Haven, Conn.: Long River Books, 1986.

Enszer, Julie R. "'Fighting to Create and Maintain Our Own Black Women's Culture': *Conditions* Magazine, 1977–1990." *American Periodicals* 25, no. 2 (2015): 160–76.

Enszer, Julie R. "Lesbian Books Are No Longer Just for Lesbians: Legacies of Lesbian Print Culture." *Continuum: Journal of Media and Cultural Studies* 32, no. 1 (2017): 62–72.

Enszer, Julie R. "Night Heron Press and Lesbian Print Culture in North Carolina, 1976–1983." *Southern Cultures* 21, no. 2 (Summer 2015): 43–56.

Espinoza, Dionne, María Eugenia Cotera, and Maylei Blackwell, eds. *Chicana Movidas: New Narratives of Activism and Feminism in the Movement Era*. Austin: University of Texas Press, 2018.

Ewing, Leslie. "Longtime Pacific Center Executive Director Leslie Ewing Announces Retirement." *San Francisco Bay Times*, April 18, 2019. http://sfbaytimes.com/longtime-pacific-center-executive-director-leslie-ewing-announces-retirement/.

Farmer, Joyce, Lyn Chevli, Mary Fleener, and Samantha Meier, eds. *Tits & Clits, 1972–1987*. Seattle: Fantagraphics Books, 2023.

Farmer, Joyce, and Mary Fleener, eds. *Tits & Clits* #7. San Francisco: Last Gasp, 1987.

Fawaz, Ramzi. *The New Mutants: Superheroes and the Radical Imagination of American Comics*. New York: NYU Press, 2016.

Fawaz, Ramzi. "A Queer Sequence: Comics as a Disruptive Medium." *PMLA* 134, no. 3 (2019): 588–94.

Fawaz, Ramzi. "Stripped to the Bone: Sequencing Queerness in the Comic Strip Work of Joe Brainard and David Wojnarowicz." *ASAP/Journal* 2, no. 2 (May 2017): 335–67.

"Flyer: *Witnesses: Against Our Vanishing* Readings in Conjunction with ACT UP," November 28, 1989. MSS 291, Box 31, Folder 7, Artists Space Archive, Fales Library and Special Collections, New York University Libraries.

Foss, Sonja K., and Cindy L. Griffin. "Beyond Persuasion: A Proposal for an Invitational Rhetoric." *Communication Monographs* 62 (March 1995): 2–18.

Foss, Sonja K., and Cindy L. Griffin, eds. *Inviting Understanding: A Portrait of Invitational Rhetoric*. Lanham, Md.: Rowman & Littlefield, 2020.

France, David, dir. *How to Survive a Plague*. New York: MPI Media Group, 2013.

Franklin, Cynthia G. "Another 1981: From *This Bridge Called My Back* to *Making Face, Making Soul / Haciendo Caras*." In *Writing Women's Communities: The Politics and Poetics of Contemporary Multi-Genre Anthologies*, 31–55. Madison: University of Wisconsin Press, 1997.

Fuchs, Elinor. "Staging the Obscene Body." *TDR: The Drama Review* 33, no. 1 (Spring 1989): 33–58.

Gallo, Marcia M. *Different Daughters: A History of the Daughters of Bilitis and the Rise of the Lesbian Rights Movement*. Emeryville, Calif.: Seal Press, 2007.

Galvan, Margaret. "Adjacent Genealogies, Alternate Geographies: the Outliers of Underground Comix, and *World War 3 Illustrated*." In "The Counterpublics of Underground Comix," edited by Margaret Galvan and Leah Misemer, special issue, *INKS: The Journal of the Comics Studies Society* 3, no. 1 (2019): 92–113.

Galvan, Margaret. "Archiving Grassroots Comics: The Radicality of Networks and Lesbian Community." *Archive Journal*, no. 5 (Fall 2015). http://www.archivejournal.net/issue/5/archives-remixed/archiving-grassroots-comics-the-radicality-of-networks-and-lesbian-community/.

Galvan, Margaret. "Archiving *Wimmen*: Collectives, Networks, and Comix." *Australian Feminist Studies* 32, nos. 91/92 (April 2017): 22–40.

Galvan, Margaret. "Finding Feminist Comics Histories in Grassroots Periodicals." *American Periodicals* 32, no. 2 (2022): 121–27.

Galvan, Margaret. "From Julie Doucet to Gabrielle Bell: Feminist Genealogies of Comics Anthologies." In *The Comics of Julie Doucet and Gabrielle Bell: A Place inside Yourself*, edited by Tahneer Oksman and Seamus O'Malley, 3–22. Jackson: University Press of Mississippi, 2019.

Galvan, Margaret. "Making Space: Jennifer Camper, LGBTQ Anthologies, and Queer Comics Communities." In "Lesbians and Comics," edited by Michelle Ann Abate, Karly Marie Grice, and Christine N. Stamper, special issue, *Journal of Lesbian Studies* 22, no. 4 (2018): 373–89.

Galvan, Margaret. "Resource: Open-Access Digitized Grassroots Media." *Margaret Galvan—Archives. Comics. Feminisms. Queer Theory. Digital Humanities*, September 14, 2020. http://margaretgalvan.org/archives/open-access-digitized-grassroots-media/.

Galvan, Margaret. "*Servants to* What *Cause*: Illustrating Queer Movement Culture through Grassroots Periodicals." In *The Comics of Alison Bechdel: From the Outside In*, edited by Janine Utell, 214–29. Jackson: University Press of Mississippi, 2020.

Gardiner, Judith Kegan. "Queering Genre: Alison Bechdel's *Fun Home: A Family Tragicomic* and *The Essential 'Dykes to Watch Out For.'*" *Contemporary Women's Writing* 5, no. 3 (November 2011): 188–207.

Gebbie, Melinda, and Dot Bucher, eds. *Wimmen's Comix* #7. San Francisco: Last Gasp, 1976.

Goldin, Nan. "Afterword." In *The Ballad of Sexual Dependency*, by Nan Goldin, edited by Marvin Heiferman, Mark Holborn, and Suzanne Fletcher, 145–46. New York: Aperture Foundation, 1996.

Goldin, Nan. "Afterword." In *The Ballad of Sexual Dependency*, by Nan Goldin, edited by Marvin Heiferman, Mark Holborn, and Suzanne Fletcher, 145–46. New York: Aperture Foundation, 2012.

Goldin, Nan. "Afterword." In *The Ballad of Sexual Dependency*, by Nan Goldin, edited by Marvin Heiferman, Mark Holborn, and Suzanne Fletcher, 145–47. New York: Aperture Foundation, 2021.

Goldin, Nan. *The Ballad of Sexual Dependency*. Edited by Marvin Heiferman, Mark Holborn, and Suzanne Fletcher. New York: Aperture Foundation, 1986.

Goldin, Nan. *The Ballad of Sexual Dependency*. Edited by Marvin Heiferman, Mark Holborn, and Suzanne Fletcher. 2nd ed. New York: Aperture Foundation, 1996.

Goldin, Nan. *Couples and Loneliness*. Edited by Taka Kawachi and Nan Goldin. Kyoto: Korinsha Press, 1998.

Goldin, Nan. "'Nan Goldin on Cookie Mueller' (2001)." *AMERICAN SUBURB X* (blog), April 10, 2012. http://www.americansuburbx.com/2012/04/theory-nan-goldin-on-cookie-mueller.html.

Goldin, Nan. *The Other Side*. Expanded ed. Göttingen, Germany: Steidl, 2019.

Goldin, Nan, and David Armstrong. *A Double Life*. New York: Scalo, 1994.

Goldsby, Jacqueline, and Meredith L. McGill, eds. "Black Bibliography: Traditions and Futures." Special issue, *Papers of the Bibliographical Society of America* 116, no. 2 (2022).

Gomez, Betsy. "She Changed Comics: Roberta Gregory Interview." *Comic Book Legal Defense Fund* (blog), March 29, 2017. http://cbldf.org/2017/03/she -changed-comics-roberta-gregory-interview/.

Greenwood, Eve, Alex Assan, and Spire Eaton, eds. *When I Was Me: Moments of Gender Euphoria*. Edinburgh: Quindrie Press, 2021.

Gregory, Roberta. *Dynamite Damsels*. Long Beach, Calif.: self-published, 1976.

Gregory, Roberta. "A Modern Romance." In *Wimmen's Comix* #4, edited by Shelby Sampson, n.d. San Francisco: Last Gasp, 1974.

Groeneveld, Elizabeth. "Letters to the Editor as 'Archives of Feeling': *On Our Backs* Magazine and the Sex Wars." *American Periodicals* 28, no. 2 (2018): 153–67.

Groeneveld, Elizabeth. *Making Feminist Media: Third-Wave Magazines on the Cusp of the Digital Age*. Waterloo, Ont.: Wilfrid Laurier University Press, 2016.

Groeneveld, Elizabeth, and Samantha C. Thrift, eds. "Thinking beyond Backlash: Remediating 1980s Activism." Special issue, *Continuum: Journal of Media and Cultural Studies* 32, no. 1 (2017).

Hall, Justin. "No Straight Lines." In *No Straight Lines: Four Decades of Queer Comics*, edited by Justin Hall, n.p. Seattle: Fantagraphics Books, 2013.

Hall, Justin, ed. *No Straight Lines: Four Decades of Queer Comics*. Seattle: Fantagraphics Books, 2013.

Halsall, Alison, and Jonathan Warren, eds. *The LGBTQ+ Comics Studies Reader*. Jackson: University Press of Mississippi, 2022.

Harker, Jaime. *The Lesbian South: Southern Feminists, the Women in Print Movement, and the Queer Literary Canon*. Chapel Hill: University of North Carolina Press, 2018.

Harker, Jaime, and Cecilia Konchar Farr, eds. *This Book Is an Action: Feminist Print Culture and Activist Aesthetics*. Urbana: University of Illinois Press, 2015.

Heifler, Sydney. "Teen Age Temptations: How Romance Comic Books Condemned Precocity." *Prized Writing, 2015–2016*, 2016, 97–111.

Heresies Collective. "Editorial." *Heresies #7: Women Working Together* 2, no. 3 (Spring 1979): 3–5.

Heresies Collective, ed. "Heresies #12: Sex Issue." *Heresies #12* 3, no. 4 (1981).

Herrera Rodríguez, Celia. "A Sacred Thing That Takes Us Home: Curatorial Statement." In *This Bridge Called My Back: Writings by Radical Women of Color*, edited by Cherríe Moraga and Gloria Anzaldúa, 3rd ed., 279–87. Berkeley, Calif.: Third Woman Press, 2002.

Hesford, Victoria. *Feeling Women's Liberation*. Durham, N.C.: Duke University Press, 2013.

Hilty, Joan. "Joan Hilty Letter to Alison Bechdel," September 14, 1993. Alison Bechdel Papers, Sophia Smith Collection, SSC-MS-00633, Smith College Special Collections.

Hogan, Kristen. *The Feminist Bookstore Movement: Lesbian Antiracism and Feminist Accountability.* Durham, N.C.: Duke University Press, 2016.

Holert, Tom. "Nan Goldin Talks to Tom Holert." *Artforum* 41, no. 7 (March 2003): 232–33, 274–75.

House, Penny, Liza Cowan, and Roberta Gregory. "Criticism, Feedback and Changes." In "Ethnic Lesbians," special issue, *Dyke A Quarterly*, no. 5 (Fall 1977): 4–5.

Howard, Yetta. *Ugly Differences: Queer Female Sexuality in the Underground.* Urbana: University of Illinois Press, 2018.

Hubbard, Jim. *United in Anger: A History of ACT UP.* San Francisco: United in Anger, Inc., 2012.

Hubert, Craig. "Behind the Camera: A Portrait of Nan Goldin." *Blouin Artinfo*, October 3, 2014.

Hunter, Nan D. "Contextualizing the Sexuality Debates: A Chronology." In *Sex Wars: Sexual Dissent and Political Culture*, by Lisa Duggan and Nan D. Hunter, 16–29. New York: Routledge, 2006.

Hunter, Nan D. "The Pornography Debate in Context: A Chronology of Sexuality, Media and Violence Issues in Feminism." In *Caught Looking: Feminism, Pornography and Censorship*, edited by Kate Ellis, Beth Jaker, Nan D. Hunter, Barbara O'Dair, and Abby Tallmer, 26–29. East Haven, Conn.: Long River Books, 1986.

Hunter, Nan D., and Sylvia A. Law. "Brief Amici Curiae of Feminist Anti-Censorship Taskforce, et al., in American Booksellers Association v. Hudnut." *University of Michigan Journal of Law Reform* 21, nos. 1/2 (1988): 69–136.

"Interviews with Women Comic Artists: Aline Kominsky." *Cultural Correspondence*, no. 9 (Spring 1979): 15–18.

"Interviews with Women Comic Artists: Lee Marrs." *Cultural Correspondence*, no. 9 (Spring 1979): 22–26.

"Introduction to the Third Edition." In *Borderlands / La Frontera: The New Mestiza, Third Edition*, by Gloria E. Anzaldúa, n.p. San Francisco: Aunt Lute Books, 2007.

Jesanis, Renie, Kyri Lorenz, and Steph Rose Glass, eds. *Being True: LGBTQ+ Comics from the Boston Roundtable.* Cambridge, Mass.: Boston Comics Roundtable, 2018.

"John Simon Guggenheim Foundation: Alison Bechdel." John Simon Guggenheim Memorial Foundation, 2012. https://www.gf.org/fellows/all-fellows/alison-bechdel/.

Jordan, Tessa, and Michelle Meagher, eds. "Feminist Periodical Studies." Special issue, *American Periodicals* 28, no. 2 (2018).

Joy, Phillip, Stephanie Gauvin, and Matthew Lee, eds. *Rainbow Reflections: Body Image Comics for Queer Men.* Toronto: Ad Astra Comix, 2019.

Junge, Sophie. *Art about AIDS: Nan Goldin's Exhibition Witnesses: Against Our Vanishing*. Translated by Laura Radosh. Berlin: De Gruyter, 2016.

Kaplan, Carla. *The Erotics of Talk: Women's Writing and Feminist Paradigms*. New York: Oxford University Press, 1996.

Kaplan, Louis. "Photography and the Exposure of Community: Reciting Nan Goldin's *Ballad*." In *American Exposures: Photography and Community in the Twentieth Century*, 81–107. Minneapolis: University of Minnesota Press, 2005.

Kastor, Elizabeth. "The Content: Political Paintings, Plays That Plead." *Washington Post*, May 20, 1990. MSS 291, Box 33, Folder 1, Artists Space Archive, Fales Library and Special Collections, New York University Libraries.

Keating, AnaLouise. "Archival Alchemy and Allure: The Gloria Evangelina Anzaldúa Papers as Case Study." *Aztlán: A Journal of Chicano Studies* 35, no. 2 (Fall 2010): 159–71.

Keating, Ana Louise, ed. *Entre Mundos / Among Worlds: New Perspectives on Gloria Anzaldua*. New York: Palgrave Macmillan, 2005.

Keating, AnaLouise. "Introduction: Reading Gloria Anzaldúa, Reading Ourselves . . . Complex Intimacies, Intricate Connections." In *The Gloria Anzaldúa Reader*, edited by AnaLouise Keating, 1–15. Durham, N.C.: Duke University Press, 2009.

Keating, AnaLouise, and Gloria González-López, eds. *Bridging: How Gloria Anzaldúa's Life and Work Transformed Our Own*. Austin: University of Texas Press, 2011.

Ketelaar, Eric. "Tacit Narratives: The Meanings of Archives." *Archival Science* 1, no. 2 (2001): 131–41.

Kirby, Rob, ed. *QU33R*. Seattle: Northwest Press, 2014.

Kirtley, Susan. "'A Word to You Feminist Women': The Parallel Legacies of Feminism and Underground Comics." In *The Cambridge History of the Graphic Novel*, edited by Jan Baetens, Hugo Frey, and Stephen E. Tabachnick, 269–85. Cambridge: Cambridge University Press, 2018.

Koegeler-Abdi, Martina. "Shifting Subjectivities: Mestizas, Nepantleras, and Gloria Anzaldúa's Legacy." *MELUS* 38, no. 2 (2013): 71–88.

Kominsky, Aline, and Diane Noomin. *Twisted Sisters*. San Francisco: Last Gasp, 1976.

Korinek, Valerie J. "*voices* of Gay, Lesbian, and Feminist Activists in the Prairies." *American Periodicals* 28, no. 2 (2018): 123–38.

Kumbier, Alana. *Ephemeral Material: Queering the Archive*. Sacramento: Litwin Books, 2014.

Lacayo, Richard, and Lev Grossman. "10 Best Books." *Time*, December 17, 2006. http://content.time.com/time/subscriber/article/0,33009,1570801,00.html.

Laing, Olivia. "A Fold in Time." *Aperture*, no. 239 (Spring 2020): 92–95.

Lambert, Bruce. "Rockettes and Race: Barrier Slips." *New York Times*, December 26, 1987. http://www.nytimes.com/1987/12/26/nyregion/rockettes-and-race-barrier-slips.html.

"Lavender Menace Action at Second Congress to Unite Women." NYC LGBT Historic Sites Project. Accessed February 1, 2021. https://www.nyclgbtsites .org/site/lavender-menace-action-at-second-congress-to-unite-women/.

LeMieux, Kathryn, and Lee Binswanger, eds. *Wimmen's Comix* #8. San Francisco: Last Gasp, 1983.

Leng, Kirsten. "Readers Respond to Alison Bechdel: Fan Letters and the Emotional Afterlives of *Dykes to Watch Out For.*" *Feminist Media Studies*, January 30, 2023. https://doi.org/10.1080/14680777.2023.2171084.

Leschen, Caryn, and Rosemary Dinegar, eds. *Wimmen's Comix* #9. San Francisco: Last Gasp, 1984.

Lopez, Erika. *Flaming Iguanas: An Illustrated All-Girl Road Novel Thing*. New York: Simon & Schuster, 1998.

Lopez, Erika. *The Girl Must Die: A Monster Girl Memoir*. San Francisco: Monster Girl Media, 2010.

Lopez, Erika. *Lap Dancing for Mommy: Tender Stories of Disgust, Blame and Inspiration*. Seattle: Seal Press, 1997.

Love, Heather. "*Diary of a Conference on Sexuality*, 1982." In "Rethinking Sex," edited by Heather Love, special issue, *GLQ: A Journal of Lesbian and Gay Studies* 17, no. 1 (2011): 49–78.

Love, Heather. "Introduction." In "Rethinking Sex," edited by Heather Love, special issue, *GLQ: A Journal of Lesbian and Gay Studies* 17, no. 1 (2011): 1–14.

Lubow, Arthur. *Diane Arbus: Portrait of a Photographer*. New York: HarperCollins, 2016.

"Lynn R. Hansen Underground Comics Collection, 1899–1994." Archives West. Accessed September 9, 2021. http://archiveswest.orbiscascade.org/ark:/80 444/xv17739.

"MacArthur Fellows Program, Class of 2014: Alison Bechdel." MacArthur Foundation, September 17, 2014. https://www.macfound.org/fellows/class-of -2014/alison-bechdel.

Macy, Jon, and Tara Madison Avery, eds. ALPHABET. Walnut, Calif.: Stacked Deck Press, 2015.

Mangels, Andy, ed. "Alison Bechdel." Special issue, *Gay Comics* #19. San Francisco: Bob Ross, 1993.

Mangels, Andy, ed. *Gay Comix* #14. San Francisco: Bob Ross, 1991.

Mangels, Andy, ed. *Gay Comics* #21. San Francisco: Bob Ross, 1994.

Mangels, Andy, ed. *Gay Comics* #25. San Francisco: Bob Ross, 1998.

Mangels, Andy. "A History of Contributors." In *Gay Comics* #25, edited by Andy Mangels, 72–82. San Francisco: Bob Ross, 1998.

Mankiller, Wilma P., Gwendolyn Mink, Marysa Navarro, Gloria Steinem, and Barbara Smith, eds. *The Reader's Companion to U.S. Women's History*. New York: Houghton Mifflin Harcourt, 1999.

Marcus, Greil. "Songs Left Out of Nan Goldin's *Ballad of Sexual Dependency*." *Aperture*, no. 197 (Winter 2009): 76–81.

Marrs, Lee. *The Further Fattening Adventures of Pudge, Girl Blimp* #1. Berkeley, Calif.: Last Gasp Eco Funnies, 1973.

Marrs, Lee. *The Further Fattening Adventures of Pudge, Girl Blimp* #2. Hayward, Calif.: Star*Reach, 1975.

Marrs, Lee. *The Further Fattening Adventures of Pudge, Girl Blimp* #3. Hayward, Calif.: Star*Reach, 1977.

Marrs, Lee. "Interview with Lee Marrs." *Sipapu* 6, no. 2 (July 1975): 5–10.

Marrs, Lee, ed. *Spit in the Ocean* #4: *Straight from the Gut*. Pleasant Hill, Ore.: Intrepid Trips Information Service, 1978.

Marrs, Lee, ed. *Wimmen's Comix* #2. San Francisco: Last Gasp, 1973.

McChesney, Kit. "Hot Throbs: A Conversation with Alison Bechdel." *Circles* 1, no. 5 (Summer 1997): 40–46.

McCloud, Scott. *Understanding Comics: The Invisible Art*. Northampton, Mass.: Kitchen Sink Press, 1993.

McHenry, Elizabeth. *To Make Negro Literature: Writing, Literary Practice, and African American Authorship*. Durham, N.C.: Duke University Press, 2021.

McKinney, Cait. *Information Activism: A Queer History of Lesbian Media Technologies*. Durham, N.C.: Duke University Press, 2020.

McKinney, Cait. "Newsletter Networks in the Feminist History and Archives Movement." *Feminist Theory* 16, no. 3 (2015): 309–28.

Meagher, Michelle. "'Difficult, Messy, Nasty, and Sensational': Feminist Collaboration on *Heresies* (1977–1993)." *Feminist Media Studies* 14, no. 4 (2014): 578–92.

Meagher, Michelle, and Roxanne Loree Runyon. "Backward Glances: Feminism, Nostalgia and Joan Braderman's *The Heretics* (2009)." *Feminist Theory* 18, no. 3 (2017): 343–56.

Meier, Sam. "The Forgotten History of Outrageous Women-Made Comic *Tits & Clits*." *Bitch*, October 10, 2014. https://bitchmedia.org/post/the-forgotten-history-of-outrageous-women-made-comic-tits-clits.

Meier, Sam. "On Teenage Abortions and the *Facts o' Life*: An Interview with Lora Fountain." *Women's Comix* (blog), March 3, 2013. https://womensco mix.wordpress.com/2013/03/03/on-teenage-abortions-and-the-facts-o -life-an-interview-with-lora-fountain/.

Melia, Don, and Lionel Gracey-Whitman, eds. *Strip AIDS: A Charity Project for London Lighthouse*. London: Willyprods / Small Time Ink, 1987.

Mendes, Willy. *Illuminations*. Edited by Willy Mendes. Berkeley, Calif.: Print Mint, 1971.

Mendes, Willy. "Wiley Willy's Realm of Karma Comix." In *All Girl Thrills*, edited by Trina Robbins, n.p. Berkeley, Calif.: Print Mint, 1971.

Mercado-López, Larissa M., Sonia Saldívar-Hull, and Antonia Castañeda, eds. *El Mundo Zurdo 3: Selected Works from the 2012 Meeting of the Society for the Study of Gloria Anzaldúa*. San Francisco: Aunt Lute Books, 2013.

Miller, Nick. "Why Nan Goldin, Pioneer of Lo-Fi in-the-Moment Photography, Hates Insta." *Sydney Morning Herald*, November 8, 2020. https://www .smh.com.au/culture/art-and-design/why-nan-goldin-pioneer-of-lo-fi-in -the-moment-photography-hates-insta-20201108-p56cjv.html.

Miller, Rachel R. "When Feminism Went to Market: Issues in Feminist Anthology Comics of the 1980s and '90s." In *The Oxford Handbook of Comic Book Studies*, edited by Frederick Luis Aldama, 419–36. New York: Oxford University Press, 2019.

Misemer, Leah. "Hands across the Ocean: A 1970s Network of French and American Women Cartoonists." In *Comics Studies Here and Now*, edited by Frederick Luis Aldama, 191–210. New York: Routledge, 2018.

Misemer, Leah. "Serial Critique: The Counterpublic of *Wimmen's Comix*." In "The Counterpublics of Underground Comics," edited by Margaret Galvan and Leah Misemer, special issue, INKS: *The Journal of the Comics Studies Society* 3, no. 1 (2019): 6–26.

Moraga, Cherríe. "Catching Fire: Preface to the Fourth Edition." In *This Bridge Called My Back: Writings by Radical Women of Color*, edited by Cherríe Moraga and Gloria Anzaldúa, 4th ed., xv–xxvi. Albany: SUNY Press, 2015.

Moraga, Cherríe, and Gloria E. Anzaldúa. "Introduction, 1981." In *This Bridge Called My Back: Writings by Radical Women of Color*, edited by Cherríe Moraga and Gloria Anzaldúa, 4th ed., xliii–xlvii. Albany: SUNY Press, 2015.

Moraga, Cherríe, and Gloria E. Anzaldúa, eds. *This Bridge Called My Back, Fourth Edition: Writings by Radical Women of Color*. 4th ed. Albany: SUNY Press, 2015.

Moraga, Cherríe, and Gloria E. Anzaldúa. *This Bridge Called My Back, Fortieth Anniversary Edition: Writings by Radical Women of Color*. 40th anniversary ed. Albany: SUNY Press, 2021.

Morgan, Robin, ed. *Sisterhood Is Powerful: An Anthology of Writings from the Women's Liberation Movement*. New York: Random House, 1970.

Muñoz, José Esteban. *Cruising Utopia: The Then and There of Queer Futurity*. New York: NYU Press, 2009.

Murphy, Annie. *Gay Genius*. Portland, Ore.: Sparkplug Comic Books, 2011.

Murphy, Michelle. "Immodest Witnessing: The Epistemology of Vaginal Self-Examination in the U.S. Feminist Self-Help Movement." *Feminist Studies* 30, no. 1 (Spring 2004): 115–47.

Murray, Simone. *Mixed Media: Feminist Presses and Publishing Politics*. Sterling, Va.: Pluto Press, 2004.

Natalie, Andrea. *The Night Audrey's Vibrator Spoke: A Stonewall Riots Collection*. Pittsburgh, Pa.: Cleis Press, 1992.

Natalie, Andrea. *Rubyfruit Mountain: A Stonewall Riots Collection*. Pittsburgh, Pa.: Cleis Press, 1993.

Natalie, Andrea. *Stonewall Riots*. Gutenberg, N.J.: Venus Press, 1990.

Nelson, Marybeth, and Hannah Alderfer. "Re: Caught Looking Etc." Email message to author, May 9, 2022.

Nestle, Joan. "Who Were We to Do Such a Thing? Grassroots Necessities, Grassroots Dreaming: The LHA in Its Early Years." *Radical History Review*, no. 122 (2015): 233–42.

Nestle, Joan. "The Will to Remember: The Lesbian Herstory Archives of New York." *Feminist Review* 34 (1990): 86–94.

Nolan, Michelle. *Love on the Racks: A History of American Romance Comics.* Jefferson, N.C.: McFarland, 2015.

Noomin, Diane. "Wimmin and Comix." *ImageTexT* 1, no. 2 (2004). https://imagetextjournal.com/wimmin-and-comix/.

Oksman, Tahneer. *"How Come Boys Get to Keep Their Noses?": Women and Jewish American Identity in Contemporary Graphic Memoirs.* New York: Columbia University Press, 2016.

Oksman, Tahneer. "Mourning the Family Album." *A/b: Auto/Biography Studies* 24, no. 2 (Winter 2010): 235–48.

O'Neill-Butler, Lauren. "Out of Sheer Rage." *Aperture*, no. 239 (Spring 2020): 96–101.

"PanelxPanel #36—Romance." Gumroad. Accessed February 1, 2021. https://gumroad.com/l/PXPNO36.

Perez, Domino Renee, Larissa M. Mercado-López, and Sonia Saldívar-Hull, eds. *El Mundo Zurdo 5: Selected Works from the 2015 Meeting of the Society for the Study of Gloria Anzaldúa.* San Francisco: Aunt Lute Books, 2016.

Pérez, Elle, and Marvin Heiferman. "The Original Ballad." *Aperture*, no. 239 (Spring 2020): 52–57.

Pérez, Laura E. "Spirit Glyphs: Reimagining Art and Artist in the Work of Chicana 'Tlamatinime.'" *Modern Fiction Studies* 44, no. 1 (1998): 36–76.

Perlson, Hili. "Nan Goldin on the Changing Aesthetics of People with HIV." sleek, August 7, 2017. https://www.sleek-mag.com/article/aids-through-nan-goldins-eyes/.

Peterson, Gregory J. "The Rockettes: Out of Step with the Times? An Inquiry into the Legality of Racial Discrimination in the Performing Arts." *Columbia Journal of the Art and Law* 9, no. 351 (1985): 351–78.

Piepmeier, Alison. *Girl Zines: Making Media, Doing Feminism.* New York: NYU Press, 2009.

Pinckney, Darryl. "Nan's Manhattan." In *I'll Be Your Mirror,* edited by Nan Goldin, David Armstrong, and Hans Werner Holzwarth, 203–11. New York: Whitney Museum of Art, 1996.

Pinckney, Darryl, and Nan Goldin. "The Ballad of Nan Goldin: A Conversation with Darryl Pinckney." *Aperture*, no. 239 (Spring 2020): 22–33.

Playbill Staff. "*Fun Home* Breaks Box Office Record after Five Tony Wins." *Playbill*, June 8, 2015. https://www.playbill.com/article/fun-home-breaks-box-office-record-after-five-tony-wins-com-350886.

Precup, Mihaela. "The Wound Which Speaks of Unremembered Time: Nan Goldin's *Cookie Portfolio* and the Autobiographics of Mourning." american suburb x (blog), April 12, 2012. https://americansuburbx.com/2012/04/nan-goldin-the-wound-which-speaks-of-unremembered-time-nan-goldins-cookie-portfolio-and-the-autobiographics-of-mourning.html.

Prosser, Jay. "Testimonies in Light: *Nan Goldin: Devil's Playground.*" *Women: A Cultural Review* 13, no. 3 (2002): 339–55.

Ramírez, Sara A., Larissa M. Mercado-López, and Sonia Saldívar-Hull, eds. *El Mundo Zurdo 6: Selected Works from the 2016 Meeting of the Society for the Study of Gloria Anzaldúa.* San Francisco: Aunt Lute Books, 2018.

Ramírez, Sara A., Larissa M. Mercado-López, and Sonia Saldívar-Hull, eds. *El Mundo Zurdo 7: Selected Works from the 2018 Meeting of the Society for the Study of Gloria Anzaldúa*. San Francisco: Aunt Lute Books, 2019.

Raymond, Claire. "Performances: Nan Goldin, Nikki Lee, Catherine Opie, and Zackary Drucker." In *Women Photographers and Feminist Aesthetics*, 120–41. New York: Routledge, 2017.

Reuman, Ann E., and Gloria E. Anzaldúa. "Coming into Play: An Interview with Gloria Anzaldúa." *MELUS* 25, no. 2 (2000): 3–45.

Rich, Adrienne. "Compulsory Heterosexuality and Lesbian Existence." *Signs: Journal of Women in Culture and Society* 5, no. 4 (Summer 1980): 631–60.

Rich, Adrienne. *On Lies, Secrets, and Silence: Selected Prose, 1966–1978*. New York: Norton, 1979.

Rich, Adrienne. *On Lies, Secrets, and Silence: Selected Prose, 1966–1978*. Rev. ed. New York: Norton, 1995.

Rich, B. Ruby. "Feminism and Sexuality in the 1980s." *Feminist Studies* 12, no. 3 (Fall 1986): 525–61.

Robbins, Trina. "Babes & Women." In *The Complete Wimmen's Comix, Volume 1*, vii–xiv. Seattle: Fantagraphics Books, 2016.

Robbins, Trina. *Babes in Arms: Women in the Comics during World War Two*. Neshannock, Pa.: Hermes Press, 2017.

Robbins, Trina. *The Brinkley Girls: The Best of Nell Brinkley's Cartoons from 1913–1940*. Seattle: Fantagraphics Books, 2009.

Robbins, Trina. *A Century of Women Cartoonists*. Northampton, Mass.: Kitchen Sink Press, 1993.

Robbins, Trina. *The Flapper Queens: Women Cartoonists of the Jazz Age*. Seattle: Fantagraphics Books, 2020.

Robbins, Trina. *From Girls to Grrrlz: A History of ♀'s Comics from Teens to Zines*. San Francisco: Chronicle Books, 1999.

Robbins, Trina. *The Great Women Cartoonists*. New York: Watson–Guptill, 2001.

Robbins, Trina. *Last Girl Standing*. Seattle: Fantagraphics Books, 2017.

Robbins, Trina. *Nell Brinkley and the New Woman in the Early 20th Century*. Jefferson, N.C.: McFarland, 2001.

Robbins, Trina. *Pretty in Ink: North American Women Cartoonists, 1896–2013*. Seattle: Fantagraphics Books, 2013.

Robbins, Trina. "Wimmen's Studies." In *Underground Classics: The Transformation of Comics into Comix*, by James Philip Danky and Denis Kitchen, 31–34. New York: Abrams, 2009.

Robbins, Trina, and Alison Bechdel. "Watch Out for Alison Bechdel (She Has the Secret to Superhuman Strength)." *The Comics Journal*, no. 237 (2001): 82–88.

Robbins, Trina, and Terry Richards, eds. *Wimmen's Comix #5*. San Francisco: Last Gasp, 1975.

Robbins, Trina, Bill Sienkiewicz, and Robert Triptow, eds. *Strip AIDS USA*. San Francisco: Last Gasp, 1988.

Robbins, Trina, and catherine yronwode. *Women and the Comics*. N.p.: Eclipse Books, 1985.

Rosenkranz, Patrick. *Rebel Visions: The Underground Comix Revolution, 1967–1972*. Seattle: Fantagraphics Books, 2002.

Rubenstein, Anne, and Alison Bechdel. "Alison Bechdel Interview." *The Comics Journal*, no. 179 (1995): 114–23.

Rubin, Gayle S. "Blood under the Bridge: Reflections on 'Thinking Sex.'" In "Rethinking Sex," edited by Heather Love, special issue, *GLQ: A Journal of Lesbian and Gay Studies* 17, no. 1 (2011): 15–48.

Rubin, Gayle S. *Deviations: A Gayle Rubin Reader*. Durham, N.C.: Duke University Press, 2011.

Rubin, Gayle S. "Thinking Sex: Notes for a Radical Theory of the Politics of Sexuality." In *Pleasure and Danger: Exploring Female Sexuality*, edited by Carole S. Vance, 267–319. Boston: Routledge & Kegan Paul, 1984.

Rudahl, Sharon, ed. *Wimmen's Comix #3*. San Francisco: Last Gasp, 1973.

Ruddy, Sarah. "'A Radiant Eye Yearns from Me': Figuring Documentary in the Photography of Nan Goldin." *Feminist Studies* 35, no. 2 (Summer 2009): 347–80.

Russ, Joanna. "What Can a Heroine Do? or Why Women Can't Write." In *To Write Like a Woman: Essays in Feminism and Science Fiction*, 79–93. Bloomington: Indiana University Press, 1995.

Sabin, Roger. *Comics, Comix and Graphic Novels: A History of Comic Art*. London: Phaidon Press, 1996.

Saldívar-Hull, Sonia, Norma Alarcón, Rita E. Urquijo-Ruiz, and Rita E. Urquijo-Ruiz, eds. *El Mundo Zurdo 2: Selected Works from the 2010 Meeting of the Society for the Study of Gloria Anzaldúa*. San Francisco: Aunt Lute Books, 2012.

Sammond, Nicholas. "Comix." In *Keywords for Comics Studies*, edited by Ramzi Fawaz, Shelley Streeby, and Deborah Elizabeth Whaley, 58–62. New York: NYU Press, 2021.

Sammond, Nicholas. "Meeting in the Archive: Comix and Collecting as Community." *Feminist Media Histories* 4, no. 3 (2018): 96–118.

Sante, Lucy. "All Yesterday's Parties." In *I'll Be Your Mirror*, edited by Nan Goldin, David Armstrong, and Hans Werner Holzwarth, 97–103. New York: Whitney Museum of Art, 1996.

Scott, Darieck. *Keeping It Unreal: Black Queer Fantasy and Superhero Comics*. New York: NYU Press, 2022.

Scott, Darieck, and Ramzi Fawaz. "Introduction: Queer about Comics." In "Queer about Comics," edited by Darieck Scott and Ramzi Fawaz, special issue, *American Literature* 90, no. 2 (2018): 197–219.

Scott, Darieck, and Ramzi Fawaz, eds. "Queer about Comics." Special issue, *American Literature* 90, no. 2 (2018).

Scott, Linda M. "'For the Rest of Us': A Reader-Oriented Interpretation of Apple's '1984' Commercial." *Journal of Popular Culture* 25, no. 1 (Summer 1991): 67–81.

Sedgwick, Eve Kosofsky. *Epistemology of the Closet*. Berkeley: University of California Press, 1990.

Sedgwick, Eve Kosofsky. *Touching Feeling: Affect, Pedagogy, Performativity*. Durham, N.C.: Duke University Press, 2003.

Sellie, Alycia, Jesse Goldstein, Molly Fair, and Jennifer Hoyer. "Interference Archive: A Free Space for Social Movement Culture." *Archival Science* 15, no. 4 (December 2015): 453–72.

Sharpe, Susanna. "Anzaldúa across Borders: A Traveling Thought Gallery." *Portal: Web Magazine of LLILAS Benson Latin American Studies and Collections*, August 27, 2017. https://llilasbensonmagazine.org/2017/08/27/anzaldua -across-borders-a-traveling-thought-gallery/.

Sheffield, Rebecka Taves. *Documenting Rebellions: A Study of Four Lesbian and Gay Archives in Queer Times*. Sacramento: Litwin Books, 2020.

Sheklow, Sally. "Letter to Alison Bechdel," July 10, 1990. Alison Bechdel Papers, Sophia Smith Collection, SSC-MS-00633, Smith College Special Collections.

Sherman, Bill. "An Interview with Trina Robbins: The First Lady of Underground Comix." *The Comics Journal*, no. 53 (1980): 46–54, 56–58.

Sherman, Bill. "Sex and the 60-Second Warning." *The Comics Journal*, no. 77 (1982): 109–10.

Smith, Barbara. *Ain't Gonna Let Nobody Turn Me Around: Forty Years of Movement Building with Barbara Smith*. Edited by Alethia Jones and Virginia Eubanks. Albany: SUNY Press, 2014.

Smith, Barbara, ed. *Home Girls: A Black Feminist Anthology*. New York: Kitchen Table: Women of Color Press, 1983.

Snitow, Ann. *The Feminism of Uncertainty: A Gender Diary*. Durham, N.C.: Duke University Press, 2015.

Sontag, Susan. *On Photography*. New York: Farrar, Straus and Giroux, 1977.

Sousanis, Nick. "A Life in Comics: The Graphic Adventures of Karen Green." *Columbia Magazine*, Summer 2017. https://magazine.columbia.edu/article/ life-comics-graphic-adventures-karen-green.

Springer, Kimberly. *Living for the Revolution: Black Feminist Organizations, 1968– 1980*. Durham, N.C.: Duke University Press, 2005.

Springer, Kimberly. "The Soul of Women's Lib." In *Living for the Revolution: Black Feminist Organizations, 1968–1980*, 1–44. Durham, N.C.: Duke University Press, 2005.

Stein, Arlene. "Introduction to Barnard Special Issue." In "Commemorating the Barnard Conference," edited by Arlene Stein, special issue, *Communication Review* 11, no. 3 (July 2008): 199–201.

Stein, Marc. *Rethinking the Gay and Lesbian Movement*. New York: Routledge, 2012.

Stephenson, Heather. "Alison Bechdel: 'I Would Love to Be the Lesbian Norman Rockwell.'" *Vermont Sunday Magazine*, June 4, 1995. Sunday *Rutland Herald* and the Sunday *Times Argus* edition. Box 10, Folder 30: n.d., *Hot, Throbbing Dykes to Watch Out For*: Promo Materials, Firebrand Books records, #7670, Division of Rare and Manuscript Collections, Cornell University Library.

"Steve Willis Underground Comics Collection, 1966–1997." Archives West. Accessed September 9, 2021. http://archiveswest.orbiscascade.org/ark:/80 444/xv00903.

Stoler, Ann Laura. *Along the Archival Grain: Epistemic Anxieties and Colonial Common Sense*. Princeton, N.J.: Princeton University Press, 2010.

Sussman, Elisabeth. "In/of Her Time: Nan Goldin's Photographs." In *I'll Be Your Mirror*, edited by Nan Goldin, David Armstrong, and Hans Werner Holzwarth, 25–44. New York: Whitney Museum of Art, 1996.

"Third World Feminist Speakers List for Women's Studies," 1981. Box 43, Folder 15: This Bridge correspondence, speakers list, Collection on Gloria Evangelina Anzaldúa, Nettie Lee Benson Latin American Collection, University of Texas Libraries, University of Texas at Austin.

Townsend, Chris. "Nan Goldin: Bohemian Ballads." In *Phototextualities: Intersections of Photography and Narrative*, edited by Alex Hughes and Andrea Noble, 103–15. Albuquerque: University of New Mexico Press, 2003.

Townsend-Bell, Erica E. "Writing the Way to Feminism." *Signs: Journal of Women in Culture and Society* 38, no. 1 (2012): 127–51.

Triptow, Robert. *Gay Comics*. New York: Plume, 1989.

Vance, Carole S. "Epilogue." In *Pleasure and Danger: Exploring Female Sexuality*, edited by Carole S. Vance, 431–39. Boston: Routledge & Kegan Paul, 1984.

Vance, Carole S. "More Danger, More Pleasure: A Decade after the Barnard Sexuality Conference." *New York Law School Law Review* 38 (1993): 289–318.

Vance, Carole S., ed. *Pleasure and Danger: Exploring Female Sexuality*. Boston: Routledge & Kegan Paul, 1984.

Village People. "Ready for the 80's." *Live and Sleazy*. New York: Casablanca Records, 1979.

"Visual AIDS: Day Without Art." Visual AIDS. Accessed October 3, 2020. https://visualaids.org/events/detail/day-without-art1.

Walters, Suzanna Danuta. "Introduction: The Dangers of a Metaphor—Beyond the Battlefield in the Sex Wars." In "Pleasure and Danger: Sexual Freedom and Feminism in the Twenty-First Century," edited by Suzanna Danuta Walters, special issue, *Signs: Journal of Women in Culture and Society* 42, no. 1 (September 2016): 1–9.

Warren, Roz, ed. *Dyke Strippers: Lesbian Cartoonists A to Z*. Pittsburgh, Pa.: Cleis Press, 1995.

Warren, Shilyh. "Consciousness-Raising and Difference in *The Woman's Film* (1971) and *Self-Health* (1974)." *Jump Cut: A Review of Contemporary Media*, no. 54 (Fall 2012). http://www.ejumpcut.org/archive/jc54.2012/War ren70sFemstDocs/index.html.

Webster, Paula. "Pornography and Pleasure." In *Caught Looking: Feminism, Pornography and Censorship*, edited by Kate Ellis, Beth Jaker, Nan D. Hunter, Barbara O'Dair, and Abby Tallmer, 30–35. East Haven, Conn.: Long River Books, 1986.

Westfall, Stephen. "The Ballad of Nan Goldin." *BOMB*, no. 37 (Fall 1991): 27–31.

Wilshire, Mary. "More Nasty Women's Humor." In *After/Shock: Bulletins from Ground Zero!*, edited by Becky Wilson, 36–39. Berkeley, Calif.: Last Gasp Eco Funnies, 1981.

Wojnarowicz, David, James Romberger, and Marguerite Van Cook. 1996. *Seven Miles a Second*. New York: DC Comics.

WomaNews Collective. "Persephone Press Passes." *WomaNews*, July/August 1983. Newsprint Collection, *WomaNews*, Lesbian Herstory Archives.

Women's Center. "Women's Center Annual Report: 1981–1982," August 1982. Box 1, Folder 12, Barnard Center for Research on Women records, 1962–2019, Barnard Archives and Special Collections, Barnard Library, Barnard College.

Wyatt, Susan. "Attendance Records," 1989. MSS 291, Box 31, Folder 6, Artists Space Archive, Fales Library and Special Collections, New York University Libraries.

Wyatt, Susan, Nan Goldin, David Wojnarowicz, Linda Yablonsky, and Cookie Mueller. "Catalog: Witnesses: Against Our Vanishing," 1989. MSS 291, Box 32, Folder 5, Artists Space Archive, Fales Library and Special Collections, New York University Libraries.

Wyatt, Susan, Nan Goldin, David Wojnarowicz, Linda Yablonsky, and Cookie Mueller. "Catalogue Drafts," 1989. MSS 291, Box 31, Folder 7, Artists Space Archive, Fales Library and Special Collections, New York University Libraries.

Zaytoun, Kelli D. *Shapeshifting Subjects: Gloria Anzaldúa's Naguala and Border Arte*. Urbana: University of Illinois Press, 2022.

INDEX

Margaret Galvan is assistant professor of visual rhetoric in the Department of English at the University of Florida.